PRAISE FOR

THE HISTORY OF MEN'S SOCCER AT COLORADO COLLEGE

1950-2015

Horst Richardson has assembled a unique collection of stories, as told by the players, documenting 65 years of soccer at Colorado College. This book includes entertaining, humorous, and heartwarming accounts of how the beautiful game played a significant role in the lives of young athletes. These players' memories shed light on how their experiences with college soccer were so much more than just being about wins and losses. A must-read for soccer enthusiasts!

**Jay Engeln, past president of United Soccer Coaches;
1970-73 CC Tiger; 1973 team captain**

The story of Colorado College men's soccer needed to be told. Coach Richardson and his wife, Helen, put the same energy and love into this historical account as they did throughout each of their 50 years at the helm of our storied program. You'll enjoy many entertaining tales from the 'good ole days' and come to appreciate the tight-knit soccer family that continues to grow stronger. Above all, you will be reminded of what collegiate athletics are supposed to be all about.

Scott Palguta, head coach of men's soccer at Colorado College

The story of Colorado College soccer under the wonderful leadership of Professor and Coach Horst Richardson is a marvelous example of what Plato in The Republic *described as the balance between mind and body in education: "And so we may venture to assert that anyone who can produce the perfect blend of the physical and intellectual sides of education and apply it to the training of character is producing music and harmony of far more importance."*

Maxwell Taylor, former CC dean of students and athletic director

THE HISTORY OF MEN'S SOCCER AT COLORADO COLLEGE

1950-2015

I had the singular good fortune to have been employed at Colorado College for half a century, teaching German and coaching men's soccer. Now in retirement, my wife Helen and I have written a narrative about CC soccer, not primarily based on records, statistics, and championships, but more on stories and memorable moments told by players, staff, and friends of the program. This history — **all proceeds from which will go to The Boddington/Richardson Endowment for Men's Soccer** — is our way of saying thanks and *Auf Wiedersehen*.

— Horst Richardson
August 2018

THE HISTORY OF MEN'S SOCCER AT COLORADO COLLEGE

1950-2015

Horst & Helen Richardson

Helen Richardson

East of the Mountains and West of the Sun

RHYOLITE PRESS LLC
Colorado Springs, Colorado

⌘

Published in the United States of America
by Rhyolite Press, LLC
P.O. Box 60144
Colorado Springs, Colorado 80960
www.rhyolitepress.com

Richardson, Horst and Helen
The History of Men's Soccer at Colorado College 1950-2015
1st edition: March, 2019
Library of Congress Control Number: 2018963950

ISBN 978-1-943829-09-5

⌘

PRINTED IN THE UNITED STATES OF AMERICA

Cover design, Book design/layout
by Kirk Woundy and Laura Tiller

DEDICATION

This history of men's soccer is dedicated to all the players I have coached during my half century at CC, to the many assistant coaches, trainers, and volunteers who have helped me along the way, to the parents who entrusted me with their sons, to my fellow coaches whom I faced in competition, to the referees who blew their whistles in the almost 1,000 games I coached, and to my mentor, Bill Boddington.

ACKNOWLEDGMENTS

Helen and I want to express our thanks to the following people who helped us along the way with this narrative:

Jessie Randall and Amy Brooks in the CC Library Special Collections for helping me plow through old *Catalysts* and innumerable yearbooks;

Charlie Lengal and Bill Parent, sports photographers *extraordinaire*, for their many memorable action pictures;

Judy Kanagy and Justin Freeman in the CC alumni office and records department, for identifying many a "lost" player;

former CC Athletic Director Ken Ralph, Associate Athletic Director Greg Capell, current Head Coach Scott Palguta, and Sports Information Director Dave Reed, who encouraged me along the way;

Tom Fitzgerald, Bob Scarpati, and Paul Bernard, who helped fill in the blanks from the early club years;

longtime referee Dick Burns and former captain Jay Engeln for historical perspectives on local youth and high school soccer;

Bill Hochman, CC professor, friend, and super soccer fan, for valuable writing feedback;

Don Jones, hiking buddy and professional photographer, for scanning 63 team pictures into digital format;

Elaine Freed, for finding us Don Kallaus, our enthusiastic publisher;

Kirk Woundy and Laura Tiller, our design and layout team;

our daughter, Stacia Arcila, and our good friend, Jody Atkinson, for assisting in proofreading;

the former players who engaged with us in the difficult detective work of identifying old photos;

and most importantly, all the players, staff, and friends of the program, who sent in over 200 stories and memorable moments to make this enterprise possible.

CONTENTS

INTRODUCTION

As early as the days of the gold and silver rushes, soccer was played in the mining towns of Colorado. In 1892, the Denver Association Football (soccer) Club was founded by British immigrants. After World War I, soccer activity boomed as waves of European immigrants made their way to Colorado.

So writes G.K. Guennel, longtime commissioner of the Rocky Mountain Intercollegiate Soccer League (RMISL), in his sketch of "Soccer in Colorado."

In 1927, in late February, 23 years before the start of men's soccer at Colorado College, there was a championship game played in Denver between Clan Gordons, representing Northern Colorado, and Pueblo Rovers, the Southern Colorado representative. The Clan Gordons, presumably a team made up of Scottish immigrants, handily defeated the Rovers by a score of 5-1, thereby claiming the state soccer crown. In the *Steel Works Blast* newspaper, the weekly publication of the CF&I Pueblo Steel Mill, a major article describes this epic battle played in inclement weather before a "large number of spectators." The hero of the game for the Rovers was Freddie Johnson, who was brilliant in goal.

A decade later, at the Fountain Valley School, a private school south of Colorado Springs, soccer was well-established as an intramural sport, as documented in the FVS history book. By the end of the 1950s, FVS, coached by Lew Perry, was a powerhouse amongst the few prep schools playing the game in Colorado. At Camp Carson, a military base south of Colorado Springs, German prisoners of war played recreational soccer from 1944 to 1946. A film about the POWs, starring Walter Matthau, called *The Incident*, includes several background shots of POWs kicking the ball.

Although soccer was played in the Denver area fairly consistently since the 1920s, mainly in an ethnic environment of Brits and Germans (the German Turnverein comes to mind), soccer in Southern Colorado was spotty at best. The adult game tried to gain a foothold in the Pueblo Steel Mill and in the various coal mining towns, but it was ultimately an effort which failed.

During my time in soccer I have witnessed the growth of the sport from its infancy to a mainstream sport for boys and girls, for high school and college students, and for amateurs and professionals. For our family it has been most gratifying to have been associated with so many players, coaches, parents, volunteers, and alums who all participated in the game. Now in retirement, my wife Helen and I want to document memorable stories from our soccer experience, which have enriched our lives and provided us with excitement and joy, apprehension and tense moments, and above all, lasting and meaningful relationships.

What follows are personal reflections, recollections from old and young alums, anecdotes from staff and faculty members, and tales true and embellished. Articles from the CC student newspaper, *The Catalyst* (before 1969 called *The Tiger*) and CC yearbooks, as well as from local newspapers, will supplement our history.

SCRAPBOOKS, ROSTERS, SCHEDULES, AND STATS

Helen has put together a scrapbook for every season since 1965. These annual projects became a labor of love for her, and she conscientiously completed a scrapbook every year, just in time for the annual banquet. With the help of Seth Newby, a player who graduated in 2016, and with the assistance of Dave Reed, the current CC Sports Information Director for Division III Sports, we were able to photograph every page of all the books and insert them into the men's soccer archives on-line. So you can pull up the following link and scroll through the books of your seasons:

www.cctigers.com/sports/2015/9/30/MSOC_0930155224.aspx

While you are on cctigers.com, under MEN'S SOCCER, you can also explore the ROSTER, SCHEDULE, and STATS sections for each year.

THE EARLY YEARS
1950-1958

In the fall of 1950, a foreign student from Jordan assembled a motley crew of CC students to form a club team. Several members of that early effort have written extensively about that time.

Saad Sahawneh '51, on the occasion of his induction into the CC Sports Hall of Fame, writes *in absentia* from Amman, Jordan, in March of 2001:

> *Soccer started on CC grounds over 50 years ago. We were then a bunch of interested students; about six were Americans and six foreigners. We were on our own for about two years and we managed to keep the team playing ...*
>
> *I am glad and gratified to see soccer at CC where it is now. For me this is a dream fulfilled. I was following the news and how loyal coaches and leaders kept the sport alive. My tribute to them, and a special tribute to Coach Horst whose gray hairs are among the penalties for success. A job well done. I feel sad that I am not in person present for this ceremony, but I am greatly gratified and I am proud of the honor bestowed on me ... Hopefully I will be back to see my name in the Hall of Fame at CC. Thank you all and good luck.*

Saad was a student in the college's then-engineering program. He did attend the 2000 Fifty-Year Reunion at CC, at which time he invited me to visit him in Jordan, an offer which I accepted. He was indeed a gracious host in his home country and frequently spoke with fondness about his years at the college. Somehow Saad had found a coach, one Michael Cares, who had moved to town from New York City, where he had worked for the Nestle Corporation. Coach Cares was not connected to CC in any way. Upon the occasion of the first-ever game, he sent the following letter to all members of the team:

SPECIAL NOTICE TO THE SOCCER PLAYERS

Our Sunday training sessions have not been in vain in as much as we are now on the eve of our first soccer game. Soccer finally will be introduced in Colorado Springs for the first time. Remember that the first impression is always a lasting one, and it is up to you to make a good showing. I do not expect miracles as we are facing the strongest team in the State of Colorado. Do your utmost at all times and do not be discouraged if the score is against you. Results, presently, are only secondary. The main object is to play the game. It is only a beginning which should augur well for the future.

It is imperative that our team is presentable on the field as we do not want to look like an army in "rags." Borrow football shoes from the athletic department. Everyone should wear white shorts and a white T. shirt. High sox of a uniform color for all players should also be worn.

In conclusion, I would like to say: win, lose, or draw, always play the game fairly and be a good sportsman on the field. Good luck to you.

— Michael Cares

1950 | 5-4-1

Front row, left to right: Frank Kin-Maung, Helmut Schlemmer, Walt Stone, Frank Daly, Mel Smith. **Middle row:** Jack Annan, Phil Walther, Russell Laechelt, Coach Mike Cares. **Back row:** Saad Sahawneh (captain), Georg Ruschitzky, Jimmie Hill, Bo Bergh. **Not pictured:** Mike Burr, Eric Drexler, Werner Koss.

1951 | 3-5-1

Front row, left to right: Mel Smith, Jack Hattstaedt, Saad Sahawneh (captain), Walter Stone, Frank Kin-Maung, Horst Hergel, Frank Daly. **Back row:** Emanuel Ekunseitan, Paul Trietsch, Milton Nichols, Jim Hill, Coach Dr. Richard Fox, Edward Wardwell, Mid Gammell, Russell Laechelt, Durrant Kellogg. **Not pictured:** Chuck Bacon, Eric Drexler, Pete Jowise, Victor Koa, Werner Koss, George Krause, Georg Ruschitzky.

Jim Hill '52, who resides in Colorado Springs, has come to many a CC soccer banquet and has regaled young and old with his stories from the past. Jim remembers the genesis of soccer as follows:

> *It seems impossible that it has been 60 years since Saad Sahawneh asked me to come out and play soccer. Saad was a Christian from Amman, Jordan, and was one of the five foreign students at Colorado College in 1950. All of them played soccer, but we were way short of having enough players to field a team, so Saad took the initiative and rounded up other students to fill the gaps. He taught us the fundamentals of the game and put us in positions where we could do the least amount of harm.*
>
> *Somehow Saad found a coach, Mike Cares, and we practiced on Sundays. Our first game was against Colorado School of Mines, which we lost 2-1, but we were off and running. We continued to play mostly club teams in Denver (Denver Kickers, Turners). Our record was not great, but we had fun.*
>
> *Looking back over 60 years, I consider Saad the father of soccer at Colorado College. It was his effort to form a team for a new sport the school had never played before.*

Teams improved over the years thanks to Bill Boddington and the present coach, Horst Richardson. They have brought the team a long way to where it is today and have done an excellent job. Keep up the good work.

Bo "Gus" Bergh '51 was a foreign student from Finland and a member of the very first team. On the occasion of the 60th anniversary of soccer in 2010, he sent this letter:

Thank you for your kind invitation to the 60th Anniversary Celebration of Men's Soccer at Colorado College. I am so proud that I, a foreign student from frosty Finland, was asked to be a member of the first-ever CC soccer team.

Our CC team finished second in the first-ever year of soccer university competition at the beautiful surroundings of Pikes Peak. If I remember correctly, we were three students from Europe on that first-ever soccer team, two German boys and myself, an optimistic Finn. (By the way, several of the Yankees were better players than me.) It was a fantastic year of "great fights" at CC home games and on the road to Denver and Pueblo.

Today, at the age of 79, unfortunately, I do not have the possibility to travel to the anniversary celebration, but you can be sure that my thoughts will be with you during the weekend starting on Friday, September 17th. GO TIGERS GO!

Please give my best regards to Horst Richardson and to the present team. Also to alums and students of CC plus possible other friends I was acquainted with during my year abroad in the U.S.

Best regards from an old foreign student.
— Bo "Gus" Bergh

One of the Americans, Mel Smith '52 from Pasadena, California, was small, but fast and quick. Saad had recruited him to play wing on that 1950 fledgling team. Mel had collected and kept lots of memorabilia from his years at CC, and communicated with me on several occasions about the early years. Here are his reflections:

Wow! My mind is really having trouble with 60+ years of memory. Here is what I do recall, fuzzy as it is. I played wing - what else at 5'7", 120 pounds, and new to the game, but I was pretty quick. We played a 2-3-5 formation in short, short pants and hard-toed high ankle shoes. The coldest game I remember was on our football field, light snow, and 3 degrees F.

Saad Sahawneh was one of my good friends. We were both civil engineering majors; he played center forward and was our primary scorer. Saad had coached an all-Arab team and was a great mentor for me. Frankly, I don't remember Mike Cares doing much coaching but then again, I started from ground zero. Our team, I believe, only had twelve players: six Americans and six exchange students.

I played right wing and by the end of the first season I learned to pass well enough to receive Saad's pass and return it as he ran up to shoot. I went on to play at Caltech grad school in Pasadena, California, my hometown, with players from all over the world. I wasn't any star, but I was happy to be one of the 15 players to letter there ....

I found my old college student directories but still can't remember who was on the team. Saad, of course, from Transjordan, and his friend, also a Jordanian. Frank Kin-Maung was an exchange student from Rangoon, Burma. He apparently was on, or tried out for, the 1948 Burma Olympic team. He lived with us in the Beta House in 1950-51 and was the driver to form the college soccer team. He recruited me (that was during the few years that CC offered a five-year Civil Engineering BS major), and a freshman, Frank Daly '54 from Wayne, Pennsylvania. I told Saad, and he brought his friend.

We also had two German exchange students. One was Georg Ruschitzky from Stuttgart, then West Germany. I don't remember the name of the other student, maybe Helmut Schlemmer from Munich. They played defense, and I didn't interface with them outside of soccer. Of course, Walt Stone '53 from Chicago was our goalie, the only American who had any previous experience.

Thank you for tackling the stories of the beginning of the CC soccer program. It was fun playing, and it didn't require being over 6' tall, over 150 pounds, or able to run a 4:20 mile. Soccer certainly has been a positive influence and provided a lot of good times in our family. Thanks to Frank Kin-Maung, to CC, and to you, Horst, for building such a successful program and pride at CC.

— Mel Smith '52, submitted January 15, 2013

The goalkeeper on the team was Walt Stone '53, who hailed from Cincinnati and was the only American with soccer experience. He has been an ardent supporter of CC soccer over the years, so much so that our annual MVP award is named in his honor. In a lengthy letter from 1969 to Bill Boddington, Coach in 1953, he details the early years:

Dear Bill - There currently is a bit of graffiti which says that "Nostalgia isn't what it used to be," but after you called and I was able to locate the scrapbook from soccer at CC, a lot of nostalgic memories came flooding back.

I can't recall in detail how we got started, but it was in the fall of 1950. I had transferred to CC and was a sophomore at the time. I think the nucleus of the team centered around Saad Sahawneh who was a bit older than the rest of us; I think he was 27, and had some leadership experience before coming to the U.S. In addition, there were about six rather good and experienced foreign players in school at the time, and as I recall Georg Ruschitzky, Frank Kin-Maung, Helmut Schlemmer, Bo Bergh were the nucleus. I think I was the only American with any experience, but there were some talented athletes on the first-year team.

We played a couple of exhibition games with Colorado Mines to start off with. I was really surprised as I recall the loss of only 2-1 in our opening game at home. With the reputation they had I thought we would be killed. Then we went up there and tied 1-1. I recall the party afterward when they took us over to the local pub and we all got high on Coors beer.

I really recall very little about the first coach we had, except that he worked at Nestle's and got mad and quit. There are some references to his resignation in the clippings, and I think that Juan Reid (Athletic Director) is quoted perhaps a bit defensively.

As I mentioned on the phone, I used soccer as a wedge to pry a car from my parents over the Christmas holiday, partly in a realistic fashion so that we could have adequate transportation for the Sunday games in Denver. (The first coach provided a car, and Mel Smith and Jim Hill had vehicles as well.) I also think that my parents contributed money for the uniforms, although I think that the quote was correct that the College paid for the shoes. We were literally hand-to-mouth that first year, because I think many of the foreign students were barely making it financially.

Nevertheless, that first year I recall we had the best team that we had in the three years that I played. In the second and third year we just could not provide that experience which the six experienced and talented foreign students provided that first year. I think it showed as we played, because I remember it was quite a thrill when we made the play-offs at the end of the first season and reached the finals, only to lose to Mines. Our victory over Colorado A&M (now Colorado State) was tremendous as far as we were concerned.

1952 | 2-5-1

Top left: Coach Bill Boddington. **Players in order of last name:** Bjorn Aarkarmark, James Deyo, James Duque, Mort Forster, Mid Gammell, Ben Haggin, Martin Hanrahan, Gordon Hatch, George Krause, Dan Mulford, Milt Nichols, John Price, Dave Rodriguez, John Sibilia, Walt Stone (captain), John Taylor, John Terplan, Paul Trietsch.

I cannot recall who picked up the coaching reins after Mike Cares quit. I think it was Dick Fox, who was a Zoology professor in 1951-52.

You (Bill) appear in the picture in the fall of 1952 and you must have taken over permanently.

I cannot recall very much about the second year except that we clearly were not as strong with some of the foreign students missing. I know that we never had enough to practice a full game and we would improvise with our modification of "half-court," which would both give the defense and the offensive line an opportunity to scrimmage, with the halfbacks thrown in on both sides. I think that the situation became even more grave at the beginning of the third year when, as you can see from the clippings, we nearly folded.

I do remember our exhibition game at the half-time of the football game in the middle of the second year. We only had the 20-minute half and had to use football goal posts, which made it a bit difficult for the goalies - you couldn't stop the high ones. They scored two quick ones in front of a rather good size football crowd. We then restarted the game on Stewart Field and got a 3-3 tie. Georg Ruschitzky played a tremendous game that day. He was a great big fullback and I think he moved to center forward sometime during the game and was in the midst of all of our goals - whether he scored them or not I don't remember,

The third year, your first, was painful. We had no depth or experience, and I can remember wondering on many a Sunday how badly we would get trounced, like the 7-1 at U-Colorado. It wasn't the score; it was the field and the weather conditions that were so appalling. The field was literally a matchbox, and if we thought that we had poor support from our college, it was clear to us that CU soccer didn't fare any better. The other part of it was the enormous snowstorm that we played in. There were a couple of inches on the ground by the end of the game and I think I stayed up in Boulder overnight, partly for the fun of it and partly because of the roads. We played the other colleges on a Saturday that third year, a bit out of the tradition of Sunday soccer in the Denver area.

You can see from the newspaper clippings of the third year (fall of 1952) that we had received some recognition from the College and were included in the fall sports banquet. But I really don't remember many players from that year.

If I were to pick any outstanding performance in those first three years, it was the five goals that Saad scored against Colorado U, even though it was their second team. The other games that stand out so clearly are those first two against Mines, including the tie. I would compare it to the Mets or the Jets wins, at least in terms of my own reaction.

There were also two overtime wins in the first year in the Spalding Cup play-offs. I think that Colorado A&M played with only 10 men, and then they had one more hurt. It was at that point that we scored the only goal in the overtime win, a David vs. Goliath win as far as our experience in soccer was concerned.

During the first two years we went through the wintertime with postponements when the weather was too bad, but by the third season we had limited the competition to the fall.

There is one other person we might mention in an historical survey of the game. That was Thomas Brandt, the German professor. He served as an official in some of the games and I think added a bit of prestige to the local game. As I recall, he was a real authoritarian official — but aren't they all.*

My promise of a contribution to the College for the soccer team was made with every intention of following through when the time is right.

*As an interesting note, let me add that it was the very same German professor, Thomas Brandt, who hired me in 1965 to teach German and thus it was he who brought me to CC.

1953 | 3-3-1

Front row, left to right: John Sibilia, Howard Heffernan, Hassel Taylor, John Taylor, Dan Smith, John Zengerl, Leonard Cole. **Back row:** Coach Bill Boddington, Mort Forster, Mid Gammell (captain), George Miller, Ian Clark, George Krause (captain), Ted Arbaugh, Tom Gentry. **Not pictured:** Martin Hanrahan, Gunther Rinsche, Ed Roy.

The 1953 season was ably led by two captains, Mid Gammell and George Krause, but the number of foreign students, who had been stalwarts the years before, had diminished. An indication of the tenuous condition of the program is the fact that from 1954 to 1958 there were four different coaches.

Bill Boddington, who was in charge of the team in 1952 and 1953, had done an outstanding job with the squad and the number of participants had grown. For medical reasons, however, he had to withdraw.

In 1954, Scotty Russell, a CC groundskeeper, took over and in 1955, Paul Bernard, who had played for the CU Boulder club, was hired by our CC History Department and volunteered to guide the team for two years. Actually it was Lew Worner, then Dean of the College, who "talked" Paul into accepting the coaching position because the previous coach, who worked for the Physical Plant, had been hospitalized.

Professor Bernard recalls that Professor Thomas Brandt assisted him for a while until Paul and he had a confrontation about post-game socializing. Brandt insisted that on road trips post-game recuperation, by the customary means of drinking beer with the host team, should be disallowed. Coach Bernard, fresh out of CU-Boulder, indicated that such a rule would be unenforceable. Assistant Coach Brandt left the squad and focused on refereeing.

1954 | 5-3-0

Front row, left to right: Glenn Nelson, John Zengerl (captain), Tom Fitzgerald, Dave Neill, Henry Taylor. **Back row:** Coach Allen "Scotty" Russell, Ed Klinck, Mort Forster (captain), Gerhard Poehlmann, Martin Hanrahan, Chuck Lundberg, Tom Gentry, Clinton Ferris. **Not pictured:** Howard Heffernan.

Tom Fitzgerald '57, still an active and supportive CC alum, remembers the mid-'50s in a recent note to me:

> *I am not sure what I can contribute to our history of soccer at CC. I do have a scrapbook from my days at CC. It does have some small notes from the Colorado Springs paper about some of our games and a few photos. I'd be happy to share those with you.*
>
> *The biggest memory is that we were a bit of a rag-tag team. We did play C.U., Colorado A&M (now Colorado State), D.U., Mines, Wyoming, and the Air Force Academy. We also played or scrimmaged against a group called the Denver Turnverein, a German social club. We would also scrimmage Fort Carson from time to time. I don't remember a Pueblo team.*
>
> *The first time we played Air Force, it was a big deal for them. It was their first varsity game of any kind in any sport. There were lots of photographers and brass assembled along the sidelines. We won 1-0. Some of their pictures ended up in one of the Academy's publications. In a later game that year in Denver, at Lowry Air Force Base, I went into their locker room for some help. All the team was stretched out on couches, fully dressed and they were being talked to by a coach/psychologist about the importance of winning and the beginning of establishing a winning reputation*

1955 | 3-3-0
Front row, left to right: Ted Klinck, Gerry Van Tienen, John Zengerl, Chuck Lundberg, Bill Flickinger, John Jepson. **Back row:** Hans Bjornen, Bob Scarpati, Tom Fitzgerald (captain), Coach Paul Bernard. **Not pictured:** Mort Forster, George Miller, Kenneth Smith.

for the Air Force Academy. After hearing most of the remarks, I thought we might just surrender and not play and get back to CC early.

Paul Bernard played for CU when we played them and then he became a faculty member and our coach the next year at CC. My roommate at the time was Mort Forster, who was one of the co-captains of the team in 1954. He was a Golden Glove fighter from Detroit and from time to time, going up for a head ball against someone, the opponent would end up on the ground. Mort would have whacked him in a way so it went unnoticed. (Rumor has it that Mort also "whacked" a referee once!)

There were some good players on the team and the rest of us filled in. As you know, it wasn't until later in the early 60s, when Bill Boddington returned to coach, that the program began to take off.

Tom Fitzgerald, captain in 1955, John Zengerl, co-captain in 1954, and Chuck Lundberg were the leading figures on the team in the middle of the 1950s.

In 1956, when Glenn Nelson was captain, there was an uprising against communist control in Hungary. Soviet military might occupied the streets of Budapest. Two university students, with military training behind them, hijacked a tank, drove through the established army blockade, made it to the Austrian border and crossed over to the West.

Somehow Paul Szilagyi and Lotzi Torma ended up at CC, where they were housed and fed by the Phi Gamma Delta fraternity. (A sizable number of Hungarian refugees were enrolled at CU-Boulder as well.)

Paul and Lotzi started for the team and in fact became co-captains in 1958. Professor Paul Bernard provided his recollection of an Air Force game from that era, which reflected the growth of the club program:

Hi Horst,

Good talking to you last night. I subsequently recalled one story which you might like to include in your opus. This was in the mid-50s. We were playing at Air Academy and the league title was on the line. The ref, as it turned out, was an Air Force lieutenant on active duty and I feared the worst. Still, we grabbed a goal early and thereafter hung on grimly. Then, deep into the second half, our friendly ref made a truly outlandish call. Our goalie made a save on a well-struck high ball and, before going to ground, made a couple of baby steps to keep his balance (at the time there was a rule preventing goalies from running with the ball in their hands, running being defined as taking at least three steps). The ref blew his whistle and awarded Air Force an indirect free kick deep inside the box, on which they almost scored. But, with literally seconds to play, one of our central fullbacks (I don't recall his name, but he was nicknamed "Heff," Scarpati will doubtless remember him) took a blast from just inside his own territory which, with some help from the ever blowing Academy wind, sailed right into the upper right hand corner of the goal, and we won 2-0. It seems that, at least on that day, God was not on the side of the cheaters.

Best regards, Paul

1956 | 1-3-1

Front row, left to right: George Irving, Glenn Nelson (captain), Tom Loughlin, Bruce Batting, Mike Taggert, Philip Moran. **Back row:** Coach Paul Bernard, Tom Love, Doug Art, Don Hansen, Tom Fitzgerald, David Fessenden, Mike Tilma, Howard Heffernan, Orest Kinasewich, Bill Flickinger.

Bob Scarpati '59, an All-American high school player from Summit, New Jersey, became player/coach in 1957. It was also in 1957 that Juan Reid, then Athletic Director and longtime staff member of the College, had the foresight to help organize the Rocky Mountain Intercollegiate Soccer League (RMISL), and Colorado College became one of the league's founding members. In a brief statement to me, Bob Scarpati remembers his 1957 season as follows:

THE BAD NEWS TIGERS OF 1957

The 1957 CC soccer team consisted of approximately a dozen former high school and CC soccer players. The balance of the team was made up of players who had little or no soccer experience and were acquired through "conscription." The team had one Italian exchange student and two former Hungarian freedom fighters.

As coach and co-captain (Jim Neumann being the other), I ruled with an iron hand; extended practices and physical conditioning were high on our priority list. Although in reality we were a pretty rag-tag group, we all had a great time and played good soccer for at least the first half of every game.

Doug Corley '58, a member of the 1957 team, submitted the following narrative from his times on the pitch:

Roster

Mario Amadio
Douglass Corley
Thomas Crouch
Peter Henkels
Oreste Kinasewich
William Master
Philip Moran
Pieter Myers
Glenn Nelson
James Neumann *Captain*
Bob Scarpati *Captain/Coach*
Ed Starr
Paul Szilagyi
Leslie Torma
Donald Young
Peter Young

Scarpati, Moran Pace Soccer Team Over C. U.

Although bothered by occasional lapses in teamwork, the Colorado College soccer team picked up their first victory in regular season play last Sunday by defeating Colorado University, 2-1, on Stewart Field.

The Tigers evened up their record in the Colorado Association with the win, and currently sport a 1-1-1 slate after three games.

The Free Press Sports

Colorado Springs, Colo. Thursday, October 31, 1957 Page 5

In My Opinion

By K. S. CHANG
Free Press Sports Editor

A Sport Worth Developing

It's interesting to note that the higher educational institutions in Colorado have taken up soccer—the English type of football. Colorado College, Air Force Academy, Colorado University, College of Mines and Colorado State College all have soccer teams which have started official competition under the ... Colorado Collegiate Soccer Association.

[illegible]

Scarpati Replaces Bernard as Soccer Mentor for 1957

Professor Paul Bernard of the history department has recently stepped down from his post as coach of the soccer team. Bob Scarpati, a junior, will take up the job of coaching, in addition to his playing duties.

The tentative soccer schedule includes Colorado School of Mines, the Air Force Academy, Colorado U. which sports a number of Hungarian refugees in its line-up, U. of Wyoming and Denver U.

Colorado College Drops Soccer Tilt To Colorado Buffs

In a return game after beating the University of Colorado in the first of the set, Colorado College was defeated by the Buffs Sunday, 4-1.

Colorado scored the first goal midway in the half and then the Tigers retaliated with a goal to tie the score. Phil Moran punched the ball thru the goal from a cross pass from Bob Scarpati.

With six minutes remaining in the contest, CU scored three quick goals to wrap up the game.

Altho on the losing side, Tom Crouch played a fine game as the CC goal tender.

With the record now standing at 1-3-1 for the season, the Tigers will travel to Lowry AFB next Saturday for a game with the Air Force Academy and then finish out the schedule at home against the University of Wyoming on Nov. 24 and then host the Falcons on Dec. 7.

1957 | 1-4-1 News clippings

That fall of 1957, Bob Scarpati was organizing the soccer team. The problem he was having was trying to round up enough players to field a team. He finally talked a bunch of our Phi Delta Theta fraternity into playing. With the exception of a few players, mostly from back east, most of us had never played the game before, but with Bob's help and the coaching from Bill Boddington, we sort of figured out where we were supposed to be on the field.

I don't suppose we had more than three or four practices before the first game. I just looked at the 1958 year book which only has six small action pictures that don't help with my roster memories, but Tom Crouch was the goalie. The season record has been long forgotten. I do remember a blowout loss to CU and an Air Force Academy game on Stewart Field in a snowstorm that might have even been a win. The only reason I remember the Academy game is because I managed to score the one and only goal of my soccer career. Actually, I was offside, but it was snowing so hard the ref could not see me.

Good luck with your book! I know that the soccer program made great improvement after 1957.

1958 | 0-3-0

Front row, left to right: Paul Szilagyi (captain),Werner Schwarz, John Haney, Don Lavers. **Back row:** Tom Crouch, Phil Moran, Junior Prescott, Tuck Ingham, Fred Placzek, Bill Master, Pete Henkels, Coach Norry Djoudi, Lotzi Torma (captain).

Professor Emeritus of History, Bill Hochman, now in his 90s, has probably attended more CC men's soccer games over all these decades than anyone else. He submitted a number of anecdotes; here is a witty observation about players who were most likely his students as well:

> *In those early days, Tom Fitzgerald and Mort Forster were leading players. I was told that in an away game against the Air Force Academy, Mort punched the referee. I did not see that game. In later life, Mort became a judge!!*

At a recent lunch with Tom Fitzgerald, the then-goalkeeper, Tom set the record straight:

> *It was in that Air Force game when Mort Forster socked the ref. I had made a save on a shot and was hit by two Air Force kids. They drove me into the goal and when I looked up, the ref was holding his arms up indicating a goal. The next thing I saw was his whistle leave his mouth as Mort socked him. Bill Hochman for years told people it was me, not Mort, who did the socking. Last fall at Homecoming was the first time I ever heard Bill make a correction.*

Tom also remembered that on away-game days, usually a Sunday morning, the team would have to report to Juan Reid, the Dean of Men and Athletic Director, to pick up their food money for the road trip. Each player received 1 dollar and 25 cents!! And Tom insists today that in 1956-57 that was a good amount of cash!

Tom also relates an interesting incident in the days before red cards:

> *At the end of an away game to Colorado A&M, the referee called the game early because of fighting. The next day, Dean Juan Reid called in Tom, the captain, and presented him with a list of several players whom the referee apparently had reported to the athletic director with a recommendation that those individuals should be suspended for the next game. Tom looked at the list and was amazed to ascertain that all of those on the list were substitutes. So Tom agreed to the suspensions, saving the team's good relations with the AD.*

After a core group of players graduated, the enthusiasm for the game could not be sustained at the end of the decade, and soccer at CC became dormant until 1962.

GAINING VARSITY STATUS

The 1960s

There were a couple of unofficial scrimmages of no consequence against the Fountain Valley School in 1961, but a huge watershed moment occurred a year later in the fall of 1962. The resurrection of soccer began with a student lobbying effort for varsity status.

Tony Bryan '65 led the charge. As a transfer student and collegiate player, he sensed that the moment was right to confer with the Athletic Department about their support of a soccer effort, both in recognition of the team and a budget for the squad. Furthermore, there were two brilliant players enrolled, both foreign students from Africa: Solomon Nkiwane '64 from Rhodesia, (now Zimbabwe), and Abiodun Afonja '64 from Nigeria. Steve Prough '66, a freshman goalkeeper from California, was eager and experienced; two dozen or so students had expressed interest, and a faculty duo, Paul Bernard and Alex Malyshev, was willing to step in as coaches.

Professor Bernard had had an earlier stint with the team, and Professor Malyshev, who taught history and Russian, brought knowledge of the game from his native Prague, the capital of then-Czechoslovakia.

Solomon Nkiwane continued his academic career to obtain a Ph.D. in political science and taught on occasions at CC as a guest instructor. Abi Afonja, whose facial scars attested to his princely tribal past, returned to the USA in 1996 with the help of the African Lecture Fund to pursue his lifelong ambition to become a lawyer. He took the ceremonial kick-off on CC's Stewart Field for the 2000 Homecoming game.

1962-64

Tony Bryan was the most mature American player on the team. He had played at Cal-Berkeley as a freshman and after two years away from college transferred to CC. He drove a Porsche Cabriolet, as teammate Kent Drummond '65 remembers, "with no driver's seat. The bottom of the floorboards had rusted out, so all he had to sit on was a board spanning

1962 | 2-3-0

Front row, left to right: Dave Mauritz, Tony Bryan, Va Chounramany, Solomon Nkiwane (captain), Ted Eliopoulos, Steve Prough, Roger Weed, Jon Hetzel, Mike Pleasants, Rudolf Giesinger. **Back row:** Coach Alex Malyshev, Coach Paul Bernard, Abiodun Afonja, Gerhard Jansen-Venneboer, Kent Drummond, Serge Trubetsky, Jay Shideler, Steve Terry, John Pasley, Bob Conrad, Ernie LeMelle, Hans Neumann, Jim Railey, George Moore, Rich Brooks, Tony Placzek, Colin Pease. **Not pictured:** Nick Bourg.

---

from the doorsill to the gearshift tunnel. Beneath the board was exposed street." Tony has been a longtime ski instructor in Vail and remembers that early and critical week in the fall of '62:

> *Maybe I am more senile than I am aware, but I have no recollection of Ray Boyce in the fall of 1962. I remember discussion that someone had tried to start a team one or two years earlier, but there had been little interest.*
>
> *I do remember Paul Bernard and Alex Malyshev. And I very much remember my meeting with Carle and Flood. (Jerry Carle was the athletic director and head football coach, and Frank Flood was his assistant.)*
>
> *Wondering if the penciled date on your enclosure is correct. Nice project you and Helen have undertaken. If you are ever up this direction and feel like a hike, please be in touch.*

Even though Tony couldn't recollect Ray Boyce (he ended up playing J.V.), the record of the Athletics Board meeting of September 13, 1962, shows that it was he who approached the board with a formal request for varsity recognition.

13 September 1962

Mr. Carle also reported that a group of boys led by Ray Boyce (a student) had asked for $712.00 to finance a soccer team this year. The soccer team proposes to play in the Colorado Soccer Association which includes Denver University, University of Colorado, Air Force Academy, Colorado State University and Colorado School of Mines. Colorado College would also be a member of the Association. Ray Boyce is ineligible to play because of scholastic difficulties but would act as coach. Mr. Carle said he believed the $712.00 could come out of this year's athletic budget if it were approved. Certain savings on pre-season meals have already been made and other savings are probable.

Mr. Reid moved that the soccer group be given the $712.00 out of the current athletic budget subject to the following conditions: 1. Every effort be made to secure a faculty sponsor. 2. Faculty eligibility rules must be observed. 3. Soccer must be considered as an intercollegiate sport.

The motion was seconded by Mr. Peterson. Mr. Johnson asked if the above motion would permit foreign students to play and Mr. Werner stated that it would be interpreted to allow foreign students to play unless they were ineligible because of scholastic reasons. The motion was approved.

Mr. Carle asked that a new statement of athletic policy be made up and distributed to the faculty.

The meeting was adjourned at 2:00 p.m.

The team had received intercollegiate status and a budget for travel. A giant step in the evolution of soccer at CC had occurred. And the squad experienced some success during the season.

For the 1963 season Professor Alex Malyshev began as the coach. Bill Boddington had taken Russian classes from Alex and noticed his interest in soccer. Bill convinced him to coach, but the story goes that early on in the fall Alex twisted an ankle badly in practice and was incapacitated. That's when Bill, by then a successful businessman in Colorado Springs, returned to take over the coaching reins.

Bill had a lumber business in town, focusing on moldings, doors, and windows. He spent a lot of time, energy, and money to make sure that the fledgling soccer program not only survived, but also that it flourished.

Steve Prough, who tended goal for the Tigers from 1962-1965, remembers his days in the nets with fondness. Steve, the goalkeeper then, has been a 50-year supporter of the Tigers. On a number of road trips to California, Steve extended hospitality to the team, including a memorable BBQ on a beach near Corona del Mar. When I asked him to recount his netminding days at CC, he submitted these memories:

As I look at my college days, what are my memories? I do not remember classes. I do not remember professors (except Doc Stabler. But that is lacrosse related). My memories are of soccer and those experiences and lessons learned on the field.

My memories of Colorado College Soccer start before I even knew of CC's existence.

I played two years of prep school at Desert Sun School, Idyllwild, California. My senior high school year, 1961, we played a friendly as a warm up for our season

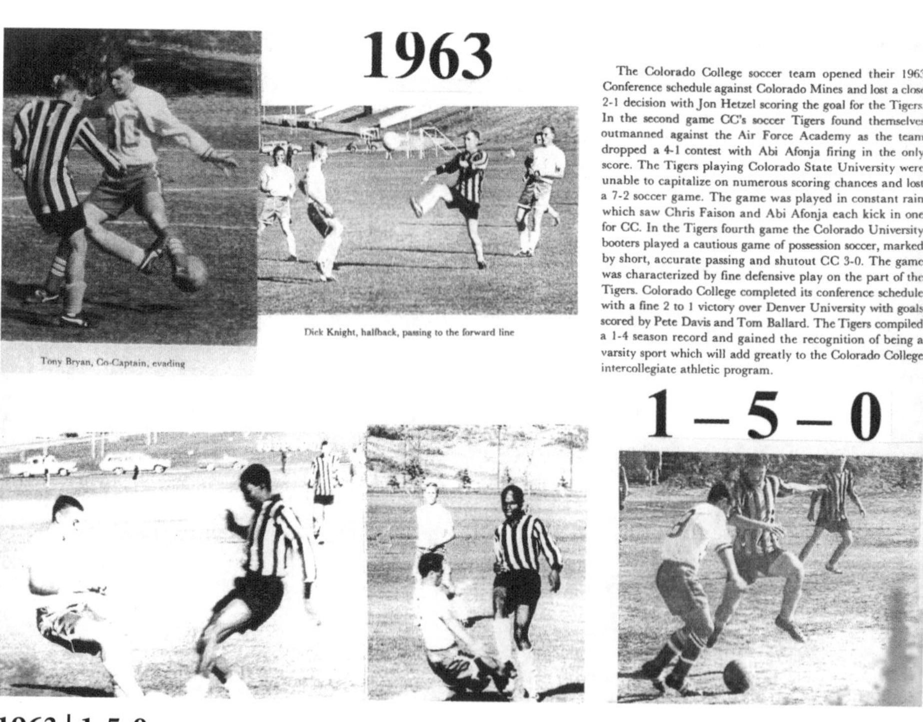

1963

Tony Bryan, Co-Captain, evading

Dick Knight, halfback, passing to the forward line

The Colorado College soccer team opened their 1963 Conference schedule against Colorado Mines and lost a close 2-1 decision with Jon Hetzel scoring the goal for the Tigers. In the second game CC's soccer Tigers found themselves outmanned against the Air Force Academy as the team dropped a 4-1 contest with Abi Afonja firing in the only score. The Tigers playing Colorado State University were unable to capitalize on numerous scoring chances and lost a 7-2 soccer game. The game was played in constant rain which saw Chris Faison and Abi Afonja each kick in one for CC. In the Tigers fourth game the Colorado University booters played a cautious game of possession soccer, marked by short, accurate passing and shutout CC 3-0. The game was characterized by fine defensive play on the part of the Tigers. Colorado College completed its conference schedule with a fine 2 to 1 victory over Denver University with goals scored by Pete Davis and Tom Ballard. The Tigers compiled a 1-4 season record and gained the recognition of being a varsity sport which will add greatly to the Colorado College intercollegiate athletic program.

1 – 5 – 0

1963 | 1-5-0

Players in order of last name: Abiodun Afonja, Thomas Ballard, Tony Bryan (captain), Philip Davis, Christopher Faison, Rudolf Giesinger, Nixon Hare, Jonathan Hetzel, Louis Jaramillo, Richard Knight, Hans Neumann, Solomon Nkiwane (captain), Colin Pease, Mike Pleasants, Steve Prough, James Railey, Roger Weed, Coach Bill Boddington, Coach Alex Malyshev, Manager John Pasley.

against the team from the University of California at Riverside. I do not remember the score, but I do remember seeing a midfielder on my left side (obviously playing right midfield) dribbling the ball, and I can now say he never scored on me. This midfielder became a much more familiar face later in my junior year at CC: his name was Horst Richardson. (I was a student at UC Riverside then.)

Later in December my Principal said, "Steve, Colorado College is perfect for you." I said, "Yes, mam." It is the only school to which I applied.

During my first week at CC, I was informed that CC had a club soccer team which just became a varsity sport. I showed up and as luck would have it, a goalie was needed. I started in goal the first game of my freshman year and played all four years in the goal, never missing a game.

We have all seen games played at a higher level and plays made watched from a distance. But I quickly learned how the sport changes from high school to college.

First game, it appeared that an attacker had a break away on me. As I started to commit on breaking from the goal, our center midfielder overtook him at full speed, doing a back flip scissor kick clearing the ball. I had never seen such a move up close in any game. Fifty years later, it is still a vivid memory.

The guy who did that was from Nigeria. Tribal scars of three cuts on each side of his face. Ran the 100 and 220 as league champ. Fastest player on the field. Abi became a

1964 | 5-1-0

Front row, left to right: Rory Weed, Sandy Heitner, Steve Egan, Tony Bryan (captain), Steve Prough, John Primm, Mike Jones, Nick Hare, Jonathan Hetzel. **Back row:** Coach Bill Boddington, Wink Davis, Jim Railey, Kees Van Slooten, Hans Neumann, Chris Faison, Tony Jonker, Leon Orcutt, Peter Morse, Nick Binkley.

good friend and my coach that freshman year. Abi knew I was inexperienced at this level and we would work together after practice an extra half an hour. I remember him giving me a better understanding of when I should commit on coming off the line. I still smile about him taking penalty shots. In very proper colonial English, "Stephen, left foot accuracy and right foot power. Which one do you want?" I went for accuracy, since power just plain hurt.

Abi would show up at our Sunday games after church wearing his full flowing colorful tribal dress with his soccer uniform underneath, as he changed on the field. Singing and chanting, with full robes and tribal scars, he was an intimidating force for any team we would be playing that day. He knew what he was doing as he sent his message.

Solomon from old Southern Rhodesia, now Zimbabwe, was another intimidating force with his tribal scars. Quiet spoken and polite with his colonial English. Very fast on the right outside attack. His presence as our captain talking in proper English usually received the attention desired on the opposing team.

Sophomore year, 1963, my memory is about my worst game at CC against Colorado State as we lost 4-2. The game was played on the football field at CC and as I am walking home, Coach Boddington drives up and asks me to sit in his car. He gives me two sticks of gum and he put the game in perspective. A few years later I saw the same scene played in a TV advertisement for Juicy Fruit.

Bill Boddington coached the last part of freshman year and then my sophomore year. Bill was listed as our coach my junior year, 1964. But Horst Richardson really ran the coaching as Bill's son, John, became an important part of our team. The example I gave earlier is one of many teaching moments by Bill as a 'father figure' for me while I was at CC. Talking about business and his experience in the Olympics are very fond memories.*

In 1964, junior year, we had a shot at winning the league in our last game against Wyoming in Laramie in the wind. Score tied with about three minutes left. A lot of activity in front of me and I end up with the ball. This exchange caused Wyoming to pinch in and as I looked up I see Nick Binkley by himself just inside midline wide left. I clear the ball over his head. He runs it down and hits a fantastic left foot fading away in the upper left corner as we win the league. A vivid exciting moment that I have enjoyed for the last fifty years.

We won't talk about the fact that we were not allowed to accept an NCAA bid by our Athletic Director. I just remember what he said to me. It was a great teaching moment for me in understanding fairness and jealousies.

My senior year, 1965, the right midfielder I played against in high school during the UCR game became officially my head coach. I therefore claim I am the only player in CC history who played against and for Horst Richardson!

Our last game of that year was against Air Force. The outcome would determine the league championship and an NCAA bid. Four days before the game, our star and high-scorer forward was asked to leave the school. As I understand, he was bowing politely to a CC authority figure, but maybe he had been facing the wrong way.

Unfortunately CC lost that game to Air Force. 50 years later I remember that match as if it had been played yesterday, especially their first goal. I was screened by two players but saw the swinging foot only and I reacted in a dive about three feet parallel to the ground on my left. The ball touched my right pinky finger and I can still see the ball rising upward into my goal. The second goal was a penalty kick by their all-league striker. I guessed right and the shot came to my right but it was an excellent shot up high and six inches outside my reach in the left corner. I still wish I had moved before the kick just to get another chance.

My best memories were traveling to and from the games and all the relationships built in cars and buses during those hours on the road. Building relationships, understanding the importance of teamwork and dealing with adversity and success are lessons learned at Colorado College.

My senior year was a great experience as Horst was now recognized and in full control of coaching responsibilities. Losing the NCAA bid that year was a great lesson for me. I know I could have and should have worked harder and I have always wondered if that would have made a difference. That concern has stayed with me my entire business career as I remember perfect practice makes perfect and we don't get a second chance. Thank you, Horst, for the memories, and for being my friend for 50 years.

*A slight correction here: Steve has me coaching in 1964. He is off by a year. I arrived in the fall of 1965.

Months after graduating from CC, Steve received notification that he had been selected for an Olympic try-out. By then, however, he was serving in the U.S. Navy in Vietnam.

As we look back on those formative years, it is fitting to include the 1962 Athletics Board minutes from the end of the fall sports season. Mr. Carle, the Athletic Director, recommends a number of soccer players for letter awards, and Professor Ray Werner, Economics, President Louis Benezet, and Dean of Men, Juan Reid, react to Carle's recommendation.

> *4 December 1962*
>
> *Mr. Carle reported that the following men participated in football but did not earn letters: Tom Brindley, Stevens Frink, Tony McGinnis, Ben Melton, James Ware, Joseph Caldwell, Edw. Huwalt, Rolf Hiebler, Herman Whiton, Peter Richards*
>
> *Mr. Carle recommended the following men for letters in soccer on the basis of their participation in 1962: Abiodun Afonja, Anthony Bryan, Valounna Chounramany, Theodore Eliopoulos, Rudolf Giesinger, Jonathan Hetzel, Solomon Nkiwane, Michael Pleasants, Stephen Prough, Gerhard Venneboer, Roger Weed*
>
> *Mr. Werner stated that he felt the awarding of letters for soccer would destroy the spontaneity of the sport and put too much emphasis on soccer. Mr. Benezet stated that he felt that we had given them a challenge and that they had met the challenge. Mr. Reid felt that we should look for a coach for the soccer team with perhaps the possibility of paying him a bonus to coach the team.*
>
> *Mr. Reid moved that the above-mentioned men be awarded letters in soccer. The motion was seconded and approved.*

Fortunately, the well-meant comments by Athletic Board member Ray Werner proved to be unfounded, as the game of soccer began its climb upward to become a mainstream American intercollegiate sport.

Foreign student Solomon Nkiwane was enrolled in Bill Hochman's history class. Bill often watched him play and reflects on a game which we lost:

> *In those early days, soccer appealed to the eastern preppies, more familiar with the game. Of course, I remember Solomon Nkiwane. He was a student in my class and I was delighted to see him play. He looked like an African God. I remember after a*

game we lost by one goal, he was standing on the sideline and saying in a soft voice: "It's a pity! It's a pity!"

Kent Drummond '65, a teammate, submitted this anecdote about Solomon:

I can't remember the specific year or game, but it seems like we were in Boulder for a tournament. When we got to the field, one member of the team had an orange and commenced to peel it and throw the peel on the grass at the touchline. Solomon Nkiwane immediately stooped over to pick up the orange peels and said, "You must keep America clean!"

HORST JOINS THE TEAM

I was hired in 1965 to teach German at Colorado College for one year. A faculty member of the German Department had been granted a sabbatical leave and I was to replace her. Well, that one-year appointment turned into a half century of employment at the college.

The events, which led to my involvement with the soccer program, are quickly told. My college efficiency apartment overlooked the playing fields to the west. One day in mid-September, while grading papers, I heard shouting and yelling on Stewart Field. I looked out and noticed a number of students playing soccer.

I had grown up with the game in my native Germany and had been a varsity player during my undergraduate years at the University of California, Riverside. Naturally I was attracted to the soccer activity on the field, went outside, and watched the boys play.

An older gentleman came over to the sideline and asked if I wanted to participate. "Of course," I replied, and joined in. Once I told the group that I was not a student, but an employee, the older gentleman, who was none other than Bill Boddington, asked me if I wanted to help him coach, and before I knew it, I was the assistant coach.

He seemed to be pleased with my work, because sometime thereafter he indicated that I, being a faculty member, ought to take over as coach. Bill, whose son John was by then a member of the team, assumed the duties of JV and freshman coach, and in 1966 I became the head coach.

Bill and I had a most productive working relationship for over 25 years. He was my mentor, and I owe him a lot. He, as a former officer in the 10th Mountain Division and a World War II veteran, gave me the opportunity to develop leadership skills.

SOCCER TEAM ENDS SEASON WITH 5 – 2 – 0

1965 SCHEDULE

CC	4	WYOMING	3
CC	2	C.S.U.	0
CC	6	REGIS	1
CC	2	MINES	0
CC	2	C.U.	1
CC	0	D.U.	7
CC	0	A.F.A.	3

A 5-2 record for the 1965 season was compiled by the C.C. soccer team by defeating Wyoming, C.S.U., Regis, Mines, and C.U. Eight players on the C.C. team have finished their college soccer careers by making this very acceptable record. Fourteen of the team members lettered out of 50 students who started at the beginning of the season.

Coach Boddington, with his assistants Chris Rich and Horst Richardson, guided the soccer men through a very successful beginning of the season. The momentum of the team slackened toward the end, but not before five straight wins were tallied.

Steve Prough, in his goalie position, aided the C.C. team by defending well, and two outstanding offensive players were Norman Heitner, fullback, and John Primm, halfback.

Returning lettermen included Nicholas Binkley, Philip Davis, Christopher Faison, Nixon Hare, Norman Heitner, Jon Nicolayson, John Primm, Stephen Prough, and Roger Weed.

1965 SOCCER TEAM

Norman Heitner
Richard Knight
Hans Neumann
Colin Pease
Stephen Prough
Roger Weed
Chris Faison
Nixon Hare
Michael Jones
John Primm
Stephen Andrews
Nicholas Binkley
Philip Davis
Jon Nicolayson
Leon Orcutt, manager

1965 Yearbook

Most importantly I learned that there was more to coaching than spending two hours daily training the team; equally as important, if not more so, was to build meaningful relationships with the players, which would help motivate them to inspiring performances on the field during games.

1965-70

Today, the athletic facilities at Colorado College are impressive. The fields, the courts, the locker rooms, the training and equipment rooms, and the offices for coaches are showpieces which are tops in the collegiate world. That was not always so.

When I became associated with the team in 1965, our locker room was the old coal cellar of the Cossitt gymnasium. The field space, Stewart Field, allocated to soccer on occasions, was really a baseball field and the football training ground, and many of our home games were played north of the campus in Bonny Park, which, as I remember distinctly, had a drainage ditch traversing the pitch on a diagonal.

Instead of having a number of dedicated trainers assigned to the various sports teams, as is the case today, one man ran the show in the training room, Roosevelt Collins. He was a black man who wore the thickest lenses I had ever seen in his steel-rimmed glasses and had intuitively-educated hands in treating his injured athletes. At first, he had a tough time warming up to this new "associate" varsity sport of soccer, since he had grown up in the football, basketball, baseball, and hockey culture of CC, but he soon became the friend of many a soccer player, including me. After a serious car crash, "Rosie," as he was affectionately called, applied his magic and thoroughly rehabilitated me.

Bonny Park, during a "Homecoming game" vs. CSU, was the site where I met my future wife, Helen, for the first time. She was an elementary school teacher at Steele School, close to campus, and had also accepted a position at CC as a head resident. The mother of one of her pupils and her best friend, who was the secretary of our foreign language department, were spectators at this Homecoming game. Helen, who had never seen a soccer game before in her life, attended the game on a whim.

When the parent mom and the German Department secretary noticed Helen at the game, they conspired to introduce us at the end of the match, and this match-up on the field has now lasted over 50 years. As I recall, we won the game 2-1, I asked Helen out to dinner, and the rest, as they say, is history.

The CC Tigers also won the next game against the AFA, which earned us a berth in the NCAA championships. Excitement ran high as the Tigers prepared to face powerhouse Saint Louis University. Inexplicably, we were declared the host for this first-ever play-off game. Bill Boddington purchased several thousand square feet of sod to lay grass over the broad jump pit and over much of the track to bring Washburn Field in compliance with NCAA width regulations.

After our last practice before the big game, there was much hooting and hollering in the locker room, and the boys in the shower room (there were only three working shower heads) were jumping up and down. Nick Hare, one of the few players who could head the ball accurately, hit one of the shower heads in the relatively low-ceiling room with his forehead and required stitches, which Rosie Collins supplied. We lost the game the next day 5-1.

The Tigers roared back from this defeat during the next season to a second consecutive NCAA bid, but this time we were the traveling team, and once again, the opponent was

Saint Louis University. Unlike in 1965, when the team was chosen for post-season play and was unable to go because of lack of support from our athletic department, this time around the squad was funded and embarked on its first out-of-state trip, on an airplane!!

The players, dressed formally with coat and tie, beamed with pride. Unfortunately, the field our hosts provided was anything but hospitable. A bumpy surface, with exposed dirt and patches of weeds, was not an inviting site, and the opposition had pumped up the game ball so hard, that we, heading their high balls away, suffered from near concussions. They, of course, were skilled enough to keep the ball on the ground, and were in possession for most of the match. Once again we lost, and by a similar score.

In the *Colorado Springs Gazette-Telegraph* sports section there appeared an article the day before the game which deserves mentioning. It was entitled "Wedding Plans in Doubt for Coach." Helen and I were to be married the week after the first play-off game. Had we won the game, the groom would have missed the wedding. So the wedding came off as scheduled. Sitting in the front pews of the church were Helen's fifth-grade students from Steele School on one side and the CC soccer team across the aisle on the other side.

1966 | 5-2-0

Players in order of last name: Steve Andrews, John Boddington, Craig Clayberg, Philip Davis, Jerry Dyson, Chris Faison, Eliot Field, Nixon Hare (captain), William James, James Kubie, William Lockhart, Charles Matteson, Peter Morse, Jon Nicolaysen, Frederick Norcross, Edward Pike, John Volkman, William Whipple, Blake Wilson, with Coach Horst Richardson.

During those first two years with varsity soccer, I worked with some remarkable young men. I was just a couple of years older than the players, and the bonding which occurred with these athletes has lasted for a lifetime.

Steve Andrews '68, an environmental engineer who lives on the banks of the Arkansas River now, checks in on occasions. When talking about his soccer years, he remembered the line-up for the DU game in 1966!! And then additional memories come to his mind, about our goalkeeper, and about that fabled win over archrival AFA:

Here are numbers, positions and player names listed in the program for the CC-DU game, October 14, 1966—your first year as head coach, if memory serves. It's listed as starting at 8 p.m.—a night game? I don't ever recall playing a single game under the lights during my three years on the team.

STARTERS

1	**James Kubie, So.**	*goalie*
2	**John Volkman, So.**	*left fullback*
16	**Philip Davis, Jr.**	*center fullback*
11	**Steve Andrews, Jr.**	*right fullback*
10	**Jon Nicolaysen, Jr.**	*left halfback*
13	**John Boddington, So.**	*center halfback*
14	**Ned Pike, So.**	*right halfback*
4	**Nick Hare, Sr.**	*left wing*
15	**Peter Morse, Jr.**	*right wing*
12	**Eliot Field, So.**	*left inside*
5	**Blake Wilson, Jr.**	*right inside*

A few names on the DU side of the ledger that definitely ring a bell, about 45 years later: goalie George Krog, So.; Oivind Skauerud, Sr.; Arie DeGroot, So.; Willy Schaeffler, coach.

My senior year? The only name that jumps off the page would be Craig Clayberg. Frankly, I thought he came out late in our junior year, because Kubie wasn't getting the job done.

1. Craig Clayberg's role as goalie our junior year, 1966. We had a good team that year, lots of promise. But our goalkeeper, though he had some experience, couldn't change his body type … which was on the short side. About 1/3 of the way through the season, someone approached Craig, a good pitcher on the CC varsity baseball team, and pointed out that we could use an additional goalie. Though he had never played the game, Craig was a very skilled athlete with multi-sport experience back in high school.

From the time he showed up at his first practice, three things stood out: his sure hands, his leaping ability, and his quiet confidence. He quickly picked up the game, and he earned a game-time try in the goal, maybe entering after half-time when we were up a couple of goals.

In his first game, I think it was up in Wyoming, he got caught out of position and was scrambling on his hands and knees after a pass-type shot that bounced in and scored. He was a bit embarrassed by the mistake, but it was the last one he made for the next four games. At least two, maybe three, and maybe all four of those games were either shut-outs or one-goal-allowed games.

He did so extraordinarily well that we considered sending in his photo to Sports Illustrated. *They had a small section of "new faces in the crowd" or something like that; they featured 3-4 amateur athletes each week who had done something noteworthy. We certainly felt Craig's incredible start qualified. And the lopsided scores in the play-off games in both his junior and senior years — both against national champs St. Louis University — would have been much worse had he not played as well as he did.*

2. The goal I scored against Air Force may be worth a write-up because I think it decided the league title (with DU disqualified?) and because it's the only goal I ever scored.

Context from my perspective: If you'll recall, in those days (fall of 1966, if memory serves) the halfbacks and fullbacks didn't get to shoot that much. It wasn't our job. We didn't push up and do wall passes with forwards. In fact, I hadn't really seen a wall pass executed until St. Louis schooled us in the play-offs. It was our job to stop the other team's offense, then carry and-or pass the ball up to our forwards — who were quite skilled passers, ball-handlers and shooters — and let them work their magic. The game has progressed a ton since that era.

Of course, center halfback John Boddington, being the superb player and complete student of the game that he was, could and did collaborate with and sometimes dictate a ball-control offense, running forever on Ever-Ready batteries. I suspect Ned Pike, the right halfback, tended to cheat a little towards defense. But over at left halfback I know I tended to cheat a lot towards defense.

About half way through the second half on Air Force's field, the game was tied 1-1. I forget how those two scores were pushed through. Of the two teams, on that day and in that era we had the better skills but they had the advantages of greater endurance, speed, physiques, and the inclination towards non-disciplined contact, and even a slight elevation advantage on us, and I doubt that any of their players smoked (our smokers probably could be counted on one hand, but maybe it would require two hands). My sense is that the game was trending in their favor.

Yet there we were, pushing the ball up the field. At one point, maybe 15 minutes left, I was well outside the penalty box — maybe 10-12 yards — shaded towards the left side of the field. Our offense may have lost the ball to their defense, or maybe it was shoved to me as a desperation pass by one of our forwards. However it happened, the ball came well out of a scrum in front of me, rolling smoothly on nice grass towards my right foot. Since I had rarely taken a shot on goal and had never scored a goal in high school or college to that point, and since I was so far out, my inclination was to pass the ball. I saw Rick Norcross (aka "Goat") cutting in from the right wing. I lined up and … well … made contact. Was it really intended as a shot or a crossing pass to Goat? I can't really say.

I made really good contact, sort of extraordinary for me. Nice ball. Their goalie was on the short side and I think I caught him out a ways and he may have been back-pedaling once I shot, reducing his leap. The ball cleared him untouched and squeezed just below the post and crossbar into the upper right-hand corner. Goal!

I was dumbfounded. No jump for joy, no pre-planned celebration. I probably went into severe shock right then and there. My now-famous roommate and sports photographer Dave Burnett captured on film both a photo of my shot, then one of me slowly turning away from the goal and pointing to myself as if to say "me? I did that? No way …" The caption on the cover of the school newspaper read something like, "Who, me? Yes, Lurch baby, YOU!"

We won the game not just because of that shot but because when we went up 2-1, John Boddington almost single-handedly took control of the game and the defense. He would not be denied and by the end of the game he appeared exhausted.

After the game, there was also a picture of our team and our melee of fans on the field. Burnett captured a look of joy on Peter Morse's face, and several of us were

> *celebrating with him … with over 200 student fans on the field. Quite a celebratory moment, to steal the championship game on their field.*
>
> *It was a thrill, and decades later still a fond memory, to have scored that one and only goal in my three-plus decades of playing organized soccer, one that helped move CC into the national play-offs for the first time ever. I think we got clobbered 5-1 on our own Washburn Field by St. Louis University — the eventual national champs. But we were league champs that year and the next.*

David Smith '70, who was in his first year at CC and thus, under the-then NCAA rules ineligible to play varsity, was an enthusiastic spectator at that AFA game and submitted his recollection of that blockbuster event:

> *A bitterly cold blustery Saturday afternoon, late fall 1966 … all of us cheering ourselves hoarse standing on the steep hill overlooking Air Force Academy's varsity soccer field. "Us" being the 1966 CC men's "Freshman Soccer Team," a team necessitated due to the then-NCAA rule prohibiting freshmen from playing varsity … a team very ably coached by Bill Boddington with Horst (also very ably) taking on (for the first time) varsity coaching duties … and "us" being (seemingly) the entire CC student-faculty body.*
>
> *Our varsity competed in a league composed of Rocky Mountain rivalries … DU (essentially ski and soccer coach Willy Schaeffler's national championship Nordic ski team), Colorado School of Mines, CSU, Regis, AFA, Wyoming and more. The league championship and a potential NCAA play-off bid hung in the balance as the chippy game, punctuated with pure beauty, unfolded … but nothing was as beautiful as the very late-in-the-game shot that still is crystal clear to CC players and fans present that bitterly cold afternoon: Steve Andrew's monstrous wondrous shot from midfield carrying for an eternity then over the lunging AFA goalie's outstretched arm and burying into the back netting … the remaining minutes endlessly ticking off … all of us joyously rushing the field.*
>
> *That day CC men's soccer program set their sights higher … as the program and teams still do to this day. True, we got (resoundingly) knocked out in the first round of the play-offs by the University of St. Louis (national champions 1965 and 1967) that year, and the following year (when I along with others formerly on the "Freshman Team" got to play), but the takeaway for us was going for it … individually and as a team. A treasured memory … and a life lesson too.*

John Boddington '69 and Peter Morse '68 from that squad, both standout players, were even invited for an Olympic Team try-out in Chicago. What an honor for the program and quite a boon for our fledgling recruiting efforts!

After graduation, John served his country with distinction in Vietnam, and Peter found a career in the petroleum world and ended up being an expatriate living in exotic places. He wrote to me in 2001 from the Indonesian Island of Sumatra, where he worked as a geophysicist in a "jungle" environment and coached three local youth soccer teams on the side!! (Our son Erik taught at a private school by then in Jakarta and was well on his way to becoming an expat as well.) Peter concludes his letter by extending greetings to the Boddingtons:

> *Please give my regards to John and Tim Boddington. I remember fondly all our soccer get-togethers at their house after soccer games. I will never forget how Bill Boddington pleaded my case with Dr. Worner (then president of the College) to allow me to return to CC after my sophomore year of exile. I hope I have a chance to travel to Colorado sometime in the near future and visit all of you.*

Peter's subsequent work assignment brought him to Nigeria where, after a competitive squash game, he unexpectedly and tragically died of a heart attack in 2011.

Evan Griswold '70 was a freshman in 1966 and as such under the then-NCAA rules, ineligible to play varsity ball. But it was evident in his first year that he would be a force on the field to be reckoned with. From his freshman year Evan remembers an eventful road trip:

> *Freshman year: The NCAA in 1966 still separated Freshman and Varsity teams, so although we all practiced and scrimmaged together, we had different game and traveling schedules. Bill Boddington was our Freshman coach that year and he had arranged for us to play the Colorado Rocky Mountain School (a secondary, boarding school) in Carbondale, Colorado.*
>
> *On a golden Friday afternoon in Colorado Springs, the team piled into several cars for the drive to Carbondale, about four hours distance through the mountains. The route took us up past Pikes Peak, shining with a dusting of early autumn snow, and west across South Park to Buena Vista on the Arkansas River. Mr. Boddington determined that since the weather was fine and Independence Pass was still open, we should take the short route over the pass, through Aspen, to Carbondale.*

1967 | 5-2-0
Front row, left to right: Coach Bill Boddington, Peter Morse (captain), David Smith, Simon Salinas, Craig Clayberg, Wink Davis, Coach Horst Richardson. **Middle row:** Eliot Field, Nick Rutgers, Tom Shuster, Mark Dunn, Peter Shidler, Steve Andrews, Manager Walter Bacon. **Back row:** Evan Griswold, John Boddington (captain). **Not pictured:** Ned Pike, John Volkman, Blake Wilson.

Up we went, higher and higher into the Collegiate Range, on a narrow and winding road bordered by stone walls built sometime in the 1930s by the WPA. While the sun shone brightly, the temperature dropped with altitude and we were riding in Mrs. Boddington's convertible with the top down. I was behind the wheel, with my knuckles showing whiter at each new hairpin turn and 1000-foot drop on the other side of the flimsy looking walls. Our teammate from Bogota, Colombia, Simon Salinas was tucked in the back seat and he had come prepared with a blanket.

Approaching the top of the pass, at nearly 12,000 feet above sea level, Simon decided to deploy his blanket for warmth. Unfortunately, the breeze caught the blanket and whipped it straight over my (The Driver's) head. Darkness! Fear and Panic! Instant thoughts of plunging through the wall and into the abyss!

Screaming to "Get this f#%^ing thing off my head," I gripped the wheel and stomped on the brake. The quick thinking and action by Tom Shuster, who was sitting beside me, restored my sight of the road and prevented an accident. The remainder of the trip down the other side of the pass and on to Carbondale was blessedly uneventful.*

Evan became an unbelievably athletic competitor whose speed and aggressive play struck fear into the hearts of our opponents. At an away game against Regis, the taunting home crowd and our bench almost got into a fight. Here is Evan's recounting:

The other memory I have is the story of the famous brawl at Regis College, precipitated by my throw-in from the sidelines into the face of one of the Regis players who was trying to prevent me from throwing the ball to one of my teammates. The ensuing melee is probably best described from the standpoint of a bystander rather than from that of one of the participants. It was ugly!

The first person off our bench to "defend" the encircled Evan on the other side of the field was none other than Assistant Coach Bill Boddington. He had a leg injury at the time and hobbled across the field swinging his cane, eager to knock down any Regis fan who came close to him. The referees eventually settled the melee and the game continued. We won the game 5-2.

Eliot Field '69 was a teammate of Evan Griswold and also a member of that NCAA squad which traveled to St. Louis for a play-off game. Eliot writes about that weekend:

Our trip to St. Louis: up the Arch (Gateway to the West), which was just under construction when we were there. I recall that we went up the elevator on the north side. What an adventure getting to the top and looking at the Mississippi below! And I think that was the trip that saw us lose to St. Louis on a hard-packed dust bowl, when the ball would bounce, and bounce some more, and bounce some more. A bad day at Black Rock!!

And from a memorable AFA victory, a game that I (Horst) remember as if it had been played yesterday, Eliot recalls the victory:

The game against AFA during our/my junior or senior year, I think. Goals were scored by guys who had never scored before, namely Rick Norcross and Steve Andrews, alias "Lurch," and our supporters, huddled together in the cold weather, flooded onto the field after we scored, and I think the final score was 2-1, and we likely went on to the NCAA tournament, after the victory over AFA.

May 12, 1968, marked a major milestone in the evolution of Colorado Springs soccer as an open soccer clinic for children, organized by Bill Boddington, Dieter Hentschel, and me attracted 200 youngsters to CC's Washburn Field. Chief attraction, of course, was the participation of CC varsity players.

Shortly thereafter, the Soccer Organization for Colorado Springs Youth (SOCSY) was formed. SOCSY experienced phenomenal growth, so much so that City Parks and Recreation

1968 | 5-5-0

Front row, left to right: Coach Horst Richardson, Simon Salinas, Craig Skowrup, Tom Shuster, Thomas Amory, Marc Lowenstein, John Boddington (captain), David Patton, Ned Holloway, Manager. **Back row:** Scott MacGregor, James Foster, David Rutherford, Carl Wheat, Jim Hopkins, Evan Griswold, Eliot Field, Ned Pike, Peter Shidler, Coach Bill Boddington.

---

struggled to find enough playing fields and volunteer coaches. Ten years after that initial clinic, there were close to 200 youth teams, both boys and girls, competing in town.

Another major milestone that year was the completion of the new El Pomar Sports Center, which brought gym, locker room, and training room facilities into the 20th century. Unfortunately, within years of opening the sports center, it became clear that the building was not user friendly to the accelerated participation of women in sports under Title IX, nor was any consideration given to handicap access. Also, there was no elevator in the three-story building, which made moving heavy equipment around a challenge.

Bill Boddington and I had settled into a routine of coaching. He managed the junior varsity effort and I coached the varsity. There were about 20 players on each team! Who will ever forget those wonderful post-game parties at the Boddingtons, with Bill serving the beer, and his wife, Jo, preparing homecooked *Himmlische Brulette*. The Boddingtons were also gracious hosts for the annual awards banquets. Bill's longtime and dedicated efforts on behalf of CC soccer earned him induction into the CC Sports Hall of Fame!

Tom Shuster '70 was a freshman in 1966. Not only was he a clever and versatile player, but also a dedicated and able student in several of my German classes. His excellence in the German language prompted me to cast him in leading roles in two German plays which I directed. He remembers an incident in his freshman year where his "acting" talents came in handy:

> *In my freshman year we played a "friendly" with the Air Force Academy. They were very fit and we felt we needed to seek some special advantages. To put them off we arranged for one of the CC students, who played the bagpipes, to pipe us on the field as we marched onto the pitch. We also had empty beer cans which we were apparently swigging down, but which were actually empty. It all did serve to lift our spirits a bit but I am afraid they did "take us to the cleaners." The painful part of the memory is the score which I am happy not to be able to recall.*

Tom also pays tribute to freshman coach Bill Boddington, who not only coached, but also provided summer employment to some of the players:

> *Being on the freshman team with Bill Boddington as coach did come with special privileges. Most important was, of course, access to their fridge with all the beer after the match. A close second was Bill's helpfulness in providing jobs for soccer players during semester or summer breaks at his lumberyard. (You were certainly worked hard but I think he figured that was a contribution to the next season's fitness!)*

1969 | 5-5-1

Front row, left to right: Jim Foster, Ward Hillyer, Mohammed Dalhoumi, Todd Brown, Evan Griswold (captain). **Back row:** David Rutherford, David Smith, Shahdad Zandford, David Ramsdell, William (Tad) Creasey, Craig Skowrup, Mike Young, Richard Johnson, Simon Salinas, Peter Shidler, Jim Hopkins (captain), Thomas Amory, Scott MacGregor, Bill Pugh. **Not pictured:** Ben Nitka and Charles Hosley.

EARNING NATIONAL RECOGNITION

The 1970s

In the early summer of 1970, Tom Shuster and I traveled together to the World Cup in Mexico. We actually managed to obtain press credentials, writing articles for the *Colorado Springs Sun*, whose sports department was somewhat partial to soccer.

We drove all the way to the colonial town of Guanajuato and made our headquarters there. Colorado College had a Spanish program there, and thus we had a couple of contacts to make our stay comfortable. No doubt the highlight of our stay was attending the England-West Germany game in Leon, which the Germans won in an overtime thriller 3-2. At the end of the second half, England was ahead 2-0 and substituted one of their stars, Bobby Charlton, assuming that the game was well in hand. Bobby walked to the bench, asked for a cigarette, and began to smoke to relax!!

1970-74

As we transition from the '60s to the '70s, mention must be made of four other players who left their marks at the turn of the decade.

David Rutherford had come from England with his mother and two brothers to live in Denver. His older brother started working for Bill Boddington's lumberyard in Denver and Bill became aware of the brothers' excellence in soccer. The youngest of the three, David, not only was keen on soccer, but was also looking for a college education. Bill brought him to campus, and arranged an interview with the head of the admission office, Dick Wood. Mr. Wood was impressed and admitted David. That proved to be a major recruiting coup, since David ended up being a major force on the field, an elegant midfield general alongside of John Boddington, whose energy was inexhaustible.

Ben Nitka, of Polish descent and needy family background, had come from Philadelphia. He had the strongest pair of legs I had ever seen. He would delight in kicking 50-yard field goals for the football team, but his heart was in soccer. He scored some amazing goals,

1970 | 8-5-2

Front row, left to right: Steve Wong (reclining), Charles Vogel, Jay Engeln, Tom Turner, Mike Young, Richard Johnson, Richard Burns, Bill Cramp, Jeff Jones. **Back row:** Scott MacGregor (captain), Peter Fairchild, David Rutherford (captain), Andre Zarb-Cousin, Todd Brown, Charles Hosley, Jim Hopkins (captain), Tad Creasey, Ben Nitka, Tim Boddington, Coach Horst Richardson, David West.

---

but somehow ended up in Boettcher Health Center too often after games to "recover" from competition, feigning injury. We all thought that he preferred the health center environment to his dorm room. He also became a card shark and won more poker games than soccer matches. He was one of the few soccer players who didn't graduate, preferring a try-out with a professional football team as a kicker.

Andre Zarb-Cousin was born in Malta, but by the time I met him he lived in Southern California and was already married. He had served in Vietnam with the U.S. Air Force and now played club ball in the Pacific Coast League in the sunny southland, where he averaged 2.5 goals per game. My dad, Walter Richardson, a high school teacher, became acquainted with Andre at a track meet and notified me of his athletic and soccer abilities. Dick Wood in our admission office, to whom Andre had written numerous times, took a chance on Andre, and Andre turned out to be a scoring machine for us. He once scored 8 goals in a single game and held the high-scoring record for nearly 20 years! He settled in Colorado Springs and now works with high school drop outs, channeling them back to school to learn a trade so the adolescents can become productive citizens, a most laudable enterprise.

And who could forget Steve Wong, our indomitable goalkeeper then. He had the capacity to make an easy save look spectacular. He would leap into the air, have the longest hang-time imaginable, snare the ball, and land gracefully, even on the hardest of surfaces. He was also a terrific cook of Chinese food, a skill which he often exhibited when we worked soccer camps in Vail together in the summers. In an alumni game at CC he and Tony Bryan, who by then was playing for the alums, had an unfortunate collision in front of goal, and Tony broke his leg. This incident put alumni games on hold for a while.

After graduating, Steve Wong '73 became goalkeeper coach for several years. He now is a Jungian psychotherapist. When I asked him to submit a memory, he wrote, in retrospect, about a Heidegger moment:

THE GATHERING

Players, coaches and friends are gathering together on Stewart Field for soccer practice. The cool, crisp air of fall with its deep blue sky, rich green grass, and the rustling yellow aspen leaves twinkling in the sunlight. The cotton balls from the cottonwood trees float and mix in with the laughing and smiling faces of soccer players running around the field, chasing the soccer ball and each other.

The whistle blows. "Form two lines!" bellows Coach Richardson, and a platoon of young men run laps around the field. Separating into small groups we practice passing, movement and ball control. Beads of sweat forming and dripping down our temples and foreheads as we sprint, stop and turn. Then shooting practice: players lining up with soccer balls ready to shoot. Boddington, Hopkins, Nitka, Cousin, Creasey, Turner, the whole team, even Bill Boddington, the 60-plus-year-old assistant soccer coach. All there to take a crack at the goalies.

Gathering around and behind the white netting draped over the back of the goal, are young kids, among them, Bruce Finley and Spencer Gresham (who would later grow up to be talented soccer players). Nitka hits a powerful shot and others follow suit. MacGregor and I take turns stopping the shots. We jump, stretch and catch or deflect the incoming bullets. Our bodies flying high and crashing into the ground. Soon a rhythm sets in. A shot, exploding off our feet, we stretch and snatch the ball with our fingertips but this time we hang in the air and float to the ground. Another shot ... spring, catch, hang and float. Over and over. The moment, the catch, a moment that defies gravity, suspended, a moment of freedom and of pure contentment.

1971 | 3-9-1

The closest thing to a 1971 team photo is one featuring a Colorado Springs All-Star team that took on visitors from Herford, West Germany, at Washburn Field on July 10, 1971. Tigers participating include Peter Fairchild, Tad Creasey, Andre Zarb-Cousin and Tim Boddington (CC captain), with Coach Horst Richardson. **Other 1971 Tigers in order of last name:** Peter Armstrong, Alan Carroll, Jay Engeln, Gary Gilligan, Zelfgang Guerrero, Richard Johnson, Jeff Jones, Olamide-Nelson-Cole-Agboola, Dave Patz, Gary Peterson, Richard Schulte, Peter Schwarz, Eric Smith, Tom Turner, Tony Visconsi, Charles Vogel, Larry Weisgal, Steve Wong and Mike Young, with coach Bill Boddington.

A number of years later, I went onto campus and, on impulse, went to Cossitt Hall, the old gym. Walking in the front door and past the rotunda, I went downstairs to the spacious dance room with all the polished mirrors and freshly sanded floor. I paused to take in the natural light coming from the windows up high. Stepping into the dark hallway I catch sight of a person out of the corner of my eyes. She said, "May I help you?" A bit awkwardly I replied, "I am here for memories." A pause. Then she said, "I remember you. I used to bring my dance classes to watch you during soccer practice. You flew up high and were suspended in the air before floating down." All these memories of the faces of teammates, coaches, friends and the fall season came rushing back! This was the first time we met and at such a unique moment formed by a memory. A pause, but such a sweet pause. My eyes teared up with gratitude and thanks as we nodded to each other and quietly departed into the dark hallway.

Walking out of Cossitt Hall, I suddenly realized it was Ursula Gray, the wife of distinguished philosophy Professor J. Glenn Gray. Professor Gray was instrumental in translating Martin Heidegger's favorite but complex word "versammeln" *into "the gathering." Heidegger's fourfold: "Earth, sky, mortals, divinities," i.e., "The Gathering," all this coming together on the practice field in the fall, "belonging-together."*

David Rutherford '71, the midfield general and Wong's teammate, is back in England now, but we stay in touch. In 2010, he sent me a CC soccer-related story which merits inclusion here:

Got to tell you this little story. Was in a crowded pub in Bath last Thursday with friends. Just got our drinks at the bar when a couple of young guys with an accent asked me where the action spots were in town. Well, there aren't many in Bath, and you certainly don't ask a 60 year old. I asked what they were doing in Bath and they said they were on a football tour. I thought they were from Oz, so I said is that Rules Football, they said no they were from the States and it was Football. I said Oh American Football, since they both had swollen noses. They said no, real football, soccerfootball. We finally found the Right sport! We laughed. So they were from Washington State, their coach is English, from Weston Super Mare, so they were playing a few English clubs. I said how did you get the swollen noses, and they both said by being elbowed! So much of that in the World Cup.

I said I lived and studied in the US, at CC, and they said ooooh we played them pre-season last year and beat them 2-1. Wow! What a small world; in a packed pub they find me. Do you know the college? I mean, really small, 1500 kids, by the Puget Sound? Would like to get hold of them to see if they survived the Bath night life!!

Soccer had become popular. In the '70s, the team began to take out-of-state road trips and competed against big-time opponents like SMU, UCLA, South Florida State, BYU, Cal-Santa Barbara, U-Chicago Circle, Southern Illinois, North Texas State, and U-Nevada at Las Vegas.

One opponent, the University of British Columbia, traveled here for six years in a row. We only beat them once. After their fourth trip here, I asked the coach what attracted them to return every year. "Well," he said, "we come to bet on the dogs at the race track, and the post-game parties at the Boddingtons are fabulous." Several times Bill Boddington discovered UBC players sleeping soundly on his lawn in the morning after a late party!

Peter Fairchild '73, a most determined defender for us at the turn of the decade, remembers the UBC post-game parties at the Boddingtons with fondness:

It would be very difficult to take a look back at the early '70s and not remember the memorable games played against the University of British Columbia – or more specifically, the absolutely incredible parties at the Jo and Bill Boddington residence after the matches. To say that the boys (and coaches) from UBC enjoyed adult beverages would be a monumental understatement. Those were some great times.

Although the team from Vancouver provided somewhat of an international flavor, the first "real" international matches were played on Washburn Field in the summer of 1971. A team from West Germany and one from Austria were on sports tours of the U.S. and included stops in Denver and Colorado Springs. The games in town were somewhat of a CC affair, as Professor Dirk Baay was one of the linesmen, I coached the Colorado Springs All-Stars, and five members of the CC squad were on the All-Star team: Tim Boddington, Tad Creasey, Peter Fairchild, Mike Young, and Andre Zarb-Cousin.

Another feather in the soccer cap of CC that summer was the hosting of one of the very first United States Soccer Federation (USSF) licensing clinics. The USSF had hired a

1972 | 9-3-2

Front row, left to right: Peter Schwarz, Dave Pertz, Richard Johnson, Jon Roberts, Mike Young, John Middleton, Larry Weisgal, Bob Shook (reclining). **Back row:** Peter Fairchild, Andre Zarb-Cousin, Mark Johnstone, Steve Wong, Tad Creasey (captain), Peter Gordon, Dick Schulte, Todd Brown, Dave Patz, Gary Peterson, Jim Terrall. **Not pictured:** Jay Engeln, Nick Houston, Doug Obletz, Tom Turner, Tony Visconsi.

world-renowned coach from Germany, Dettmar Cramer, to be the first National Director of Coaching. Coach Cramer, only 5'4", conducted intensive field and classroom sessions for 30 certification candidates, most of whom passed the course, including me. Becoming acquainted with Dettmar that week paid off several years later when he, as the Bayern Munich coach, extended an invitation to me and my son Erik to attend a Bundesliga game, VIP seating.

In rummaging through old soccer correspondence from those years, I discovered to my surprise several letters I had written to the U.S. State Department in which I request assistance to organize a soccer tour of Indonesia! These fledgling efforts came to naught; our first foreign tour would have to wait until 1988.

The Colorado College Block Plan was adopted in 1970. During the first block break ever, in late September, the squad took a road trip to Provo, Utah, for a doubleheader. And what a road trip it was!

We didn't have enough of a budget to rent cars, so we drove our own vehicles. Tim Boddington drove his mom's car, I took our VW bus, and two more vehicles were loaded up. Because of final exams we couldn't all leave at the same time, and we were going to spend the first night camping at Dinosaur National Monument on the Colorado-Utah border.

So the advance party left yellow headbands tied up on critical junctures on the highways to guide the rest of the crew to Echo Park on the banks of the Yampa River. Amazingly, we all made it by 8 p.m., even though the steep and twisty dirt road down the canyon to the campground was slow going. We had a cook-out and found spots for tents. Outdoorsman Jay Engeln had found an abandoned raft along the bank of the river and figured if he tied it to a tree and gave the line some slack, he would be sleeping in a comfortable water bed. During the night the water level rose, and Jay almost drifted down to rapids below. Even worse was the fact that it drizzled a bit that night, and I didn't sleep a wink because I worried that the next morning we wouldn't be able to drive up the canyon road because the rain might have turned it into slick mud. But we made it, arrived in Provo in time for the game, tied the first one and won the second by a good margin.

Peter Fairchild, who probably sported the longest hair on the team and wore a yellow headband proudly, has this to say about that Salt Lake City trip:

> *I should also mention the trip, in personal vehicles, to Salt Lake City for a game with Brigham Young University. Vague memories of standing at a burger stand seemingly out in the middle of nowhere on a very windy and cool day, and Tim Boddington warming his hands between the burger buns. A late night arrival to our camping site in Dinosaur National Park – only discovered because of the CC gold headbands left tied by teammates to trees and bushes along the route. The interesting looks and comments from the BYU fans – the entire team, regardless of hair length, wore the previously mentioned headbands. Quite a sight.*

That BYU trip was one of our first extended road trips, and it was done on a shoestring. Once we arrived there, though, and started to play, any hardships of travel were forgotten and the competitive juices began to flow. Andre Zarb-Cousin '73, our high-scorer and threat up front, remembers the encounter:

> *Our four-car cavalcade slowed as we entered the Brigham Young University campus the afternoon of the game. It was 1970, but the 60's hippie movement was still alive and well...just not at BYU. Our team's long hair, beards and bandannas sent an instant shockwave across the faces of the well-groomed Brigham Young students who stopped in their tracks to gawk at the aliens from another planet. Tom Turner decided we should really give them a jolt and walk straight down the middle of their lush, green, perfectly manicured campus lawn.*
>
> *By the time the game started that night, it was obvious that word had spread like wildfire and BYU fans were calling for blood. They saw us as an easy win. Within a few minutes of the start of the game I scored our first goal. After the kickoff BYU's sweeper ran up and shoved me, saying, 'You were lucky. That won't happen again!' Pointing my finger at him I retorted confidently, 'Next time I touch the ball I'll score'; and to my surprise, I did. Minutes later I scored a third goal. About twenty minutes into the game it was 3-0 and the fans' fury was electric. On our next attack the referee called an off-side on me from midfield, so I yelled loudly 'No!' I think he hydroplaned at me waving a red card and just like that, I was out of the game — much to the joy of the BYU team and fans. Our awesome CC team finished up with a 5-3 win. Unforgettable day!*

(By the way, in those days we played 22 1/2-minute quarters!!)

Tom Turner '73, a freshman along on that fabled road trip, has fond memories of that adventure. In addition, he adds a political dimension to the trip which I had totally forgotten:

> *Between Andre Zarb-Cousin, Ben Nitka and David Rutherford and others, I was dumbstruck with the caliber of play. The team was scheduled to go to Provo in mid September but I hadn't really made the team. Fortunately for me, I was not as politically savvy as some of the older players who decided to boycott BYU because of their stand on race issues … and I was included in the traveling team with the aforementioned, Scott MacGregor, Steve Wong, Tim Boddington, Tad Creasey, Todd Brown, John Middleton, Peter Fairchild, Alan Carroll, et al.*
>
> *We piled into 3 or 4 station wagons and headed west. Probably more than the game or games we played, most indelible in my mind was the trip to and the night we spent on the Green (or was it the Yampa) River. It seemed just a tad bit disorganized, where to camp, what to eat, even a small question as to "Where were we, really?"*
>
> *Remember, this is 1970 and as a team, we were a motley crew … very long hair, pony tails and army surplus green pants with hand-sewn patches. Stepping on to the BYU campus was akin to stepping back in time — say 10 or 15 years, give or take. Male students with very short hair and all wearing coats and ties. Female students all in dresses and coiffed hairdos. Todd Brown and Tad Creasey were escorted out of the Student Union. I am sure they were in cutoffs and barefooted. It was decided that we would all wear homemade black armbands as a protest of LDS doctrine regarding Blacks.*
>
> *I think we may have won or at least tied them in one game. I do remember a few of the BYU players remarking about our '70s look, "We didn't know that long haired hippies could even play soccer."*
>
> *We were given a small slick-looking book about the history of the LDS. My copy later became the perfect shim to our refrigerator in our Tejon St. apartment.*
>
> *The soccer may not have been as much fun as I remember but I always get a huge grin on my face thinking about CC soccer. To this day, I think you were the perfect coach. You were knowledgeable about the game and your calm demeanor really set the tone for the game. Thank you, Coach.*

This first block break trip to BYU, to be sure a memorable one, was the beginning of a tradition of block break soccer journeys. The block breaks in the fall provided opportunities to schedule intriguing road trips against key regional opponents. Initially these trips were made in private cars and then in College vans. As the budget increased, we could afford the CC highway bus, and eventually we traveled by air.

I could write a whole chapter on my days as bus driver for the team, sitting behind the wheel of the "Desert Shark," driving to Grinnell, Iowa, or Las Cruces, New Mexico. As we get into the '80s, I will return to this topic.

Jon Roberts '74, now in the Psychology and Neuroscience Department at the University of Colorado, Boulder, was a total novice to soccer when he tried out in the early '70s. CC Professor Salvatore Bizzarro, on whose recreational team Jon had played, recommended to me that I should give him a try-out, and he managed to make the cut. Jon writes:

> *The first weeks were grueling, with training runs and intense drills, and one time, walking back from the field to the locker room after practice you (Horst) told us that before we got to go shower, we had to run 220s on the track until one of us could make it in some number of seconds that seemed, and was, unattainable. You had mercy on us and after a few tries let us off …*
>
> *I loved it all! Walking back to the dorm exhausted after practice … flying to Kansas to play Benedictine University in heat and humidity I had never experienced … driving CC vans over Independence Pass to play a "friendly" in the Aspen Tournament … beating the University of British Columbia 2-1 the year they were Canadian national champs (we got help from the fact that they arrived late and had to sleep on the floor of the astroturf room in El Pomar; they came back and kicked our asses in a snowstorm the following year!) … flying to Chicago to play Northern Illinois and Wheaton — we were picked up at the airport by limousines arranged by North Shore Chicago parents (probably arranged by the Engelns, Schultes, and Shooks, parents who were most generous hosts) … and then the team parties at the Boddingtons' house …*

It would be fair to say that in the early varsity years, and well through the '90s, we received more press coverage than we get today. All you have to do is look at the scrapbooks for those seasons and compare them with recent ones.

Well, first of all, there were two newspapers in town, and *The Colorado Springs Sun* had a sports reporter, Greg Lathram, who really gave the relatively new game extensive coverage. Karl Licis at *The Gazette* was similarly inclined. And, no doubt, the two were aware of the enormous growth of the sport at the youth level. In the '70s, women's and girls' sports weren't covered. The AFA sports program was in its infancy, and UCCS was not yet a factor in local sports.

I regularly and judiciously would call both the sports desks of *The Gazette* and *The Sun* after each game. While the players were showering, I would find a phone and would make collect calls to report the score, some statistics, and a few highlights. I think the reporters appreciated the fact that I checked in with them, helping them learn about that new game of soccer.

One event, which occurred in Chicago in the early '70s, I did not report to the papers. We had a number of players from Chicago's north shore on the team and made successive appearances against Lake Forest College, Wheaton College, University of Illinois, both at Chicago Circle and De Kalb. The parents of our Chicago players were stupendous hosts, providing generous room and board. One of the parents had a membership in the Playboy Club and enabled a visit for the team to see the "bunnies." Two teammates, injured and on crutches, also went to the club. Someone took a picture of them next to a buxom "bunny." The photograph appeared in the campus paper the following week, which increased the injured players' popularity considerably.

George Jackson '76, who was a sophomore on the team and wrote for *The Catalyst*, still has his *Catalyst* articles on file at home and reviewed his journalism days to submit his summary of that event:

> *Most of my old articles were too boring even for me to read, but one stands out because of the picture that ran with the story. The picture shows (immortalizes) Jon Roberts and Mike Dennis posing with their crutches with a Playboy bunny. I recall that somehow we left our Chicago host families, drove downtown, and we were admitted into the famous Playboy Club — most of us under age. We all chipped in to pay a hefty fee for the picture to be taken of the guys in the 'pose with a bunny' Polaroid picture booth. I will take the liberty of editing my original 1973* Catalyst *article to tell the tale:*
>
> *"The Bengal booters booted and bunnied over the block break as they traveled to Chicago for a two game stand. The Tigers met Wheaton College Thursday ... blah blah blah, blah blah blah, blah blah blah ... Then with the help of Mr. Shook's Playboy credit card the team went out for some evening entertainment. The bunnies and refreshments proved to be especially therapeutic for cripples Dennis and Roberts.*

Saturday saw the team traveling to play Northern Illinois University ... blah blah blah ... blah blah blah ... blah blah blah blah blah."

Ok, so where was Horst? What kind of college allows this? A good one, obviously.

Dick Schulte '75 adds: "After arriving in Chicago on Wednesday, the Tigers were superbly hosted by the Engeln, Peters, Shook, Schulte and Weisgal families. The hosts all saw to it that the team members were well fed, entertained and never thirsty."

Also, there is a quote from Bill Boddington in the article as he was interviewed at the end of the road trip. Asked his opinion of the trip, Bill said, "We played some good soccer ... and the drinks were quite good." Priceless.

An incident, memorable in quite a different way, occurred in 1973 on a road trip to the Kansas City area. We were competing against St. Benedictine College in Atchison, Kansas, on a field up on a bluff overlooking the beautiful Missouri Valley. On our team was John Grenardo, a black player, originally from Guyana. He was a bit older than the average student and was a veteran. At half time he came off the field, visibly upset. Apparently the referee had

1973 | 6-8-4

Front row, left to right: Coach Horst Richardson, Alan Carroll, Jay Engeln (captain), George Jackson, Jeff Jones, Brad Turner, Jim Terrall, John Grenardo, Don Clark. **Back row:** John Middleton, Coach Bill Boddington, Dave Patz, Randy Millian, Larry Weisgal, Jon Roberts, Mike Dennis, Doug Obletz, Bob Shook, Charles Hosley, Dick Schulte, Manager Lee Weisgal. **Not pictured:** Nick Houston, Dave Pertz, Jamie Peters, Gary Peterson, Peter Schwarz, John Weiss.

called him derogatorily "Boy" a couple of times, and John was going to slug him. John kept his cool and continued playing, and I admired him for his controlled behavior.

Coaching soccer was becoming a full-time job. My primary employment at CC, of course, was teaching in the German Department. I didn't have an office in the Athletics Department, but conducted soccer correspondence, recruiting phone calls, and scheduling out of my German office. How lucky I was to have supportive secretarial staff there to be understanding about my "second" job. And Jerry Carle, the Athletic Director, was also patient with me and allowed me to conduct soccer business without much interference or supervision from him.

In September 1974, I sent him an interoffice memorandum, from my German office, to address the "state of affairs" as I saw them then:

> *Dear Jerry:*
>
> *I would like to voice my concern about the lack of playing field space at Colorado College. This matter is not only of importance to Varsity and Club Sports, but also to the entire College community. Recently the Rugby Club approached me with the request to play their home games on Stewart Field. ..... Stewart Field is heavily taxed already. In the fall, varsity and j.v. soccer games are staged there, and now rugby as well. In the spring, there is lacrosse and rugby and some soccer activities. Add to that early football practice and all the practice time for soccer and lacrosse, and pretty soon Stewart Field will be a dirt lot.*
>
> *We do have a number of dirt lots on campus already, and I propose that they be turned into playing fields. Unquestionably, the need exists. CC coeds have practically no opportunity to engage in field sports, although there is demand for field hockey, soccer, and touch football. The intramural program is handicapped by lack of adequate playing fields. The baseball team hasn't been on campus in years. I propose that the dirt lot west of Mathias and parallel to Uintah, as well as the College property to the east of Nevada, be considered for playing field spaces. .....*
>
> *An alternative would be astroturfing Washburn Field and installing adequate lighting. In this way Washburn Field could be used round the clock and absorb much athletic traffic.*

1974 | 13-6-1

Front row, left to right: Bill Scott, Bob Shook, Dick Schulte (captain), Ken Millian, Bruce Petterson. **Middle row:** Peter Schwarz, Guy Jackson, Jim Terrall, Brad Turner, John Grenardo, John Monteiro, Larry Weisgal, George Robb, Karl Soderstrom, Ron Edmondson, Goalie Coach Steve Wong. **Back row:** Manager Lee Weisgal, Coach Bill Boddington, Dave Dietel, Tom Lee, Chris Marks, George Jackson, Chuck Donley, Steve Paul, Alan Carroll (captain), Jamie Peters, Randy Millian, Coach Horst Richardson. **Not pictured:** Don Clark, Jeff Jones.

My German Department secretary helped me send this memo to all the important entities on campus; the Athletic Board had some discussions on the matter, but nothing came of it for years.

Bill Boddington had his own solution to improving the parched turf of Stewart Field. Our stellar fullback, Peter Fairchild, who worked at Boddington's lumberyard on occasions, submitted this anecdote about Bill's subversive activities:

> *One of my earliest memories of Colorado College soccer occurred immediately after my arrival at CC. As an incoming Freshman in the first year of the block plan, I was also working afternoons at the Boddington Lumber Company when not at soccer practice.*
>
> *In that fall of 1970, Stewart Field for some unexplained reason was not receiving irrigation priority when compared with football's Washburn Field. It really wasn't in great shape. In the back of Bill Boddington's green Ford station wagon (we all remember it fondly) were several lengths of 100' garden hose. After work, Bill and*

> *I would drive down onto the edge of the field and park out of sight in the northeast corner. I would quietly climb up through the bushes and hook up the hose to one of the sorority houses and we would set up a couple of sprinklers. I am not quite sure that we had the blessing of the CC physical plant for this activity!*

Coach Boddington employed a number of players in his lumber company, mostly in Colorado Springs, of course, but sometimes also in Denver. I distinctly remember working at his yard in Denver during the Christmas break in 1970 with his son Tim, unloading railroad cars full of moldings and door frames. Bill gave me a chance to earn badly needed funds to pay for the birth of our first child, Erik. There were no maternity benefits extended then to college employees!

John Middleton '74, a novice player from Texas, ended up being co-captain in his senior year. He speaks highly of Bill Boddington in his reflections on his soccer career at CC:

As a freshman, I wasn't really skilled enough for the varsity group, but I was fortunate and blessed to spend time with Coach Bill Boddington on the junior varsity. He was kind enough to take me on as a personal project (one of his many acts of kindness to young players, I'm sure). He would meet me at the kick boards for shooting practice and other drills. With time, practice, and his patient coaching, I was able to make the varsity squad my junior year.

John is now an M.D. in Denver. Of his teammate David Rutherford, John offers the following comments:

> *One of the best was a tall lanky Englishman who played center mid, David Rutherford. He seemed to have eyes in the back of his head, and if you tried to get inside his space, he simply executed one of the many options he had been processing and passed the ball off successfully to a teammate. After a while, most people kind of gave up on trying to challenge "the field general."*

(John Middleton, by the way, married one of my favorite German majors, Melinda Smith. They met each other in my German Abroad class. At their wedding, our son, Erik, was the ring bearer, and our daughter, Stacia, was the flower girl.)

An important person on campus was Robert "Bob" Brossman, vice president of the college. On occasions I would meet him in "The Hub" in Rastall Center prior to a morning's class, and he, in his inimitable way, would give me some advice on my beginning career as a coach at a distinguished Division III liberal arts college. "Horst," he would say, "you are winning too many games!" I guess he implied that victories are important, but much is to be learned from losing, and from recovering from defeat. A solid lesson from a wise counselor!

Wisdom of a different kind was offered by player Gary Peterson '75, who remembers the work-hard, play-hard spirit of CC soccer which made it unique. But even during intense practice sessions, there were moments to pause for reflection:

> *We would be in the middle of an intense practice session and then suddenly stop for five minutes to watch and admire an amazing purple and orange sunset over Pikes Peak! Purple mountain majesty indeed!!*

We won the first of three successive Rocky Mountain Intercollegiate Soccer League (RMISL) championships that year, and also broke into the national rankings for the first time. With success on the field, recruiting outreach became more widespread. New England, Chicago, the Twin Cities, and the Northwest were principal providers of talented student athletes, and soccer grew in Colorado, and indeed in Colorado Springs. And, of course, I always had my eye open to international prospects.

One of the most far-fetched recruiting stories of a foreign student ever began when a West German high school graduate visited the beaches of southern Spain on a summer camping trip.

Kornel Simons '79 and a high school buddy had pitched their tent in a campground close to the beach and in the evening had gone out on the town. When they returned around midnight, they noticed to their surprise that two young women were sleeping soundly in their tent. They gently awakened the two ladies, who were totally embarrassed and explained that they had been to a party and, a bit tipsy, apparently mistook the boys' tent as theirs. The next morning the two gals, who turned out to be rookie teachers from Colorado Springs, apologized and as a gesture of goodwill invited the two Germans to "come visit us sometime."

Well, the two Germans came to the U.S. the next summer and hitchhiked their way across the American West, eventually wanting to visit their "tent" friends in Colorado Springs. The two Germans had been stuck in Hartsel, in South Park, for a while until they got a ride. Once in the vehicle, Kornel and his friend asked the driver if she had heard any news about the World Cup, which was staged that summer in West Germany. The German team was in the final with Holland, and the two hitchhikers desperately wanted to find out the result. Well, the driver, as it turns out, was an acquaintance of mine and didn't know, but she said that she would drop them off in Colorado Springs at the house of someone who surely would know. And 90 minutes later, the boys were at our house!

And a year thereafter Kornel Simons started his extraordinary career at CC. Not only was he a supreme player but also a true student of the liberal arts. He ended up marrying a CC coed and lives in Chicago. By the way, he never did hook up with the two "tent" ladies from the Spanish beach.

In 1974, we won the RMISL and awaited a bid to the NCAA tournament. However, as was the case in 1970, the expected invitation to post-season play did not materialize. This time it turned out to be a "strength of schedule" issue. The RMISL commissioner, Dr. G. K. "Joe" Guennel, explained in an article in *The Denver Post*: "The loss to the AFA will probably keep them out of the NCAAs, even though they won the league. Actually, I don't think that anybody from the RMISL will be invited. Now that our league is in the Midwest Region, it's tougher."

In 1970 there were, I believe, two issues: One was an identity issue. In those days there were two NCAA divisions, the University and the Collegiate division. Even though CC, a small, private liberal arts institution, obviously should have been considered "collegiate," it was not so designated because west of the Mississippi no distinction was made between "collegiate" and "university" brackets. The other consideration from the NCAA's point of view was, and to a degree continues to be true today, that CC is simply too isolated geographically to be in the running for post-season play unless the season record is so overwhelmingly successful that the team undeniably warrants an invitation to the "big dance."

Here is a letter from 1970, which I wrote to the team after we were "disinvited":

> *With some misgivings I wish to explain the reasons which brought about the anticipated California trip fiasco. When Mr. Paul Fardy, the coach from California State-Fullerton, invited us to participate in the first Western NCAA Collegiate Tournament, I naturally accepted.*
>
> *To appreciate what follows, it needs to be pointed out that CC Soccer, under the efforts of Coach Boddington, has repeatedly requested to participate in the NCAA Collegiate bracket instead of the University Division, but was always informed that west of the Mississippi, a division between University and Collegiate in soccer did not exist; competition here was restricted to University Division only.*

Naturally I was somewhat upset when the tournament chairman in California informed me that CC was ineligible to compete since it was listed as "university division" in the NCAA tournament handbook. I attempted to explain that this designation was due to our hockey program and certainly did not apply to soccer. Thereupon I was informed that a year ago there was an NCAA change in rules, which stated that an institution must declare itself whether it wishes to compete in the NCAA Collegiate or University division at the beginning of the fall season. This decision then applies to ALL sports in the institution. This I did not know.

Mr. Boddington and I contacted Mr. Carle, our athletic director, who in turn contacted the head of the NCAA in Kansas City to see if we might appeal this ruling. Our effort proved to be futile.

In late November 1970, the CC student paper, *The Catalyst*, ran a headline in the sports section: "CC SOCCER TEAM IS TOURNEY BOUND." It was disclosed on November 18 that the CC fighting Bengal Soccer Team has been invited to participate in the NCAA COLLEGE Division Soccer Tournament to be held in Fullerton, California, at the site of the host team, Cal-State Fullerton. Chico State, and either U-Cal Davis or Pomona College, were to be the other three teams. A week later the headline in *The Catalyst* read: "TIGER SOCCER TEAM DECLARED INELIGIBLE FOR COMPETITION IN NCAA TOURNAMENT." The reason for the ineligible status, as stated above, was the discrepancy between university vs. collegiate status.

Today, when a college team wins its conference, as was the case with us in 1974, the NCAA extends an automatic bid to the post-season tournament. Not so then. Selection was made by a committee of coaches and administrators who attempted to select the best teams. In 1975, with a 15-3-2 record, the RMISL championship in hand, and the first national ranking (No. 19) in the sport's history, there was no question about being invited to post-season play. But more about that in a minute.

With the arrival of Jay Engeln on campus in 1970, there began a fruitful recruiting effort from Chicago's North Shore, which culminated with the presence of the "Chicago Seven" on the team in 1974. These players, Don Clark, Larry Weisgal, Jamie Peters, Tom Lee, Bob Shook, Jeff Jones, and Dick Schulte, spent their high school playing careers at New Trier and Evanston secondary schools. They were a competitive, experienced, and skillful group who provided the backbone for many a Tiger victory. (And their parents were super hosts for us on away trips to Chicago.)

Every year at our awards banquet we present an "Animal Award" to the most aggressive player in honor of Jay Engeln, who earned the "animal" moniker during an AFA game. In colliding with an opponent, remnants of blood from the "Zoomie" spotted his jersey. For the rest of the season, Jay refused to wash his uniform, preferring to sport those battle scars during subsequent contests. As a senior, Jay marked out the AFA All-American sensation, Lenny Salvemini, helping us protect a hard-fought 2-2 tie.

Jay became a high school biology teacher and successful soccer coach, a National Principal of the Year at Colorado Springs Palmer High School, and eventually president of the National Soccer Coaches Association of America. He is also a CC Athletic Hall of Famer. Jay, prompted to submit the genesis of the "Animal Award," sent in this history of how the award came to be:

> *The first Animal Award was presented in the fall of 1973. The Animal Award was established by graduating senior soccer captain Jay Engeln '74 and presented to junior Jamie Peters at the end-of-the season team banquet held in the living room of the Boddington residence. The award consisted of a dog collar with an "Animal" dog tag attached. The instructions that accompanied the award were that Jamie (and then future recipients) would pass the award on to the CC junior soccer player who was most deserving of the honor by exhibiting all-out effort and determination on the field and in practice. The holder of the Animal Award dog collar would be the person to select the next recipient. Presentation of the Animal Award has been an ongoing tradition at the annual CC soccer team banquet since 1973.*
>
> *Where did the name 'Animal' originate? A story in* The Catalyst *following the CC vs. Air Force soccer match in 1970 included the following:*
>
> *"Jay Engeln, the freshman wing who has proven to be a consistently good player throughout the season, received a concussion in a head-on collision with an Air Force cadet. The concussion, ('just say that I was shook up') was serious enough to send Engeln from the remainder of the game and to the Academy hospital [along with the Air Force player] for a checkup and rest. The loss of the freshman wing was another contributing factor to the inability of the CC offense to put in more goals. (CC lost 3-1.)*
>
> *"Upon returning to practice later in the week, CC teammates teased Engeln about the incident. Peter Fairchild and Tom Turner, fellow freshmen on the team, were relentless in their comments. As the team was gathered around Horst Richardson*

> *and Bill Boddington at the end of practice, Horst expressed concern (always worried about the budget) that Engeln's jersey was torn down the front and was permanently stained by the AFA player's blood. Tom Turner joked, 'Jay, you are such an animal.' Well, the name stuck and the tradition of the Animal Award still carries on."*

An animal of a different sort ended up in my shorts one day at a game in the '73 season. It is common knowledge that I become nervous before every game. In order to relax before the important first game of that season, I started to chop some wood in our backyard. I wore long overalls for this activity and noticed at one point a curious itch along my left leg. Not giving it much thought, I walked over to the college, met the team in the locker room, gave an invigorating talk, and then coached the game. I also had a habit of crouching and kneeling during games, and during this match I became annoyed by an occasional twitch in my lower stomach area. I attributed this to muscle fatigue from chopping wood. We won the match vs. Wyoming 3-1. Once the game was over, and the players had dispersed, Helen and I visited friends, sitting comfortably in their living room. All of a sudden I jumped up, clutched my groin, reached into my underpants, and pulled out a small and very dead lizard!! The critter had been enjoying my body warmth for hours but died of fright when I grabbed my lower stomach region.

On an annual basis an outstanding CC midfielder is recognized with the Dick Schulte "Midfielder of the Year" Award. This award is given in honor of Dick Schulte, who was one of the "Chicago Seven" and a superbly gifted central player. Dick scored the only goal in a 1-0 victory against AFA in 1974, which produced the first win over the Academy in six years. He was agile, determined, deceptive, and he could run forever. Upon graduation he was employed at Boddington Lumber, and eventually became a successful entrepreneur. Dick's support of our program over time has been truly outstanding. Dick Schulte '75 remembers the AFA game vividly and recounts the events leading up to the goal:

> *So, the Air Force game — my most memorable game at CC, a 3 p.m. match at Stewart Field in mid-September. We beat them 1-0 on a goal that I scored about 15 minutes into the second half. First defeat of the Zoomies in 6 years that "the Tigers relished with the enthusiasm of a World Cup win." Quotes are from an article in* The Gazette Telegraph *written by Joe Navarro about the game.*
>
> *I took a pass from left wing Larry Weisgal and fired a right-footer upper ninety left-hand corner from about 25 yards out. One of those shots you take when the*

moment you strike the ball, you know it's going in. Their keeper had no chance. And, you (Horst) had given the job of marking Zoomie ace Lenny Salvemini to Bobby Shook and he basically marked him out of the match. One helluva game and a great victory for us.

We went on to win the RMISL that year as well by beating DU 2-1 away on the final game of the season. We had an 11-1 league record in 1974 and won the league for the first time since 1967. I think beating Air Force that year was literally a game-changer for the team and gave us the confidence that we could beat anybody that year. Horst, your quote after the DU game: "Obviously I am pleased with the performance of the squad. It's the first time we have played 19 games in a season and the first time we've won 13 games."

(Our dynamo midfielder Bob Shook had broken his leg in the '73 away game at D.U., and in '74 he played with a fractured wrist which was cast and bandaged. What a competitor he was!!)

The defense in the mid '70s featured George Jackson, Tom Lee, Bob Shook, Don Clark, and Bruce Petterson. What a hard-nosed group they were! George, aside from being a part-time magician and better known as "Jorge the Magnificent," also wrote clever and witty articles about the team for *The Catalyst* to document our successes and occasional failures.

Jorge and I recently met and chatted about the "good old days." He reminded me of a lousy night game played on the rain-soaked astroturf at De Kalb, Illinois. Here is his account of that evening:

Then there was the miserable night game in the rain in De Kalb, Illinois, when I realized that there was a God. We lost the game, and I was responsible for two goals against us and I knew it just wasn't my night. After the game, Horst gathered us in the dripping concrete locker room under the bleachers and announced that he did not have enough airline tickets for everybody for the flight home. He would conduct a drawing of straws to choose one of us who would return to Colorado Springs in the back of a Volkswagen bug driven by some non-soccer CC students who had journeyed the 15 hours to Illinois for the block break.

I was absolutely certain that it was my night to lose that lottery. But, the short straw went to our captain that year, Alan Carroll. I realized that it could only have been divine intervention that spared me my just penance. Alan, with incredible graciousness, accepted the dreadful fate that was rightfully mine. Puzzlingly, I never thought to question Horst as to why he did not have enough airline tickets ...

Brad Turner '77 remembers a road trip out West, where the guys had to sleep out on the ground camping style:

Then there was the road trip to Las Vegas in 1974. Tom Lee's station wagon had a third seat facing backwards in the rear. John Grenardo, my best friend, and I rode in this seat, watching the road move away from us as we caravaned through the Southwest.

We camped that night in a state park in the San Juan Mountains. John, having grown up in Guyana, was not about to sleep on the ground in a sleeping bag because "There's bears out there!" So John slept, or tried to, sitting up in the back seat of Tom Lee's station wagon. I tried to sleep on the ground in my sleeping bag but I kept thinking about what John had said: "I am not sleeping on the ground. There's bears out there!"

It wasn't an hour of lying there in my sleeping bag listening for rustling sounds in the bushes, remembering John's scary voice saying: "There's bears out there!" before I was knocking on the window of the station wagon for John to let me in. Of course he had locked the doors — "You never know if a bear might open the door while you're asleep," said John after I got into the car. So the both of us tried sleeping, sitting up in the back seat of Tom Lee's station wagon, because "There's bears out there!!"

1975

As we enter the fabled 1975 season, three men deserve mention: Bill Scott, Kornel Simons, and John Monteiro.

Bill Scott discovered CC on a cross-country trip from Massachusetts to the West Coast. He stopped at CC to see a friend, who encouraged him to "kick the ball around" with the team. Clearly, he had "what it takes." After he was admitted, I discovered that he had written part of his application in blank verse! He was an effective and articulate leader of men and competed tirelessly to win, but always with a twinkle in his eye. He was one of two players ever to be selected Most Valuable Player three times and captain once. (The other player to be honored in such a way was David Rutherford.)

Here's a story which has to be unique in the annals of CC soccer history: During the first block break of the 1975 season, our squad had entered a tournament in Santa Barbara,

1975 | 15-3-2

Front row, left to right: Bill Scott, Jim Balderston, Bob Shook (captain), Ron Edmondson, Bruce Petterson. **Middle row:** Coach Horst Richardson, Richard Chilcott, Pablo Lorca, Don Clark, Kornel Simons, Randy Stein, Goalie Coach Steve Wong. **Back row:** student trainer, Frank Lane, Dave Dietel, Brad Turner, John Monteiro, George Jackson (captain), Tom Lee. **Not pictured:** John Grenardo, Sam Harper, Nick Houston, Guy Jackson, Chris Marks.

California. The opening match for us was against Chico State. We lost the game 3-1, in a physically grueling contest. No wonder that the team wanted to visit the beach to relax.

Once on the golden sands of the Pacific shore, we walked south, dipping our feet into the water. Imagine our surprise when we suddenly discovered that we had stumbled into a nude beach area. The nude sun-seekers were stretched out in the late afternoon sun, away from the beach at the bottom of a cliff. What an opportunity, thought Bill, to go skinny dipping! And so most of the team stripped and jumped into the waves.

Once we were back at the parking lot, a police cruiser was there to meet us. The officer approached me, guessing correctly that I was the adult, and proceeded to show me a Polaroid picture of Bill in the nude, indicating that this individual was going to be charged with indecent exposure. The police were in the habit of surveying the nude beach from the top of the cliff where they could easily take telephoto shots of the skinny dippers. The savvy nude sunbathers tucked themselves in against the slope below the cliff, thus not visible from above. Our team, of course, was fully exposed.

It took all my diplomatic skills in the parking lot to convince the officer that the "mountain boys" from Colorado, never having been at an ocean, went a bit overboard in trying to forget a tough overtime loss. When Bill Scott retired from coaching soccer at Phillips-Andover prep school, I told this story at his party, evoking a hilarious response.

By the way, in the second tournament game against the host, UC Santa Barbara, we played exceedingly well for 110 minutes. The 0-0 tie was settled in favor of the host after the ninth penalty shot.

In a previous anecdote, we met Kornel Simons already. Kornel, affectionately called "Connie," might have had a professional career in his home country of West Germany, but his priorities were to see the world. Once he became a member of our team, it was immediately evident that we had found a jewel. During our 1975 blockbuster season, we received quite a lot of newspaper coverage, and Connie was featured in most of the articles. I am quoted in one at the end of the season praising Connie:

> *Kornel is unquestionably one of the most skillful players I have coached at CC. He immediately jelled with the rest of the squad even though he is a foreign player and has a skill level above them. He was not the typical prima donna foreign student. He scored 19 goals and had 8 assists, and was selected to the All-America Far West First Team. Only one other CC player ever got on the All-America Far West Team, and that was Dick Schulte, who received Honorable Mention in the previous year. George Jackson, a well-deserved recipient in 1975, completed our regional recognition.*

(Receiving outright national All-America recognition always was a challenge for CC, since most of the collegiate soccer programs, and thus the voting block, were located east of the Mississippi River.)

The ultimate highlight of the year was a 1-0 victory in the "soccer war" over the AFA, a repeat 1-0 performance from the year before. This time around, however, the sports writers in town had heightened the hype and an unbelievable crowd of 1,500 spectators — that's one thousand five hundred — ringed the field standing four deep.

An iconic, award-winning picture of the game appeared in *The Gazette*, which featured Brad Turner, our goal scorer, squished between the AFA goalie and a defender, and Kornel Simons, the assist-man on the goal, about to collide with the huge AFA keeper. This picture, which now hangs in our locker room, has been a motivational mainstay for years. Interestingly, Kornel's son, Matt, an incoming recruit for 2017, will be able to see his dad every day as he enters the locker room. Brad Turner '77, on the left side of the picture, has vivid memories of this incident:

> *This picture brings me back to memories of the AFA game at our Stewart Field in 1975. Our team my junior year was an awesome team. Men's soccer at CC was then Division I and we finished the season ranked 15th in the country. The morning of the game we had a team get-together at the Richardson home with Helen providing breakfast. We were a closely-knit team with a wide spectrum of personalities and we had some exceptional players like Connie Simons, John Monteiro, Bobby Shook, George Jackson, and others, but our real strength was the way we got along and played together as a team.*
>
> *The picture of the midair collision in* The Gazette *newspaper sports section (See p. 140) documents the seconds after a perfect crossing pass from the right corner, chipped in by John Monteiro. I got a good header on the ball and I thought I was going to score on this play, but the ball went a few inches wide of the right post by the upper corner. I had just completed the header when Schulze, the AFA goalkeeper, and Landman, the defender, hit me at the same time. I remember flying backwards and hearing every vertebrae in my back crack as I hit the ground. But I was fine, got up, and regulation time ended 10 minutes later. We went to overtime tied 0-0.*
>
> *With five minutes left in double O.T., Kornel Simons gave me the perfect pass from the left flank. The ball bounced once and I blasted it with my left foot. I immediately thought I had kicked it over, but somehow it dropped into the net, grazing the underside of the crossbar in the upper corner by the left post. Without Connie's pass, there would not have been a goal and a stupendous victory in front of an overflow crowd on Stewart Field.*

John Monteiro '78 was featured in a *Gazette* sports page article at the midpoint of the 1975 season. He comments that he "blundered onto CC. When looking at colleges, I searched for a school with both strong academics and a good soccer program, which CC has, and, of course, the mountains." From St. Paul, Minnesota, he had spent eight years of his life in Brazil and had become hooked on soccer there. He was tall and strong, sported long hair, wore thick glasses, and was a magician with the ball. He coached a youth team in town on the side and was known to be gentle and patient with his young charges, who adored him. He probably was the one who introduced the joy of the "nutmeg" move to our squad, as he demonstrated that ability quite often.

Once John had the ball, it was tough for defenders to take it from him because he shielded the ball so well. And he delighted in scoring goals in accordance with the Brazilian motto of the "beautiful game." Once, in Texas, against the "Mean Green" of North Texas State in a tight game, he could have easily scored with a simple push pass in front of the opponent's goal, but he wanted to tickle the net in style and with flair and attempted a chip over the keeper's outstretched hands. "A goal has to be satisfying to be truly meaningful," he told me after the game.

John became a Fulbright Scholar after graduation and, fluent in Portuguese, accepted a teaching position at a Brazilian university where he became an authority on Amazon indigenous people. Tragically, outside of the city of São Paulo, John was killed in an automobile crash in 2013.

The 1975 NCAA post-season play-off game vs. Cal State-Fullerton on their field put us on the national soccer map. Although we lost the game 1-0, it could have gone either way.

The match was played while the Santa Ana wind was blowing in from the Mojave Desert, elevating the ambient temperature to nearly 95 degrees. Suffice it to say, it was an awfully hot day. In spite of the heat, we pressured their goal with consistency, and only the terrific saves of their keeper, Morrison, kept the score at 0-0 at half-time. Kornel twisted his knee early on in the second half and had to leave the field, and the Tigers began to fatigue. A fluke goal settled the contest in their favor. We had, however, shown the collegiate soccer world that Rocky Mountain soccer was alive and well. The season ended with an impressive 15-3-2 record.

George Jackson, co-captain at the time, remembers a fun incident on the flight out to Southern California:

> *One day while we were waiting for the bus to take us to the airport to fly to the Far West Regionals, we learned that it was (good old Assistant Coach) Bill Boddington's birthday. Bob Shook and I determined that it was our duty as co-captains to honor the occasion, so we ducked into the nearby 7-11 store and bought a Sarah Lee cake and some candles and smuggled them onto the airplane. Incredibly, by today's standards, we engaged the stewardesses during the flight to help prepare the cake with lighted candles in the galley. Then, we brought the cake into view at the front of the airplane compelling all the passengers to sing happy birthday. Bill had to reluctantly come forward to blow out the candles. We knew he would be embarrassed — but in a good way! — we hoped.*

As I peruse the old scrapbooks, two other items stand out. One is the beginning of women's soccer on campus. About a dozen CC coeds took an interest in the game while watching the men and decided to form a team of their own. Their enthusiasm for the sport became such a noteworthy event that the local *Gazette* sent out a reporter to observe and interview me.

"It's just getting off the ground," I said. "They have a game scheduled against Loretto Heights this week. The way it started was that some girls showed an interest in playing soccer and we told them they could come out and work out with the varsity. I expected three or four, but twelve showed up, which was enough for a team. I assigned my manager, Lee Weisgal, to give them basic instructions when he was not busy with varsity assignments. He was obviously delighted with the assignment."

A year later, two players from the men's team, Steve Paul '78 and Doug Obletz '77, continued the effort of instructing the women and even staged a women's tournament at CC. Steve wrote to me about his beginning struggles with the women's effort:

> *As I look back on those early days, several things come to mind. I remember having to ask the parents for donations in order to buy uniforms (the College did not know that and did not want me to solicit funding for the program). I remember hand washing those uniforms in the dorm. I remember working/volunteering with Bruce Kola, head ATC, in order to learn something about athletic training and taping so we would be OK on our own. I remember helping the grounds crew do the lines on the field. Also, that is why I got a commercial driver's license in order for us to afford to take the school bus on road trips. We also shared some trips with men's teams (CC and Regis) in order to afford trips. We used to go to California, often UCSB, for spring break. The highlight was the year we raised money to fly …*
>
> *We bounced around a lot from spring to fall, balancing field space and equipment. (I had lots of battles with football coach and AD Jerry Carle, getting field space, use of Washburn Field and eventually funding.) We had good support from people like you, (Horst). You helped us wherever you could with equipment or field space, even just moral support — along with the men players.*

And the rest, as they say, is history.

Another pertinent matter focused on our pre-season practice. Unlike football, the other fall sport, which was well-funded, our soccer budget did not allow for pre-season expenses of room and board. I tried to stretch the budget as much as I could toward scheduling and playing away games against strong opposition in order to improve our competitiveness. We also skimped on meals on the road, frequenting mostly fast food joints. In order to make a meaningful pre-season period possible, I charged the players $40 per person to cover half of the pre-season expenses. We also had a policy of not supplying soccer boots to the players. They had to bring those from home. After the success of the 1975 campaign, the budget increased somewhat!

And lest I forget: The appointment of Bruce Kola to the training room in 1974 began a longtime and fruitful working relationship with me and the soccer effort. The two of us could write a separate book about working at CC!

A lecturer in sports science, he instructed many a CC student and guided them to careers in health and fitness, as well as in medicine. With a real innovative break with convention, female students became student trainers and worked with athletes on the field and in the training room. A huge *Gazette* article, entitled "WOMEN TRAINERS BRAVE TIGER LAIR," on September 12, 1976, devoted extensive coverage to female student trainers, attending to CC football and soccer players. It stated:

> *Of all places, one would not expect a locker room to be an incubator for women's rights and acceptance, but at CC things are different. Sexist jokes, snapping towels, and other characteristics of the average locker room are almost nonexistent, Kola said. The women have been completely accepted, Kola continued. Our athletes are intellectually and socially mature. Their acceptance has been overwhelmingly positive.*

Local soccer fans were able to observe soccer at its highest level in Colorado Springs, as the U.S. National Team trained here for a month. The team was housed at the Colorado Springs School and practiced at the AFA and CC. The National Team needed high-altitude training for their World Cup qualifying match against Mexico, which was to be played at 7,500 feet in Mexico City. The 20 candidates for the squad had been mainly selected from the relatively new North American Soccer League (NASL). Iconic coach Walt Chyzowych was in charge of the preparations. While in Colorado, the team staged a walk-out, demanding an increase in pay.

1976-77

Our 1976 campaign produced another 15-victory season, but unlike in the year before, no NCAA invitation was forthcoming even though at one point in the season we were ranked No. 15 nationally. The balanced squad had a terrific start, outscoring opponents handily, including a 17-0 drubbing of Regis.

With a 5-0 record to our credit, we faced Benedictine College in a home game. It was a rough one. In three newspaper articles, one from *The Gazette*, a second one from *The Sun*, and a third from *The Catalyst*, the sports writers focused on the "rugged" play of the opposition. Rich Director '80, a tenacious defender for us, describes the game and the opponent's tactics:

> *It was my freshman year and we were undefeated (5-0) going into the Benedictine College game. We had played five competitive and physical games to that point, but nothing nasty like the boys from Benedictine. In fact, in my recollection they were*

1976 | 15-3-0
Front row, left to right: Frank Lane, Doug Jewell, Ron Edmondson, Jim Balderston, Chris Lehrecke, Randy Stein. **Middle Row:** Kornel Simons, Bill Scott (captain), Sam Harper, Richard Director, Tom Lee, Dave Dietel, Pablo Lorca. **Back row:** Coach Horst Richardson, Jeff Beckley, Eddy Dietz, John Monteiro, Brad Turner, John Grenardo, Don Clark. **Not pictured:** Chris Clifford, Bruce Petterson.

talented — but dirty and I think it was part of their game plan. Especially with regard to Connie (Simons). If my memory serves me, red cards back then DID NOT mean you played a man down. And this blew me away. They were free to hack Connie (and the rest of us for that matter) and able to simply sub in for the penalized player. Frightening.

Benedictine were called for 22 fouls against our eight and clearly were the more physically aggressive team. At the end of the game, tempers flared and there was a brief scuffle.

A road trip during Block Break I to a U Nevada Las Vegas tournament produced a win against the host, but in a foul-filled game vs. Cal State-Fullerton, we had to settle for a disappointing loss. The defeat, undeserved, we thought, was so depressing that we left Sin City immediately after the game and drove straight home, my loaded VW bus trying hard to keep up with the rest of the caravan.

Sam Harper '79, then on the team and now writing scripts for the movies, has vivid memories of the Vegas road trip:

In 1976, I was a sophomore forward, having made the team by the skin of my teeth. Being a pine-riding back-up, I was thrilled to be included in the September road trip to Las Vegas for a three-team tournament with Cal Fullerton and UN Las Vegas, my first road trip as a Tiger.

When transportation assignments were handed out, I had the great fortune of landing in the back seat of Bruce Petterson's hard-charging, gold Camaro. These days, the drive is a solid 12 hours. Back then, with the 55 mph speed limit, and the lack of interstate through a portion of Utah, it was more like 16, even with Bruce and his Camaro challenging the sound barrier.

I have no memory of where we stayed that first night on the road, or if we drove straight through, but I do remember stopping for a cookout dinner in a camping area where we attempted to grill foil-covered baked potatoes. They didn't quite get cooked and, suffice it to say, local wildlife carb-loaded that night. Food drama became a theme after we arrived and ate at a local buffet. A group of us, including the late, great John Monteiro, got food poisoning and spent the night on a relay circuit to the bathroom. Connie Simons, Eddy Dietz and Jeff Beckley remained healthy, and led us to victory against UNLV the following day.

The next day, Cal Fullerton, the team that had eliminated us from the NCAA play-offs in 1975, beat us again, this time 5-2. What was truly annoying was that

1977 | 13-5-0

No team photo was taken during the 1977 season, though the photo above features various members of the varsity team. These "Peppers" played off-season, in the spring (alongside others not on the varsity team). **Front row, left to right:** Erik Richardson (Horst's son), Jeff Beckley, Jim Balderston, Joe Ellis (with Horst's daughter, Stacia Richardson, in his lap), Chris Lehrecke. **Back row:** Meril May, guest player, Coach Horst Richardson, Eddy Dietz, John Williamson, Jon Hulburd, Mike Slade, Rich Director, Mike Maisonpierre, Kal Kaliban, Gordon Jackson, guest player. **Not pictured**, but on the 1977 varsity roster: Steve Barron, Toby Borst, Chris Clifford, Dave Dietel, Ron Edmondson, John Grenardo, Sam Harper, Mitch Hoffman, Tom Lee (captain), John Monteiro, Chris Nawn, Bruce Petterson, David Randall, Kornel Simons, Randy Stein, Kamau Thugge, Peter Wilhelm.

UNLV, the team we'd easily handled, went on to beat Cal Fullerton. Everyone went home, 1-1.

In terms of wins and losses it was a disappointing trip, and Horst reminded me that he was so angry at losing to Cal Fullerton again that we drove straight back to Colorado Springs after the game. But the indelible memories, like so many I have from CC Soccer, are only good ones: Blazing through the Rocky Mountains toward Utah, howling with laughter as we chucked those baked potatoes into the woods, and Beckley's goal against UNLV, a beautiful shot from 18, into the upper right corner.

The team recovered and won the rest of their matches, until we faced the AFA away in the last contest of the season. "Cadets Top Tigers in Snowfest" read the headline in the paper. A memorable event at half-time of that frigid encounter was a CC marching column, led by Doug Obletz, presenting the CC mascot dog, Levi, to the spectators. It was a bit of levity during a tense and cold afternoon.

But the real blockbuster event of the time was the realignment for soccer to NCAA Division III status. The entire matter hinged on our Ice Hockey program which in 1977, when divisional alignments in NCAA Hockey came about, had to choose between Division I, II or III.

Since it had been a scholarship program since its inception, and since soccer had never received a scholarship at all, hockey became our D-I sport, an allowable exception in our D-III institution. The discussions about this realignment, both in the papers and in committees, were extensive, but I maintained that in the end-effect, D-III for men's soccer was the right place to be.

You can read all about the transition to D-III in the 1978 scrapbook. Go to www.cctigers.com/sports/2015/9/30/MSOC_0930155224.aspx.

Now it's time to write about Eddy Dietz. To put it mildly, Eddy was a complicated individual. A German immigrant like me, he was born in East Berlin during the cold war and moved to West Berlin with his proletarian family before the Berlin Wall was built. His mother, divorced, met and married an American soldier who brought the family to Fort Carson. At Palmer High School in Colorado Springs, Eddy quickly established himself as a standout athlete and his soccer prowess garnered my attention.

At CC he distinguished himself in the classroom and, even as a freshman, became a force to be reckoned with on the field. He played like a bull, and, if necessary, would have banged his head into the goalpost to score a goal. Because of his family's financial hardships, he carried a grudge against the CC elite and thus made damned sure that he showed "those preppies" how the game was played from the blue collar side. He could become enraged at a perceived injustice and made no bones about letting you know that.

Once, after a game at Chicago-Circle in a dilapidated neighborhood, Eddy discovered that his wallet had been stolen from the locker room. Even though I had told the team to leave no valuables in the locker room, he became so angry about his loss that he nearly took the locker room apart. And then he would try to atone for his sins.

He and teammate Mike Haas were our first two professional players, having been drafted to play in the North American Soccer League, the NASL. Eddy played for the Detroit Express and Mike for the Dallas Tornado. Eddy once told me that his greatest moment in soccer occurred when he played against the NY Cosmos, featuring Pele and Franz Beckenbauer. Eddy made money in the pros, traveled internationally, and came back to CC to graduate in History, cum laude. He coached high school for a while and then, in 1992, was hired by UCCS to be their soccer coach. For ten years we had a terrific crosstown rivalry going, and nothing made Eddy's season more successful than a victory over CC. He later fell on hard times, and two days before his 59th birthday, he died of heart failure as a homeless person here in town.

Dave Moross, longtime sports information director at CC, now retired, heard of Eddy's athletic feats when he attended Palmer High School. He and Eddy also were employed together at the Hatchcover Restaurant in town, Dave as a waiter, and Eddy as a busboy. Here are Dave's recollections of Eddy:

> *Then there's the sad tale of Eddy "Great Solo Effort" Dietz, who passed away late in 2016 at the young age of 58.*
>
> *I happened to know Eddy back when he attended Palmer High School, when we both worked at a local restaurant — The Hatchcover — during the mid-1970s.*
>
> *I was particularly impressed to hear that Eddy had kicked a field goal for Palmer's football team from something like 50 yards, and we got along very well as co-workers. I was a waiter, he a busboy.*
>
> *Eddy's playing career with the Tigers began and ended well before I started working for CC in 1986, but I know he was a very dominant player with a burning passion for soccer. He just didn't pass very often!*
>
> *At any rate, he remained involved with the game in some shape or form for most of his short life. In addition to his share of opponents as a player and coach, however, he also seemed to fight a constant battle with demons in his own head. And I, for one, wish I could have done more to help him.*

And History Professor Bill Hochman, who taught Eddy in class, had this to say about Eddy on the field:

> *I remember watching Eddy Dietz play with admiration. I can still see him speeding down the field, with flashing legs and a wonderful ground-covering stride. Eddy was a beautiful player. He was a student of mine too, and I was sorry to see the tragic misery of his later life.*

Our junior varsity program in those days was very active. Bill Boddington was in charge of the effort, and trained 12-16 players throughout the year. These reserve squads played games against local teams along the front range. Both Harold Thurman and Mike Slade, JV players then, remember an intriguing encounter in Pueblo against a team of steel mill workers. Here is Thurman's '78 account of that game:

> *I remember that with the JV squad we played games against local college club teams in Colorado Springs and Pueblo, and our toughest games were against the Air Force JV — they were always super fit and hard-nosed — and against a factory team of Iranian steelworkers from the CF&I mill in Pueblo — those games were intense, taught me something about blue collar soccer!*
>
> *I remember one away game where it seemed like we were out-skilled by the Iranian steelworkers on their home field, and we managed to score a late goal to win 1-0, and we were scrambling to get to our cars and get out of there while the steelworkers were chasing the referee over a hill.*

Mike Slade '79, in charge of the spring club program, elaborates:

> *That spring, as usual, we had a spring team that under the rules you (Horst) couldn't supervise, so as I recall for that spring ('77) and the next one ('78) I ran the team, probably with help from Tom Lee. I also recall that you played on the team once or twice! How cool!*
>
> *Anyway, sometime that spring we were playing a team from Pueblo at some field in downtown Pueblo. I recall driving down to the game with Rich Director and Chris Lehrecke.*
>
> *The team we played was, as I recall, composed of an ethnically diverse soup of Arabs, Hispanics and God knows what else. We had a couple of guys from the real team including Rich, Eddy, Lee, Gordon Jackson, and Joe Ellis. I played some defense as did you; in fact, I seem to recall you and I splitting playing time at left D. Anyway, in the first half the other team was playing really dirty soccer and kicking us in the shins, tripping, swearing, you name it. At one point I yelled at this one Arab guy to knock it off and he screamed at me, "You motherfuckerrrrrrrrr!!" I simultaneously recoiled and laughed at his rolled r, a joke Rich and Joe and I still laugh about.*
>
> *At half-time you got mad at me for engaging with these guys and kind of scolded me, telling me to cool it and keep it mellow. I felt chastised and pissed off but kind of*

agreed with you. Towards the end of the game, (we were ahead 1-0) one of their guys tripped Eddy and he twisted his ankle. Another guy actively then stepped on Eddy's injured ankle right in front of an uncaring ref, who was probably the guy's brother. I was on the sidelines and you were playing. You got in the guy's face and yelled at him to "knock it off!" and then the guy threatened you. At this point you showed me a totally different side of our head coach — a true pragmatist. You looked at all of us and uttered these memorable words: "Let's get the hell out of here!"

And we left the field (5 minutes remained maybe), got into our BMWs, and drove home! I always felt very justified and proud when you got angry. Like I was in the right in the first place.

Bill Boddington's development efforts in local soccer were recognized by our Colorado Springs Parks and Recreation Department in 1978 when a former reservoir site in Monument Park was refurbished as a youth soccer field and dedicated in Bill's honor on April 15 that year. During informal off-season sessions the CC boys would jog up Monument Creek from campus to kick the ball around there.

In the mid '70s, from '74 to '77, the team had four banner years, accumulating a combined record of 57-17-3. We had grown accustomed to success, even against university programs like U Texas Austin, BYU, North Texas State, Cal-Santa Barbara, Cal State-Fullerton, U Nevada Las Vegas, SMU, U Illinois Chicago Circle, U South Florida, U Wisconsin Milwaukee, and, of course, the annual emotional encounters against DU and AFA.

A game for the ages was our unfortunate 1-0 loss to the AFA on October 12 on our Stewart Field in front of a huge crowd of spectators. The game winner came off of an AFA free kick, which the referee awarded after our keeper, Jim Balderston, had been called for "too many steps" while releasing the ball. It was a controversial call in a tight game and decided the contest. Inexplicably, two shots by Kornel Simons for us seemed to have scored, but weren't counted. "I really thought Simons' shots should have been goals," I was quoted in the paper, "one of them for sure dropped into the net and then rolled out. And that's a goal."

Kornel Simons, "Tuna Boat" Monteiro, Eddy Dietz, and Rich Director and Tom Lee played exceptionally well, but it was the AFA goalie, Greg Schulze, who made several astounding saves to walk away with MVP honors for the game.

In the crowd that day were two distinguished CC professors, Ric Bradley, Physics Department and then Dean of the Faculty, and George Drake from the History Department, whose son played youth soccer in town and who a couple of years later would become president of Grinnell College. They wrote to me after the game:

> *"That was a real heartbreaker! Our guys outplayed the other team the whole time ... and then to lose on what almost seemed to be a minor technicality was really tough to take ... You have a great team, you played a great game, and you should have won." — Ric Bradley*
>
> *"Now that the emotions are beginning to settle, I want to write to you and the team to congratulate all on a marvelous game against Air Force. ... From the point of view of the spectator, it was a terrific game, and it did a great deal to advance the cause of soccer in the Pikes Peak region. All of us are grateful to you and the team for showing us such a high level of play, and sportsmanship. I was impressed by the self-control showed in the face of bitter and undeserved defeat; and this was perhaps the most impressive thing about the game ..." — George Drake*

1978-79

The last two seasons of the decade, at least in terms of record, were marginally successful, with two fall campaigns of only nine victories each. One explanation may be that the CC men's soccer program was realigned from D-I to D-III and still played against many D-I opponents who in the course of time were developing strong scholarship programs. We remained a member of the RMISL, a conference with not one D-III team. In fact, as I frequently pointed out, we were the only D-III non-scholarship team in the entire Rocky Mountain time zone area, a fact which is still true today.

Most other D-III teams competed in D-III conferences where the winner of the conference would receive an automatic qualifier to the national tournament. We, on the other hand, needed to prove ourselves through our strength of schedule.

The 1978 Tiger squad featured a strong defense, with Mike Haas and Spencer Gresham anchoring the defense, and tested goalie Jim Balderston in the nets. Rich Director, Gordon Jackson, and Joe Ellis were solid in midfield, but forwards Kornel Simons and Eddy Dietz, now well-known to most opponents, had a tough time scoring. By the time we rolled out of town for a BYU road trip during the first block break, we had only won one game. We were a motley crew arriving on their campus, as Jim Balderston '79 remembers:

Ah, Utah. I have fond memories of playing the BYU squad through the years, including a number of 8th-year seniors that seemed to infest their team until the NCAA put the kibosh on such shenanigans. We traveled to the BYU campus to play our Mormon adversaries and this presented us with the opportunity to see and be seen. I remember as we watched an endless stream of Donny and Marie Osmond clones walk past our chosen position on campus. The men all with pressed slacks (no jeans!) flowered shirts, (with collars!) and polished, shiny shoes. They were all clean-shaven. Their hair was perfect.

The women, following suit, wore dresses (NO pants) and modest collared shirts. They were prim and proper. They were Marie Osmond's back-up singers. They exuded wholesomeness.

And then there was us.

1978 | 9-7-3

Front row, left to right: Dan McCarthy, Jim Balderston (captain), Steve Barron. **Second row:** Joe Ellis, Eddy Dietz, Kornel Simons, Rich Director (captain), Gordon Jackson (captain), Randy Stein, Mitch Hoffman. **Third row:** Mike Haas, John Williamson, Spencer Gresham, Doug Bell, Jeff Beckley, Kal Kaliban, Jon Hulburd. **Fourth row:** John Winsor, Jeff Karas, Don Remlinger, Mark Shira, David Hoag, Kamau Thugge, Randy Morrow, Toby Borst. **Back row:** Coaches Steve Wong, Bill Boddington and Horst Richardson.

We lounged. We wore shorts and flip-flops. T-shirts advertising various beers. Our hair was long and not particularly combed. Our faces sported an array of beards, goatees, fuzz and stubble.

We were The Unclean.

And then we beat them handily, another triumph for slack and bad habits.

This victory on the field was a morale booster for us, but it didn't last very long. U-Nevada Las Vegas beat us the next day. We just couldn't find the winning formula.

Jim, also known as Baldy, concludes his reflections:

There are some powerful memories, some wonderful bonds between a broad range of people from many, many, different backgrounds. We have lost several teammates tragically (that I am aware of) and I sense that loss of those people who I spent time with screwing around in locker rooms, taunting in practice, smiling in victory and consoling in loss.

There were (and are) some damn fine people on those rosters; it was a pleasure and an honor to be on teams with them. Thanks, Horst, for holding it all together (and holding the bail money).

Mike Slade, the *Catalyst* sports editor, in an interview with the 1977 captain and standout defender Tom Lee, conjectured that the team lacked "cohesion." Tom Lee continued: "The 1978 squad is lacking intestinal fortitude. In the last four years, we were winning those 1-0 games because we had had enough people who wanted to win — this year the same intensity is not coming through."

One important lesson I learned that year is that I needed to better balance our D-III philosophy of participation in a popular program with my desire to put a winning team on the field. I guess that deep down in my soccer gut I was always too much of a nice guy when it came to making tough player personnel decisions.

Another dilemma I struggled with over time was a recognition that playing attractive soccer should trump efficient soccer, knowing full well that efficient soccer at our level would produce more wins than advocating an elegant style of play. So sometimes you have to deal with criticism ...

And then we beat the AFA 5-2 away. Behind at the end of the half 2-1, with a Dietz penalty shot giving us a lifeline, we came out in the second half with gusto. It was sophomore Mitch Hoffman who sparked the comeback with spirited play and then, with a half an hour to play, we scored three goals, Director, Simons, and Ellis, in under three minutes. It was a wild one! Jeff Beckley put the game out of reach with a fifth goal. We were 6-0 in the RMISL standings, and the CC soccer world was back in order.

Somewhat of a mysterious incident deserves mention relevant to the epic AFA game. The AFA cadets had painted a huge "WE WILL BEAT CC" sign on their kick board at the south end of the field, obviously bragging about an expected win. Several CC night owls had snuck on academy ground the night before the game and had changed the lettering to "WE WILL BEAT AFA." And so we did. After an end-of-the-season loss to DU, however, the RMISL championship was out of reach for us.

Mitch Hoffman '81, a sophomore on the team then and now a judge, submits his recollection of the subversive activities which made the kick-board incident possible:

> *I saw in the scrapbook the reference to the 1978 game in which we defeated Air Force 5-2. There was a mention that the Air Force Kick Board had been mysteriously re-painted by some unknown "C.C. Night Owl." Well, it's possible that I was along on that particular night mission, along with a couple of other Sophomore players. Led*

1979 | 9-9-1

Front row, left to right: Jon Hulburd, Spencer Gresham, Mike McMenamy, Kal Kaliban, Bill Riebe, Bill Rudge, Peter Scott, Chuck Lundberg. **Back row:** Coach Horst Richardson, Eddy Dietz, Gordon Jackson, Jeff Beckley, Mike Haas (captain), Mark Friederich, Peter Armstrong, Mark Shira, Mitch Hoffman, Don Remlinger, Bryan Erickson, Rich Director, Joe Ellis, Chris Lehrecke. **Not pictured:** Kelly Kirks.

by a player, who would later go on to become team Captain in his Senior Year, (with the initials JH), and another player who hailed from Long Island (with the initials KK), our "Special Ops" team took extreme measures to avoid detection by Air Force security patrols.

This was not a mission for the faint of heart. Having successfully completed the "re-branding" of the Air Force kick-board, we had to exit back out past the Sentry post at the east end of the Academy. As several of us crouched down in the back seat, our driver (JH), wearing a gorilla mask to hide his identity, respectfully saluted the sentry as we sped past on the way to the safety of the CC Campus. I'm pretty sure the anger of the Zoomies when they saw their precious kick-board the next day had something to do with their poor play and our thrilling victory! I hope the statute of limitations has run out on any "real or imagined crimes" that may have been committed. But, if we must go to prison, we will go proudly, wearing black and gold.

In 1979, 48 candidates tried out for the Tiger squad, the largest number ever. A 2-2 tie with Air Force, and a late season OT win over DU crowned us co-champions of the RMISL, but on two block break trips to the west coast, where we played five games, including one against UCLA, we didn't win one contest and only scored two goals.

Eddy Dietz and Mike Haas were drafted to the NASL and became our first two professional players.

The decade ended with a festive awards banquet at the home of the Boddingtons. After the players had headed home, Bill and I strategized about initiating a fund drive to establish a men's soccer endowment. This effort became a tremendous success, and the current teams benefit considerably from this now handsome endowment fund.

ACHIEVING SUSTAINED SUCCESS

The 1980s

Soccer had grown tremendously in the country, especially youth soccer. In Colorado Springs, the Soccer Organization for Colorado Springs Youth (SOCSY) had thousands of kids kicking the ball.

With the help of Steve Paul and Dennis Hoglin, Helen and I started a summer camp at the Colorado Springs School in 1979. The next summer we moved the camp to a bigger facility at Memorial Park, providing pick-up and drop-off transportation for some of the youngsters. Colorado College had never offered any youth camps of any kind during the summer months; we convinced the administration of the value of community outreach and staged successful camps on campus for nearly 20 years. Many a player from the Tiger men's or women's teams worked as counselors and coaches in these camps.

Tim Schulz, not a CC student, but a local soccer player who basically grew up practicing on Stewart Field, was the darling of the campers, winning cookies and fruit from their lunches in skill contests. I still see him coaching on the field in the afternoons with bananas sticking out of his socks! Tim now runs the Rush Soccer Club, one of the largest clubs in the U.S., if not in the entire world.

Judy Sondermann, a CC graduate and member of the first women's team, became an elementary school teacher in town and a most effective coach for us. She always took on the six- and seven-year olds and turned them on to soccer! Emily Varley, the senior citizen equipment manager for CC, was on the job during all the camps providing motherly TLC. Helen, the camp administrator, took care of registration and public relations with the parents and made dozens of nourishing lunches every day to feed the starving counselors.

In our last years of the camps, we had up to 600 kids enrolled in camp, utilizing every available mini-field of grass we could find on campus, since the varsity fields were off limits to us. Some of the profits from the camp were used to enhance the Stewart Field environment. We were able to replace the fences along Monument Creek, straighten out the embankment on the east side of Stewart, and install water fountains on the field.

Pat Shea '84, then CC freshman on the team and Palmer High School graduate, submits a camp story to illustrate how much fun we had working with the kids:

> *On the first day of camp I walked into the El Pomar indoor turf, where the kids had gathered. Horst, who had a flair for drama, had prepared a little skit with me to entertain the campers on opening day with some humor and improvisation. He asked me who I was and I replied, "Arthur Greengroin, the janitor around here." Horst followed up with a number of questions to establish a fake identity for me, gave me my cues, and I knew my role was to be clueless about soccer, particularly about the bicycle kick. He built up the scene like a Broadway show finale, providing instructions until I eventually biked the ball into the net.*

(Pat knew the indoor turf at CC well. He and his Palmer High School buddies would routinely sneak into the facility after school to knock the ball around, telling CC student monitors tall tales to let them stay.)

As State Coach of Colorado, I staged many a coaching and refereeing course in our athletic facilities, providing opportunity for adults to learn more about the game and earn badges in USSF state level courses. CC soccer players helped to demonstrate the finer points of playing the various positions on the field. And Colorado Springs became the central location for U.S. soccer when the National Federation decided to move its headquarters here from New York.

Fewer of our collegiate athletes engaged in multiple sports, preferring to concentrate on their chosen sport. However, no off-season training existed. Even though the NCAA provided for such opportunities, CC and a couple of other comparable liberal arts institutions had policies in place, which barred coaches from becoming engaged with their players off-season.

Instead, some of the players organized their own team to compete locally in the adult league. One enterprising student obtained T-shirts from Dr. Pepper, and the "Peppers" were formed. In another year, they had T-shirts printed with "Si Si" across the chest, since they couldn't register as CC. These off-season efforts were marginally successful because, during every block break and spring break as well, the guys would inevitably prefer the ski slopes to the local fields and thus had to forfeit a number of games.

The CC women's club team was granted varsity status in 1978. In 1980, CC hosted the first National Collegiate Women's Championship Tournament the week before Thanksgiving. Cortland State drove 1,700 miles in two vans from New York to participate, and they won it all, beating UCLA 5-1. (By the way, a senior on that Cortland team would return to CC 15 years later, because her husband, Marty Scarano, had accepted the position of Athletic Director here.) One year later, our women's program received scholarships and headed for NCAA D-I status.

Our men's program, on the other hand, still playing some tough D-I opponents, started to outreach to established D-III programs from west of the Mississippi to the Pacific coast. Our 1980 team, for instance, traveled close to 6,000 miles during the season, trying to complement its RMISL schedule with D-III opponents.

In order to afford these travels, I had to become creative and frugal when on out-of-state trips. Southern California was a good destination for us, not only because of D-III opposition there, but also because my parents lived there. They and their friends hosted many a CC team, providing lodging and barbecues. Bill Riebe '82, the giant goalkeeper of the team, reminisces about a stay at my parents' home:

> *Road trip to California, when, I think, Rudge and I were freshmen and Rudge and I had the opportunity to stay with you and your parents at their house. We had to shower outside in the backyard, naked behind a shower curtain, so the water could be used to water the garden and the fruit trees. It was a real pleasure to meet your Mom and Dad!*

Bob Wessen was a CC graduate who owned a Buick dealership in the heart of Los Angeles. If it hadn't been for his generosity to offer courtesy cars for our team whenever we came to the Sunny Southland, we could have never afforded to travel there. The team would arrive at LAX, and a couple of seniors and I would hail a taxi and hurry on to Century Boulevard in downtown LA to get the vehicles. In the meantime, the rest of the guys would retrieve the bags and buy some food. If the traffic on the freeways was reasonable, we could be back to the airport within an hour to pick up the squad.

After a couple of years of doing this, we had the pick-up and delivery down to a routine, and Bob Wessen's secretary would greet us with car keys in hand as we jumped out of the taxi. Then we would caravan along the freeways, weaving in and out of traffic. It seems absolutely amazing to me today, with cellphones and GPS standard devices, that we never lost any vehicle on these excursions!

Before we return to our chronology of stories, a few words about our pre-season practice sessions. In the '70s and '80s, we were into circuit training during pre-season. I would devise eight to 10 stations of various difficulty levels around the perimeter of the field and groups of players would rotate through.

These stations would become ever more esoteric over time — so much so that one year the players added one of their own, replicated on p. 139.

THE TEAM IN THE 1980s

As we enter the '80s, we started to benefit from local recruiting. A number of large high schools in Colorado had adopted soccer as a varsity sport by then, including our local Colorado Springs school district. In the first four years of the decade, we were blessed with a number of talented players from Colorado Springs: Spencer Gresham, Kelly Kirks, Pat Shea, Rick Hibbard, Jamie Hull, Tom Hyland, Jim Grice, and Todd Walker. Add to that list the following standout recruits from the Denver area: Bill Riebe, Mike McMenamy, Bill Rudge, Charlie Stanzione, Mitch Green, Tom MacKenzie, Greg Kazemi, Richard Lyford, and Danny Moe, and now you have a strike force to reckon with.

A number of these Colorado players, while still in high school, had been with me on a foreign tour of Germany, and thus I already knew them well. A California quartet of exceptional athletes complemented the Colorado nucleus: Scott Evans, Jacques Lemvo, Brigham Olson, and Brad Wolf. With this core group of Coloradoans and Californians we experienced incredible success in the first half of the '80s.

1980

1980 witnessed the beginning of a lengthy series of annual games against Grinnell College. Whenever we played there, we would stay in their wrestling room and sleep on the mats, and since the swimming pool was right next door in the gym, it was actually a comfortable environment. I drove the 24-passenger CC bus, the "Desert Shark," for the 800-mile journey. Right above my head was an onboard TV monitor; I can't remember

1980 | 12-8-2

Front row, left to right: Kelly Kirks (captain), Jon Hulburd (captain). **Second row:** John Hennessey, Bill Riebe, Randy Morrow, Chuck Lundberg, Bryan Erickson, Marco Della Cava, Peter Scott. **Third row:** David Hoag, student trainer, Peter Armstrong, Gordon Jackson, Bill Rudge, Tony Puckett, Carl McCluster. **Back row:** Coach Horst Richardson, Mitch Hoffman, Kal Kaliban, Spencer Gresham, Mike McMenamy, Don Remlinger, John Moderwell, Kevin Director, Pat Shea, Charlie Stanzione. **Not pictured:** Bruce Atkinson, Doug Ebner, Mark Friederich, Chris Jackson, Steve Larson, Chris Lehrecke, Chris Peel, Mark Shira, Kevin Sweeney, John Weiss, John Williamson.

---

how many times I heard the dialogue from the film, *The Outlaw Josie Wales*, but Clint Eastwood kept me awake!

Fortunately the much larger CC highway bus was available later in the decade. More about these and other bus trips later in the narrative.

Grinnell College, by the way, in 16 encounters, never beat us! Once, in 1980 away to Grinnell, we had the game in hand and were awarded a penalty kick. In a rather cocky move, I instructed our goalkeeper, Bill Riebe, to take the spot kick. He remembers this incident:

> *When we played in Iowa (I think Grinnell), you had me take a penalty shot and I choked! Their keeper caught the ball and proceeded to kick it down field over my head as I was running back to my goal. Fortunately, Rudge and friends stopped them, giving me a chance to recover and they didn't score.*

On a block break away trip to Texas in '81 that same Bill Riebe was called upon to execute a totally unforeseen responsibility. We had beaten Texas Christian in Fort Worth and needed to find a place to eat. As it turned out, we ended up at an establishment in a dilapidated and black neighborhood on the other side of the tracks and, having found the address, stopped in front of a dimly lit building, which looked like an abandoned Texaco gas station. I, somewhat apprehensive, asked Bill Riebe, 6'5", to come with me to inspect the place. Here is Riebe's take on this incident:

> *Road trip to Ft. Worth. We played well. Rudge, me and a couple others went to the TCU campus, met some girls and in the course of the late afternoon were informed of a good place to eat steak. Short story is we confused the name and ended up at a joint with a similar name in a part of Ft. Worth where the houses had bars on the windows. You (Horst) and I went in first (you made me) to see if we were at the right place and sure enough, we were. Everything was set up, people were fantastic, food was outstanding, and everyone had a great time! — and I think we all learned a little bit that night about other people and their circumstances.*

I distinctly remember that the proprietress had the longest fingernails I had ever seen, that the World Series was on TV, and that the food was exceptionally delicious.

1981

The 1981 season started off with an international youth tournament between Mexico, USA, Canada, and Bermuda at our field and at the AFA. The Under-19 national teams of these nations practiced and played here. The U.S. team was coached by Walter Chyzowych and Bob Gansler. Mexico won the tournament.

During pre-season, for entertainment and motivation, I decided to take the team to the recently released soccer film *Victory*, starring Sylvester Stallone and Pelé. The movie is about a group of allied prisoners in a German POW camp during World War II who are allowed to form a soccer team to play against the German National team in Paris as a Nazi propaganda scheme.

When we came to the theater the manager greeted us, shouted out that the soccer team had arrived, thanked us for coming, and seated us in reserved seating, even though I had not reserved any seats at all. As the film started, another college team showed up, all

1981 | 15-6-1

Front row, left to right: Randy Morrow, Marco Della Cava, Tom Hyland, Sam Schwartz, Bill Riebe, Brad Wolf, Bryan Erickson, Rick Hibbard, Charlie Stanzione. **Middle row:** Coach Bill Boddington, Scott Evans, Brad Lundberg, Mark Friederich (captain), Spencer Gresham (captain), Tom MacKenzie, Carl McCluster, Jamie Hull. **Back row:** Richard Lyford, Pat Shea, Jacques Lemvo, Brigham Olson, Gunther Karstens, Don Remlinger (captain), Mitch Green, John Moderwell, Bill Rudge, Coach Horst Richardson, Dave Hoag. **Not pictured:** Greg Mendoza, John Van Allen.

---

dressed in military uniform. It was the AFA, who actually had made reservations, but it was too late to change seating. So they had to make do with whatever seats were available. A small moral victory for us!!

Another military story of much greater impact was my recruitment of Jacques Lemvo. The various branches of our military have very selective sports teams, including soccer. Fort Carson, the military base just south of Colorado Springs, hosted the annual services soccer tournament that summer. I had met the Army coach at a soccer coaches convention, and he had invited me to come to watch the competition, indicating that I would be pleasantly surprised by the level of talent.

A powerful, black, athletic forward, 6'2" immediately caught my eye, and when he scored a dazzling goal, a full volley laser cannon shot into the upper 90, I was eager to meet him. To my delight and surprise I found out that he was born in Zaire (now Congo), grew up in Belgium, served in the U.S. Army in Germany, and spoke four languages. Furthermore he was an accomplished artist and dancer. I immediately went to our admission office, spoke with Director Dick Wood, and indicated to him that CC couldn't afford not to enroll this veteran. Dick agreed, and Jacques came to CC.

Suffice it to say, it didn't take long for Jacques to not only establish himself as a force on the field, but also to become a popular person on campus. He would saunter out to practice, stop on the football field to kick a couple of 50-yard field goals, and then continue on his way to Stewart Field, juggling the soccer ball all the way. To Frank Flood, the assistant football coach who was eager to enlist his services as a kicker, Jacques would reply: "Soccer is my life!" And that was that.

1981 was also the first year that we handed out game programs. It included pictures of all the players, vital statistics, our schedule, some recent soccer history and even a couple of ads.

The second weekend of the season featured a six-team tournament, co-hosted by CC and AFA. And believe it or not, it was called the "First Annual BUDWEISER Soccer Bowl" and was publicized with a fancy program. Participating teams were AFA, CC, Southern Methodist, Creighton, Eastern Illinois, and Rockhurst College. CC came in second behind Eastern Illinois. Not only were the visiting teams powerhouses, but the opposing coaches, Luis Sagastume at AFA, Jimmy Benedek at SMU, Wayne Rasmussen at Creighton, Schellas Hyndman at Eastern Illinois, and Tony Tocco at Rockhurst, all became towering figures in the sport.

By the way, the annual BUDWEISER soccer bowl only lasted one year. It morphed into the Pikes Peak Classic Tournament the following year. The reason for this change may be explained by Brad Lundberg's '83 comments regarding an intense game during the first Budweiser Bowl:

> *We always had great crowds and one year while we were playing our archrival from the Midwest, Rockhurst College, we decided to create an incentive to bring more fans to watch the weekend home stand at Washburn field, and held a banner contest to see which fans ended up using their bed sheets showing their support. The winner got a free keg of beer. (Budweiser?) Our biggest mistake was announcing a winner and awarding the keg at half-time. By the end of the game the crowd was a bit unruly, and if you remember we were put on some sort of probation for derogatory comments some of the fans made to the opposing players. I can't remember but that may have cost us a home game in the first round of the NCAA's, which I think was my senior year 1982?*

Mid-season we participated in a tournament at Wooster College in Ohio. As part of the hospitality arrangements for us, we had to commit to a soccer clinic for local boys and girls.

We demonstrated some drills and got the kids involved. During a rest period I assembled the children at the top of the box and announced that our team was now going to demonstrate the difficulty of hitting targets with the ball. I challenged our players to step up to the 18-yard penalty box and with a chip shot hit the cross bar of the goal. Well, Rick Hibbard steps up and with his very first try hits the target. The kids and I were amazed!!

For the first time CC assigned a sports information director to cover us. Pat Haley did a terrific job promoting us by writing stories and taking exciting action shots. He even released pre-game announcements and supplied interesting statistics in fliers for the spectators. And we had a squad to be proud of! By the end of October we had run up a 13-1-1 record and were ranked No. 8 in the entire country for D-III.

And then came the infamous AFA game, which we lost 2-1 in OT. I consider myself to be a very reasonable person and display no violent tendencies, but on that afternoon I could have killed the referee. AFA was ahead 2-1 as we entered the second 10 minute overtime period. Here is the way Karl Licis, the sports writer for *The Gazette*, reported the incident:

> *Both teams knew it, the coaches knew it, and the crowd at Stewart Field knew it. With less than 10 minutes remaining in OT, the ball was rebounded back in front of the AFA net. CC forward Jacques Lemvo raced back for the ball, and in a spectacular individual effort reminiscent of some professional team's all-time highlight film, lifted his leg high, and in one fluid motion kicked the ball with his back to the goal over his head, suspended in mid-air, into the net. From all appearances, CC had tied the game. …*
>
> *Everyone seemed to know except referee Dieter Sulzbach. He arrived on the scene, blew his whistle, and signaled DANGEROUS PLAY. Lemvo's goal had been disallowed. ….*
>
> *"That's incredible! How can he possibly call that back?" the irate CC coach Horst Richardson fumed after the game. "I don't complain about officials, but this is ridiculous. I've never seen anything like this, anywhere. He'll never referee another game here at CC."*

And thus, the most acrobatic goal ever scored at CC didn't count. By the way, in all of my 50 years of coaching, only once did I receive a yellow card and never a red one. But on that day I could have punched the ref so hard that he would have tumbled into Monument Creek!

With that win AFA won the RMISL that year, but we went to the NCAAs! The 1981 season was the first of four incredibly successful back-to-back years, and every year was highly competitive for the participants.

Pat Shea, standout defender from Palmer High School in Colorado Springs, remembers that as a freshman in 1981 he spent the night in his sleeping bag on Washburn Field prior to the competitive pre-season 12-minute run, which was conducted early in the morning. He apparently was so nervous about passing the test that he wanted to be first in line when the trial runs were conducted!!

Much of the credit for the success of those years goes to a young man named Brigham Olson. Although Brigham listed his hometown as Los Angeles, he spent much of his young life at a boarding school in England and at a prep school on the East Coast. He was a natural athlete and participated in several sports. He later told me that during his first pre-season at CC, he was terribly afraid that I would stick him in goal, because he was tall, courageous, and had good hands. But it was clear from the start that we needed him as a central defender. His signature move was to leap sky-high and head away any ball that was crossed into our penalty area.

Handsome and gregarious, he became a huge promoter of our team, both on campus and in town. He convinced my wife Helen to start videotaping our games. Bill and Jo Boddington had made a generous gift to the program so that we could purchase a video camera. At the end of each season, Brigham would come over to our house, sit on the cold floor of our downstairs and spend hours on end splicing together highlight tapes for the enjoyment of the squad at our awards banquets. No one had ever done that before! He became the older "brother" of our two kids, Erik and Stacia, and, in a word, was family!

1981 was the last time that our post-season awards banquet was held at the Boddington residence off campus. I am certain that I speak for dozens and dozens of players who enjoyed their tremendous hospitality over time when I express my sincere gratitude to Bill and Jo for all the good times at their home. It was also Bill's last year as an assistant coach. In the summer of 1982 we staged our first CC soccer camp on campus.

1982

The 1982 season started off with two strikes against us: We had no assistant coach, and three integral starters from the previous season, Jacques Lemvo, Charlie Stanzione and Pat Shea, had decided to study abroad. Nevertheless, we fielded a spirited and formidable team. Brigham Olson, Tommy Hyland, and Jamie Hull anchored our defense, with freshman Brad Wolf showing his stuff in goal. Local star and attacking midfielder Jimmy Grice, a freshman from Palmer High School, was a huge presence in midfield alongside of Scott Evans. And Tom MacKenzie, an agile gymnast, had a wicked flip throw in!! One of the highlights of that fall was, no doubt, the 1-0 victory over D-I Cal-Berkeley. Bill Rudge '83, our captain then, has these memories of that encounter:

> *Their captain was six inches taller than me, and they had lots of talent. After John Cook had scored in the 18th minute for us on a floater of a shot, we held on for the remainder of the game with pure guts. We just outlasted them, chased them all over the field, Brad made some key saves, and they finally felt the altitude and became exhausted. 6000' worked in our favor!!*

Brad Wolf '85, our keeper from California, also remembers the Berkeley game as a high point of the season:

Not pictured: Peter Armstrong, Shep Davis, Greg Gale, Tom Penzel, John Petersen, Peter White.

Clearly the win over UC Berkeley was stupendous for us. 1-0. They were nationally ranked in D-1 and they wrote us off until half-time when they realized we were the real deal. They had two U.S. National Team players (one I knew) and I remember Jimmy Grice just torturing them. Great effort defensively by the team.

In a mid-season game against SIU-Evansville, a D-I powerhouse whose coach Fred Schmalz was a good friend of mine, we were down 1-0 at half time. In the second half, Scott Evans "caromed a free kick off the crossbar and into the net" to even the score. But it was the stunning execution of a pretty tricky set piece which is noteworthy. A teammate flicked the ball up into the air, and Scott shot a right footer on a full volley with spin that dropped the ball over the wall and into the net. I was quoted in the paper: "And I was so happy to see Evans score on that free kick. He has practiced that move 257 times. It's something that is not that easy to do, and it's something that he has practiced and practiced."

An adventurous coed road trip in the aging CC highway bus all the way to St. Louis deserves mention. A bit over 800 miles in a crowded bus can be a bore, but with songs and games, and ample food from our food service, it didn't seem so long. Besides, it was a block break!

The men's team beat Maryville and Washington University, and the women's squad split. And now the long trek home, which, because of the success of the teams, turned into a heck of a party. The vintage CC bus, with a manual transmission, was lumbering along, and we were not going very fast. Steve Paul was the licensed relief driver, but had trouble shifting gears on this old vehicle, especially from second to third. In the middle of Kansas, the terrain flat as a pancake, the bus driver needed to catch a couple hours of sleep. What did the two of them do to let Steve drive for a while without having to get the bus up to speed from a stop? Here is Steve's confession:

The bus driver, what a great guy, was this thin fellow who wore cowboy boots, and he drove that bus effortlessly ...

I, on the other hand, even with my soccer-thunder thighs had a really hard time double-clutching on gear shifting. (Shifting gears was second nature to him.) Anyhow, on a previous trip, I took over at night and when I shifted, everyone woke up and said, "Yup, Steve is driving" because I was not very good at it. So on that trip, we decided to save all the embarrassment of me trying to double-clutch shift, and we changed drivers on the fly — which was actually a whole lot easier than grinding the gears!

Bill Rudge chuckles when he thinks of that road trip and adds:

> *I remember how mad the Wash-U coach was after losing. He threw the team bench out onto the field at the end! But the trip home was a swell victory party in the back of the bus. I guess we smuggled a couple of beers on board and sang a lot of songs. Horst didn't want us to stop at a gas station until we got to western Kansas. So we had a rest stop right on the side of the road. And it was: Girls to the right, boys to the left.*

We lost to Wheaton in Chicago in the NCAA play-offs and also away to AFA thereafter in a late-season match in the snow and ice. Brigham Olson cut his leg badly on an ice chip while executing a sliding tackle, and Brad Lundberg almost bit off his tongue in a collision with a Zoomie. Lundberg remembers this incident vividly:

> *It was my last game ever as a CC player against our arch nemesis AFA and I had a tussle with one of their players close to their sideline. I bounced up first and had an unobstructed sideline, but I had to navigate around two of their players so I took two steps off the field into their bench area, and an AFA player on the sideline gave me a hard upper cut under my chin, and the motion drove my front teeth through my tongue hanging out, and it was almost severed. I immediately walked up the hill to the parking lot, knowing it was bad, and jumped into the waiting ambulance, which had just loaded up Brigham Olson with his severe shin injury suffered moments before my tongue injury. That was my last play of my CC career.*

1983

1983 was a banner year not only for CC but also for the Colorado Springs soccer community. In May of that year we hosted the Far West Regional Olympic try-outs on Stewart Field. Steve Paul and I were on the coaching staff, Eddy Dietz had returned for this event, Tommy Hyland, Scott Evans, and Charlie Stanzione remained in the top 24, and Jimmy Grice was selected and traveled to South Korea and Malaysia with the U.S. Olympic soccer effort.

A huge plus for our soccer program was the appointment of Greg Ryan as assistant coach. Greg received All-America status at SMU, had played against CC during his collegiate years, was drafted to the NASL and played for the New York Cosmos, the Tulsa Roughnecks, and the Chicago Sting. And he wanted to take biology courses at CC! He brought professional experience to enhance our performance. Several years later he ended up as CC's women's coach and thereafter became the coach of the U.S. National Women's Team!

Our three studs who had been studying overseas had returned to beef up the roster, and a solid recruiting class reported for pre-season. Jacques Lemvo, our artist and dancer, provided levity in the locker room, as Dean Campbell '87 remembers:

> *I imagine that Jacques will feature prominently in many anecdotes from the mid-'80s. One day after practice, I encountered him in the shower. He used to call me Mandraque, the French pronunciation of Mandrake, the comic-book Magician. "Mandraque," he said, "show me your chicken." The chicken was something akin to his corner flag victory dance, after scoring a goal, that basically involved short, rapid movements of the pelvis. After he demonstrated, I reluctantly followed, and my underwhelming effort (and endowment) elicited his trademark booming laughter.*

1983 | 15-6-3

Front row, left to right: Brad Wolf, Rick Hibbard, Tom Hyland (captain), Dickie Hertel, Dan Moe, Matt Slothower. **Middle row:** Jim Grice, Todd Walker, Scott Evans, Sam Schwartz, Tom MacKenzie, Jamie Hull, Greg Kazemi. **Back row:** Coach Horst Richardson, Pat Shea, Richard Lyford, Brigham Olson (captain), Jacques Lemvo, Alec Rekow, John Cook, Michael Friederich, Robert McAnulty, Charlie Stanzione, Mitch Green.

Our third game that year, a 3-3 tie against SMU, surely goes down in the annals of CC soccer as one of the most exciting ones ever. Scott Evans had scored for us, and SMU equalized. Then Brigham Olson put in a sweet header, and SMU equalized. And then they went ahead, 3-2. Brad Wolf was spectacular in goal.

The clock kept ticking away. With 10 seconds left, Sam Schwartz, substitute and back-up goalkeeper, broke through on the right wing and delivered a Hail Mary cross which, miraculously ended up in the goal with one second left on the clock. Bedlam ensued! The entire team ran out on the field and piled on Sam to celebrate. SMU refused to play overtime because of a close flight connection out of Denver. I guess they never expected anything but a win vs. CC. By the way, Helen captured every precious final second and the ensuing celebration on video.

Sam Schwartz '85, when I asked him to send me his rendition of this spectacular incident, submitted the following recollections:

> *It was late in the second half with only a minute or two remaining. We were down one goal in a game that we were not really supposed to do well in. The crowd was a full house for CC and the atmosphere was electric. My roommate Tom Hyland had been doing battle all game against SMU at fullback. Suddenly he, Tom, went down with an injury and Coach was looking around for a sub. I'm not sure why he picked me, as I usually played reserve goalie or midfield, but that is what he did.*
>
> *Honestly, I about threw up from nerves, but I managed to pull it together and get onto the field. After all there was only a minute left, how bad could I mess things up? They came at us one more time and we got the ball and moved onto attack. It started on the other side from me but then moved into their end. There were a few guys pressuring at attack on my side and the ball went out for a corner in our favor.*
>
> *I remembered in high school we used to run a play where the fullback came up and received a set up ground ball and shot at distance hoping that the ball might rebound and a striker would finish it. As the ball was played in short to a CC midfielder I could see he was in a panic, and with only 10 seconds left I screamed for the pass.*
>
> *He passed it back about 15 meters and an SMU defender came out to stop me from shooting. I kept my head down and shot the ball as hard as I could hearing the timing officials counting at 4, 3, 2 ... etc ... I never looked up.*
>
> *The defender got just enough of the ball to put a wicked top spin on it. It went towards the goal with the announcer saying "2," "1" ... and somehow, I'm not sure*

> *how, it went over the keeper's hand and dropped down like a baseball sinker, and just as the guy says "1" ... it hits the back of the net.*
>
> *The entire spectator side cleared and within a second or two I found myself on the bottom of a huge pile of players and fans! People were screaming, laughing, shouting my name and other creative phrases. After all in our sport it is VERY rare for a goal to be scored in the last second. It wasn't until Coach showed me the video that I honestly even saw the goal. It was my 15 minutes of fame and I am proud to be a part of a rich tradition of Colorado College soccer.*

Scott Evans not only ruled in midfield for us, but he also wrote some pretty good *Catalyst* stories about our soccer exploits. On the Utah trip to BYU and Westminster he reported about the bizarre refereeing at BYU, where the off-side rule seemed to have been suspended, and a score was allowed, even though it was clear that the ball went into the goal through a hole in the side netting. He further pointed out the value of liberal arts learning by driving there in private cars and camping out along the way. And, of course, the mudslide!

Let me elaborate: After camping Friday night in the Colorado National Monument outside of Grand Junction, we hit the road early to arrive in Provo by noon for an afternoon match. Just after Green River, Utah, the road north to Provo over Soldiers Pass was closed due to a major mudslide, which had washed away a portion of the highway. For us that meant a 100-mile detour. We drove on relentlessly and arrived in Provo 20 minutes before kick-off. Anyway, we tied BYU, beat Westminster, and made it back to campus in time for Monday morning classes.

Brigham Olson had begun a tradition for home games. He had secured sponsorship from Skodack and Turner, a florist on Tejon Street, to provide 11 red roses for every home game. The starters would take these out to the center circle during player introduction and then present them to their favorite ladies in the stands. This ceremony increased our popularity!

The mid-season bus trip to Grinnell was much more comfortable than the road trip to Utah, although the scenery left much to be desired. Brigham, the seasoned traveler, brought his hammock along and strung it up in the bus between luggage racks. John Cook, as Jim Grice remembers, "made the miles melt away with his magic fingers on the guitar."

We scored 15 goals in three games at the Grinnell Invitational and allowed only one. No wonder that the guys socialized a bit at our sister school. Jimmy Grice '86, a man of few words, put it succinctly in a rhetorical question: "Anyone ever been to a toga party in Grinnell, Iowa?" Jacques obviously had; he nearly missed the bus on the way home, probably because of talking to some toga-clad Grinnell coed he had met the evening before.

The week after we returned to campus, there was a memorable weekend wedding in Shove Chapel, folded in between two home games. Assistant Coach Greg Ryan married his sweetheart Janet Schwartz. It was a festive affair and impressive to see the entire squad in attendance dressed to the hilt in coat and tie.

In the second half of the season the team pursued its ambition to once again qualify for the NCAAs and rolled from one victory to the next, including a battle for an away win to Metro State. Our valuable defender Mitch Green ended up with a cast on his ankle after a bad Metro tackle and furthermore, unheard of in college soccer, our entire team received a yellow card upon protesting this injury! A festive meal provided by Mitch Green's parents at their home in Denver restored the squad's physical and mental health.

A homecoming of sorts for me occurred when, during the second block break, we traveled to Southern California for three games, including one against my alma mater, U-California, Riverside. We beat them 3-0. Their alumni magazine was gracious in lauding their graduate and his team upon his return to campus.

We were selected for the NCAA play-offs for the third year in a row and once again had to travel to Chicago to face Wheaton College. The local crowd was large and vociferous, and the freight trains kept rattling by the field, just behind the press box. You couldn't hear yourself think! But the third time against Wheaton was the charm for us, as we defeated the host 2-1.

What a game it was! Brigham Olson had scored on a header early in the first half, and freshman left winger Dickie Hertel had threaded his way into the box before half-time and finished off the solo run with a magnificent goal. We knew that the second half would be a nailbiter, but we hung on. Hertel hyperventilated in the second half from all the tension and had to breathe into a paper bag for 10 minutes, and Charlie Stanzione, who dazzled his opponents a number of times with his signature hip swivel move, had to come out with a severe thigh strain. Our substitutes carried the day!! For the first time in five NCAA outings we had advanced to the next round!

Riding back to the airport in our Lincoln Continental town cars, courtesy of the NCAA, of course, we felt elated. Brad Wolf '85, who tended the goal for us and, as a surfer from Southern California, nearly froze to death on that cold afternoon, had this to say about the game:

> *Playing Wheaton in Illinois on a fiercely cold day was hard. We played our hearts out. I was shaking the entire time, from the cold and from the nerves, and it was difficult to concentrate. I will never forget the lads crying on the field after our victory. That was our year.*

Klemens Hertel was a foreign student from Freiburg, West Germany. In a manner of speaking, the CC German Department needs to get credit for his recruitment. As part of my duties in the German Department, I had instructed a group of our students in Germany during the spring of 1982. An acquaintance in Freiburg hosted us there for a couple of days, showing us the town and the adjacent Black Forest.

One day we were guests at a high school in Freiburg and participated in their English classes. Since I was introduced as German professor and soccer coach, this little guy approached me after class, indicating that not only did he play soccer, but also that he wanted to study in the U.S. after graduation. I didn't pay much attention to him at first, but when I watched him walk down the hallway I noticed his bowed legs and his quick sidestepping as he accelerated through the crowded corridors. Our host and I checked out his youth soccer career in Freiburg, and he had stellar credentials. He also turned out to be an outstanding student, and so he applied to CC and was accepted. He became our "Garrincha."

The win at Wheaton and our record had catapulted us to No. 5 in the country, the best ranking ever. So our hopes were high to host the next round, and we were granted that honor. (The first home NCAA game since 1966.) However, nemesis Claremont from California loomed on the horizon, and they had eliminated UC San Diego, a formidable feat.

Our grounds crew worked hard to get Washburn Field ready for the play-off event. In spite of a wonderfully supportive crowd of 1,400 and our 30 shots vs. their 10, we lost the game 3-2. Brigham and Jacques had scored for us, but their keeper, a Colorado native from Denver, had an incredibly strong performance in the nets.

We ended the season with a festive banquet for both the women's and the men's teams at the Press Box restaurant downtown. And Dang Pibulvech, the women's coach, and I were named Midwest coaches of the year.

A final comment about the '83 season: The November 18 issue of *The Catalyst*, the Friday before the play-off game, featured a full-page side shot of three nude torsos on the front page. The provocative caption below read: "What's on everyone's mind?" The answer, presumably, was to attend the game. I know who the models on the left and right were, but I never did figure out the identity of the middle figure.

1984

In 1984, the Tigers, with 17 wins, again had an NCAA play-off year, for the fourth year in a row. By now, coaching at CC had become a family affair. At every home game Helen shouldered the heavy video camera and from her perch on a 12' tower, taped the competition. Our son Erik worked in our camps and came to practice in the fall when his high school schedule permitted, and our daughter Stacia took stats from the stands.

An incredible story of player development was exemplified in the case of Jamie Hull, a local athlete. In '84, Jamie was a senior and a stalwart defender. Four years earlier, he had barely made the team and spent most of his time retrieving balls which had been shot over the fence into Monument Creek. I have never witnessed a work ethic stronger than his, and the positive attitude he brought to every practice session was nothing short of admirable. In his sophomore year he was voted "Most Improved Player" by his teammates, and during his last two seasons our defense would have been unthinkable without him. After his graduation, he wrote me a personal note:

> *There are so many things to look back on with fondness during these four years: My trips to the creek to secure a drowning ball — The many hours of practice — The great games we played — Those sumptuous meals Mrs. Richardson prepared for us — The plus and minus instructional film sessions — The great hamburger cookout on a road trip …*

Jamie made the job of coaching a rewarding enterprise. And his three sisters played for our Tiger women's team!!!

1984 | 17-6-1

Front row, left to right: Greg Kazemi, Dan Engster, Tom Hyland (captain), Brigham Olson (captain), Charlie Stanzione (captain), Rick Hibbard, Jim Grice. **Middle row:** Kelly Atkinson, Sam Schwartz, Andy Henderson, Klemens Hertel, Jamie Hull, Teddy Mattera, Dan Moe, Scott Evans, Michael Blaxill. **Back row:** Volunteer assistant coach, Mark Nordby, Jim Henderson,Todd Walker, Michael Friederich, Matt Slothower, Brad Wolf, Richard Lyford, Mitch Green, Tom MacKenzie, Steve McDougal, Coach Horst Richardson. **Not pictured:** Jacques Lemvo, Robert McAnulty.

We had taken the usual block break trip to Grinnell, Iowa, to compete in their invitational, but did not play the host. In an overtime thriller we topped St. Olaf of Minnesota, with Jacques scoring two. Tommy Hyland, who notched his 81st consecutive career start in that game, was hospitalized after the match with a possible broken rib. Richard Quincy, who traveled with us as our trainer, not only took good care of T HY, but also of all the other bruised warriors.

In mid-October, a freak snowstorm dumped eight inches of wet snow on Colorado Springs, forcing a cancellation of our DU contest. More importantly, though, was the fact that our Division III tournament was in doubt for the weekend.

The whole team came out with snow shovels Thursday, trying to clear Stewart Field, but we barely got one penalty area uncovered. What to do? Knowing Lou Sagastume, the Air Force coach, quite well, I was able to make arrangements with him to move the entire tournament into the Academy Field House. So instead of playing in the snow, we played indoors, 8 vs. 8. All teams had agreed on that format. CC came away with three victories, defeating Trinity, Pomona, and Grinnell. And Tommy Hyland, whose rib was fortunately not broken, got his 86th career start.

Stewart Field was getting crowded. Both men's and women's teams were highly successful and carried large rosters. Thus, field configurations and improvements were high on my to-do list. With the help of the supportive physical plant and grounds crew, we kept chipping away at the east slope of the field to gain more practice space. We built a kick board on the east side and realigned the large sandstone blocks to provide for a parallel line for the sidelines and seating for the spectators. A 20-by-20-yard indentation in the hillside, called "The Pit," provided a valuable 3-on-3 "torture" area and also was storage for our bleachers, which the team had to put in place before each home game. A huge success was constructing a steep retaining wall in the northeast corner of the field, which allowed for two teams to practice cross-field simultaneously. Every year we also gained space in the north end. Finally, we were able to obtain a couple of storage sheds for our practice equipment.

Speaking of Stewart Field: A number of things happened there that year that are firmly embedded in my mind. One day during practice, while I was talking with the players on the west side of the field near the Monument Creek fence, an errant Canadian goose crashed into the fence in full flight. That incident disrupted practice as we were trying to get the bird back on its feet.

Another incident, once again during an instructional talk, occurred when Scott Evans, the prankster, snuck up behind me and pulled down my shorts all the way to my knees in one swift action. I deflated his prank considerably, though, by continuing my talk uninterruptedly and pulled up my pants as if nothing had happened at all!

A rather shocking event one afternoon spooked the whole team: A young woman stumbled along the path on the creek-side of the fence with bloodied hands. She apparently had slashed her wrists in a suicide attempt. Brigham and Teddy Mattera comforted her until medical help arrived.

Even though we had suffered narrow losses to both UC San Diego and Claremont away, our strength-of-schedule index warranted an NCAA appearance. At Claremont in the Sunny Southland we defeated St. Olaf from Minnesota in overtime. BUT, with four minutes to go in regulation time we trailed 2-0.

At 85:47, Charlie Stanzione booted home a loose ball in front of their net, and with 90 seconds left, Brigham Olson hammered home a hanging header off of a Stanzione free kick. "It was one of the most beautiful head-ball goals I have ever seen," I was quoted in the paper. What an unbelievable comeback!!

But the hero of the game was a foreign student from South Africa, Teddy Mattera. He had seen limited playing time, but when he had his chance, he took it. He beat their keeper five minutes into the second OT with a low shot to the far post from 18 yards out. "That was the best come-from-behind victory in my time at CC," I said.

Unfortunately we lost to Claremont on the next day and were out of the play-offs. A small consolation at home the next weekend was a solid win over DU in a make-up game.

Pat Shea, fellow defender to Brigham, pays homage to Brigham with this memory:

> *Fellow center back Brigham Olson was a leader with constant humor and dedication. He started 91 games in four years, helped ensure shut-outs, scored 16 goals, and registered nine assists. We've all heard about players who make their teammates play better and assist scoring. Brigham took it to a higher level by helping teammates score off the field as well. How else can you explain Brigham's Starting 11 Flower Project?*
>
> *Brigham worked with a flower shop downtown to have 11 roses for every home game. Each starter would deliver his rose to a fan. I gave mine to my mom (sentimental). Other players used the roses to woo new girls (or strengthen relationships with existing girlfriends). By the end of the season, my mom still loved me, but my teammates reaped a higher love yield.*

The four-year stretch from '81 to '84 was magnificent! The team had acquired national prominence. Traditions were born and expectations were set, which are still with us today. I think all players from that era would agree that much of the credit for this success must go to our co-captain Brigham Olson, whose 91 career starts set a record which will most likely never be challenged.

At the '84 awards banquet, Brigham presented his teammates with an 84-page booklet he had compiled, detailing all of their accomplishments and statistics in their four years, including pictures and every press release and *Catalyst* story. What a class act!

Brigham died in 2003 of a brain tumor. His tragic death devastated his family, friends, and teammates. My saddest duty ever was to render a eulogy, on the day he died, upon his induction into the CC Athletic Hall of Fame. His wife, Leslie, a CC graduate, leaves us with this remembrance:

When we first started dating, Brigham was spending countless hours sitting in the Richardson's basement working on the CC highlight tapes. Other than as a spectator, that was my introduction to the CC men's soccer program.

I realize that Horst and Helen have been the "second set of parents" for countless of these young men and, for many, the CC soccer program was the most important part of the college years. That was the case for Brigham. I don't recall specific moments about the team, but I will never forget observing the strong bond among the players. They had that easy-going camaraderie that you expect from a strong team; they teased each other, sometimes to the point of giggling like young children, and they supported one another. This was particularly evident when Brigham became sick. Players sent letters and videotapes with words of love and encouragement. Those living close by visited Brigham regularly. Many of the players traveled to California for an early celebration of Brigham's 40th birthday, surprising him when they ran in wearing their CC soccer jerseys. It was the epitome of a bittersweet moment. At that party, Horst announced that Brigham would be recognized as a CC Hall of Fame recipient the following May.

Here is my most memorable moment about the program — Brigham's health had been deteriorating rapidly to the point that he was no longer communicating with us. I'm not sure why I asked the question but, on the morning of May 10, 2003, I asked my mom if she thought Brigham would die that day. She looked at me with tears in her eyes and said, "Absolutely. He does not want to miss his CC Hall of Fame Induction Ceremony tonight for his beloved soccer team."

She was right. He briefly regained consciousness that day so I know he knew and then passed away just hours before he was inducted into the CC Athletic Hall of Fame. I truly believe Brigham chose May 10th as the day he would pass so he could have as much time as possible with his family but still be able to be with Horst and Helen at the moment he was inducted into the Athletic Hall of Fame. That is how much the CC men's soccer program meant to Brigham.

To honor the memory of Brigham, the College named the north-end practice area "Olson Field" in 2004.

1985

I am inclined to call 1985 the "Year of the Jacques." But we started off the season with aerobics on the astroturf surface in the basement of the El Pomar gym. Stephanie Pell, a wisp of a woman, put all the guys to shame with her workouts. We were huffing and puffing, and she hardly broke a sweat. We needed to get in shape and become competitive quickly.

Eleven seniors had graduated from the previous team, and rebuilding was very much on my mind. We did have four seniors on the squad to lead us. Jimmy Grice, our captain, Dickie Hertel, our dangerous and quick left winger, Danny Moe, a diminutive midfielder, who could jump higher than most guys six inches taller than he, and Jacques Lemvo, who was breaking our all-time scoring records. And then we had our new secret weapon, Kristian Sundborn from Sweden.

We started off well with a couple of victories, even beating Claremont by a good margin. Then Dan Engster broke his leg in the Bethel game, and we lost to Washington University, a big-time D-III opponent. Freshmen Wiley Bland, Andy Dorsey, and Chip

1985 | 15-8-0

Front row, left to right: Matt Slothower, Tim Kienitz, Steve McDougal. **Middle row:** Andy Henderson, Dickie Hertel (captain), Paul Schmidt, Chip Sagal, Ricky Garcia, Jim Grice (captain), Greg Kazemi, Dan Moe, Coach Horst Richardson. **Back row:** Assistant Coach Tom Hyland, Mike Blaxill, Todd Walker, Wiley Bland, Alexis Donahue, Kristian Sundborn, Dean Campbell, Andy Dorsey, Jacques Lemvo, Mike Fraterelli. **Not pictured:** Dan Engster, Teddy Mattera, Richard Van Noy.

Sagal showed their stuff against crosstown rival UCCS in a narrow win, and then it was off to the St. Mary's Invitational in Winona, Minnesota.

We ended up winning this tournament. Noteworthy here is the fact that I refereed our second game there, a match against St. John's University, since the assigned referees didn't show up for the game. We won, and there were no controversial calls!

Mike Fraterelli '88 and Dan Engster '87 wrote wonderfully witty articles for *The Catalyst*. Here is a quote from their reporting on our block break trip to Grinnell: "Over block break the team traveled 16 hours via the luxury first-class CC bus to everybody's favorite vacationland — Grinnell, Iowa. Playing an inspired home team in front of hostile farmers armed with 12-foot pitch forks, the Tigers were lucky to escape with a 1-0 victory, on a penalty shot by Jacques Lemvo."

We stayed in the Grinnell gym wrestling room again and enjoyed the sister college's hospitality. Their coach, John Pfitsch, had become a good friend of mine. I have a telling picture of him talking with Jacques after our game, which we humorously captioned: "Grinnell coach trying to convince Jacques to transfer."

Jacques had elected to become a studio art major and had a significant exhibition of his art work in early October. *The Gazette* sports writer, Karl Licis, devoted almost the entire sports section on October 10 to this exhibit. His article was called "The arts and soccer!" It included large pictures of Jacques playing soccer and close-ups of his abstract, confrontational, and somewhat disturbing paintings.

Certainly Jacques considered playing soccer an art form, but as the season stretched into the fall, he seemed to shift his focus from the field to the studio. And it came as no surprise to me when he told me then that he was going to quit the team to spend more time in the studio. The team was disappointed, if not shocked, when I told them. Two weeks later he changed his mind and wanted to return to the squad. In fact, he announced his intention minutes before a road trip to Albuquerque. The boys were already settling in on the bus when he came aboard. I left it up to the team to decide whether or not to take him back. They voted "Yes," with the proviso of a one-game suspension.

So we left with Jacques on board. I drove the 24-passenger bus, the "Desert Shark." And this trip turned into one of the most bizarre and taxing ventures ever.

The plan was to drive to Santa Fe, spend the night there, and then continue to Albuquerque for a game against UNM, a member school of the RMISL. That evening we were to fly on to San Antonio, Texas, for a two-game series at Trinity University. Then on Sunday, we would return by air to Albuquerque and bus back to CC.

Thirty miles out of Santa Fe I ran out of gas. I had switched to the second fuel tank once we were well into New Mexico, assuming that the second tank had the same capacity as the first. That was a faulty assumption. The second tank was just an emergency tank. It was 10 p.m.; the guys were hungry and needed to be in bed at the motel, and here we were on I-25, all alone under a full moon.

Fortunately we had a player on the bus who lived in Santa Fe. So I directed Alexis Donahue to hitchhike into town to get fuel. He caught a ride and came back two hours later with a five-gallon can of diesel. Our bus, however, had a gasoline engine. By now the guys were muttering! There was hardly any traffic on the freeway, and the boys used the shoulder markings to play soccer tennis!

In desperation, I set up a couple of guys along both freeway lanes, north and south bound, to hail down any and every vehicle in the hope that someone might carry extra fuel. And we were lucky! A diesel trucker had five gallons of gasoline in his cab. We made it to the motel by two in the morning.

Exhausted and with Jacques sitting out the DI UNM game, I figured our chances of success there were low, to say the least. But David beat Goliath in this match. They might have had much more possession of the ball than we did, but we played awesome defense, with goalkeeper Matt Slothower stopping multiple shots. Mike Fraterelli and Dickie Hertel scored, and we dug in deep to protect the victory.

"We might have run out of gas on the road," I was quoted, "but we didn't run out of gas on the field." In Texas, we picked up two more shut-outs. I was extremely proud of the team to turn a potentially disastrous road trip into a supreme success story!

This adventurous road trip left such a lasting impression on Todd Walker '87 that he submitted a short story entitled "Horst, the King of the Road." Here it is:

> *Discarding his German roots in favor of his Western surroundings, Horst stood before the 16-man traveling squad sporting dusty boots and a large cowboy hat. Horst always seemed to love road trips, and he sported a big smile as we boarded a small bus headed to Albuquerque to play UNM in the fall of 1985.*
>
> *In those days, commercial drivers were not in the soccer budget. But our Autobahn veteran, Horst, was at the wheel, so why worry?*
>
> *Horst drove with cowboy confidence into the late evening. All seemed to be going well, until the engine sputtered and the bus stopped running on a dark and very quiet*

stretch of I-25, about an hour short of our destination. Horst, taking charge, assessed the situation and discovered the obvious: he had run out of gas!

We had a really good laugh at Horst's expense while he worked to regain control of a potential crisis. He decided to send one of the guys to hitchhike his way to a can of fuel. And even though Horst's very job was to offer guidance to his young men, he provided no detailed instructions to our hitchhiker, Alexis Donahue.

A lot of time passed before Alexis returned. We were relieved to see that he made it back safely, and we were happy to see that he had a can of fuel. There was, however, one small problem: He had brought back diesel, but the small bus took gas. Back to square one!!

A trucker, in a diesel rig who stopped, luckily had a can of gas on board. We started driving again; bodies were scattered along the floor and on the seats of our bus as we tried to get some sleep. After getting to our budget motel in Santa Fe sometime after 2 a.m., we crashed.

An all-you-can-eat breakfast buffet awaited us in the morning: rice with sweet and sour pork?? It didn't seem very cowboy-like to us, but we made the best of it and ate what we could. At the field in Albuquerque, we had no illusions of playing well under the circumstances and knew that Horst couldn't very well criticize us for a lackluster effort that day. But then the strangest thing happened!! Within minutes of the kick-off, we scored. And scored again, and I think we might have even scored a third one before the half was over. That day we handed UNM a crushing defeat, which cost them an expected bid to the NCAA D-I play-offs.

The strong finish to our season, though, earned us another trip to the NCAAs, an unprecedented fifth year in a row. In San Diego, UC San Diego, with an enrollment five times that of CC and no football program, defeated us 3-1.

As an addendum to the San Diego trip, Kristian Sundborn '90, our Swede, recalls how five members of the team snuck across the border to Tijuana, Mexico, to "relax from the stress of the game!"

After a tough game against the always difficult team UCSD, one of us had a splendid idea. We are going to Tijuana! Five of us decided to jump into a small car. Somehow, I figured the reward is greater than the risk, although I had no passport and my visa did not permit me to leave the U.S. during the semester and year.

> *So, the emotional Swede decided to take the risk. I remember, we decided to put me in the trunk. It was obviously uncomfortable, risky and stupid.*
>
> *I remember my thoughts and my nervousness: it was like a movie. I really thought I was in a movie, probably about to get busted for some minor offense.*
>
> *We had a typical college time in Tijuana, and the trip going back made me even more nervous since it was quite late. We managed to get to the hotel safe and sound.*
>
> *I realized it was a risk, but it was exciting. I will not put it on my CV.*
>
> *CC Tigers have given me great experiences in many ways; I guess this was one that was educational in a different way. Thank you again, CC, Horst and Helen.*

It was a risky trip for that quintet. But border controls were lax then, and Kristian was lucky!

1986

1986 was a World Cup year. Mexico hosted the tournament, and some of the games there were to be played at high altitude. To train for 6000' and more, three World Cup participants, England, Canada, and South Korea, spent time in Colorado Springs, exercising and adjusting to altitude. South Korea trained on our field, and in return agreed to have a scrimmage against the Tigers. We played the game at the Fountain Valley School. Even though we lost 7-0, it was a memorable experience. Especially for Todd Walker, our pillar of strength on defense. Here is his rendition of defending against their star forward, Bum Cum Cha:

> *I did brutally foul Cha as he beat me badly just outside the top of the box in the South Korean friendly in 1986 that we played at Fountain Valley HS. We got the "Friendly" (as I am sure you recall since you arranged it) in exchange for us being so gracious to let them train at altitude on Stewart Field as they prepared for the Mexico City World Cup. It turned out that I was not so "Friendly" and apparently missed the memo on proper protocol, although I only fouled him because he was so quick to get the ball out of the way of my lumbering tackle. So it was kind of his own fault. Cha was uninjured on the play and they promptly scored on the ensuing free kick. So I think it all worked out fine for everyone.*

1986 | 9-9-4

In '86, we flew half the team to California — but couldn't afford tickets for the other half. Those who traveled by van are featured in this year's photo. **Front row:** Paul Schmidt, Andy Henderson, Chip Sagal, Wiley Bland, Alec Rekow, Coach Horst Richardson. **Back row:** Jim Schuster, Scott Reynolds, Andreas Klohnen. **Not pictured:** Mike Blaxill, Doug Corkran, Alexis Donahue, Andy Dorsey, Derek Fehmers, Mike Fraterelli, Ricky Garcia, Steve Herzog, Tim Johnson, Greg Kazemi (captain), Teddy Mattera, Steve McDougal, Nedim Ogelman, Steve Patrick, Matt Slothower, Richard Van Noy, Todd Walker (captain), Brian Weslar.

South Korea were eliminated in the first round in Mexico, but their enthusiastic and diligent play, which they exhibited on our field, was inspirational. By the way, the then-UCCS coach, my good friend Bruce Atkinson, and I attended the World Cup in Mexico.

Jacques Lemvo had become our all-time scoring leader in his senior year with a career 65 goals, breaking the 62 goal record, which Andre Zarb-Cousin had established in 1972. And our midfield ace, Kristian Sundborn, had to take time off from CC to fulfill his military service requirement in Sweden. Kristian returned to CC to graduate and complete his playing eligibility. He even became my assistant after graduation and a year thereafter was named assistant to the CC women's team.

Jacques, on the other hand, did not graduate, electing to leave campus in the spring of his senior year to pursue his art in Los Angeles. Two years after his departure, he called at our house to read us his Easter poems, in English, German, and French. Since that phone call, aside from two rambling letters, we never heard from him again.

1986 was the year in which the Tigers took their first trip to the East Coast, playing in a tournament at Elizabethtown College in Pennsylvania. After beating Carnegie Mellon in the first game, we faced the host the next day. After a 1-1 tie and double overtime, the tournament winner was settled on penalties. Scott Reynolds' spot kick settled the matter and we traveled home with a huge trophy.

Paul Schmidt, Andy Dorsey, Chip Sagal, and Alec Rekow provided steady and intelligent play to make the first East Coast trip a success. A rumor exists that Paul Schmidt '90 ruined the trophy at the airport by letting it slip out of his hand and dropping it to the floor. Here is Paul's humorously evasive answer to this incident:

> *If you send me a copy of that "rumor report" (aka flagrant misrepresentation), I will be glad to make any necessary corrections. If you can't send the particular flagrant representation of the incident for the specific correction, I can only say this: check the airport video.*
>
> *Did the perpetrator have a pre-mullet hair trim? Was he wearing blue Adidas? Was he carrying a heavy-studied look, even extreme consternation, i.e., the somber-CC-stare of a person about to face a Music in Western Culture mid-term exam? Then yes, it might have been me, or probably Chip Sagal or Kristian Sundborn.*

A block break trip to the land of 10,000 lakes, however, was not as successful. I won't ever forget our match against St. Thomas in the Twin Cities. Ahead 1-0 for the entire game we were awarded a free kick on the edge of their penalty area with 12 seconds left in regulation time. We took the free kick, it bounced off their wall, and on a breakaway counter they scored with one second left. Absolutely dismal!

The annual alumni game had become a cherished tradition. At Homecoming that year, 28 alums, the most ever, showed up for the encounter, all fit and eager to play. It was a festive occasion and heartwarming for me to see so many former players return to their alma mater for this event.

Our annual jaunt to Grinnell College in Iowa proved to be a painful experience for Andy Dorsey, our dominant and essential player in midfield that year. In a game against Wooster College, on a rain-soaked pitch with standing water and pockets of deep mud, he literally "got stuck in the mud" to such a depth that he twisted his ankle so badly it sidelined him for the rest of the season.

The ultimate road trip that year, though, was a split one to Southern California. To keep the cost down, I decided that half of the team would fly out and the other half would drive with me. On the way back we would exchange boarding passes and reverse the travel group. (That procedure, believe it or not, was legal and possible then.) I, of course, drove both ways.

Wiley Bland '89, outdoorsman from Alaska, remembers this adventure with relish:

> *Some of my best Colorado College Soccer memories can be summed up in two words, ROAD TRIP. The year was 1986. I think it was mid-season in October. Horst announced to the team we were going to be playing some games in Southern California. Half the team got to fly and half drove in the van with Horst. The deal was that the van ride to California included an overnighter in the desert. I thought, "He's crazy!!!" My other thought was, "I'm in!"*
>
> *The road trip began with the usual card games, joking on each other, and food breaks. We had just passed through the Four Corners region and night was falling. We found a campsite, pulled out the sleeping bags, and figured out the best spots. Some slept in the van, some slept on the desert floor, and one (Scott Reynolds) slept on top of the van. Huh? Why on top of the van? He told us, "scorpions." Uh-oh.*
>
> *Needless to say, many of us on the desert floor then crammed into the van. I don't think anyone saw a scorpion, but we didn't sleep well. I think the guy on top of the van made the right choice. Guess where Horst slept? On the desert floor! Dang. Regardless, it was my first trip to this beautiful area and gave me inspiration to adventure to more places like it ... minus a scorpion. Thanks for the memories, Horst!*

Jim Schuster '90, along on that California road trip, also remembers the overnight stay in the desert. Here is his recollection:

> *Unless you are up for serious adventure, I do not recommend booking with the Coach Richardson Travel Agency. Citing budget issues, Horst was creative in our travel arrangements, and he often kept the information about our sleeping accommodations vague until the moment of arrival. Gym floors, alumni and parent living rooms, and wrestling room mats were common fare, but the Desert Inn caught us all off guard.*

> *Horst told us to bring sleeping bags for the stay at Derek Fehmers' home in Pasadena, but he would not reveal where we would stay on the way to the Sunny Southland. Upon badgering him, he stated that we would be staying "somewhere in the desert; let's call it the Desert Inn." As the evening grew late and our crew got tired, Horst pulled off the highway and drove down a dirt road, cruising into the desert as though he had taken the road a thousand times. As the van headed into the empty desert, the team members began to realize that we would literally be sleeping "somewhere in the desert."*
>
> *Without as much as a word, Horst stopped the van, grabbed his sleeping bag and a fold-up cot, opened the van door and grabbed a place under a Joshua tree to bed down for the night. The team was stunned at our predicament, and the scramble began for the prime sleeping spots. The seats on the van were quickly claimed, and those afraid of snakes slept on top of the van, while those afraid of rain slept under the bus, and the rest spread around the comfort of the desert vegetation. Welcome to the Desert Inn, Gentlemen!!*

(I have taken many a trip out to California since then, taking my family to visit my parents and relatives in Orange County. And every time we drive by that "Desert Inn," I have told the tale of the overnight stay in the desert. And I chuckle.)

In the Rocky Mountain Intercollegiate Soccer League (RMISL) we ended up in fifth place that year, behind AFA, Regis, DU, and UNM. Metro State, Mines, Westminster, and UCCS completed the standings.

Greg Kazemi, an outstanding defender for us, was selected as our first All-American. That was a big breakthrough for CC soccer. Our geographic isolation from the heartlands of D-III soccer and our D-III independent status had always handicapped us from getting national post-season player recognition. Teammate Marc "Chip" Sagal was chosen for the U.S. team to participate in the 5th Pan Am Maccabi games, staged in Caracas, Venezuela. And at the awards banquet in Bemis Hall, the team presented me with a "King of the Road" hat. The team thought I looked like Harrison Ford. Cool!

1987

Let's dedicate 1987 to two integral persons of the CC soccer effort: Bruce Kola and Weidou Xu.

Bruce, CC's head trainer and faculty member in sports science, was reducing his availability to the hockey team and elected to spend more time with men's soccer. His relationship with the team and with me personally was most productive and based on respect and friendship. His undivided attention to injured athletes was decidedly professional, and the health and readiness of our varsity players remained his priority. What a luxury in a D-III soccer program to have one of the finest trainers in the collegiate world out on the field with us or on arduous road trips to distant places in the West!!

The appearance of Weidou Xu from the People's Republic of China on the CC athletic scene is a marvelous liberal arts story. Weidou was a professor of sports at the distinguished Beijing Institute of Physical Education, who somehow obtained a sabbatical leave to spend a semester at Boston University. After his time at BU, Weidou was eager to remain in the U.S.

1987 | 12-10-0

Front row, left to right: Scott Zeman, Andreas Klohnen, Steve Herzog, Steve Patrick, Doug Corkran, Andy Schwartz, Craig Fukushima. **Middle row:** Brian Joseph, Scott Reynolds, Mike Blaxill, Nedim Ogelman, Chip Sagal, Jim Schuster, Andy Henderson. **Back row:** Coach Horst Richardson, Than Acuff, Alec Rekow (captain), Derek Fehmers, Wiley Bland, Sean Hurley, Alex Ayers, Bob Hartman, Andy Dorsey (captain), Assistant Coach Weidou Xu. **Not pictured:** Brian Burke, Mike Fraterelli, Tim Johnson, Michael Konsek, Richard Van Noy.

I had become well-acquainted with the BU coach, Hank Steinbrecher, at coaches conventions, and was intrigued when he called to ask if CC soccer would be interested in offering Weidou an assistant position so that he could extend his visa. Weidou's credentials were stellar; not only was he a student of the game, but he also brought a wealth of knowledge in acupuncture, massage, stretching, and Chinese medicine. He quickly established himself as an invaluable assistant coach and representative of a distant culture.

"Weidou gives the best massages," said Andy Dorsey '89. "I really can't play a game without a leg massage from him. I've become addicted."

Pre-season started off with an ascent of Pikes Peak in the rain, led by captain and iron man Alec Rekow. He honed his persuasive leadership skills on that hike, I am sure.

Andy Dorsey, Wiley Bland, Chip Sagal, Mike Fraterelli, Andy Henderson, Mike Blaxill, and Jim Schuster were veterans. Weidou worked with the three goalkeepers, and Steve Patrick got the nod to start in the nets. Andy Schwartz was new, a razzle-dazzle player from New Jersey, and Steve Herzog and Andreas Klohnen provided speed up front.

We drove off to Salt Lake City on Labor Day weekend before instruction at CC even started. We picked up a win and a forfeit at Westminster College. The forfeit gave us a chance to sightsee in SLC and visit the Mormon Temple. I was always eager to take advantage of educational opportunities on road trips!!

I thought we were off to a good start, but a close loss to AFA put a damper on our ambitions. With a mere 500 season at the halfway point of the campaign, I announced the "October Revolution" and encouraged all the guys to wear red socks to keep up their spirit as we approached Homecoming. We were rewarded with a win against Mines and a new scoreboard on Stewart Field!!

But the temporary high didn't last long, as we not only lost to DU at the second Homecoming game, but also our keeper Steve Patrick to a dislocated kneecap. The up-and-down season continued. A mysterious writer for the *Catalyst* reported with gusto on our trials and tribulations. His alias was Slobodan Yukovylitchski, better known as Jim Schuster. Great fun!!

For the next game we had lost our back-up keeper to a field trip. Alex Ayres stepped up to the plate, a freshman from Lander, Wyoming. Had they ever seen a soccer ball on the high plains up there?? Alex was an incredible athlete and had super fast reflexes, developed as short stop in high school. I praised him in an interview: "I mean here is a freshman from Lander, Wyoming, who has no game experience at all, and he comes out and records two straight shut-outs. He is a natural, a competitor, and doesn't get excited when under pressure. We just worked with him for a week …"

During that week the stock market fell 508 points (as Helen had documented in the scrapbook for that year), but Alex's stock soared!

We traveled to Southern California during Block Break II, and our athletic director, Dick Taber, chemistry professor and sports enthusiast, came along. All the players wore coats and ties!

In the first half of our game against Occidental College, Scott Reynolds had received a red card, and I sent him to the locker room to take an early shower. After the game we couldn't find him. He had disappeared. He wasn't at the motel either, and had not returned by the following morning. Naturally we were worried, and the AD had reason to question my supervision of the team. As we arrived on the Pomona College field for our second game, here is Scott, dressed to play! Well, we suspended him for the rest of the season.

Funny thing, though. We gave him a second chance a year later, and our relationship was much improved. And today Scott is heavily involved with soccer promotion at the MLS level, and we meet frequently at national coaching events. He is ardently interested in the welfare of CC soccer and has become a supportive alum.

The season ended with a road trip to Las Cruces, New Mexico, where there was no collegiate soccer at all. But they had a very active youth soccer program there, and with the help of Chip Sagal, whose home was Las Cruces, we convinced the youth soccer folks in town to let us stage a collegiate tournament for the benefit of their players and parents in exchange for housing and food. Through my connections in the collegiate soccer world, I convinced Trinity from Texas, Cal State-San Bernardino, and Glassboro State from New Jersey to participate. For several subsequent years we continued that format and helped promote the game in that New Mexico/Texas border town.

By the time of our awards banquet at the end of the season, Weidou had established himself at CC. In my German and Russian foreign language department, I had convinced my colleagues to allow Weidou to teach a Chinese adjunct course, which proved to be quite successful. In a manner of speaking, Weidou initiated our now active East Asian language program.

Weidou also worked on the grounds crew at CC, and several times a week in the post office of the United States Soccer Federation, which had relocated from New York City to the Colorado Springs Olympic quarters. And, most importantly of all, he and I were planning a team trip to China. We announced our intentions at the banquet with much fanfare and encouraged the players to start raising funds for this foreign adventure.

1988

1988 began with a team tour of Communist China! Marc "Chip" Sagal '89, who was on the trip, and who produced an award-winning video of the epic journey, began his video commentary by asking: "Take the CC soccer team to China? Are you kidding me? We couldn't even go to New Mexico without running out of gas!"

In 1988, taking a group of 23 to Communist China was an out-of-the-ordinary trip, to say the least. Weidou Xu, our then assistant coach, used his China connections to organize the trip, but, being a defector, he obviously couldn't accompany us. His instructions to

1988 | 14-6-2

Front row, left to right: Steve Herzog, Andy Schwartz, Colin Chisholm, Marc Sagal (captain), Conan Bliss, Alex Ayers, Assistant Coach Weidou Xu. **Middle row:** John Carranza, Brian Joseph, Jim Schuster, Paul Schmidt, Kristian Sundborn, Zibusiso Ncube, Scott Reynolds, Derek LaTour, Ricky Garcia, Erik Richardson. **Back row:** Andy Dorsey (captain), Alexis Donahue, Wiley Bland (captain), Scott Zeman, Derek Fehmers, James Rankin, Jon Ahern, Chris Lee, Chip Stanley, Coach Horst Richardson. **Not pictured:** Bill Thomas.

me were: "Just give all the money to my friend at the Beijing airport!" And, with some hesitation, that's what I did. $10,000 in cash! And it was a most memorable adventure from then on.

Our oldest member of the group was Lou Henke from the class of '38. He documented the entire tour on video. Our youngest participant was my daughter, Stacia, then 16. A parent, a CC secretary and her friend, who was a nurse, as well as Helen and our son, Erik, completed the travel roster.

We traveled by bus, train (steam engine!), boat and plane and covered quite a bit of territory. From Beijing to Xian, through the Yangtze Gorge to Wuhan, on to Changsha, Guilin, Guangzhou, and finally to Hong Kong. The adventures we encountered are too numerous to list here, and the memories of that trip could fill a separate book.

China then was a third-world country, trying hard to make its economy competitive in the 20th century. Everyone wanted to practice their English on us — once we read a statistic that there were more people in China learning English than there were English speakers in the entire world. That says it all.

The hospitality we received was enormous, and we met lots of dignitaries and attended several receptions. Helpful at these functions was an official letter from the Dean of CC, David Finley, which I presented to party officials at these meetings:

TO OUR CHINESE HOSTS AND FRIENDS

The Colorado College is pleased to be represented by its men's soccer team under the supervision of Professor Horst Richardson on a goodwill tour of the Peoples Republic of China.

For many years, dating back to 1920, the Colorado College has had a special interest in China and association with its people. Students from China made a distinctive contribution to our student body between 1920 and 1930. In the past decade we have been very pleased at the reemergence of those old ties of friendship and respect. This spring we are grateful for the hospitality of our Chinese friends who have helped arrange this tour. We regard it as one more step in the new consolidation of mutual understanding that serves our two great peoples well in the common cause of world peace.

Signed David D. Finley, Dean of the College

As far as soccer competition was concerned, we came home with a paltry record of four losses and one tie, but the adventures encountered and memories collected will last the participants a lifetime.

At the Beijing Institute of Physical Education, after our first game, I tried to recruit a player whom Weidou had recommended to me. Of Mongolian descent, he had the largest thighs I had ever seen, his English was tolerable, and his playing abilities were Olympic. For a year after our return I worked diligently with our college administration, with the State Department and with religious organizations, trying to obtain entry and exit visas for him and we were on the verge of getting him when the Tiananmen Square incident occurred and all our efforts came to naught.

A number of players remember that overseas trip to China. Jim Schuster was along, and he submits his recollection:

> *One early morning during our trip through China, our bus collided head on with a man driving a tractor who had fallen asleep at the wheel. The crash sent our bus down an embankment, turning over and sliding through a rice paddy field. Fortunately, the only injuries were minor bruises.*
>
> *A farmer ran through the field with a ladder to help us exit the floor of the bus, which now laid above us (no idea what a farmer was doing with a ladder in the middle of a rice paddy field). Through translation, we were being asked if anyone had been bitten by a king cobra snake, which was clearly not part of the trip itinerary.*

Within 30 minutes of the crash, we were all loaded into a local bus, and along with peasants, chickens and ducks, we were on our way to our next destination, the city of Guilin. Derek Fehmers recently found a translated note from the Chinese government about this accident:

THE CASE CONCERNING THE TURNING OVER OF A HUNAN PROVINCE 01-06099 BUS

> *On June 22, 1988, at 7 a.m., a 01-06099 bus from Changsha University, Hunan Province, driven by Mr. Guo Zhenhua, collided in the area of Quanzhou County, Guilin, against a 40/31294 tractor driven by Mr. Luo Rongkun from Luokou Village, Shaoshui Town, Quanzhou County of Guangxi Province. The bus overturned*

> *laterally into the rice field which was 1.7 meters deep. The above-mentioned 01-06099 bus carried 21 people from Colorado College Soccer Team on their way from Changsha to Guilin. The accident has been settled according to our country's traffic regulations.*
>
> *— Traffic Accident Office, Security Department of Guilin*

As if one bus crash wasn't enough, we had a second one just a few days later when another bus driver tried to beat the arm coming down over a train track crossing. The driver made the first arm on the near side of the track, but the arm on the far side of the track blocked the bus, stalling us on the train track. Schuster remembers the tense moments:

> *With a train within sight and heading our way, a bit of panic started to set in. Fortunately, the driver got the bus restarted in time, and we were able to get off the track. Horst, in his true nature, was immediately on task and had tracked down a passing military truck and commandeered it to our next destination, where a party awaited us.*

We have, of course, lots of pictures from this epic journey. One photo always stood out in my recollection: Andy Dorsey, a tall blond from Minnesota, and Andy Henderson, an African-American, standing in the midst of a class of Chinese elementary students at a rural school, attempting to get the kids to say a few English phrases. The youngsters, however, were more interested in touching Dorsey's blond hair and Henderson's black skin to find out if both were real, because they had never seen any two men like these two CC players!

Derek Fehmers '90 sums up the China trip with this three-liner:

> *When I think of China, the memories flood. The Tsingtsao beer at half-times, the crash, the desolate landscapes, the heroin recovery center in Hong Kong, the river cruise at Guilin, the one victory in HK, running with Dorsey.*

Our soccer tour of China prepared us well for the season because the teams there had demonstrated skills we needed to practice, such as speed of play, shielding the ball, and receiving and distributing the ball. After an average start and a dismal 7-3 loss to the AFA, a respectable season of 14-6-2 followed.

In spite of that AFA loss, I have a distinctive memory of the first goal we scored there that afternoon, already down 6-0. We had a foreign student from Zimbabwe on the squad named Zibusiso Ncube. He was somewhat older than our players, of slight build, awfully polite and unassuming, and fast on his feet. We called him "Zet the Jet." He entered the game as a substitute, and shortly thereafter headed in a goal off of an Andy Dorsey cross. He jumped up into the air, and like an inverse corkscrew, propelled himself higher and higher. I will never forget the incredible smile he had on his face after he scored. "Zet the Jet" only stayed at CC for a year, but he had set his mark with that goal.

A source of much joy and satisfaction for me was the fact that my son, Erik Richardson, had enrolled at CC and joined the squad. His skill, wit, and determination to always do his best were a source of much admiration for me. The four years we spent together on the CC soccer field were perhaps the best times in my coaching career.

The team started to jell, and supportive tongue-in-cheek articles in *The Catalyst*, anonymously written by one John Roach, promoted the team on campus. (I suspect that John Roach was the alias for team member Jim Schuster.) After an early season loss to St. Olaf in Minnesota, "John Roach" wrote:

> *The humiliating defeat to St. Olaf left the team in a state of shock. One theory put forth to explain the loss was that the team had spent too much time trying to locate each of the 10,000 lakes in Minnesota and was thus too tired to play efficiently.*

Jim Schuster also remembers a psychological ploy we used when the team exited the bus on road trips in front of the opponents' gym:

> *Colin Chisholm was our back-up goalkeeper whose size and physique resembled Michelangelo's David. Upon the bus arriving at an away game, Horst believed it important to mentally defeat the opponent before the game started by having Colin lead the team off the bus. As Colin walked down the aisle to put his jersey on to lead the team, Horst had one more request: "Colin, keep your shirt off!" And so Colin went off the bus with no shirt on to lead the team to victory.*

During the first block break, that tactic must have worked on a three-game road trip to Iowa because we came home with 27 goals to our credit. That sure made the long bus trip home much more tolerable.

Block Break II saw us travel to Las Cruces, whose youth program once again had invited us to a college tournament. Somewhat unique was that we traveled to southern New Mexico together with UCCS in one large highway bus. My good soccer friend, Bruce Atkinson, had become the coach of the fledgling program at the University of Colorado in Colorado Springs, and we decided to travel together and share the cost of the bus trip.

Bruce remembers the fall colors on the trees as we headed south along the Rio Grande, but more importantly he couldn't believe the publicity we received at the tournament where he was interviewed by local TV. I think it made him realize that soccer was on its way and that UCCS, although just beginning with soccer, had a future in the sport.

Our player "Chip" Sagal made his home in Las Cruces, and he arranged for his younger brother, also a talented player, to visit CC on a recruiting trip. He came to our campus with a soccer playing friend, Arron Lujan, totally unknown to us. As it turned out, Chip's brother went elsewhere to college, but Arron applied and was accepted. What a gold-mine find for us, because four years later Arron Lujan had not only become an All-American, but also our highest scorer ever!

I am much indebted to Chip for alerting us to Arron Lujan. Marc "Chip" Sagal, who graduated in 1989 with a degree in Philosophy, was highly verbal and an astute observer of the game. We didn't always agree on matters pertinent to soccer and team chemistry, and his criticisms were well-constructed and objective. I was more focused on subjective issues and player relations. Chip today is a most successful sports psychologist and works with high-profile teams. When I asked him to submit a contribution to our CC soccer narrative, he delivered:

> *It was 1987 or 1988, I can't remember exactly (years of childhood heading ...). Horst had been on one of his many trips to Germany and returned with any number of insights. If it was physically possible for eyes to roll out of one's head, mine would have fallen down on Stewart Field's perennially hard and uneven surface.*
>
> *At the time, this was heresy. The importance of the critical Beckenbauerian role as a sweeper was still in full swing here in America. Where would Dorsey ("White Andy") play? Who would tell the back line when to move up? Who would chase down the opponent's unskilled but very fast center forward?*
>
> *You see, I knew everything back then. I think most everyone I played with during those magical college years ('85-'89) could have told you that Horst and I didn't exactly see eye-to-eye. Whether it was our formation, travel logistics, lineup or his*

unwillingness to allow me to heel the ball incessantly, I could find fault with just about anything. The turf room of my mind destroyed by those ridiculous pillars. I realize now that my truth never really set me free. Instead, my truth created an unintended barrier between me, my coach and those idiot teammates who seemed to be willing to go along, like lambs to the proverbial slaughter, with the strategies and tactics that our fearless leader concocted in the dark of night.

Four years came and went. I went on to play professionally (ok, so it was the Swedish third division), get my "A" coaching license (long-since lapsed) and a graduate degree in Sport Psychology (not a Ph.D.). I've spent the last 25 years helping athletes and teams be at their best (when it matters most). Poetically enough, one of my clients was CC. Called back to the scene of such fond memories to help others deal with various sporting slings and arrows that I was only too familiar with … With each return visit, I got the opportunity to know Horst and Helen in a different and more complete way.

It became increasingly clear how much they really cared about the team. I'm not sure why I didn't seem to appreciate this at the time. For them, it wasn't just about winning, it was about the importance of experiencing the world. Soccer was the vehicle.

There were slideshows at their house, beers at "The Bee," and spirited conversations about players up in that makeshift crow's nest perched precariously above the pitch. They put me up in the Alumni House where beautiful ghosts of my CC comrades reminded me of what a special time and place I had. I returned for homecomings with my family. My sons playing eagerly in the faintly falling snow as yet another Horst-led team handed roses to a thin but eager crowd. Even then Horst had one eye on his team and another on a boy (my boy) who one day might boost the chances of a future crop to fulfill a destiny. Wasn't it just yesterday with Lemvo? With Lujan?

Fast-forward to today, where two of my central tenets are Identity and Alignment. Identity as the clear and compelling philosophy and set of values for a team and Alignment being the willingness for all the members of the team to be "on the bus" (or Shark as the case may be). As far as Identity, I suppose it wasn't perfect. We seemed always to be searching for the key that would unlock our potential, that magic "Black Attack" with Hendo and with Teddy that would deliver that all-too-elusive NCAA Division III trip to the promised land.

And now, somewhere between a million years ago and yesterday, I realize that you can be right and still be wrong; that perspective shines a light that reveals the essence of a man (and a woman) who devoted their lives to a sport and a place and a family beyond their own. Buses run out of gas (and get stuck on tracks and fall into rice paddies far away from home). The important thing, that Horst knew then and I know now, is that you must be on the bus, aligned with a destination that may be further than you think. So, let this serve as a warning to all those that come after; to a sophomore (or a junior) who hears his coach tell him that the role of the Sweeper is returning, just wait — it might be so.

During the 1988 season the team traveled as much domestically as they did journeying through China in the late spring. Trips to Minnesota, Iowa, New Mexico, and Southern California were exciting but exhausting. Lack of comparable Division III competition close to home made it necessary to travel. At the end of the season we were close to making the NCAAs, but a loss to Claremont in our final game of the season erased our ambitions.

Coming home after each road trip, win or lose, our friendly and motherly equipment manager, Emily Varley, always greeted the boys with a smile and offered to wash and mend their clothes. What a positive effect she had on our morale!!

1989

The decade of the '80s came to a close with a 15-5-2 record in 1989. To assist players from both the men's and women's teams with early fitness and training, Helen and I employed several players each year in our summer soccer camps for children. The camps, which served hundreds of local children, were scheduled for early August. A unique group of participants that summer were seven young boys and girls from the Taos Pueblo Indian Reservation, who were funded by a grant from the NSCAA. The College's Southwest Studies Program supplied room and board for the kids.

Alec Rekow, our captain from the previous year, had spent his first year after graduation volunteering in children activities on the reservation and initiated a youth soccer program there. These programs grew in popularity over the years and CC men's soccer conducted many a clinic for this worthwhile youth effort.

In the morning of one of the summer camp sessions, I noticed two young men watching us from the other side of the Monument Creek fence. I walked over to them, expecting them to be parents of one of the campers. It turned out that they were recent arrivals from England and missed soccer. They joined the practice session, showed their "stuff," and the taller one, David Jones, a Welshman, became our assistant coach that year. His nickname

1989 | 15-5-2

Front row, left to right: Sean Fitzgerald, Kristian Sundborn (captain), Alex Ayers, Ezra Bayles, Scott Reynolds, Jim Schuster (captain). **Middle row:** Coach Horst Richardson, John Carranza, Rikard Nagy, Chris Lee, Jon Ahern, Chip Stanley, Steve Herzog, Nedim Ogelman. **Back row:** Assistant Coach Dieter Sturma, Richard Farrer, Erik Richardson, Paul Giesing, Scott Zeman, Noah Epstein, James Rankin, Paul Schmidt (captain), Derek Fehmers, Assistant Coach David "Tufty" Jones. **Not pictured:** Alexis Donahue.

---

was "Tufty" and he was a diesel mechanic in real life. He was passionate about soccer, and his brash English brogue, coupled with innumerable jokes, was the source of much enjoyment.

Another unique opportunity arose during pre-season as the men's team became actors in a movie about World War II German prisoners of war!! The famous Walter Matthau played the lead in *The Incident*, a film about a murder, which occurred in the prison compound at the Fort Carson military base. Somehow the producers of the film had discovered that I had done some research on German POWs in the United States. They approached me with questions about recreational activities in camp. I told them the POWs had bands, choirs, theater productions, and played soccer. And by the way, I said, if you need extras in the film who can play soccer, I just happened to have 28 of them right here in town! They hired all of us except Noah Epstein, who refused to get a military-style haircut!

Ezra Bayles' mother, however, thanked me profusely that her son had shed his shoulder-length hair. I actually ended up in the film with a speaking part!! And I still have the soccer ball we used in the film as a souvenir.

Participating in a film was a true liberal arts experience. Observing filmmaking up close, waiting for a "take," eating Helen-made sandwiches on the set, stepping in military formation, and learning a bit of history along the way were educational opportunities. (The only member of our team with military background was our captain Kristian Sundborn, who had completed his service requirement in his native Sweden.) We actually had two Swedes on the team that year. Kristian's friend, Rikard Nagy, also a talented player, enrolled at CC for a year.

In the first four games of the 1989 season, we managed to score only three goals, and I was worried. On a trip to Southern California the trend continued, with us tied 1-1 vs. Pomona at the end of regulation. And then something spectacular happened: Freshman Noah Epstein scored three goals in 1 minute and 57 seconds, an NCAA record! (I forgave him for not getting a military-style haircut in pre-season.) We played two games in the Sunny Southland and came home with 10 goals!

Alums Brigham Olson, Scott Evans, Brad Wolf, and Tommy Hyland treated the team to a victory dinner, and Steve Prough from the class of '65 organized a super beach party/ BBQ at Corona del Mar. The mountain boys enjoyed themselves, and, in a tag football game by the Pacific shore, Jim Schuster tackled the host's daughter!

It's worth noting that nearly 30 years later, I would be reminded of this party in the most unexpected of ways. While finishing up this book in November 2018, I received an email from the Alumni Office, which had just received a 9-by-12-inch cardboard mailer containing a notecard and a printed photo. The notecard read:

> *This is the story of two friends who met in college during their freshman year. Although not always a good influence on each other, they would quite often go to the gym together. Always, they stopped at the trophy case to admire a picture of this soccer team. This was a less enlightened time and people of all genders were always objectifying each other.*
>
> *Four years went by and one of these friends turned 21. The other friend, who had never stolen so much as a stick of gum, went down to the gym in the dead of night with her Swiss Army knife and liberated the oft-admired photograph. She gave the photograph to her friend, and that friend has cherished it as the most memorable gift of her lifetime.*
>
> *Now that young woman has kids who are asking questions. It is time to return this relic of youth and friendship to its origin.*
>
> *With fondness,*
> *XXX*

The photo, taken at that Southern California beach party, can be viewed on p. 142.

But back to 1989: Our winning streak continued, leading to a spectacular Homecoming game vs. the alumni squad. Twenty goals were scored in this epic 10-10 event!

At Grand Canyon College in Phoenix, the squad provided me with my 250th win. We had entered a prestigious tournament there, with powerhouses UC San Diego and Howard University. Although we lost a close one to UCSD in the heat of the Phoenix night (101 degrees at kick-off at 7 p.m.), we beat the host the next day. Former CC captain Jon Hulburd, now a successful businessman in Phoenix, invited the team to his home for well-deserved postgame treats.

We received national ranking after that weekend, and we all got a little bit cocky. During a couple of subsequent home games, the bench grew somewhat rowdy, so much so that trainer Bruce Kola had to step in. Then-SID Dave Moross remembers:

> *Bruce Kola served forever as head of the sports medicine staff in the Colorado College athletics department.*
>
> *For many, many seasons, he assigned himself as trainer for the men's soccer team. Highly respected nationwide and even internationally among his peers, Bruce was as good as they come in his chosen field. But his duties, and authority, often seemed to span far beyond the realm of medical attention.*
>
> *I'm not certain, but I suspect he may have served as the team's travel secretary at times. That would have been somewhat "official," I suppose, as was his lightning horn that could delay games for varying lengths of time. But, also, on the sideline before and during matches at Stewart Field, he often could be heard yelling up to the press box for someone to "turn down the music" or "stop the clock." And when he did it, that someone usually complied.*
>
> *Typically very mild mannered and professional, he nonetheless had a way of striking the fear of God into people. I suspect this happened on more than one occasion, but I distinctly recall one game in which he screamed at two or three of CC's players on the bench to "Sit down and shut up. Now!"*
>
> *It seemed a bit odd for that to be the role of the team's trainer. To my knowledge, however, no one ever confronted Bruce or other members of his staff with overstepping their boundaries.*

With a respectable record and nationally ranked, a play-off spot seemed a distinct possibility for the team. The third annual Las Cruces Invitational, with Trinity University from Texas, and New Jersey Tech, both quality squads, could make us a contender. We won the tournament, "Chip" Sagal's family provided hospitality, the team was fed, and the Desert Shark bus was fueled up and ready to take us back on a 600-mile northward journey.

I was driving, and making good time, when a water hose ruptured and, on a lonely stretch of I-25 in northern New Mexico, we had to stop and investigate the damage. Alex Ayers, our goalkeeper from Wyoming, came to the rescue. He discovered a roll of duct tape in his bag and with deft keeper hands repaired the broken hose. Not wanting to push my luck, I nursed the 24-passenger vehicle along, arriving back on campus in the early morning hours.

Yes, we received an NCAA bid and were even granted a home-field advantage. The opponent was St. John's from Minnesota, a physically strong squad of meat-and-potato athletes. Our seniors, captain Kristian Sundborn, co-captains Jim Schuster and Paul Schmidt, and Derek Fehmers and Scott Reynolds, were confident, and our scoring had averaged three goals per game. It was not our day, however. We outshot the opponents 19-7. The game was tied 0-0 at the end of regulation, and went into double overtime still tied. The contest was settled on penalties, and we lost on the 10th penalty kick. It was a most frustrating conclusion to a terrific season.

For his efforts in growing soccer in Colorado Springs, Bill Boddington was inducted into the Colorado State Soccer Hall of Fame, and a youth playing field north of the college was named in his honor.

Horst Richardson

Erik Richardson

Superfan Stacia Richardson

Bill Boddington

MEN'S SOCCER

A TRADITION OF EXCELLENCE

Saad Sahawneh at the 50th Anniversary in 2000.

John Boddington

Tim Boddington

THE ALL-AMERICANS

Greg Kazemi **1986**

Noah Epstein **1990,1993**

Robert Lipp **1992**

Arron Lujan **1994**

Dan Morlan **1997**

Photo by David Bitton, The Gazette

Pat McGinnis **2004**

Matt Fechter **2011, 2012**

Max Grossenbacher **2015**

Celebrating a goal on Washburn Field in 1966 at an NCAA play-off game in front of a huge crowd.

Above: Dick Schulte, captain in 1974, dominating mid-field.

Left: Andre Zarb-Cousin, 1970, a scoring machine!

Action on Stewart Field, 1965.

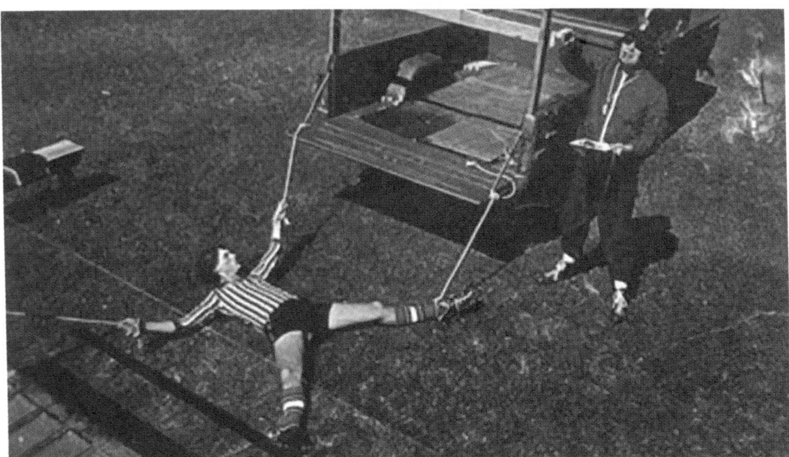

Circuit training: a station on "stretching!!"

Pre-game strategy talk in 1965 - Ned Pike, Horst, Peter Shidler, Eliot Field.

Emily Varley, longtime and beloved CC equipment manager.

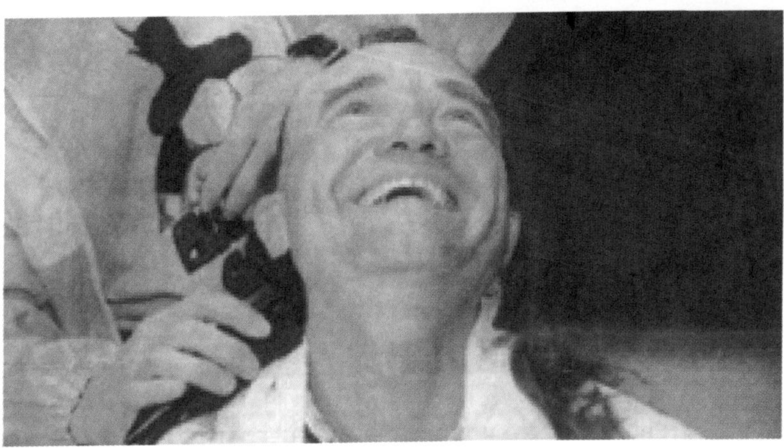

Horst's head shaved in locker room, 1995 - honoring a lost bet with the team.

Brad Turner and Kornel Simons battle AFA to 1-0 victory in 1975.

Jacques Lemvo, 1985, player *extraordinaire*, artist, and poet: "Soccer is my life."

Celebrating a goal in 1991 with a mid-air hug: Ezra Bayles and Ted Nusbaum.

Photo by Jerilee Bennett, The Gazette

below: Nick Lammers, the 'big man,' tallest player ever at 6'7". Photo by Charlie Lengal

above: Tigers in the movies, 1989, *The Incident*, with Walter Matthau. Acting as German prisoners of war in a U.S. camp are: Jon Ahern, Jim Schuster, Horst, and Alexis Donahue. Photo by Bob Jackson, The Gazette

Like a long overdue library book, we appreciate the return of this long-lost California beach picture of the 1989 team. (See story on p. 133.)

Trophy case in El Pomar Gym.

Alumni gathering on Stewart Field in 2006.

Alumni game in 2015.

Caden MacKenzie, All-American, 2016 in action photo taken by his proud dad Tom MacKenzie, who played in 1981-1984.

Goooooal!
Sean Parham scores. Ben Glass, right, and Matt Fechter, left, help celebrate. (See story on p. 286.)

October 10, 2014

Bill and Horst at Homecoming 1990.

Summer Soccer Camp 1991.

Practice under a rainbow on Washburn Field.

Photo by Dave Reed

The Field of Dreams. Photo by Bill Parent

IN MEMORIAM

THE RICHARDSON ERA PLAYERS

Peter Morse *played 1964 - 1967, captain | died 2011*

John Monteiro
played 1974 - 1977 | died 2013

Eddy Dietz
played 1976 - 1979 | died 2016

OLSON MEMORIAL FIELD

DEDICATED TO THE MEMORY OF A TRULY GREAT ATHLETE

BRIGHAM DIDRIK OLSON '85

1962 - 2003

1981-84 Men's Soccer, Co-Captain, All-Star, Hall of Fame
Skilled and graceful competitor
Disciplined and passionate player
Dedicated and inspiring leader
Noble and exemplary sportsman

"THE BEST OF THE BEST"

Brigham Olson
played 1981 - 1984, captain | died 2003

Matt Slothower
played 1983 - 1986 | died 2007

Chris Quon
played 2005 - 2007 | died 2009

NOT PICTURED

Richard Knight
played 1963 - 1965 | died 1991

Nate Walrod
played 1995 | died 2002

Sean O'Donnell
played JV 1973 - 1975,
Colorado Springs doctor | died 2018

REACHING PEAK PERFORMANCE

The 1990s

Shortly before the 1990 graduation in early May, a horrendous accident happened to Sean Fitzgerald, a promising freshman player from Cincinnati. He fell off the roof of McGregor Hall and nearly died. Sean had locked himself out of his fourth-floor room, and in attempting to enter his room through a window, he slipped on an icy ledge and fell, narrowly avoiding a concrete walkway below. The entire college community rallied to support him. More than a hundred students donated blood.

Sean underwent multiple surgeries and recovered. He returned to CC and graduated in December of 1993.

1990

The fall season commenced with an exhibition match vs. AFA at the Stetson Hills soccer stadium to benefit Colorado Special Olympics. Six starters returned from the previous year: Jon Ahern and Noah Epstein up top, co-captains Scott Zeman and Erik Richardson in the middle of the park, and John Carranza and Chris Lee on defense. Ezra Bayles had earned the starting position in goal. Andy Schwartz and Nedim Ogelman had come back from injuries, and two transfers, Jon Whitfield and Robert Lipp, were about to make a stupendous impact.

It took us two games to sort things out, but in Games 3 through 8, we scored 33 goals and we knew we had potential. We also enjoyed a little bit of luck during a home game against Pomona College. In the drizzle on Stewart Field early in the second half, Rob "Josimar" Lipp attempted a shot at goal from distance, which wasn't much more than a blooper, but the ball inexplicably hit an exposed sprinkler head, changed direction abruptly, and eluded the outstretched hands of the Pomona keeper. That turned out to be the sole goal in the contest. With Assistant Coaches "Tufty" Jones and CC legend Eddy Dietz, we had soccer expertise to prepare the squad for competition.

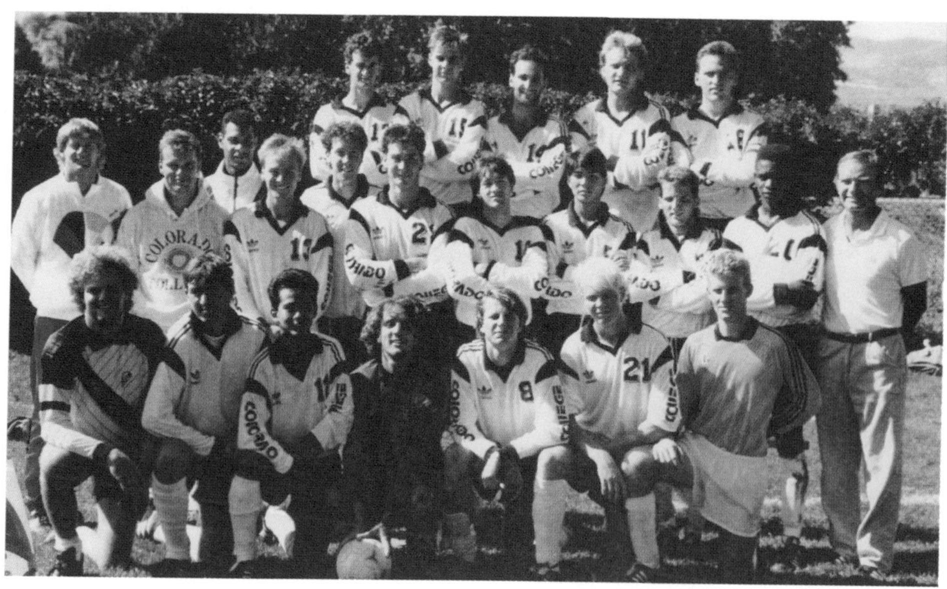

1990 | 13-6-3

Front row, left to right: Shedd Glassmeyer, Rylan North, Takuma Hayashi, Ezra Bayles, Guy Mossman, Aaron Frohnmayer, Rob Faucett. **Middle row:** Assistant Coaches Eddy Dietz and David "Tufty" Jones, Aaron Boelter, Jon Ahern, Scott Zeman (captain), Noah Epstein, Nedim Ogelman, Chris Lee, Jon Whitfield, Rob Lipp, Coach Horst Richardson. **Back row:** Matt Gregory, Paul Giesing, Andy Schwartz, Erik Richardson (captain), John Carranza (captain). **Not pictured:** Yuri Kostick, Ben Straley, Jeremy Vannatta.

Block Break I we journeyed to Iowa to participate in a Grinnell College tournament. For many years we made this 800-mile road trip every other year. We fell into a routine to go to dinner at a German restaurant in the nearby Amana Colonies. I had become acquainted with the German proprietor of the restaurant and always looked forward to the home-style food served there. We dined there on this trip as well. An outlandish bet was waged there on this road trip, which Jon Whitfield '93 describes:

AMANA COLONIES AND A POUND OF FLESH

John Carranza, class of '92, once accepted a paid dare to eat everyone's left-over fat from our dinner at the Amana Colonies — fat-only remains of roast beef, steaks, ham, pork chops ... you name it, it was in there, and it wasn't a small portion ... I can tell you that! At least a full pound of fat and pads of butter piled up on his plate ... consumed to the complete for $25. Epic.

I am inclined to call the 1990 season, my 25th year of coaching at CC, The Year of the Overtime Games, as we experienced eight OTs, and we managed to win only one of them. Three games remained ties, and of the four we lost, three of those losses were encountered at home. One of those OT losses was against Glassboro State, a team which ended up NCAA Division III champion. Frustrating indeed. Probably the most memorable OT match was the away game at Claremont in Southern California, then the perennial powerhouse team in the Southern California Intercollegiate Athletic Conference (SCIAC). Three times we were ahead, and three times they came back to level the score, their last goal caroming off one of our defender's shinguards with less than two minutes left in the OT contest. Erik Richardson and Jon Whitfield wrote for *The Catalyst* that year. Here is their spirited reporting of this game:

> *Claremont. Overtime! The offensive punch of the Tigers roared on and in the 102nd minute of the game captain Scott Zeman blasted home a twine-shredding turbo missile propelling CC into a 3-2 lead. But on this day, leprechauns, rabbits' feet, and four-leaf clovers infested Claremont's bench. In the OT's final two minutes, a shinguard deflection brought the groceries back to grandma and sent the CC men back to the Ramada Inn with an unfortunate 3-3 tie.*

An unforgettable incident occurred upon our return from California at the Colorado Springs airport. Late Sunday night, while waiting for the luggage to be spit out on the conveyor belt, three members of the team decided to ride on the moving beltway into the secured area behind the luggage door. Sirens went off, and the three were promptly apprehended by security personnel.

Andy Schwartz, always sporting a three-day growth of a heavy beard, looked like a Mideast terrorist; Nedim Ogelman, of Turkish descent, had a suspicious background as far as the investigating officers were concerned; and Chris Lee, from Hawaii, could have passed for a relative of Tokyo Rose. The three were detained; in fact, the entire team was detained. It was way past midnight, when the three were taken downtown into custody. I shepherded the team into the waiting CC bus and then told the players that "We may never see these three again." That, of course, was an exaggeration, and the three culprits were back on campus in the morning. Jon Whitfield remembers this incident vividly and submits this commentary:

The three were apprehended by airport police ... we all then realized this was no joke. The three were taken away ... The rest of us retrieved our bags and boarded the bus that was to take us back to CC. After about 20 minutes or so of waiting, Horst enters the bus, gets on the microphone and announced to the team, "Well, if you want to see your teammates, Andy Schwartz, Chris Lee and Nedim Ogelman, you can visit them at the Colorado Springs Correctional Facility downtown ... Visiting hours start at 9 a.m. Bus driver, let's go."

During the 1990 season we celebrated 40 years of men's soccer at CC at Homecoming. Fifty-six alums arrived to help celebrate this festive event, including Saad Sahawneh from Jordan who started it all in 1950. The class of 1985 had the largest and loudest representation, boasting that they could take on the varsity squad. The alums played two games: one group competed against the junior varsity, and two other squads, composed of older contestants, played each other.

At the soccer reunion dinner, Saad announced a major gift to the soccer endowment, I presented a slide show of the first 40 years, Helen brought all of her scrapbooks along, and George Jackson '76, better known as Jorge the Magnificent, entertained the crowd with a poem he composed for the occasion:

They were all of them gathered that fall afternoon,
Soccer stars of yesteryear, but now out of tune.
From the '50s, the '60s, and '70s they came
With lungs clearly aching, but legs far from lame.
It was to relive years of glory that day
And, creaky bones limbered, they started to play.
Stewart Field, remembered by some as cow fodder,
Rang with the cry of "We've never been hodder!"

There was Boddington, Middleton, Griswold, and Field,
Running like Tigers — no, they would not yield.
Not to Norcross, or Jackson, or Roberts, or Wong,
Not to Heitner, or Peters, or Evon Goolagong.
These men, they were steady. Like Ned Holloway
And even Andrews, yes Lurch, came to play on that day.
There were Smiths, Dan, Ken, and Mel, from the '50s

And Schlesinger, too, showing moves that were niftys.
There was Johnson and Engeln, and Schulte and Scott,
Fairchild and Turner arrived, some did not.
But no-one was there whose paunch grew so thick,
That I knew in a moment, it must be St. Nick.

It was a group with a bond, even strangers were friends.
It's a program so nice, that we help it meet ends.
And who do we owe for this fun so unforced?
Why, I think it's the Boddingtons and Helen and Horst.

During the middle part of the season, the varsity squad enjoyed a 13-game unbeaten streak, but it was not good enough for a post-season invitation. Noah Epstein was honored with All-America recognition, only the second CC player in the program's history to receive this distinguished honor.

1991

1991 came to be known as the year of the "Black Attack," principally because the team had decided to wear simple black T-shirts as their game uniform. Additionally, the term "toy fest" was adopted to describe the joy experienced when an opponent was overcome by deft play.

Noah Epstein, our All-American, had decided to study literature in England for the year and left a void in our attack. Veteran stopper Paul Giesing was studying abroad in Germany. But Jon Ahern's scoring abilities had propelled him into the top ten all-time CC scoring list and he had ambitions to continue this trend. And then a freshman sensation from Las Cruces, Arron Lujan, had joined the squad. "Crazy Legs" Guy Mossman was always good for a surprise or two in scoring and Paolo Villa, a veteran from Italy, added consistency in defense. Paolo was married, had two kids, and at 33 was the oldest player ever to be a member of a CC varsity squad. The anchor on defense, however, was Chris Lee from Hawaii, gleefully referred to as "The hatchet from Honolulu" in a *Catalyst* article.

Eddy Dietz, our alum assistant from the previous year, had accepted the head coaching position at crosstown rival UCCS and the other assistant, Tufty Jones, had decided to focus on fixing diesel vehicles. Two new assistant coaches helped the team: Dennis Hoglin Jr., a local high school star who played his college years at Columbia University, and Doug Stenberg, recently hired to teach Russian, whose ability to boost morale proved to be invaluable.

The team voted for tri-captains that year, and what a trio they were! Jon Whitfield, a small dynamo in the middle of the park, had boundless energy, a keen sense of humor, and his leadership qualities were appreciated by all; John Carranza was a levelheaded and steady influence during practice sessions and games and inspired his teammates with mature leadership; and Erik Richardson not only wrote the wittiest and most delightful *Catalyst* articles promoting the team, but his vision on the field, his refined tactical sense, and his incisive passing ability also made him a threat anywhere on the field.

Our Stewart Field had become much improved, in part with profits from the CC Summer Soccer Camps. A tall retaining wall in the northeast end of the field gained us more practice space and a metal kick board on the east side, with a wire mesh backstop on top, was used every day in practice sessions. A couple of metal bleachers made life easier

1991 | 14-6-2

Front row, left to right: Assistant Coaches Dennis Hoglin and Doug Stenberg, Rob Faucett, Ezra Bayles, Coach Horst Richardson. **Second Row:** Erik Richardson (captain), Andy Schwartz, Ted Nusbaum, Jon Whitfield (captain), Takuma Hayashi, Jeff Montera, Helen Richardson. **Third row:** Aaron Frohnmayer, John Carranza (captain), Jon Ahern, Matt Gregory, Josh Howell, Chris Lee, Mark Thomas, Craig Lopez. **Back row:** Rylan North, Aaron Boelter, Ben Straley, Serapio Baca, Arron Lujan, Rob Lipp, Paolo Villa. **Not pictured:** Guy Mossman, Jonathan Speare.

for spectators, although many fans preferred to sit on the eastside hill. And the tradition for the starters to hand out roses to select ladies after player introductions continued.

In late August before the start of the semester, we went out on a road trip to Salt Lake City. For most players, driving endless hours through the vast expanse of the American West was nothing more than an endurance test. Not so for Paolo Villa '94, who considered the trip a dream come true:

> *My very first road trip as a member of CC's men's soccer was a dream come true for me. I grew up in Milan, Italy. When I first moved to Colorado, the proximity and array of spectacular natural sites, and the reports of mountain lions descending to lower altitude in the hot months looking for water, occasionally helping themselves to some of the pets left alone in the backyards of houses on Cheyenne Mountain, was almost overwhelming for a city boy like me. Let me put it in perspective: in the third grade, my classmates and I were loaded onto a bus and taken to see cows — yes, cows and various other farm animals. It took me quite a few months of residing in Colorado not to start shouting and pointing each and every time I saw a deer. Squirrels, truly a pest in Colorado as I soon learned, are all but mythical creatures where I come from, their images only to be seen in books and documentaries.*
>
> *At the end of August, 1991, we departed for our first weekend of action. The views from the bus became more dramatic and breathtaking as we made our westbound progress towards Salt Lake City, Utah. Amazing rock formations, cliffs and boulders were appearing in never-ending fashion in front of my eyes. For someone like me who grew up watching old western movies and reading the adventures of Tex Willer, an Italian-made interpretation of the Old West, the showstopper occurred when a herd of American Buffalo appeared on a stretch of flat land. They were bigger than I could have ever imagined and there were hundreds of them: I had finally arrived in the wild, wild West!*

The first third of the season featured competition against top-notch Division III opposition. Wheaton College, Macalester College, Claremont College, UC San Diego, who had a four-year run in the NCAA play-offs, and Washington University of St. Louis, all tested the Tigers. One win, two losses, and two ties against this quintet provided valuable experience on the way to a 14-6-2 season.

Most rewarding was the 2-1 OT win against nemesis Claremont on an Erik Richardson penalty kick. Out in California during the first block break, Pomona took sweet revenge from their loss to CC in the year before. This lopsided 7-4 loss was a wake-up call for the sleepy Tigers, and out of the next 11 games, the team won nine!!

Under Eddy Dietz's tutelage, crosstown rival UCCS had vastly improved. At the midway point in the season the Tigers faced them at home. After the first half, with the Tigers having most of the possession, they had only a 1-0 lead to show for their efforts on a volley shot by Ted Nusbaum. In the second half, we put the game out of reach with a patented Jon Ahern head ball strike and a final one from close range four minutes from time by Takuma Hayashi.

Eddy, the former CC star from the '70s, directed the UCCS program for over 10 years and focused his efforts there on beating his alma mater, which he managed to do successfully in later years.

After a victorious Homecoming weekend and an exciting alumni game, the team headed once again to Las Cruces, home not only of Arron Lujan, but also, according to the *Catalyst* soccer writer, of the Guinness Book of World Records' longest enchilada! The road trip did not have an ideal start, since three members of the team had to take exams before leaving and thus decided to head south on I-25 two hours after the bus departure. Chris Lee '92 was on the bus but remembers the "Whitfield chase":

> *Ah, yes. Then there was the Whitfield CRX racing trip to New Mexico. Whitfield, Lipp, and Ahern had exams, so they couldn't ride the bus with the rest of the team. Whitfield's compact car got a flat tire chasing the bus, so they had to put on the small, narrow-rimmed spare on which they raced down south to meet the team in Las Cruces. Given the distance and time, they must have exceeded 80 mph for most of the way on that flimsy spare. Good thing they made it.*

Once there, the team split in two games. After the second match we had a delicious, filling meal at Lujan's grandparents, Native Americans from the Kiowa tribe. Now to the odyssey of the return trip, best documented by quoting Erik Richardson's '92 *Catalyst* article:

> *... Ten miles out of Las Cruces Assistant Coach Dennis Hoglin noticed a strange noise coming from the left side of the bus. Horst Richardson, the only man around for a straight 10-hour driving job, pulled over. Guess what, the Good Year had been slashed. Jacking up a 25-passenger van can be, and actually was, a big part of a Tiger's liberal arts education. After a mere 20 more miles, the bus acted up again — however, this time in a non-radial manner. Could it be vapor lock? Yes, it must be.*

Ten more miles and the team suddenly realized that they may not be returning to Colorado Springs for a while.

For the purpose of this narrative, Erik returned to the topic of this Las Cruces adventure in a letter to me. Here is what he wrote, titling that homeward-bound road trip "The Illegal Maneuver":

> *In the days when Horst drove the Desert Shark, an 18-passenger transport vehicle, life seemed so much simpler. The coach could drive the team for 14 hours, arrive at the field, normally win the game, and we could drive home. No fees, no fuss, and on one particular trip to Las Cruces, New Mexico, no fuel pump. Well, more precisely, the wrong fuel pump. One that caused vapor lock on a Sunday morning near Truth or Consequences. In what seemed like the Middle of Nowhere, the Tigers were very stranded.*
>
> *In his bizarrely effective style of delegation and planning, Horst sent Andrew Schwartz and me to hitchhike 18 miles to the nearest town, find a tow truck large enough for a mid-range bus, and to do all of this with $27.65, all of the money Horst's budget would apparently allow for emergencies. So, Schwartz and I sauntered out to the empty highway, no sign or backpacks, and were lucky enough to have a car stop before we were badly sunburned. It was a man, drunk, looking for some company after his all-nighter at the local tavern. Taking one for the team, Schwartz and I got in and buckled up.*
>
> *The intermittent swerving of the driver kept us on high alert, our hands ready to grab the wheel. We survived the 18-mile journey to Truth or Consequences, and were deposited at a vacant gas station with one pump. Tumbleweeds and trash blew past the Sambas, and the surreal scene mounted as we approached the glass window.*
>
> *As deserted as this place seemed, there actually was a guy sleeping inside, feet on the counter, ball cap pulled down over his face. Hesitantly, we knocked on the window, and we roused the man, who until now appeared unarmed. He seemed sober and, after producing the almost 30 bucks on the countertop, quite keen to assist.*
>
> *As the Soccer Gods would have it, this guy actually had a wrecking truck parked at a nearby lot. So, taking our money and instructing us to stay put, he disappeared in a beat-up Chevy. Schwartz and I could see how this man could*

have so easily just left us there and earned his Sunday Arby's meal money. But, (we'll call him) Hank returned.

Now, if you've never sat in a wrecking truck, it's quite a ride; the cab sits about four meters from the pavement, and you need a stepladder and some climbing skills to get into your seat. In 30 minutes, we arrived at the stranded team, crouching in the sparse shade. All of the team then piled into the Desert Shark, Schwartz and I stayed in the wrecker, and we towed the loaded vapor-locked vehicle back to where we roused Hank from his slumber. Hank then saw that the CC Tigers coach was desperate. All of the players needed to be in Monday's class in 18 hours; Truth or Consequences had very few options to offer a stranded college soccer team, and the biggest kicker of them all: It was highly illegal to tow a bus while people rode in it.

Hank explained to Horst that he could serve time taking a chance like that. But perfectly on cue and using the Darth Vader Mind Melt, Horst produced another measly wad of cash, tucked it into Hank's shirt pocket, and said: "If you get us to Albuquerque ... and an ATM, I'll buy you a case of Coors Light." That sealed the deal.

Unfortunately, as the sun started to set, Hank instructed all illegal Desert Shark riders that we all had to sit on the floor and keep out of sight from the cops. This would have been fine were it not for Jon Whitfield's 32-ounce Dr. Pepper, which had spilled onto the rubberized flooring and caused every speck of sitting space to be a sticky mess. Several agonizing hours later, we arrived in Albuquerque. Hank parked in a side alley, where we all surreptitiously slid out of the Desert Shark, and pretended to hang out in the Safeway parking lot. It was then that we noticed how terrifically bald the wrecker's tires were.

It was also at this time that we noticed Horst's disappearance. Perhaps he had gone to the ATM, or maybe he went to have a few shots of Jägermeister with Hank. Nobody knew. Lipp and Lujan started juggling, and then a game of 3 vs. 3 broke out. After half an hour, Horst and three minivans appeared. To everyone's surprise, Hertz was across the street, and Hank had an illegitimate son who was the manager there. Serendipity? Mark Thomas summed up the trip in five words: When it rains, it snows!

Then, the most mature members of the squad were given rental car keys, and we had a minivan race back to Colorado Springs. The first van arrived at 2 a.m. to El Pomar Sports Center. Hank and the Desert Shark were never seen again, and CC never played another tournament in Las Cruces, New Mexico.

Bruce Kola, our trainer, had wisely decided to bring an extra rental vehicle on this trip and he took two players, who had exams on Monday, home early, over Raton Pass in a blizzard. Helen, who was also along, suffered with the rest of us throughout the long night. The bus, of course, stayed in Albuquerque at the Ford dealership, and it needed to be retrieved in the course of the week by members of the CC motor pool.

Hank, the tow truck driver, had told me that the bus had the wrong fuel pump in it and needed to be replaced. When I told that information to the motor pool folks, they thought I was crazy, since the bus was a brand new vehicle. Hank and I were vindicated, however, because on the way back from New Mexico, the motor pool driver also got stuck with vapor lock. It was indeed an incorrect fuel pump that Ford had installed in the passenger van.

At the end of the season, after defeating UC at Pueblo, a match against AFA stood in the way of the RMISL title game. For the benefit of local spectators, the game was played at the Sky Sox soccer stadium, and it turned out to be a classic, a D-III David against a D-I Goliath. We hadn't beaten the AFA since 1978, when Carter was president, but on this day the Tigers beat the Zoomies!

Although the cadets had more of the possession, they didn't have Arron Lujan's educated left foot. Two left-footed goals by the freshman had the game tied 2-2 at the half. The Tigers continued their counter offensive strategy in the second half. On a Rob Lipp through ball to Tiger cub Lujan, Arron was brought down by an opponent's tackle. A yellow card was issued and we were awarded a free kick about 25 yards out. Erik Richardson channeled all of his desire to beat the Academy into the free kick and drilled a laser cannon at the goal. The ferocious shot bounced off the keeper and a roaming Craig Lopez put the rebound away. Needless to say, the Tigers cherished the win.

Game No. 22, the last one of the season, was the RMISL championship match played at home in inclement weather. After the stupendous victory against the AFA, the Tigers were not to be denied and buried Metro State 3-0. Rob Lipp scored one, and Ted Nusbaum added two more, but the real hero of the match, played on a muddy field, was our goalie Ezra Bayles, who made some unbelievable saves that day.

We were Rocky Mountain Intercollegiate Soccer League champs, the first time since 1979, and the sixth time in our soccer history. Erik Richardson was awarded RMISL Player of the Year, and I, his dad, was named Coach of the Year. Nice family awards and fond memories.

1992 | 18-2-2
Front row, left to right: Coach Horst Richardson, Rob Lipp (captain). **Middle row:** Jeff Spight, Jon Whitfield (captain), Jeff Montera, Jeff Lee, Ben Straley, Assistant Coaches Erik Richardson and Dana Taylor. **Back row:** Serapio Baca, Takuma Hayashi, Mark Thomas, Ezra Bayles (captain), Noah Epstein, Nick Watterson, Todd Gradek, Josh Howell, Arron Lujan, Aaron Frohnmayer, Tom Heisler, Andre Nunley. **Not pictured:** Dan Burgard, Ian Creager, Gilberto Dorantes, Mark Handy, Jeff Jurgens, Paolo Villa.

1992

Before we address the blockbuster 1992 season, a couple of words about the final days of the RMISL.

The Rocky Mountain Intercollegiate Soccer League was formed in the 1950s. Under the leadership of Dr. G.K. Guennel, it became the cradle for then-fledgling university and college programs. The RMISL served varsity and club programs, nurtured newcomers and supported established programs long before the NCAA D-I, D-II, and D-III, as well as NAIA affiliations, mattered. In the 1970s, the League also accepted women's programs and assisted in their growth.

After the 1991 RMISL championship game, the League faded away. Varsity programs up and down the front range became more interested in their respective NCAA/NAIA divisions, and the Rocky Mountain Athletic Conference (RMAC) absorbed all NCAA

D-II teams in the region. AFA and DU elected NCAA D-I status. That left Colorado College as the only D-III program in the Rocky Mountain West.

I had faithfully attended coaches conventions, served on NCAA and NSCAA committees, directed clinics and camps, and over time met colleagues from around the country. This network helped me in focusing my scheduling efforts in the Division III world. CC became good hosts to D-III teams from all around the country; we became experts at creating mini-tournaments during the season, pitting squads from the east against teams from the west, from the north against the south. We had splendid relations with D-III conferences in Southern California, in Minnesota, in Iowa, in the Northwest, and later in Texas.

No longer affiliated with a conference, the Tigers competed as Independents, competing for NCAA play-off spots against other independents like UC Santa Cruz, UC San Diego, Chapman College, Nebraska Wesleyan, and Wisconsin state programs, all located in our region. Our travel schedule became elaborate, and the "Desert Shark" van, as well as CC highway buses, logged many miles hauling our players around the West and the Midwest. Hosting teams and traveling necessitated budget support; fortunately, the growing Boddington/Richardson Endowment for CC Men's Soccer provided some flexibility in these arrangements.

1992 began with a foreign tour of Japan. Our player Takuma Hayashi had contacted his father, a prominent Tokyo businessman, to ask if he could help organize a soccer tour for us. He responded in the affirmative, and upon arrival we were overwhelmed with hospitality.

His staff had put an itinerary in place, which included visits to three Japanese Islands, multiple stays in Tokyo, imperial palaces and karaoke bars, ten games against some serious competition, soccer clinics for elementary school children, historic tours of Hiroshima, Kyoto, and Samurai castles, a grandiose stay at the base of Mount Fuji in Fujioshida, sister city to Colorado Springs, and recuperative baths at famous hot springs. We had memorable homestays, multiple receptions, and received so many gifts that our suitcases must have weighed twice as much when we returned. The captain of our team, Jon Whitfield, was interviewed on national TV, we hurled through the countryside from city to city on bullet trains, and in a Buddhist shrine in the holy city of Kyoto, we almost lost Ted Nusbaum, whose CC major was religion. Takuma translated at receptions.

At an event on June 11, Jon Whitfield, ever the diplomat, complimented our hosts on their exceptional hospitality and mentioned that it was Coach Richardson's birthday.

Ironically, the city's mayor, in attendance, also celebrated his birthday on June 11. He invited the whole team to a local hotel for an incredible meal of local delicacies and sake.

Later upon returning to our hostel, we found four cases of beer waiting for the thirsty Tigers, compliments of the mayor. We came home to the U.S. with a 3-5-2 record. Thanks to the Hayashi family for a memorable sports tour of Japan!

For Ted Nusbaum '94, this foreign trip is still firmly embedded in his mind. He writes about his fond memories:

SUSHI, SAKE, SAPPORO AND SUCKERS

It was the summer of 1992 and the Colorado College men's soccer team traveled to Japan for one month of culture and competition due in large part to the ingenuity of one of our teammates, Takuma Hayashi, a Japanese native. We visited ten cities and played a robust schedule of games against a vast array of high-level competition, including a professional team, Yanmar Diesel. We were helmed by the seasoned and steadfast Horst Richardson and our captains were Jon Whitfield, Robert Lipp and Arron Lujan. And while this memoir does claim to be a faithful record of our one month together, it is by no means complete, and in many respects, hazy, due to the blurring effects of sushi, sake and Sapporo that linger to this day.

I can't recall all of the ten cities we visited, but I do remember Sendai, Kyoto, Fujiyoshida, Yokohama, Osaka, and of course, Tokyo. I was struck by the beauty, the history, the religion, and the incredible generosity and warmth of the Japanese people. From the moment we arrived we were welcomed with open arms, served lavish dinners, and in many respects, treated like celebrities.

Our hosts, whether in coordination or individually (we still don't know to this day), created a well-oiled routine to greet us upon our arrival at each new city. It went something like this: We pulled up in our bus to a throng of onlookers and city officials in what amounted to a welcoming party. There was often a band of musicians or drummers dressed in ceremonial garb, the opposing team, several well-dressed government employees, and on occasion, the town's mayor, who would give a speech and welcome the team and Horst with a hearty handshake. I could swear there was an explosion of confetti but don't quote me on it. We were then ushered to our hotel to prepare for a banquet given by the city, or separated into pairs and portioned off to kind hosts who would take us to their homes to settle in before the big night.

When we arrived to dinner, we were overwhelmed to discover a feast fit for an emperor. Tables overflowed with sushi, sashimi, octopus and pickled vegetables to cleanse the palate. We quenched our thirst with what seemed like an endless supply of Sapporo beer in 32-ounce cans and carafes of top-shelf sake that would make any fan of the distilled grain delirious with joy. And alongside every feast there came with it the eager and friendly opposing soccer team whom we would be playing the next morning. These able-bodied and gregarious young men became our drinking partners — and best friends — for the night. Chugging beers, downing shots of sake, challenging each other to swallowing chunks of whole natto (fermented soybeans), our genteel banquets quickly devolved into an odd and hilarious mixture of fraternity party meets Model U.N.

The next morning, we would awake bleary eyed, dry-mouthed, and completely hungover. At the field, we struggled through warm-ups and once the game began, did our level best to be competitive. However, we learned early on that our opponents, skilled and extremely fit, ran circles around us. By the time we sweated off the alcohol, we found ourselves behind by a few goals. The second half was usually closer than the first, but by then, the game was over.

Afterwards, we good-naturedly shook hands, piled onto the next bus, and drove to the next city. Sometimes it was a bullet train, once it was a plane. But by any mode of transportation we found ourselves speeding through the Japanese landscape, marked by jagged mountainsides populated with pines, fertile valleys teeming with rice paddies, and modern cities that appeared out of nowhere, peppered with ancient temples and yet spotlessly clean.

This pattern persisted for the first couple of weeks: warm welcome, magical feast, binge drinking, then losing to another team in the morning. By the two-week mark we were worn out. We had seen and experienced so much — from traditional Japanese saunas to visiting Zen Buddhist temples, to seeing our goalkeeper, Ezra Bayles, emerge from the fog one morning after a home visit, clad head to toe in a ceremonial Japanese kimono — but we still hadn't won a game. And while winning wasn't our main goal in the summer of '92, it was something we strove for as college athletes, and so finally, a little thing called pride began to stir in our breasts.

After a speech from Horst, we decided we'd go easy at tonight's banquet. We enjoyed the delicious meal and the lively company, but we held our drinking in check. I clearly remember a player from the opposing team remark something to the effect, "We heard you guys were big drinkers." When we took the field the next day, we noticed it for the first time: the players we lined up against were not the same young men we shared our previous evening's repast with — in fact — those guys were on the bench! Sure, they were dressed in soccer uniforms but by no means were they expected — or allowed — to play. This began to sink in… mingling with two weeks' worth of sushi, sake and Sapporo … we had been played. This was our turning point. We exploded that game for four goals and won our first match of the trip.

I'm sure you'd like to believe we went undefeated after that but this isn't a Hollywood movie. This was real life, and in reality, when you come up against a team like Yanmar Diesel the next day, a team made up of Brazilian and Japanese professionals, you lose 8-0 in an absolute drubbing (to our credit, we held them to only two goals in the second half after Horst installed a low-pressure defense). But after that tough loss, we gathered momentum and began to win games.

I can't remember our final record — perhaps I blocked it out — but random memories remain to this day: the team's guest-starring in a fast food commercial on live Japanese TV … Jon Whitfield attempting a bicycle kick and just missing … taking on the Japanese Junior National Team and beating them 3-1 (They were made up of 8th and 9th graders but man, were they good!) … visiting the ancient temples of Kyoto … mastering the art of using chopsticks, and how could I forget, experiencing heated toilet seats for the first time.

One month after we landed in Tokyo, we boarded our plane back home. Who would have thought, that just fifty years prior our two countries were embattled in one of the worst wars the planet had ever seen. I thought about the Japanese friends I had made, the players we had competed against, the hosts who had welcomed us into their homes. I was truly moved by their love of our common humanity and their generosity in welcoming us into their world.

The 1992 team compiled an 18-2-2 record on the way to the NCAA Final Four. It was the most successful team ever at CC.

After a strenuous pre-season period and subsequent player selection from a competitive pool of candidates, the squad stood at 1-1-1 against three quality opponents in the opening contests. With Ezra Bayles in the nets, we knew we had an exceptional keeper. (Ezra also played goalie for the CC lacrosse team.)

The defensive unit in front of him, however, had to be rebuilt. Serapio Baca, Ben Straley, and newcomers Jeff Spight and Tom Heisler ably fulfilled defensive responsibilities. A sturdy Jeff Montera, a talented Andre Nunley, an experienced Aaron Frohnmayer and superman Robert Lipp provided midfield dominance. All-American Noah Epstein had returned from his year abroad to join high-scorer Arron Lujan on offense to strike fear into the hearts of our opponents.

Andre Nunley '96, in a note to me, credits the success of the team to pasta dinners at Old Chicago:

> *My favorite and most meaningful memory with CC soccer was during the 1992 season. After every win Horst took the entire team to Old Chicago for dinner. This tradition Horst apparently started before my time and I doubt he planned on what happened during the1992 season. That year the team won 15 games (I believe) in a row. Meaning, Horst had to pay for the entire team and Bruce Kola to eat as much pasta as possible!*
>
> *As a freshman I naively thought every season we'd win enough games to spend several weeks eating together at "Old C's," but 1992 was a special season and the winning streak was not repeated during my time at Colorado College. My favorite memories are of those dinners. So many laughs were had; and the camaraderie and friendships the team developed were outstanding. Horst also showed he is a man of his word, no matter the outcome.*

Our assistant coaches from the year before had moved on. I was fortunate to acquire the services of the competent Dana Taylor, who was then the director of coaching for the Colorado Springs Chargers Soccer Club. (Dana has since then become a most distinguished college coach.) But best of all, my son Erik stuck around at CC to enroll in the Masters of Arts in Teaching program, and became an integral part of the development of our Final Four team.

The first three games of the season pitted us against top-notch Division III opponents: a tie against Washington University from St. Louis, a perennial play-off contender; a win vs. St. John's from Minnesota, also a play-off team; and a loss in the last 50 seconds in double overtime against powerhouse Muhlenberg College from Pennsylvania. Keeper Ezra Bayles picked up three well-deserved shut-outs in the following three matches and the Tiger attack had scored 20 goals in six games.

By the middle of the season, after victories over Wooster, Trinity and Messiah colleges, our team had achieved national ranking, occupying the No. 14 national spot. Jon Whitfield and Erik Richardson entertained the campus with hilarious *Catalyst* articles and the tradition of presenting red roses to favorite ladies at the start of home games continued.

Thus, we had supportive and vocal spectators at our home games. Here is an excerpt from a *Catalyst* article after the Messiah game:

> *Combining earthly forces of air, fire, and ice, Bible brothers Ezra Bayles and Noah Epstein sermoned the opposition into pious persecution and liberal arts inquisition in their quest to seek the true messiah. Climbing the holy stepladder to high scoring heaven, proud pulpiteer Arron Lujan heroically hallelujahed as he happily hammered a high-speed Hail Mary. Lujan's free kick licentiously lofted above a listless line of ludicrous loafers into the back of the net, thus lifting the large C.C. lads to a laudable 1-0 lead.*

(Noah Epstein, by the way, had been out of action for a while with an injury, but contributed with morale boosting from the bench.)

In front of a large Homecoming crowd, a fired-up Tiger squad beat Pomona College 2-1 and extended its unbeaten streak to nine games. All-American Noah Epstein, who was back on the field, scored the winning goal. An NCAA play-off spot seemed like a distinct possibility.

On a three-game road trip to Iowa, we extended our unbeaten streak to 14, and the team had already scored 72 goals, a school record. To celebrate this achievement, we dropped in on the German restaurant in the Amana Colonies to fortify ourselves for the long bus trip back to campus. From his seat behind the bus driver, trainer Bruce Kola encouraged the driver with one of his one-liners:

"Bob, don't spare the horses!!"

And off we were on I-80 to leave Iowa and Nebraska behind us.

We concluded the regular season with a narrow victory over crosstown rival UCCS, and earned a forfeit against Metro. The Tigers had climbed to No. 1 in the West region, and No. 8 nationally. And yet, when the NCAA selection was made, we were not granted the expected home berth but had to travel to Southern California. CC Athletic Director Max Taylor sent in an official protest, but to no avail. NCAA cost-saving trumped fairness. As Whitfield pointed out in *The Catalyst*: "We got screwed!"

But a far more difficult problem had arisen. Noah Epstein, while recovering from injury, and as a comparative literature major, had tried out for a CC play production and had been cast in the role of Romeo in Shakespeare's *Romeo and Juliet*. And the play opened on the same weekend as the scheduled first round of the play-offs. A liberal arts dilemma!!

This dilemma was featured in a retrospective article by Anne Christensen in a special *CC Bulletin* publication about 35 years of the Block Plan entitled "Balancing Academics and Athletics":

> *When soccer All-American Noah Epstein '94, CC's high scoring star, injured his knee early in the '92 season, Coach Horst Richardson encouraged him to audition for* Romeo and Juliet, *which was then being cast on campus. "Otherwise he had nothing to do but to go to class," says Richardson, chuckling just a little.*
>
> *The play rehearsals gave Epstein time to rehab his knee before returning to the team. Richardson, a bit of a Renaissance man himself, (German professor, actor, sometime philosopher), wanted Epstein to try something new during his "time off" from athletics, something else with which to balance his academic load.*
>
> *When cast as Romeo, injured soccer star Epstein got a poignantly pertinent line: "Courage, man; the hurt cannot be much!" Even without Romeo — er, Epstein — for much of the season, the team earned its spot in the regional play-offs in Southern California at Claremont College. By tournament time, Epstein was healed, but alas, the play and the play-offs were scheduled on the same weekend, and Noah was expected to star in both — 1,100 miles apart. As Romeo asked himself, "Can I go forward when my heart is here?"*
>
> *The drama department, no doubt reluctant to hear Juliet's "Wherefore art thou, Romeo?" speech remain a monologue without Romeo before her balcony, worked with Richardson to find a way to share their mutual star. The compromise: If the soccer team won its first game Saturday without Epstein, the drama department would reschedule Sunday's play from afternoon to evening to allow Epstein to fly back after the 1 p.m. game out west. The plan worked, as Epstein caught a predawn flight on Sunday.*
>
> *"But soft! What light through yonder window breaks?" (Airport shuttle service provided by Helen, the coach's wife.) Noah assisted on the winning goal in the second game, then flew back to campus to die on stage Sunday night.*

Yes, that was quite a logistical coup to allow Noah to perform on stage and on the field over 1,000 miles apart within 24 hours. In the first game vs. St. Olaf College of Minnesota, we eked out a 1-0 victory on a Lujan goal, his 25th of the season, on a double assist from Jeff Spight and Rob Lipp.

In order for us to have a chance in the second game vs. California Lutheran, it was necessary to mark out their midfield general, Preben Krohnstad, a stud from Norway. Aaron Frohnmayer accepted this assignment and executed it to perfection. Man-to-man marking all over the field and deft counterattacks put the opponents on their heels. Two goals by Lipp on assists from Epstein and Lujan, and the Tigers were Far West champions. The victory also marked my 300th win!

Our opponent in the final eight turned out to be Washington University of St. Louis, whom, coincidentally, we had played against in the first game of the season to a 2-2 tie at home. Once again the Tigers had to travel, even though we were seeded higher than Wash U. Oh well, at least we were spending some of the NCAA's money on good food and comfortable hotels.

Wash U's coach, Ty Keough, was a former U.S. national team player and son of soccer icon Harry Keough, a member of the 1950 U.S. national team, which had beaten England in a 1-0 shocker in the World Cup in Brazil. Playing Washington University on their well-worn football field was going to be a similar "English World Cup" challenge for us. Our athletic director, Max Taylor, accompanied the team to St. Louis. Here is how he remembers the game:

> *We had advanced to the final eight against Washington University, an old nemesis, in St. Louis. A trip to the Final Four was on the line. What an amazing game it was! CC scored first and led 1-0. As AD I sat with the small CC contingent of fans, yelling myself hoarse in anticipation of a victory. Wash U attacked relentlessly. CC defended its lead staunchly. The second half wore on, it seemed to me, at a snail's pace. Finally, the intense pressure was more than I could bear. I got up, paced up and down for a while, and then in anxious anticipation finally left the stadium to walk nervously around the entire sports complex. My angst was overwhelming in anticipation of a victory, in fear of a defeat. Not to worry! We won!*

Our lone goal didn't come until the 82nd minute. Noah Epstein scored on a Robert Lipp assist. The last eight minutes were the longest eight minutes in my life! Wash U swarmed around our goal and were awarded four corner kicks in succession. But if I had to single out one of the players as the hero of the game, it would have to be our keeper Ezra

Bayles. He made several amazing saves at the end, stopping one point blank shot from a couple of yards out. To this day Ezra maintains that he has virtually no memory of the end of the game; gut reactions carried him to victory.

Three shut-outs in NCAA post-season competition for the Tigers, and we had made it to the Final Four. Noah Epstein, who was euphoric after the victory, summed up the joy of the players by stating: "I feel drunk, and I haven't had a beer!"

But wait, there are two more tales to tell about this epic match. The first one wasn't revealed to me until my son's wedding, when the truth about the fire alarm incident came out into the open. Whitfield relates the story:

> *This is perhaps one of the most epic CC Soccer stories of all time … We were in St. Louis for the NCAA Quarter Final play-off match against Washington University. We had gone to bed for the night, ready to get a great night's sleep for the big match the next day ... Around 3 a.m. we are all awakened by alarm bells and strobe lights in our rooms, forcing an all-hotel evacuation. 100+ hotel guests filled the cold November streets of downtown St. Louis. Three huge fire engines arrived with sirens a-blazing. Hordes of people lined the freezing downtown streets in robes, pajamas, and clothing not suitable for the low temperatures. All of our team were convinced that the Wash U Junior Varsity had come over and perpetrated the act.*
>
> *The next day we played the match and prevailed 1-0, which advanced us to the National Semi-Final to be played in New Jersey a week later. We never knew what happened and never got the full story until ... Years later, my own brother, sister, and yes, then Assistant Coach Erik Richardson came forth and admitted they had inadvertently perpetrated the dastardly act! The source of the action was apparently a fire extinguisher fight that took place amongst the three on the top floor of the hotel in the wee hours of the morning ... The fire extinguisher smoke caused the sprinklers to go off, which resulted in an all-hotel alarm and evacuation. Fortunately, we won the game, and if we hadn't, I'm pretty sure we never would've heard the real story.*

Our team, of course, was furious to have been so rudely awakened, especially since setting off the alarm might have been attributed to the Wash U j.v. team. This incident certainly helped motivate our players to play exceptionally hard the next day.

The second event to relate is of literary value, as the Tiger team became the subject of a short story. The well-known Chilean writer Antonio Skarmeta, a soccer aficionado, had taught an occasional writer-in-residence block at Colorado College. It just so happened that he was also teaching at Washington University and attended our quarterfinal match. He was so intrigued by the match that he wrote a short story about it titled "Of Tigers and Bears."

> *A freezing day in St. Louis, one of those that crack ears and blush cheeks. There were numerous spectators, since many flyers had been distributed announcing the decisive soccer game on the way to the championship. I sit in the stands with my heart divided. I have a contract that lets me teach every two years in the magnificent Washington University. Three years ago, I occupied the Maytag Chair for a semester at Colorado College, where I was impressed by the quality of the faculty and the students, where I had good times, made great friends, some of them involved with the soccer team.*
>
> *I begin with this roundabout way to convince almost everyone that they should not doubt my objectivity in this report. CC won over Wash U 1-0, thus moving to the semi-finals of the championship in one of the most dramatic games that I have ever seen in my life. Just by looking at the build of the rivals it was possible to predict how they were going to play. The Wash U Bears have had a brilliant season and you realize why by looking at them. It is an energetic, fighting, and tough team with inspired personalities, but deep down their effectiveness is based on running for 90 minutes, on harassing the adversary without rest, on shooting from wherever they can, and on a sweeper who is an impenetrable mountain.*
>
> *The CC Tigers are not less willful, with a team perhaps not as well rounded, but with a great heart and a more sophisticated technique. The players are not as robust as the Bears, but above all they know how to endure storm with stoicism. As the game moves on, they find their way, their ability to evade the adversary, and the possibility to shoot at goal with a good chance of scoring. I do not know if I exaggerate when I say that the Tigers shot straight to the goal two times: on the second shot the ball went in and they obtained the victory.*
>
> *The Bears attacked with heavy artillery, but two factors contributed to their inability to score: Bad luck that drove two shots to goal to the clouds when it was easier to put them into the net, and the inspired goaltending of the Tigers' goalkeeper, who experienced one of his best days which could be framed in gold on the current soccer season. Without that miraculous job of the net minder, the Wash U players would have had at least a tie or perhaps a win. Many times they made their fans*

stand up and cheer and made them sit down again with a breath of disappointment. Just one of those days.

On the other hand, it is important to note that during the first half, two incisive C.C. attacks were neutralized by the kind of foul that make one's teeth gnash. On balance, both teams foul equally. However, what the final score hides is that those two first half fouls committed against the Tigers stopped plays that were on the way to scoring a goal.

I think that what ultimately determined this brilliant match, of which both teams can be very proud, were the techniques used by the two coaches. Coach Richardson hardly made changes in the team, and he was motivated to change only by an injury to the right wing in the first half. On the other hand, the Bears had a carnival of changes that attracted my attention as a Latin American, since in our countries no more than three substitutions are allowed. Thus, the Wash U team was remodeled several times, maybe because of the strategy of withdrawing the exhausted forces and of sending fresh energy to attack or hold back the opponent. But such tactical maneuvers can be risky: they do not allow a team to find its rhythm and detect the weaknesses of the adversary. As the Tigers stepped up the tempo, emphasizing their more elastic and elegant play, the winning goal ensued.

It was a superb soccer afternoon that made us forget the cold weather and bound us, the spectators, emotionally in what may be a small sample of things to come in the summer of 1994 when the United States hosts the next World Cup.

— Antonio Skarmeta

(Translated from the original Spanish by CC Professor Salvatore Bizzarro and Alfredo Villegas.)

In spite of a well-crafted letter of appeal to the NCAA for a home berth in the Final Four by then-acting CC president Michael Grace, the Tigers had to pack their bags again for a long flight to New Jersey. (My wife Helen and daughter Stacia came along, but I was so nervous that I don't remember them being there! Assistant Coach Erik Richardson had accepted a position with Royal Caribbean Cruise Lines and had sailed away.) By the time we arrived at Kean College outside of Newark, we had traveled well over 6,000 miles on our odyssey to the semi-finals and we had missed only one day of class!

The semi-final game against veteran play-off team Ohio Wesleyan was played at 10 o'clock in the morning, or 8 a.m. Colorado time. Not ideal for us. We lost badly, 5-0. The headline in *The Catalyst* a week later said it all: "Ohio Wesleyan pushes Tiger soccer off a cliff!" At half-time we were still in the game, only one goal behind. And Noah Epstein was a millimeter away from tying the contest. I think in the second half travel fatigue caught up with us and we were exhausted.

But what a season it had been: from a foreign trip to Japan all the way to the Final Four in New Jersey. The accolades for the players and the team kept rolling in and the awards banquet in Bemis Hall was as festive as it could possibly get.

1992 was a record year:

- Most goals scored in a season: 78
- Most victories: 18
- Best record: 18-2-2
- Longest winning streak: 14
- Longest unbeaten streak: 18
- Rob Lipp honored as third CC All-American and signs professional contract
- Horst Richardson named West Region Coach of the Year.

1993

After three weeks of summer soccer camps with 500 or so campers, an on-campus NSCAA residential Academy course for coaching certification, and a weekend preparatory camp for alum Lance Waring's fledgling high school program in Telluride, we focused on player selection for the new season. Every year the talent level of incoming candidates for the squad improved and consequently the final selection became ever more difficult. Making "cuts" was one of my most difficult tasks as a coach.

Three key players had graduated: Ezra Bayles, Robert Lipp and Jon Whitfield. Naturally our success from the previous season had elevated interest in the program and expectations were high.

An unusual recruiting event abroad in Ukraine provided us with a foreign talent. Marco della Cava '83, who had become a staff writer for *USA Today*, was doing a story on his Jewish family's past and in Kiev, while standing in line at the post office to send a fax, overheard a soccer conversation, in English, about the World Cup. Apparently a Ukrainian university student was giving several American students a tour of his city. Marco introduced himself, one thing led to another, and sometime later the two were kicking a soccer ball around in a park. Marco writes:

1993 | 15-5-0

Front row, left to right: Ted Nusbaum, Owen Borg, Jeff Montera, Mark Handy, Rob Faucett, Jeff Spight, Ian Creager, Coach Horst Richardson. **Middle row:** Mark Thomas, Sergei Pokhilko, Jeff Lee, Matt Atencio, Tom Heisler, Tucker Drury, Serapio Baca, Assistant Coach Cory Kasten. **Back row:** Andre Nunley, Noah Epstein (captain), Arron Lujan (captain), Nick Watterson, Paolo Villa, Isaac Jones, Craig Lopez, Assistant Coach Erik Richardson. **Not pictured:** Dan Burgard, Jeff Jurgens, Sean McGuire, Guy Mossman, Andy Olds.

On Sergei: I remember it all well. It was the summer of 1992, and Ukraine was just declaring itself independent from Russia and the former USSR. I was in Kiev, living there for the summer, sending dispatches back to USA Today *and the Gannett News Service from my travels in Ukraine and around the FSU. Sending those dispatches required, in those pre-tech days, standing in long lines at the Kiev (now spelled Kyyiv) post office, so you could FAX the article to editors in the U.S.*

One day in such a line, I was next to a smiling young local; he spoke great English (my Ukrainian is passable, thanks to my mother and grandmother teaching me a bit as a kid). We started to chat as the line shuffled ahead. Turns out, he loved soccer. "Me too," I said. So we agreed to meet at a nearby field the next day to just kick around.

The next day came, and within minutes I could tell by the way Sergei Pokhilko moved around the ball, with determination and pace, that he was a talent — no mere Sunday kicker. I asked about his dreams and ambitions, and pretty soon I realized: Maybe Horst needs to hear about this young man. The rest is indeed history, and a life-changing event in Sergei's life. Horst took the proverbial ball, and Sergei joined the team and student body at CC.

Today, Sergei lives in Kiev with a daughter — we occasionally swap emails, but I haven't heard from him in a bit. It is sad the way things are devolved in that precious country, which now once again finds itself under the pressing yoke of Russian influence. I hope he's doing well; but I'm sure that his life was changed for the better thanks to coming to CC. And soccer made that all happen.

At a later date Marco added:

… one thing greater than Sergei Pokhilko's passion for soccer was his desire to see America. Setting aside fears that I might be raising Pokhilko's hopes absurdly high, I suggested that we contact Coach Richardson. A partial foreign student scholarship allowed him to enroll at CC and attend for two years.

Sergei turned out to be a solid student and a spark plug of a player. Transfer Isaac Jones added defensive stability, Matt Atencio showed promise in midfield, Owen Borg was hard-nosed in several positions, Ian Creager displayed flashes of brilliance, and Rob Faucett took over in goal. I had reason to be cautiously optimistic about the forthcoming season. Furthermore, Erik Richardson continued as a seasoned assistant coach while working on his Masters of Arts in Teaching degree at CC and his high school and club soccer buddy Cory Kasten joined up as goalkeeper coach.

On the weekend before classes began, we headed west over Independence and Soldier passes to Salt Lake City for a tournament at Westminster College. Their coach and I had a good relationship and collaborated on setting up a number of tournaments over the years. UC Santa Cruz and Chapman College, both critical NCAA independent teams, were our opponents. We split the series.

A tournament at home, the Pikes Peak Invitational, followed. Carleton College from Minnesota, Claremont from California, and SUNY-Binghamton from New York traveled to meet on Stewart Field. Since we were no longer affiliated with a conference, attending tournaments and organizing tournaments at home became our bread-and-butter scheduling efforts. We won the tournament. To create a proper tournament atmosphere, a concession stand, a pep band, and cheerleaders helped. Big time on Stewart!!

A tournament at Wheaton College in Chicago followed. Our opening game matched us up against Trinity University from Texas. Juan Valdez, alias you-know-who, reported on the game in *The Catalyst*. (You may remember Juan as Romeo from the year before. His articles were hilarious, sometimes outrageous, but always entertaining.)

> *We beat Trinity 2-1, but CC scored all three goals. We had pity on the Texans and scored one goal on ourselves to ease the pain of eternal damnation. Jeff Spight, patron saint of Lake Michigan, scored the game's first goal on an unstoppable back pass. He later redeemed himself by scoring the winning goal; this time for the Tigers. The consistent Noah Epstein, who, contrary to CC gossip, does not write for* The Catalyst, *and who, unknown to most, is the patron saint of gastrointestinal distress, also slotted home a Tiger tally.*

Host Wheaton won their own tournament.

Another bus trip followed, this time to Grinnell, Iowa, during block break. Against Wisconsin-Oshkosh the score was tied 0-0 at the end of regulation, and at the conclusion of the first 15-minute OT it was still tied, 1-1. And then something wonderful happened! Epstein from Lujan, 2-1. Lujan from Epstein 3-1. And a grandiose "golazo" on a full volley shot from Paolo Villa, 4-1. Three goals in seven minutes!! Towards the end of the contest, there was the brewing of a brawl, with Jeff Lee and Isaac Jones ready to rumble, but I stopped all that by screaming from the sideline: "Don't get into a fight! We are all staying in the same motel!"

Buoyed by the victory, we were ready to take on Grinnell the next day. But what a surprise awaited us the next morning. Athletic Director Max Taylor had traveled to Grinnell as well to see us play and visit with the then-college President George Drake, who was a former CC history professor. Max remembers the bad weather that had set in:

> *Saturday morning we were greeted by an incredibly heavy downpour of rain. The campus had been turned into a lake! Standing water was everywhere, including several inches on the major soccer pitch. I concluded quickly that no soccer could be played on this rainy day. And then I witnessed a wondrous sight! Members of both soccer teams, dressed in their uniforms and accompanied by Coach Richardson and Coach Pfitsch, carried portable soccer goals and were heroically running from field to field on the expansive Grinnell campus in hopes of finding a reasonably playable*

pitch for the game. It was not to be! After an hour or more of trying and hoping the rains would cease, the game was cancelled.

If the cancellation of the game due to excessive rain was a disappointment, the road trip home bordered on disaster. Driving through Omaha, our bus broke down, believe it or not, on the same off-ramp on which the CC football team, in the same bus a week before, had broken down. Hydraulic suspension failure was the diagnosis. That was fixed, but once back on the bus and still within Omaha city limits, the gear box failed and we had to abandon the bus. Rental cars brought us back home.

Because of age restrictions, the three oldest members of the squad had to drive the vehicles: Bruce Kola, Horst, and Paolo Villa. Paolo, our "Italian Stallion," was not too happy about that assignment and writes about the drive back through Nebraska:

On Friday, September 24, we defeated Wisconsin-Oshkosh at Grinnell College. Our scheduled second match was canceled due to a water-logged playing field. We started the trip back to Colorado, but after about three hours, just outside Omaha, Nebraska, our bus noticeably tipped to the right. The driver exited the highway and it became obvious that we could no longer continue our journey. We still managed to make it to a hotel and after a gloomy report from the local mechanics, Coach Richardson decided we would rent cars the next morning.

The next morning we started our drive. I was one of the drivers because I was over 25 years of age. Less than ten minutes from departing Omaha, the four teammates traveling with me were sound asleep and proceeded to maintain that status for the duration of the drive. Six hundred long miles of flat Nebraska landscape without exchanging a single word with a living soul.

After three years at the helm of the crosstown UCCS program, former CC star Eddy Dietz received his biggest victory in his career when the Mountain Lions beat the Tigers on CC's home turf. But if that was a lowlight in the season, the highlight arrived a week later. The defending national champion, Kean State, host of last year's Final Four, had come to town and lost to us 2-1. With his winning goal, Noah Epstein moved into the third-place spot for CC's all-time leading scorer position.

Two days later Noah scored again in our next game against Macalester within 50 seconds of the kick-off. A superb flick pass by Mark Thomas to Noah was a brilliant assist.

No wonder that Noah, after our 4-0 victory that day, was overheard saying: "We are now legends in our own minds!"

Our No. 16 game away to Gustavus Adolphus put us in contention for the play-offs, as we won 4-0. Mark Handy had taken over in goal for injured Rob Faucett and made a couple of stunning saves. A week later in California, wins over LaVerne and Pomona sealed the play-off deal.

As if we hadn't had enough excitement already while traveling this season, one more scary incident was about to happen. Arron Lujan '95 recounts this event:

> *It was the fall of 1993 and after winning two games over LaVerne and Pomona in LA on a block break weekend, the CC men's soccer team planned on having a relaxing journey back to CC. Per our normal CC travel itinerary, our flight departed very late in the evening (so Horst could save the program a few bucks).*
>
> *The plane took off from LAX and the flight seemed to be going as planned. As we reached altitude and leveled off, the plane started shaking violently back and forth. The pilot got on the intercom and said, "We are experiencing some mechanical issues and we will be making an emergency landing in Las Vegas. If the oxygen masks come down…use them." As college students, our first reaction was sheer delight. We were landing in Las Vegas!!!! We were hoping to get stuck for the evening. Then suddenly the plane takes a nosedive and heads straight down and the oxygen masks come down from the ceiling. Our delight turned to terror in seconds.*
>
> *We put our oxygen masks on and began to panic. I looked a few rows ahead of me to see what Horst was doing. He had his oxygen mask on and he was reading a book! It was like he was on the deck of a cruise ship! He was calm, almost enjoying the moment. I was sweating profusely.*
>
> *Bruce Kola yelled, "This wouldn't have happened if we would have taken a flight at a normal damn time!" Mark Thomas is in the row in front of me and he turns to me and says, "This guy (the pilot) is not messing around!" I don't know what would make Mark think this was a joke. Jeff Spight was across the aisle from me. Jeff has his oxygen mask on and he is still celebrating the fact that we will be landing in Las Vegas with no inclination that we may die! People are screaming and one lady rips the oxygen mask completely out of the ceiling. It was only a few minutes but it seemed a lot longer.*
>
> *We leveled off and landed safely in Las Vegas. Andre Nunley walked up to me in the terminal after we departed the plane and said, "That was close." Those three*

> *words tell you how scary this ordeal was, because Andre rarely spoke. Feeling that we cheated death, we all headed directly for the slot machines and emptied our wallets. I actually won a few bucks. The airline wanted us to get back on the same flight after the mechanical issues had been fixed, but Horst refused. We got on another plane and landed safely in Denver.*

At the end of the regular season we had accumulated a 14-4 record, stood at No. 15 in the national rankings, and received a bid for the NCAA play-offs, to be staged at the University of California, San Diego. Our opponent: nemesis Claremont College. We defeated them 4-1, our biggest victory ever in an NCAA play-off game. The headline in the sports section of the *Colorado Springs Gazette* read: "Epstein's ire carries CC to first-round victory!"

Noah scored two goals in the contest, placing him in a tie with previous all-time high-scorer Jacques Lemvo at 63 goals! Nunley and Lujan scored the other two. I was quoted as saying: "I'd say it was one of Noah's finest games. He was dynamic. Devastating. Especially when he gets angry." Mark Handy tended goal, and Isaac Jones, Tom Heisler, Serapio Baca, and Jeff Spight played near perfect defense.

The next day we faced UC San Diego, No. 5 in the country, at their home field and lost 1-0. It was the only shut-out against us all season. But we played them dead even in all statistical categories. What a starting 11 we put on the field that day:

Mark Handy.................... *Keeper*
Serapio Baca .... *Defense*
Tom Heisler .... *Defense*
Isaac Jones .... *Defense*
Jeff Spight .... *Defense*
Jeff Montera .... *Midfield*
Arron Lujan .... *Midfield*
Andre Nunley .... *Midfield*
Mark Thomas .... *Midfield*
Noah Epstein .... *Forward*
Sergei Pokhilko .... *Forward*

The team was invited to a splendid reception at the home of alum Nick Binkley '68. We had a most festive banquet later on campus, and Noah Epstein was honored with his second All-America Award at the annual coaches convention and got his picture taken with none other than Pele!!

1994

The United States hosted the World Cup in 1994. Huge crowds supported the month-long competition, our national team almost snuck past Brazil at Stanford stadium in the round of 16, and the publicity for soccer and the growth of the game were tremendous. We were inundated with campers in our summer soccer camps. Epstein and Lipp were playing pro ball, Erik Richardson joined us as assistant coach for a third year, and Ken White, a native of Ireland, became goalkeeper coach. Matt Atencio and Ian Creager took over as *Catalyst* reporters and kept up the hilarious reporting tradition.

For years we produced an informative annual recruiting brochure, which we sent to high school soccer coaches around the country. We also mailed lots of these to prospects and their parents. Naturally we featured all the accomplishments of our program in this publicity. With the advent of the Internet, this custom became less and less important in the recruiting process.

After an opening tournament at home, we flew to San Antonio for a tournament at Trinity University. Whenever the team played away, I made sure that we incorporated an educational segment when appropriate. Strolling the Riverwalk and visiting the Alamo became standard procedure in San Antonio.

1994 | 12-6-2

Front row, left to right: Coach Horst Richardson, Dan Morlan, Justin Sawyer, Justin Spring, Doug Bowman, Mark Handy, Sam Douglas, Matt Atencio, Justin Meade, Ian Creager, Matt Barry. **Back row:** Assistant Coach Ken White, Jeff Spight, Craig Lopez, Andre Nunley, Nick Watterson, Arron Lujan (captain), Isaac Jones (captain), Jeff Lee, Sergei Pokhilko, Serapio Baca, Jeff Montera, Assistant Coach Erik Richardson. **Not pictured:** Dan Epstein.

The 1994 squad was fairly ethnically diverse; thus, the tongue-in-cheek comments in *The Catalyst* included these comments:

> *Before the first game against Trinity University, the team made a special pilgrimage to the Alamo, where players Serapio Baca, Matt Atencio, and Craig Lopez learned about their ruthless ancestors. Several players traded their sweatsuits for priceless Alamo souvenirs, including Davy Crockett's fork, Sam Houston's razor, and Jim Bowie's knife.*

We won the tournament. Sadly, Jeff Lee suffered a concussion on a courageous defensive play. According to Atencio, the first thing Lee remembered after a temporary memory loss was: The Alamo!

The games against crosstown rival UCCS had become more and more important, especially since the local sports press had elevated these games to the level of major competition. Thus, pride was at stake. In the past, the match-up against the Air Force Academy had been the main event in the season, but AFA had become D-I.

During the previous seasons, UCCS had narrowly defeated the Tigers, but as Arron Lujan indicated, "Our players knew that was not going to happen this year." And it didn't. After shutting out MacMurray and Chapman in subsequent games behind stellar defensive performances by Jeff Montera and Isaac Jones, we inched into the national rankings.

In the 1994 scrapbook, there is a picture of my wife Helen precariously balanced on an elevated platform videotaping a game. Come rain or shine, Helen documented every home game since the early eighties, manning ever-more-sensitive video cameras for 90 minutes with one eye closed as she was looking into the viewfinder with the other eye. What dedication to the cause of CC men's soccer! As a result, we have today a collection of highlight tapes from all these seasons.

Jim Schuster speaks for many a player when he writes about Helen:

> *There are a lot of things that college can offer, but the comfort of a mother and family is not one of them. Helen filled this missing role for many of us, often served as a surrogate mother for the team. Being a senior provided the added benefit of home-made spaghetti dinners occasionally being delivered to your door the night before a game, which was something all players looked forward to coming into their*

> *senior year. It wasn't so much the food itself that made it special, but rather just the connection to someone who was looking after you and cared enough to take her time to make us feel special.*

At the half-way point in the campaign, we traveled to "the Land of 10,000 Lakes" during the first block break. Eager to build on a string of victories, we faced an athletic Gustavus Adolphus squad. Shortly into the game, it became evident, literally, that we lacked intestinal fortitude. *The Catalyst* reported on the contest, admittedly with some embellishment, as follows:

> *The Tigers came out strong in the opening minutes. But all of a sudden, Tiger forward Sergei Pokhilko collapsed and began convulsing violently, foaming at the mouth. Team trainer Bruce Kola rushed out onto the field and without hesitation padded and wrapped Pokhilko's leg, put his left ankle in a boot, gave him an elbow brace, and taped his arms together. The diagnosis: bad lutefisk and rotten lefse served in the Gustavus cafeteria!*

We didn't have enough gas in the tank to even the score in OT and lost 1-0. But our pride was restored the following day with a win over Macalester in which a Lujan goal propelled him into a tie in the all-time leading scorer category.

It's not easy to come off a tough road trip and play at home the next day. But that's just what we did, facing second-ranked Messiah College. In scheduling, I knew it was going to be difficult to play back to back, but the opportunity to compete against this top opponent was not to be missed. The guys knew what was at stake and responded with a brilliant game and a well-deserved 3-2 victory.

Even though Lujan was a marked man by now and every opponent tried to double or triple team him, he still responded with two goals, making him the undisputed scoring leader at CC. Tactically, we had moved him from forward to midfield to give him more freedom to roam, to accelerate forward with the ball, and to use his dribbling skills to penetrate into the other team's vital area where he would create much consternation for their defenders.

Soccer can be cruel! By game No. 12 in the fall campaign we had established ourselves as a force to be reckoned with. In a pivotal match against regional opponent St. Olaf, 10 goals were scored, and we lost 6-4. Unbelievable! "I can't remember a Division III match in which we were up by two goals," I was quoted as saying, "and then lost by two after four unanswered strikes by the opponent."

Our play-off hopes were draining away. But our seesaw season had more in store for us. The resilient Tigers recovered and were back to winning form by Homecoming. And then came a mid-week home game against Grinnell College, which turned out to be a real doozie: We fired 45 shots at them and it still ended up as a 0-0 tie.

George Drake, President of Grinnell College and a former CC history professor, was quite a soccer fan. He witnessed this match and sent me his recollections:

> *On October 18, 1994, I happened to be at Colorado College to lecture and during the day I met with a class that had an international student (Sergei Pokhilko) who was the striker on Horst Richardson's varsity soccer team. At that time, I was a history professor at Grinnell (having formerly been at Colorado College) and Grinnell happened to be playing CC that afternoon, so I was able to attend the game. It was one of the most memorable college soccer games that I have witnessed.*
>
> *Colorado College traditionally has better teams than Grinnell and on that day, CC was vastly superior to Grinnell. However, Grinnell had a goalkeeper who was the best in the history of the program then and today. His name is Nate Brenneman and he resides in Grinnell's Athletic Hall of Fame both as soccer goalkeeper and as a diver on the swimming team.*
>
> *The score on that October day was Colorado College 0 and Grinnell 0: a nil-nil tie. It was extraordinary that Grinnell was able to tie CC, but what was even more startling was that CC had more than 40 shots on goal, with Grinnell managing no more than five. It was a totally one-sided game, except for the score.*
>
> *After the game, I had a chance to speak to the very appealing striker whom I had met in class that morning. All of his charm had disappeared; he was beyond frustrated after all his shots, many of them brilliant, had been blocked and scooped by Nate Brenneman's exceptional goalkeeping. Soccer can be a strange sport, but never stranger than on that October afternoon.*

We ended the season with a flurry of victories and snuck into the NCAA play-offs, our third consecutive post season appearance! The Far West regionals were once again hosted by UC San Diego. We looked sharp traveling out there with coats and ties, but deep down everyone was nervous, because we were matched up with the host, who also were the defending national champion.

UCSD's playing field areas were huge, seemingly larger than the entire CC campus, their enrollment was five times ours, and since they fielded no football team, soccer was the dominant fall sport. I muttered to myself: They have no business being a D-III program!

Without veteran defender Jeff Montera, who had accumulated his fifth yellow card and had to sit out the contest, we lost 3-0.

A memorable and rewarding season nevertheless. At the banquet we had a festive time and said farewell to the graduating seniors: Arron Lujan, Serapio Baca, Jeff Montera, and Craig Lopez. Arron Lujan, our All-American, had become undisputed high-scorer of the CC program with 69 goals. We honored that incredible achievement by retiring his No. 14 jersey. It is now displayed in a place of honor in the El Pomar Sports Center.

1995

On April 8, 1995, Coach Emeritus Bill Boddington was inducted into the CC Athletic Hall of Fame as part of the inaugural class. What a festive event it was, and there was no better candidate than Bill to deserve this honor.

1995 | 15-5-0

Front row, left to right: Mark Villanueva, Andre Nunley, Justin Meade, Mark Handy, Kainoa Lincoln, Jeff Spight, Owen Borg. **Middle row:** Assistant Coach Stan Lambros, Coach Horst Richardson, Kyle Stock, Justin Sawyer, Tucker Drury, Dan Morlan, David Skillman, Luke Helm, Nate Walrod. **Back row:** Rob Goodwin, Nick Watterson, Sergei Pokhilko, Jeff Lee (captain), Isaac Jones (captain), Matt Atencio (captain), Ian Creager, Journey Herbeck, Dave Maloney.

The 1995 season, with a 15-5 record, produced an unprecedented fourth NCAA tournament appearance in a row! We started the fall campaign with five consecutive victories, had 10 shut-outs during the regular season, and scored 56 goals along the way.

Assistant Coach Stan Lambros, a dedicated long distance runner and fitness expert, got the squad in shape and kept the players fit at a high level, giving us an edge at altitude at home and providing excellent recovery rates on the road. Stan and his wife Karen, who lived in a bungalow deep into the foothills off the Old Stage Road, invited the team to a pre-season BBQ. They enjoyed their retreat there year-round, even in the cold winter months. Their lifestyle choices were eye-openers to some of the more urban-oriented players.

Matt Atencio and Ian Creager, writing for *The Catalyst*, got us off to a humorous start to pre-season with a delightful tongue-in-cheek article in the first fall issue of the student paper. Here are some excerpts from their whimsical writing skills:

> *The CC men's soccer team try-out commenced two weeks before the school year began. Dazed freshmen were seen wandering around nervously wondering if they had what it takes to be a member of the mighty CC Tigers. Would they be able to stand the fiery passion of Sergei Pokhilko, the bone-crushing tackles of Owen Borg? Could they comprehend the obscure half-time speeches of Coach Horst Richardson? Probably not. The season veteran players rolled in 20 minutes before the first practice. Junior Dan Morlan and senior Nick Watterson walked onto Stewart Field with Jaegermeisters in hand, singing "Mein Hut der hat drei Ecken ..."*
>
> *Senior striker Ian Creager fell down the steps to the field due to a leg injury incurred in a street fight in downtown Santiago, Chile... Southern boys Justin Sawyer and Justin Meade cruised up to the field in their Boss Hog white (trash) convertible Cadillac.*

These two budding sports journalists always signed off their articles with their signature: We are Audi 5000!!!

Sergei Pokhilko and Dan Morlan became scoring machines with Ian Creager flying up and down on either wing; Andre Nunley and Matt Atencio provided sparkle and deft passing in midfield; Isaac Jones, Owen Borg, Jeff Lee, and Jeff Spight played stingy defense, and Mark Handy kept the ball out of the net. Dave Moross, our SID, promoted the team to the media and Bruce Kola kept all the athletes healthy.

Matt Atencio '97, one of the tri-captains in 1995, reflects back on his CC career and his comments capture the culture of the squad and staff well:

> *My first block at CC was a Southwest studies type course out at the Crestone Baca campus. This coincided with the team's first road trip to play Westminster in Utah. So, after a few days of reading about local mythology around a campfire, it was finally time to go play soccer.*
>
> *As the team pulled up on the dusty road, there I was, ready to hop on the Shark bus and embark on my first road trip experience. Problem was, there was a miscommunication and I was without a set of uniforms. Not to worry, said Horst, we'll figure something out when we get there. I would hear this statement many times over the next four years, always with the corresponding comment that "this was all part of a Liberal Arts education" ... (like later when we drove to Grinnell College in Iowa and the field was too flooded to play, or when the bus broke down in Omaha, Nebraska, and we had to spend the night there, or when we arrived too late in Chicago to eat in a restaurant and thus walked through the White Castle drive thru with our per diem money in hand).*
>
> *Anyways, in the end, at game time, the great minds from one of this nation's most selective liberal arts institutions came together to find a solution. It was determined that I would wear a white Hanes T-shirt with my number written in black Sharpie. And the shinguards? Well, a cut up Domino's pizza box sorted out this problem.*

After a super 5-0 start to the season, we lost two close ones in OT on the road in Southern California. The loss to Chapman hurt especially since they, like CC, were independents competing for a few precious C-pool spots in the NCAA post-season selection process. And then a loss to crosstown rival UCCS, coached by former CC legend Eddy Dietz, followed. For Eddy, the game vs. his alma mater mattered more than any other. After his victory he was quoted in the local sports pages: "It is a very big win for our program. This is a measuring stick. We have arrived!"

In a locker room talk with the team subsequent to the loss to UCCS, I put forth the following challenge to the team: If we got back on a winning track and made the play-offs, they could shave my head!! Well, this challenge in addition to a festive Homecoming ceremony, honoring our four previous All-Americans, motivated the squad to a stunning 9-1 rest-of-the-season record. At the Homecoming ceremony I received a heartwarming surprise. The press release of this event describes it as follows:

> *After a brief ceremony to honor the college's four All-Americans, (Noah Epstein, Robert Lipp, Arron Lujan, and Greg Kazemi), and to retire Lujan's No. 14 jersey, Lance Lujan, Arron's father and a Kiowa Indian, presented Horst with a hand-made blanket and his wife Helen with a Native American shawl in gratitude for all they had done for his son. Coach Richardson also was named an honorary Kiowan.*

A funny thing happened on the way to Iowa during the first block break road trip. The CC highway bus had pulled up to El Pomar, the players had packed their gear and assembled in the locker room, Bruce Kola, the trainer, had spread out his four sizable duffel bags in the hallway, which the freshmen would pick up and haul out to the bus. Everything was ready for the trip, but there was no Owen Borg. The junior was nowhere to be found. We waited for 15 minutes or so, and then I said: "Time to go!" We departed and left him behind. I hated to start the trip without him, for he was a most valuable member of the team.

After the long journey, just shy of 800 miles, we checked into the motel, and shortly thereafter Owen appeared in his used VW bus. He had chased after us, but couldn't quite catch us. He was embarrassed, and I was happy to see him.

On the way home, Bruce Kola insisted that Owen ride home with us on the bus, citing some obscure college regulation that team members have to travel with the team. Having grown up with VW buses, I "volunteered" to drive Owen's vehicle back, "enjoying" the solitude of the open road.

On October 30, after two convincing wins against LaVerne and Redlands, our athletic department was informed that once again we had been selected to participate in the big NCAA dance. The team, of course, remembered my bet with the squad and were eager to get at my hair. The shaving occurred in the locker room. This event produced more coverage in the local papers than we ever had received before!! And my wife Helen complimented me by stating: "I didn't know you had such a nice shaped head!"

We met Chapman College for the second time in the season at the play-offs in Southern California and lost to them again by the same 2-0 score. The loss did not diminish the success of the fall campaign, and the players received multiple awards at the banquet, highlighted by Isaac Jones' recognition as an Academic All-American and Phi Beta Kappa recipient. Jeff Spight, who was the scholar of the year, was also elected to Phi Beta Kappa.

1996 | 9-8-2

Front row, left to right: Matt Bower, Matt Bixby, Mark Villanueva, Elliott Loftis, Kainoa Lincoln, Justin Meade, David Skillman. **Middle row:** Greg Singer, Brook Birchard, Ben Turner, Cayman Seacrest, Dan Morlan (captain), Luke Helm, Andy Olds, Assistant Coach Kristian Sundborn. **Back row:** Owen Borg (captain), Coach Horst Richardson, Kyle Stock, B.J.Wooley, Jamie Stralka, Justin Sawyer, Kyle Polanski, Journey Herbeck, Matt Atencio (captain), Andreas Wolff, Corey Milner, Tucker Drury, Trainer Bruce Kola. **Not pictured:** Nick James.

1996

In 1996, the USA hosted the Olympic Games. Our Women's National Soccer Team won it all and earned the gold medal. The final game drew a huge crowd in Athens, Georgia, and the TV viewership was enormous. What a boost for the game!

Three of CC's All-Americans, Noah Epstein, Rob Lipp, and Arron Lujan, continued playing in the pros, and Chip Sagal and Andy Henderson played third division in Sweden. At home on campus, though, our playing fields were shut down for the summer for facility renovation and recovery, and for the first time in 16 years we were not able to offer a summer soccer camp for local children. Also noteworthy here is the fact that for the first time in CC athletic history, we had hired a professional athletic director, Marty Scarano, who replaced retiring Max Taylor.

Pre-season concluded with a thrilling raft trip down the Arkansas River, organized by junior Tucker Drury, who was a river guide. Two standout former players joined the staff as assistant coaches: Kristian Sundborn, our Swede, and Ezra Bayles, ex goalkeeper. International student Andreas Wolff from Germany, an outstanding defender, joined Andy Olds and freshman Matt Bower on the back line. Borg, Atencio, and Morlan led the team as tri-captains, and this trio brought lots of experience to the job. I felt good about the forthcoming season; expectations were high. And I had devised a challenging, in fact, tough schedule for the fall.

After a 4-0 victory in the opening game against Gustavus Adolphus from Minnesota, I thought we were on our way. The second contest, a narrow loss to East Coast powerhouse Babson College, was interrupted by a long lightning delay, the first one ever at home. I think those lightning bolts were somewhat of a foreshadowing of the unexpected events that dogged us most of the season, in particular frequent injuries to key players and an excessive accumulation of yellow cards, even two red ones in two successive games! Two vs. Washington University, and two vs. UCCS! Unbelievable!

After the loss to UCCS, I was quoted in *The Gazette*, commenting about the red cards: "That's the way this whole season has gone. I have been coaching for 31 years, and never have I seen anything like this year. We just haven't gotten a break!"

Matt Bower '99, a transfer from Vanderbilt, was one of the card culprits, having accumulated a number of them. When I asked him to submit an anecdote, he focused on a rather ironic incident, which occurred during our game against Washington University from St. Louis, a team and a coach he knew well:

> *Having grown up in St. Louis, I had also visited and applied to Washington University. My family was now living in Florida, but I had a connection with the Wash U coach, Ty Keough, from early on in my soccer days. The good news was that I was accepted by both schools and I needed to make a choice. After much deliberation, I decided to head west to take on a new challenge.*
>
> *I was fortunate to make the team at CC and have some playing time while meeting a great group of guys. All was well and the transition was easy. Then, checking out the schedule, I saw Wash U was heading out to play us.*
>
> *Well, my parents came in from Florida and my brother made the trip from Baltimore — neither journey particularly short. The Wash U game was on a Friday and, as usual, we had a second game on Sunday. Well, at least that was the idea. Somehow, through no fault of my own, I managed to pick up two yellow cards in the first half of the first game against Wash U. There was plenty of irony to this, yet my*

family failed to see any of it, or find any humor in the situation. Their weekend of coming to watch me play two games was cut drastically short.

I still feel the second card was not deserved by any stretch and that possibly a coach with the last name of Keough had something to do with it.

My frustration was evident. Not only about the cards, deserved or not, but also about the multiple injuries. Matt Bower, out with a shoulder injury. Andreas Wolff, out with a leg injury. Matt Atencio, out with a broken finger and then again with a bad ankle. Starting goalkeeper Kainoa Lincoln, out with a wrist fracture. Andy Olds out, Owen Borg out, Dan Morlan out, and finally Tucker Drury out with torn ankle ligaments. It got so bad that we had no goalkeeper ready to play as we were facing powerhouse Claremont at home.

Fortunately Bruce Kola did some magic on the above field players, but neither of the two keepers, Kainoa Lincoln nor Elliott Loftis, were cleared to play. Andy Olds '98 wrote about this dilemma and the creative solution:

One of the most memorable moments and games of that season was a big match-up with Claremont. With the regular goalies injured and unavailable for that game, we were all wondering what we were going to do. Horst didn't hesitate, looking over at a tall lanky freshman defender, saying "Polanski, you ever play keeper?" Once or twice, was the answer. That was good enough.

Kyle Polanski was 6'4", 185 pounds, from Minneapolis, and had big hands. Horst and a few others took Kyle down to the field the day before the big game, gave him a quick workout, a few punts, and he was ready to go. The next day we headed out to the field with some apprehension, but the contest turned out to be one of my favorite games of all times, including a highlight tackle by fill-in goalie Polanski on Claremont's best player on a breakaway. If we could have bottled that feeling of fighting through that game, pulling out the win, and dog-piling at the end, it would be priceless now.

Dan Morlan had four goals in that game on our way to an impressive 5-2 win. Thanks, Kyle, for stepping in under pressure!!!

As the years progressed, we traveled more and more by air. In the days when you could check your bags free of charge, the boys developed a betting game, which became a tradition of sorts. Everyone would throw in a dollar during the flight to bet on whose bag would come off the conveyor belt first, or last. An enterprising team member collected the bets during the flight, kept book on the participants, and then would recognize the winner once all the bags had been collected at our destination. It injected much levity into our travel schedule.

We ended the season 9-8-2, losing three of the last four games. Losses on the field always hurt for a little while. One loss that November hurt for a long time. Coach Emeritus Bill Boddington died on November 15, 1996. A two-time Olympian, a captain in the 10th Mountain Division, a warrior veteran of World War II, a successful businessman, a lover of sports and the arts, and my mentor. We had lost an officer and a gentleman.

1997

In the summer of 1997, Helen and I offered our last sports camp for Colorado Springs youths. At the end of the three one-week sessions, we gifted the CC summer soccer camp to the CC women's soccer staff. For Helen and me, the 18 years of camps left us with lots of good memories, but also with the recognition that we had little time in the summer to spend with family and friends.

As pre-season approached, a new structure was erected on Stewart Field. Finally, we were able to point with pride at a press box!! Although there had been quite a bit of opposition to such a structure on the west side of the field, mainly because of city right-of-way issues and campus design committee criticism regarding obstruction of the important western view, Marty Scarano, our new Athletic Director, decided to have it built anyway. That decision almost backfired as we discovered during construction that a major north-south sewer line was located right underneath the press box project.

I was pleased to have the expertise of alum Ezra Bayles back as assistant and goalkeeper coach. My daughter Stacia, a recent graduate of CC and a dance major, helped the team effort by providing stretching and warm-up exercises. Bruce Kola, the team trainer, was happy because the players seemed more flexible and less prone to injury.

Whitney Wheelock '01, a freshman goalie, who resided in Colorado Springs but attended boarding school back east, reminisces about pre-season:

> *The soccer program at CC formed much of my CC experience. I was coming home, born and raised in Colorado Springs, I felt literally at home when I arrived to campus for pre-season. Not only that, but I was fourth generation at CC and my*

stepfather also attended CC. Further, I was coming from four years at boarding school on the East Coast, which hardened me to hazing and the social wrangling of such environments. Needless to say I was not the usual freshman. I was a sarcastic, trouble making thorn in the side of the upperclassmen. But, for that I was put in 'my place' early.

The first day of two-a-day pre-season training sessions I spent a few minutes in the bushes below McGregor, vomiting, after our goalie coach Ezra Bayles pushed us, uh, quite hard.

A few days later was my second memorable run-in with "the establishment." The team had a ritual of going to a Sky Sox baseball game once the final roster was set. Sky Sox are a AAA baseball team, so going to a game was going to be a fun bonding experience for all of us who had made it through pre-season in one piece.

All the freshmen who made the team were ushered into Cayman Seacrest's minivan for the trip to the game. Cayman is from Nebraska, so my CU Buffalo-Nebraska Cornhusker jokes started to flow. I asked Cayman if the N on Cornhusker

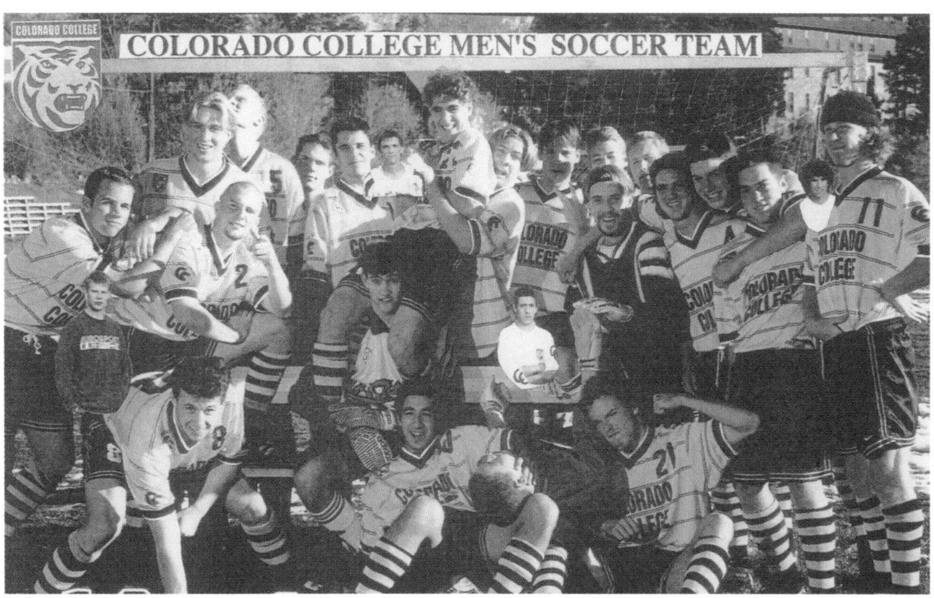

1997 | 13-8-0

Front row, left to right: Tucker Drury (captain), Fernando Regueiro, Kainoa Lincoln, Matt Bixby. **Middle row:** Matt Bower, Owen Borg, Dan Morlan, Whitney Wheelock, Greg Singer. **Back row:** Andy Hauschka, Andy Olds, Peter Strom, Brad Podolec, Journey Herbeck, Tyler Free, Jeff Slusarz, Zach Tillman, Elliott Loftis, Cayman Seacrest, David Skillman, Justin Meade (captain), Kyle Polanski, Thomas Staevski, Ben Turner, Kyle Stock.

> *helmets was really for "Nowledge?" I asked him what was the best thing coming out of Nebraska, not waiting for a response, I answered "the highway." I was making the other freshmen laugh but Cayman, not so much. Well, he did have a smirk on his face, knowing he would have his revenge.*
>
> *He and Matt Bower, the other strong-arm upperclassman there to make sure we all behaved, were less than amused. We were driving around in circles supposedly going to the Sky Sox game but I was quite aware that we were nowhere near the Sky Sox stadium. We arrived at an unknown house and Cayman and Matt said, "Okay, here we are." The others got out and looked around, wondering where in the world they were. We had driven for half an hour and as far as they knew, we were in some Colorado Springs suburb or neighboring town. We were all a bit like newborn kittens stumbling around together not knowing what to do. This was no baseball stadium, but then I looked up at the street signs and realized we were two blocks from CC campus and I said, "Hey guys, you hungry? Let's go to 7-11.'" And we all left to go to 7-11 instead of the soccer party. I was not the favorite of the upperclassmen. That turned into quite a long night for me.*

In 1997, senior Dan Morlan was selected to the All-America squad, making him the sixth CC player to receive that distinction. Dan, who hailed from Lake Oswego in Oregon, had become the second highest scorer in CC history with 65 goals, tied with Jacques Lemvo. During his freshman try-out in pre-season, I had cut him from the team. Today, that decision seems inexplicable. It was probably the worst coaching decision I ever made during my career at CC. There is no doubt in my mind that Dan would have become not only the highest scorer ever at CC, but also a two-time All-American, had he been able to play for four years. But then, the burning desire with which he joined the team in his sophomore year may have not burned as brightly had he been a returner.

Dan also was a superb German student of mine, distinguishing himself in classes and on the stage as the star in my German play production, *Biedermann und die Brandstifter*.

Halfway through the season, the Tigers had accumulated a meager 4-6 record. We had had high expectations at the outset of the fall campaign, but the soccer gods hadn't been on our side. Furthermore, our NCAA D-III independent status made it difficult to schedule comparable D-III opponents once the season got under way because most teams were then comfortably set in their respective conference competition.

My strategy to overcome this dilemma was to schedule occasional D-III tournaments at home, play against D-II opponents from the Rocky Mountain Athletic Conference

(RMAC), and travel to D-III opponents whose league schedule allowed for an open date to accommodate us. Chapman, Menlo College, Cal-Santa Cruz, and Nebraska Wesleyan were independents like us, so I tried every year to get them on our schedule.

A *Catalyst* article from late September describes the mid-season conundrum best: Staff writer Eric Martens titled his article with this headline: "ON FIRE! MEN'S SOCCER TEAM TURNS LOSING RECORD INTO WILD WINNING MAYHEM." Here is his article:

> *Few things in sports are as difficult to handle as a disappointing season. Often, when teams have high expectations heading into the year, they crumble when they fail to achieve early, leading to a disastrous year. The CC men's soccer team appeared to be heading for such a fate early this season, as they slumped to a 4-5 record with the next six games on the road. Fortunately, the team suddenly got hot, winning all six of its road games and breathing new life into its flickering play-off hopes.*
>
> *"We actually had high ambitions," said Coach Richardson, "but they were quickly thwarted because of silly mistakes and loss of confidence at key moments."*
>
> *The poor start made the squad's sudden improvement all the more unexpected. The coach attributes most of the success to lineup changes, but also thinks that the team finally found its rhythm. "The second half of the season we had a dramatic turnaround based on positional adjustments, specifically moving Matt Bower and David Skillman into midfield. We found the right chemistry."*
>
> *Another catalyst in the team's explosion was the combined leadership of seniors Tucker Drury and Justin Meade, who helped shepherd the team through its growing pains.*
>
> *"Both have lots of experience and are asserting themselves more and more as leaders," said Richardson who also cited Dan Morlan's impressive offense skills as a key factor in the team's resurgence. "Dan Morlan is on a torrid pace. He's got 20 goals this season, which, when coupled with the 38 he scored previously, puts him within reach of 2nd place on the all-time scorer's list."*
>
> *On any successful team, the goalkeeper plays a huge role. Junior Kai Lincoln has been stellar in goal and on coordinating the defense. Lincoln's abilities as goalie have been considerably augmented by the consistent play at sweeper of senior Andy Olds.*
>
> *As the play-offs approach, CC must rely on both its steady performers as well as those rare players who can ignite the entire team when called upon. Richardson believes he has such a player. "The man to watch, who's back from a nagging injury,*

> *is Fernando Requeiro, a foreign student from Mexico. He could pull a game out of the hat all by himself."*

To recapitulate, we beat six tough teams in succession: Cal-Santa Cruz and Claremont in California, Luther and Loras Colleges in Iowa, and Gustavus Adolphus and St. Olaf in Minnesota. Incredible! But an unexpected loss to Nebraska Wesleyan at Homecoming made the NCAA play-offs less likely.

In mid-October, *The Christian Science Monitor* published a picture of U.S. president Bill Clinton juggling a soccer ball while on a trip to Brazil. The weather in Rio de Janeiro was delightful, as was the smile on the president's face. The weather in Colorado, however, had turned sour as a savage snowstorm shut down the entire region. We were snowbound!

Snow drifts, several feet deep, covered CC's playing fields. Our important contest against Centre College of Kentucky started as the snow began to fall. Owen Borg '98 put us ahead with a wicked long-range shot. This snow game is firmly entrenched in Owen's memory:

> *One of my best goals ever. Left-footed pill from about 35 yards out on the right side of the field. I struck the ball and it didn't stop rising until it hit the net. Our whole team followed me as we superman-dove in the snow towards Allie in the stands. She may have been the only spectator. That was a good one.*

(Allie was Owen's girlfriend at the time. She is now his wife.)

But the referee called the game before the necessary 70-minute mark, which would have made it official. No soccer game ever had been called at CC because of snow.

We recovered from the snow, beat Metro and Mines, and our strength of schedule index was strong enough to sneak into the NCAA play-offs.

The NCAA D-III play-off pool in 1997 included an uneven number of teams, which necessitated a mid-week play-in game. Incredibly, we were granted a home berth against Chapman College from California, even though we had lost to them 1-0 in the second game of the season on a neutral site. I guess every now and then the soccer gods end up on your side!

The soccer gods continued to smile on us as the mid-week contest approached. The weather was terribly cold, and it had snowed the night before. Our physical plant crew had cleared the lines so that the field markings could be seen, but a couple of inches of snow covered the rest of the field. The game had to be played! Andy Hauschka '01, then a freshman and now a dentist, recalls the excitement:

> *The snowy play-off game against Chapman in 1997. My role didn't extend beyond providing ball boy services during the contest, but the week leading up to the game was different from any week I'd experienced in my playing career. The buzz around the facility and the focus of the team in practice was at a different level and I remember you (Horst) making all of us feel as though we were an integral part of the experience whether it was on the field during the game or as a part of the preparation for those who would play. And when the day dawned cold and snowy it just added to the electric atmosphere surrounding the game. Stewart Field could have been Old Trafford or the Camp Nou with the amount of electricity in the air that day. What a thrilling experience.*

The California team had scored in both halves to go ahead, but Owen Borg had equalized twice. At the end of regulation the score stood at 2-2. Despite the frigid weather, a sizable crowd of students and supporters had shown up, and they were exuberant when Dan Morlan scored in double overtime to win the game. Everyone celebrated by rolling and frolicking in the snow!

David Skillman '99, who had an assist on the winning goal, has a vivid recollection of the play leading up to the goal:

> *I'd like to recall the end of the play-off game we hosted against Chapman. It must have been November 1997, my junior year. It had snowed, one of a couple snow games we had during my time at CC. (In an earlier snow game — a September game, I think! — a player from Centre College confessed to me on the pitch that he had never even seen snow before.) The game against Chapman was hard fought and was a rematch from earlier in the year, which we had lost. Adding to the emotion was the memory that Chapman had also dumped us out of the NCAA Tournament in 1995 in California.*
>
> *The game was tied 2-2 during regulation, so two 15-minute halves were added. During the first half we were pinned back in our defensive third for most of the period, but just toward the end of that half, and against the run of play, Owen Borg stepped up and won the ball in front of the 18-yard box. I was playing in the midfield and had drifted to the left wing. I immediately broke forward, rushing downfield. Borg saw me and lofted a long cross toward me. I beat the Chapman defender to the ball and*

clumsily turned inside, sprinting toward the goal. But the ball was skidding too quickly on the snow, and as I crossed into their 18-yard box, other Chapman defenders were closing. I stretched and poked the ball towards the goal, and I could tell the keeper would have an easy save. I was crushed.

At that same moment, as he so often did that year, Danny Morlan swept across the goal, intercepted my rather lame shot, and pounded it into the goal. Elation! The Tigers met in a scrum on the sidelines with the fans. It was a tremendous feeling and a wonderful game!

The victory celebration was short, as we needed to prepare for the next round of the play-offs, just three days away, out in Southern California at California Lutheran University. Academic responsibilities needed to be addressed, travel itinerary and hotel accommodations had to be arranged, NCAA paperwork had to be finalized, and I had to find a substitute to teach my German class on Friday.

Our opponent was Macalester College, undefeated during their season and featuring a stud forward from Germany. Armin Heuberger, an athletic player with a deadly eye for the goal, had beaten us with a lone goal during the regular season, and he managed to do it again in our regional semi-final.

Given the fact that we started out the season 4-5, I was proud of the team to have come this far. *The Gazette* quoted me as saying: "If you had asked me in September if I thought we'd make the play-offs, I would have chuckled. I think the way we turned our season around is a credit to the fiber of this team."

Keeper Whitney Wheelock, after a first season of maturing at CC, summarized his feelings:

I do remember messing with the Juniors, but the Seniors were more mythical figures. I was pretty sure Owen Borg was in his 30s and wanted for some violent crime. Justin Meade, Tucker Drury, Dan Morlan and Andy Olds felt like my uncles from a distant branch of the family, always around at family gathering and road trips.

I remember walking away slowly and quietly after seeing Matt Bower take about a dozen Sudafed before a game because his ankles were in so much pain; yet he wanted to play. I realized then why he received the "Animal Award." I steered clear of him until sophomore year. Then I was very happy to have him in my back field defending me with blood, sweat and scars.

Being able to be part of the team my freshman year was a privilege and I still remember with a smile all these guys who became important aspects of my CC and life experience.

Throughout the years, the game of soccer has provided me with many friends, contacts and connections. Surely one of the most amazing, indeed improbable, relationships is the one I have with Hardy Fuchs. In the spring of 1998, *The Soccer Journal* devoted an article to the two of us, titled, "HARDY AND HORST: CLONED COACHES," and subtitled, "Coincidences abound for two who have almost identical lives."

Two college coaches, completely unrelated, have so many identical features, it borders on the supernatural. They are doppelganger, for all practical purposes. Hardy Fuchs and Horst Richardson are both German by birth. They both coach men's soccer at the NCAA D-III level, Hardy at Kalamazoo since 1971, and Horst at Colorado College since 1965. Neither has coached at any other college.

The principal appointment of each is as a professor of German and chair of the respective department. They were born in the same year, one month apart. They each have two children, an older son and a younger daughter. It gets more unbelievable. Horst, who took his stepfather's last name, was actually born Horst Fuchs, same last name, same initials.

In January, at the NSCAA Convention in Cincinnati, they shared the same room and the coincidences continued. It seems Hardy made a recruiting call from the hotel room and heard from his prospect that the only other college he was considering was Colorado College!

1998

In 1998, the World Cup was staged in France. Helen and I, as well as son Erik, attended. I returned full of soccer ideas and was highly motivated for the fall season. Ezra Bayles, by now a veteran assistant, and Ben Helm, volunteer assistant and brother to player Luke Helm, shared my enthusiasm. I even spent the last week of the summer putting up sheet rock in the new press box to dress up the stark structure.

Yet, many things went awry that fall, and we ended up with a meager 6-11-2 season, my first losing season in 25 years!!

1998 | 6-11-2

Front row, left to right: Greg Singer, Justin Livesay, Thomas Staevski, Austin McFeeley, Kainoa Lincoln (captain), Whitney Wheelock, Luke Helm (captain), David Skillman (captain), Jeremy Papuga. **Middle row:** Trainer Kevin Margarucci, David Fortney, Matt Bixby, Keith Connaghan-Jones, Jeff Slusarz, Ethan Anderson, Journey Herbeck, Matt Bower, Collin Eder, Brad Podolec, Trainer Jackie Rea. **Back row:** Assistant Coaches Ben Helm and Ezra Bayles, Tyler Free, Zach Tillman, Emmet Sherwood-Hill, Andy Hauschka, Scot Bilbro, Kyle Stock, Cayman Seacrest, Fernando Regueiro (captain), Coach Horst Richardson. **Not pictured:** Collin Frasier.

The opening game vs. Southern Colorado, Pueblo, set the tone: They scored their winning goal with 27 seconds left on the clock. In the second contest vs. Hope College of Ohio, we had to start the game without the referees, who arrived at half-time. Veteran player and key midfielder Matt Bower broke a bone in his heel and was out for much of the season. In the following match against Fredonia State of New York, we not only lost 3-1, but we also lost our dynamic forward Fernando Requeiro to a broken arm, and Luke Helm, a senior, who broke his leg. Three starting seniors out in a week!

It gets worse: Brad Podolec, an up-and-coming sophomore, fractured his cheekbone in the Wisconsin-Platteville game and had to go home to Hannover, New Hampshire, to have plastic surgery. Thomas Staevski, a talented defender from Bulgaria, had knee surgery during the first block break. Andy Hauschka, a giant on the field, broke his foot mid-season in his dormitory!!! Journey Herbeck and Kyle Stock suffered from strained knees and were infrequent participants on the field. And back-up keeper Emmet Sherwood-

Hill tore a ligament in his ankle. Our trainer Kevin Margarucci was kept busy that year! (Bruce Kola, regularly with men's soccer, was assigned to women's soccer that year.)

We were stingy on defense, but had trouble scoring. Kai Lincoln '99 recalls:

We have pretty solid defense, but it comes in waves, and they manage to score on us then. We are just having trouble finishing our chances, which is the main problem, because if we can't score, we can't win. There doesn't seem to be much difference in our performances at home and those on the road.

Another problem for us continues to be injuries, because we have lost seven starters just this season so far. That's tough to overcome.

We need to remain positive and support the younger players who have come in to give their all.

I had constructed an extremely difficult schedule and the players and I were excited to have quality teams as opponents. At the mid-way point of the season we faced Ohio Wesleyan and Trinity from Texas, perennial soccer powers. The Ohio team arrived to play and beat us, but Trinity was stuck at the Dallas Airport because of severe tornado disturbances. I picked them up at the Denver Airport at midnight with a CC bus nine hours after they were scheduled to play us. They played their scheduled contest against Ohio Wesleyan the following day, and our team watched, not being able to compete in the eagerly anticipated Trinity contest.

After 10 games, we were 0-8-2, and had not won a game. I was literally at the end of my rope, trying as best as I could to motivate the players. On a road trip to northern Minnesota at Concordia College in Moorhead, I resorted to voodoo! Tyler Free '01, a promising scorer in his sophomore year, remembers that incident:

The 1998 soccer season was my second year at Colorado College. I was a sophomore and not expected to get a lot of playing time when the season started. Unfortunately, the team suffered many injuries in the first few games and I was thrust into the starting lineup. The team had gotten off to a rocky start and we had not won a game yet by the time I was inserted into the lineup as the starting forward. My job was simple: Score goals.

However, things did not go as planned. We started the season 0-8-2 and I had not scored any goals and the pressure was mounting. I knew I was not fulfilling my responsibilities as a forward, and I started to have anxiety before games. I wasn't the only one not enjoying the season, and Horst could sense it. Everyone was playing with pressure and signs of nerves. We were not relaxed and we were not having fun.

So on that Minnesota road trip, in an effort to lighten the mood and help relieve the pressure, Horst took the entire team into the woods behind Concordia College to perform a seance. Coach had us collect firewood and he started a campfire! The team danced around the fire and chanted loudly in hopes of scaring away the evil soccer spirits.

We lost that game 2-0 and I had still not scored any goals in college. I felt like crying and must have shown the pain on my face. Horst pulled me aside and told me that he had faith in me and that when I did score my first college goal, it would be so beautiful that we all would feel like crying.

The next week was Homecoming and Horst's prediction came true. I scored my first goal against Ripon College and we won our first game of the season. I will never forget that first goal I scored and the ensuing celebrations that followed. I don't think anyone cried after I scored, but to me it was the most beautiful moment of my soccer career.

The two foreign students on the team, Fernando Regueiro from Mexico City and Thomas Staevski from Sophia, Bulgaria, had become bosom buddies. Fernando had come to my attention because of an uncle who lived in town. This relative promoted his soccer skills and assisted with his tuition. And Fernando was indeed an artist with the ball!

Thomas was recruited by my son Erik who, in 1995, had embarked on an international teaching career, his first job being one in Sophia. It just so happened that one of the secretaries at his private school was also the mother of Thomas. Thomas, an excellent student, received a foreign student scholarship and became a tenacious defender for us.

The two of them, when having a team meal on a road trip in a restaurant like The Olive Garden, would eat leisurely, enjoying a good conversation, having a good laugh, or sharing a good memory. They would still be nibbling away on their salads when the rest of the team, having wolfed down their main course, were already slurping ice cream cones. Fernando and Thomas had the ability to turn an average meal into a social event! A real lesson in cultural diversity!

Emily Varley, our motherly and longtime CC equipment manager, had her watchful eye on Fernando because he once suggested (in jest) that he would have to steal his uniform at the end of the season to take it back to Mexico as a souvenir. I guess the NCAA rules of turning in your player's equipment at the end of a season didn't make much sense to the big city boy from south of the border.

Game No. 17 pitted us against Wheaton College from Chicago, an old nemesis. We lost at home 3-0, and I thought that the season would end in disaster. But then something terrific happened. Just when you think you are down and out, with only a 5-10-2 record to your name, the joy and the ecstasy of a victory put a smile on everybody's face.

Our second to last game was against St. Olaf, then rated No. 6 in the country and No. 1 in the West. Obviously a team headed for the play-offs. In a thriller of a match on a chilly afternoon we beat the Olies 3-2 in overtime and everything was OK again. Matt Bixby scored the winning goal. He was exuberant and stated in a postgame interview: "This is almost as sweet as the play-offs. We have been getting better every game, and today we beat one of the best teams in the country!"

We still have a souvenir picture of our team piling on top of the goal scorer in a moment of pure bliss and satisfaction. Oh, how sweet it is!!

Unfortunately, the season didn't end on that victory. UCCS beat us 5-0 in the last match and their coach Eddy Dietz was overjoyed. For us, it was a nightmare finish.

One promising recruit, who didn't play at all that year, was Kevin Vicente '02. He had torn his ACL during the summer, and considered dropping sports entirely. Fortunately, Bruce Kola and I convinced him otherwise. Here is Kevin:

> *I am forever indebted to the Richardsons as they encouraged me to do physical therapy from my first day on campus. I had torn my ACL a few days before try-outs as a freshman and they had never seen me play in person. Regardless, they laid their faith in me to do the work to come back and play for CC. I quickly learned to tell other students that I was going to "physical therapy." When I told them I was going to "rehab," they assumed I was addicted to drugs. After a grueling 7 months under Bruce Kola doing rehab 6 days a week, I was able to play the remaining 3 years. Many, many thanks to Bruce and the Richardsons!*

Kevin, by the way, ended up being captain in his senior year.

My son, Erik, and I spent late May and early June 1999 in Kenya and Tanzania, hiking up Mt. Kilimanjaro and going on a safari. Back on campus in the summer, two major construction projects were under way. The Uintah bridge crossing Monument Creek was widened, and the Western Ridge student housing development commenced. Both projects necessitated heavy machinery; during pre-season and subsequent training sessions, it was sometimes difficult to shout loudly enough to communicate with the players on the field.

For me, having spent so many years on Stewart Field, the removal of the eastside trees, remnants of the fabled "jungle" of earlier days, and the relocation of the sorority houses lined up on the bluff, was a sad occasion, but campus-wide growth necessitated dormitory expansion.

1999

A new set of assistant coaches helped select and shape the team. Jerry McNeal, a standout player from crosstown rival UCCS, had graduated. He had distinguished himself working in our summer camps and was poised to bring his energy, talent, and enthusiasm to the Tiger lair. Bill Arbogast, an up-and-coming club coach, had lots of useful drills up his sleeve and Andy Olds, former captain and defensive strategist, volunteered his time. Ben Helm, the assistant from the year before, was off to play semi-pro soccer in Lüneburg in Northern Germany.

A most important addition to pre-season was soccer alum "Chip" Sagal. Since his graduation in philosophy 10 years ago, Chip had become a highly respected sports psychologist. He brought his cutting-edge insight and analytical skills to us in an attempt to heighten our achievement and performance. He created player and staff profiles, which allowed us to work together using our respective strengths. We learned a lot about our strengths and weaknesses; we were all prepared to engage in competition effectively.

1999 | 14-6-1

Front row, left to right: Jake Lambert, Sean McGinnis, Thomas Staevski, Austin McFeeley, Whitney Wheelock (captain), Jon Holdorf, Brian Svigel, Matt Bixby, Fernando Regueiro (captain), Assistant Coach Jerry McNeal. **Back row:** Assistant Coach Bill Arbogast, Trainer Bruce Kola, Kevin Vicente, Justin Livesay, Ethan Anderson, Tyler Free (captain), Zach Tillman, Gem McLaughlin, Collin Eder, Keith Connaghan-Jones, Martin Quinn, H.C. Martensen, Kyle Marshall, Scot Bilbro, Brad Podolec (captain), Coach Horst Richardson. **Not pictured:** Teo Benson, Kai Hilfiker, Justin Klein-Clark, Ben McVeigh, Greg Singer.

Head trainer Bruce Kola was back with us and my good German friend, Dr. Inge Schwoerer-Krais, a sports physician from the Black Forest, assisted while on sabbatical leave.

Almost half of the squad were first year or new players. A major challenge lay ahead, should we be successful in overcoming the disappointing season of the prior year. And, unlike a year ago, everyone was, and stayed healthy. Well, we experienced a magnificent 14-6-1 campaign, a superb turnaround from the year before.

Four players were selected to fulfill the responsibilities of captains: Tyler Free, Brad Podolec, Fernando Regueiro, and Whitney Wheelock. Tyler, an athletic and speedy forward; Brad, dynamic in the middle of the park; Fernando, totally unpredictable up front and exciting to watch; and Whitney steady in the nets set performance expectations for the rest of the squad, and the team responded. Noteworthy is the fact that we had only three seniors on the team, and nine freshmen. A good recruiting year, indeed.

Eight games into the season, including a road trip to Salt Lake City where a merging trucker on I-80 almost ran our bus off the road, our record stood at 6-1-1. That dangerous incident, merely a couple of seconds in length, is still on Thomas Staevski's '01 mind, as he recollects that scary moment:

> *I can't forget that bus trip we took to Utah at the beginning of the season. On the way back I believe it was, we were in the right lane on I-80 with a semi about to bypass us in the left lane, when suddenly a semi on the right shoulder in front of us decided to just merge into our lane. Without any panic and in his typical calm, steady fashion Nolan, our CC bus driver, just said, "Hold on, boys," as he maneuvered between the two semis and somehow fashioned enough space for us to safely get through and pass the truck that had merged in front of us.*
>
> *We all cheered in relief and gratitude, but those are the moments when you're thankful for sharp, alert and decisive people who know what they're doing, no matter what the job. Of course, I remember good times during our travels such as my first play-offs trip to California, but somehow that memory of Nolan just sticks with me.*

(Nolan, a Hawaiian native, still drives buses for CC today!)

And we had faced some stiff competition from Puget Sound, St. John's, St. Thomas, and Cal-Santa Cruz. In the MacMurray contest at home, after Fernando had scored the go-ahead goal in the second half, he was brutally elbowed in his face, resulting in an injury which required eight stitches. The MacMurray culprit was thrown out of the match with a red card. Three games later, Fernando picked up two yellow cards in one contest and was ejected. He did have a temper, as is the case with many a fine forward, but by the time he was a senior, he was a marked man and had to deal with much fouling.

Sean McGinnis, Brian Svigel, Martin Quinn, all newcomers, and Thomas Staevski displayed tenacious and effective play, as we shut out Cal-Santa Cruz. After a stupendous 3-0 win against a strong Linfield, Oregon, team, I singled out Brad Podolec for his standout performance in a post-game interview: "Brad really had an All-American performance in that game. He is a great leader, as well as a force on the field, and it is magnificent how well he controls the ball." Whitney Wheelock saved a penalty shot in that match early on when the contest could have gone either way.

We were blessed with camaraderie and good chemistry, morale was high, we had fun practicing and playing, and a good number of fans came out to support us. Furthermore, the three assistants were superb and deserved much credit for our success so far in the fall campaign.

Former captain Jay Engeln '74, in whose name the Animal Award is given every year at the banquet, had become principal of the local Palmer High School after a career as a biology teacher and soccer coach. Shortly before our Homecoming, it was announced that he had received the distinguished National Principal of the Year award. A well-deserved recognition for an outstanding educator and soccer coach.

Our independent NCAA D-III status necessitated extensive outreach to regional and interregional D-III teams. Southwestern University and Trinity University in the great state of Texas had excelled in D-III competition and I was able to include them in our schedule that year. Now Texas is a large state, and leaving campus mid-afternoon on a Thursday, flying to Dallas, driving four hours in two vans with all of Bruce Kola's medical gear to Georgetown, finding the La Quinta Inn before the days of GPS at 11 p.m., and then getting pizzas before lights out, required some organization. But we made it just fine. Even today, as I write this in 2018, I am amazed that with all the travel we did over time, we always "made it."

Texas was not an accommodating host on that trip. We lost both games by two goals within 27 hours, playing Trinity in San Antonio under the lights on Saturday on their postage-stamp-size field. I actually protested the outcome of the game because their small field, only 62 yards wide and slightly less than 110 yards long, did not adhere to NCAA minimum standards. Nothing came of it, of course, at least not then.

Thank goodness that once we were back in Dallas, the parents of freshman Gem McLaughlin treated the entire team to a delicious meal in their comfortable and spacious home. That hospitality helped considerably to lessen the disappointment of the two losses.

On the flight home I contemplated the weekend and decided that in spite of the two defeats, I needed to accentuate the positive. After all, we were down 3-0 to Trinity at the end of the first half and almost caught them in the second with two wonderful goals by freshmen Jake Lambert and Martin Quinn. Much more troubling was the fact that trainer Bruce Kola, captain Brad Podolec and I had agreed that Brad needed to stop playing because of nagging and recurring leg injuries. A major loss at the halfway point in the season. Greg Singer stepped in to replace Brad, and Brian Svigel was the back-up for a card-prone Fernando. We split on the road in Minnesota the following weekend and eagerly awaited the Homecoming weekend.

Just in time for Homecoming, Athletic Director Marty Scarano unveiled the newly decorated Athletic Hall of Champions in the El Pomar Sports Center, celebrating the storied past of CC Athletics. Banners highlighting the accomplishments of the various varsity teams were displayed from the ceiling, making the entry way to the sports center very festive.

After a successful start to the Homecoming games by beating Coe College on Friday, Helen served up a terrific breakfast for players and alums at our house on Saturday before the highly anticipated encounter against Pomona Pitzer College. And then it snowed, and the Pomona game that day had to be cancelled!

Pomona was committed to play a neutral game against Coe on Sunday, which we had to move south to Pueblo. Fortunately the visitors from California agreed to stay through Monday, by which time the snow had melted off Stewart Field. We were not kind to them in spite of their courtesy and beat them handily. Much of the credit for the victory goes to Zach Tillman and Kevin Vicente, who man-marked Pomona's two excellent forwards out of the game.

The Tigers dominated the last quarter of the season, posting a 5-1 record in the last six games. That was good enough to be selected to the NCAAs once again, an unprecedented sixth appearance for the decade of the '90s. Our record and strength of schedule, however, weren't good enough to warrant a home berth, and we had to travel to San Antonio to face Trinity University, a team which had beaten us in the regular season.

I was concerned to play on their mini-field; it definitely gave the home team an additional advantage. No sooner had the game started than one of their defenders, a terrific player who entered the pros after graduation, fired a shot from midfield which scored! And it was all downhill from there for us. We had no space and time to move the ball and were frustrated at every turn. Trinity was an excellent team, and has continued to be our nemesis for almost 20 years. The season, nevertheless, was an incredible turnaround from the year before, and the boys were justifiably proud of their success.

A frightening medical emergency hit freshman Martin Quinn shortly after the second semester commenced. One morning he couldn't get out of bed because of an apparent paralysis from his waist down. He was placed in the campus Boettcher Health Center for observation, and quickly moved to Penrose Hospital for emergency care. The attending physicians and specialists could not determine the cause of his ailment. They contacted a colleague at Johns Hopkins whose diagnosis led to the Epstein-Barr virus.

I was teaching in Germany at the time. Helen called me with the news of Martin's illness and I, in turn, contacted his parents who lived and worked in Germany. They immediately journeyed to Colorado Springs to be with their son. Their excellent health insurance made it possible to fly him home to Germany. On the airplane he occupied a row of seats, allowing him on his gurney to experience a fairly comfortable flight. His recovery took months.

A NEW MILLENNIUM

The Early 2000s

As we enter the 21st century in this narrative, a few comments about change and transition are in order.

By 2000, half of America was on the Internet using e-mail. Instead of writing and mailing recruiting letters, we now did so electronically. Communications speed, especially with academic records and reports, was enormously enhanced. Whereas I used to rely on distributing slick CC men's soccer brochures by the hundreds to high schools and clubs, I could now send these around *ad infinitum*. Everyone and everything could soon be instantaneously connected. The players, of course, were miles ahead of me in their ability to handle these new devices, but I adapted and surprised them occasionally with my cell phone calls and later with texting.

An annual concern was the size of the soccer budget. It seemed that it was never enough for our needs. Fortunately the Boddington/Richardson Soccer Endowment was growing, and the yield from this fund provided some budget flexibility.

Enhanced digital photography and video allowed for prospect screening and more targeted pre-season invitations. Thus, most prospects in pre-season could be expected to be legitimate contenders for the team. Helen, who had been taking game films for decades and started when movie cameras were supersized, marveled at the ever-diminishing weight and size of the new and technically complex cameras.

In the old days, I would seek a pay phone after a match and report the score and highlights to the local news media. Now, the sports information director (SID) of the opponent would shoot off an e-mail game report to our SID before the guys hit the post-game showers.

Newspaper coverage of our seasons diminished as game reports became available on our own CC website. The local paper only included a blurb with results and a few statistics. *The Catalyst*, depending on the inclination of its student editor, would give us occasional coverage. Our scrapbooks, which Helen conscientiously compiled every year, included more and more pictures from digital sources.

Finally, the CC athletic department and administration started to investigate more and more the possibility and feasibility of our D-III sports teams becoming affiliated with a D-III conference. The NCAA encouraged league affiliation over independent status.

The Tigers hadn't embarked on an international trip since Japan in 1992. Now that my administrative duties in the German Department had diminished (I was no longer chair), and after a successful season behind us, I proposed to the team at the 1999 banquet that we start planning and fundraising for a Europe trip.

Relying heavily on my friends in soccer and academia in Germany and Austria, I was able to organize a nine-game trip from North to South in central Europe. We left right after the conclusion of Block VIII and spent nearly three weeks abroad, visiting and playing in nine different cities. We traveled in vans from Hamburg in northern Germany to Innsbruck in Austria, and then through Liechtenstein and Switzerland to Freiburg in the Black Forest. From there we continued north along the Rhine River to Martin Quinn's hometown of Neunkirchen and concluded the tour in Aachen.

We absorbed a lot of culture, learned a few German phrases, ate a lot of bratwurst and sauerkraut and drank our fair share of beer, ended up with a formidable 4-1-4 record against university and club teams, and made lots of friends along the way. My German and Austrian friends outdid themselves in their hospitality, although Andy Hauschka speaks for most of the group when he remembers all the brats he ate:

> *As American visitors, our gracious hosts usually threw us a wonderful gathering after our games. Knowing we'd probably be hungry after our efforts on the field, they would go to great lengths to provide a wonderful spread of German food and drink. The only problem was that at nearly every stop this meant piles of bratwurst and other similar offerings, so that by the third or fourth stop most of us were craving something more familiar and/or plant based.*
>
> *Relief for me came in the form of one of my host family taking me to a cook out to their neighbor's house. These neighbors happened to be English and provided a wonderful spread of salad and vegetables in addition to what came off the grill. They all looked at me funny when I passed up the (again) bratwurst and instead loaded my plate with greens and several slices of tomato and cucumber. We all had a good laugh about it when I explained why I was craving salad.*

And Martin Quinn, against whose German club team we played in his hometown, had recovered well enough to travel with us for part of the journey.

It would require a separate book to detail all of our experiences. Here are a few highlights: Harbor tour in Hamburg; reception with the mayor of Lüneburg and Horst's endoscopy with Dr. Luedtke; playing against the University of Goettingen, whose captain was Andreas Wolff, formerly CC defender-of-the-year; city tour of Regensburg along the Danube, in Roman times a fortification guarding the empire; in Deggendorf visiting Burghausen, the longest castle complex ever built, where Brad Podolec almost got impaled on a torture seat (fortunately Claudia Stemmler, the beautiful CC German house head resident was there to rescue him); in Innsbruck, the Olympic ski jump and Tyler Free's 21st birthday, where he almost got arrested late at night trying to abscond with a bicycle; in Freiburg, a visit to an Adidas outlet where Horst ordered new team sweatsuits; and a hike up to the top of the Freiburg cathedral, 335 steps; in Neunkirchen and Cologne, a visit to a "Body World" corpse art exhibit, courtesy of the Quinn family, and a stint at a disco; in Bad Hersfeld, a trip to the former Iron Curtain separating the communist east from the capitalist west; and finally in Aachen, where once Charlemagne the Great ruled, where we stayed at the Karl Marx Hotel and where Andy Hauschka almost scored on an incredible diving header!

And finally, some concluding remarks by Kevin Vicente and Collin Eder:

> *Sausage, sausage, weiss beer, and soccer! Packed into three vans with Opa Horst leading the group on the Autobahn! Impressive visit to the Bayern Leverkusen stadium, courtesy of the Martin Quinn family. We remember the stern warnings of the field maintenance crew there NOT to step on the grass!! Playing in Germany we learned how important positional play and the mental aspects of the game are. Seems like we stress the physical side of the game too much back home.*

2000

The 2000 season celebrated fifty years of soccer at CC. Since its start in 1950 as a club program, it had experienced phenomenal growth. A half century of soccer in the U.S. west of the Mississippi was a big deal, and optimism and expectations abounded as we prepared for the season.

Helen, who every season and after every game posted a bulletin board outside of our locker room, made a special effort to highlight this special anniversary year. On Monday mornings while I was in class teaching German, Helen would spend an hour in the basement hallway of the gym updating records and posting motivational pictures. What a special and dedicated assistant to the program she was!!

Jerry McNeal and Bill Arbogast were back as assistant coaches and Steve Myers helped out as goalkeeper coach. Julie Soriero had become our new athletic director, the first woman in that position. She proved to be a fair and equitable supporter of D-I, D-III, and intramural sports on campus. And, at the Opening Convocation, CC soccer alum Jay Engeln '74 received an honorary Doctor of Science degree for his distinguished career in secondary education. I was proud to be able to present this degree to him in Shove Chapel. Brad Podolec had returned from injuries and was one of the tri-captains, being joined in that responsibility by Whitney Wheelock and Tyler Free.

2000 | 9-10-0

Front row, left to right: John Cropper, Tim Campbell, Jeff Stivers, Brian Svigel, Justin Livesay, Thomas Staevski, Martin Quinn, Maylon Wigton. **Middle row:** Assistant Coach Bill Arbogast, Paquito Lopez, Keith Connaghan-Jones, Joe Heinbecker, Jon Holdorf, Whitney Wheelock (captain), Ben McVeigh, Kevin Vicente, Collin Eder, H.C.Martensen, Coach Horst Richardson. **Back row:** Goalie Coach Steve Myers, Evan deSieyes, Gem McLaughlin, Zach Tillman, Jake Lambert, Sean McGinnis, Tracy Melzer, Tyler Free (captain), Brad Podolec (captain), Ethan Anderson, Assistant Coach Jerry McNeal, Head Trainer Bruce Kola. **Not pictured:** Justin Klein-Clark, Kyle Marshall, Austin McFeeley.

The Uintah bridge project had been completed, and the Western Ridge housing project had made considerable progress. Every day at practice we could witness the dormitories growing higher out of the ground of the construction site. And, to celebrate the completion of pre-season, Sean McGinnis's parents, both CC graduates and residing in town, treated us to a terrific BBQ at their home. We were all sitting on their wooden deck in the back of the house, eating and enjoying the natural setting, when the porch suddenly collapsed because of excessive weight! Fortunately, the old deck was only a couple of feet above the ground, so no one was harmed.

On the field, we experienced a rousing 3-0 start to the season and I became cautiously optimistic about our potential success in this anniversary year. We seemed to be off and running. Martin Quinn, our assist leader from the year before and recovered from his frightening illness, got some playing time as trainer Bruce Kola slowly integrated him back into competition. Bill Parent, a CC alum and an avid sports photographer, documented every game digitally so that we had hundreds of pictures to look at after each game! Bill continued to cover us for 14 more years! Many thanks to you, Bill!!

Before the crucial fourth game, a grudge match against crosstown rival UCCS, Helen had prepared breakfast for the team at our house, one of many meals she cooked for the team over the years. The good home-cooked food, of course, was the major attraction on those occasions. A close second attraction, however, was the inevitable visit of Portia, the Pig.

Portia, named after the heroine in Shakespeare's play, *The Merchant of Venice*, was a Vietnamese pot-bellied pig, which lived next door in a large semi-abandoned property. Portia would appear, snorting and belching, and would devour every piece of leftover food, which the guys would discard over the fence. When all the scraps had been devoured, Portia would grunt and waddle away on her teeny, tiny legs. It was not easy getting the attention of the team for a pre-game strategy session in our backyard while Portia was still in the vicinity.

We lost the UCCS game 1-0, but I was not dismayed. After all, UCCS had become a respectable D-II team over time, offering partial scholarships.

Then disaster struck on our first away trip to Oregon. The Pacific Northwest had become a solid recruiting region for us, so an away trip to Portland made sense. Our independent status required outreach in scheduling to all of the D-III conferences in our West region, the Northwest conference being one of four in our vast geographic area.

Two losses on the field were bad enough, but two season-ending injuries to two critical starters were much worse. Timmy Campbell broke his collarbone in the Linfield game and senior defender Zach Tillman tore his MCL in the same game. Whitney Wheelock in goal saved a PK, and maintains to this day that on Linfield's first and pivotal goal, the ball never crossed the goal line. Our early 3-0 start had evaporated, and after six matches our record stood at 3-3.

After a couple of seesaw games at home and a three-win road trip to Iowa, the Tigers looked forward to Homecoming weekend, where anniversary celebrations and a strong Haverford, Pennsylvania, squad awaited them. In front of a huge Homecoming crowd, including veteran alumni players and parents, we defeated the visitors 1-0 to the delight of the crowd. And it was a subtle goal off a rehearsed and spectacularly executed free kick. Podolec scored on a deceptive Martin Quinn feed.

Our squad member Jake Lambert '03, an intelligent and sly forward, also wrote for *The Catalyst.* He set the scene for the Homecoming anniversary in a well-written article, foreshadowing his future career in journalism:

> *I am sitting at the end of a long wooden bench in the locker room of the CC men's soccer team and there are 513 pairs of eyes looking down on me. They are those of the players who came before me. 50 years of soccer are alive in this locker room. 50 team pictures are mounted on its walls. The framing and hanging of pictures is one of several things that the men's soccer program is doing in an effort to recognize a half century of competition gone by. ...*
>
> *The next few days promise to be remarkable ones, filled with nostalgic sentiments and anticipation, as alumni representatives from many of those 50 years of soccer reminisce at a dinner Friday night, and stay to watch this year's team try to tally the 430th win for CC soccer as they match up against Haverford.*

The Friday night alumni dinner was indeed a special occasion. Saad Sahawneh, under whose leadership soccer began in 1950, came all the way from Jordan to attend with his wife Nahil. During the reunion dinner, tall tales abounded as the glory years came alive again. A highlight video of 50 years had been prepared by former captain and ex-Assistant Coach Erik Richardson, which entertained the crowd after dinner. Erik's unexpected appearance from Indonesia, where he was then employed as a teacher, brought tears to the eyes of his father, whose 35th year of coaching coincided with the reunion.

Saad Sahawneh's announcement of a major donation to the soccer program followed in the spirit of an alum fundraiser initiative. Appropriately, a team of 11 alums pledged major gifts to raise the soccer endowment considerably. Here is their initiative letter, dated August 30, 2000:

> *Dear Men's Soccer Alumni,*
>
> *The 50th anniversary of soccer at Colorado College will be celebrated in high style in conjunction with the fall 2000 Homecoming activities. During this special time, we encourage you to participate in the drive to increase the value of the Bill Boddington Endowment for Men's Soccer. Over time the fund has grown through the generous support of numerous donors to a market value of $280,715. It is our goal to increase that level to $500,000. At its current level, the endowment provides approximately $12,000 annually as an enhancement to the Men's soccer budget. The rising cost of travel, assistant coaching, visiting team guarantees, and many other program requirements have strained the men's soccer budget to the limit. With your generous participation, we will increase the value of the endowment to provide the coach and team with the funds necessary to maintain its stature as a first-class athletic program.*

The 11 alums who pledged their initial support to the fundraising effort were: David Smith '70, Dick Schulte '75, Brigham Olson '85, Thomas Clark '82, Evan Griswold '70, John Boddington '69, Jon Hulburd '81, Nick Binkley '68, Peter Fairchild '74, Steve Prough '66, and Tim Boddington '72.

The fund, now renamed The Boddington/Richardson Endowment for Men's Soccer, stands today at almost $1 million. This enormous amount could not have been raised without the generous support of former players and friends of the program.

The Homecoming and Anniversary activities concluded with a fun-filled alumni game. Two teams of alums with lots of subs chased the ball and each other with much enthusiasm and competitive spirit. Aside from Erik Richardson, who traveled all the way from Indonesia, other international travelers were: Saad Sahawneh from Jordan, Solomon Nkiwane and David Rutherford from England, Sergei Pokhilko from Ukraine, Gunther Karsten from Germany, and Duccio Faraoni from Italy. Unfortunately one injury occurred, as Peter Fairchild severed his Achilles tendon while sprinting down the field.

The concluding quarter of the season was disappointing, as we lost the last five games in a row. In the hunt for an attractive and challenging D-III schedule, I could not devise an annual schedule every year which would be advantageous to us. Instead, as independents, we had to adjust to the availability of other teams. Thus, four out of the last five games were played away, two in Minnesota, and two in California. We ended up with a 9-10-0 record. Of the 10 games lost, six losses came by one goal, and two defeats were in overtime.

Tyler Free, one of the captains, summed up the season best when he said: "We were all disappointed, I think, because we had high hopes for the year. But I had a good time this season, as did most of the players, and there were more positives than negatives."

Brad Podolec, one of the tri-captains, summed up his four years this way:

> *I have to tell you that both you and Helen helped to create incredibly fond memories of CC soccer. From the wonderful team meals at your home, to international trips through small towns in Bavaria, to intense training sessions in the CC swimming pool, and the dreaded pre-season gulley training runs, there are just so many positive memories and character building experiences. They have all played an important role in helping us CC soccer players, collectively, become better people.*
>
> *Looking back, the most life-changing memory would have to be when Coach Bill Scott at Andover went out of his way to introduce me to you, Horst, and to CC. When he shared with me that he was a former player of yours, and when he told me how much he enjoyed the program, I knew I had to come visit. I believe you had been coaching for 30+ years at the time. You were such a great host and that trip basically set my path for the next four years. They were a wonderful four years and the soccer program played a huge part in shaping my CC experience.*

For the 50th Anniversary, Helen and I had compiled an attractive booklet with pictures and highlights of the last 50 years. Each alum received this glossy 20-page brochure. This project, a trip down memory lane, motivated me to conduct further and more extensive research about the history of men's soccer.

Fortunately I had saved and filed away every roster and stat sheet beginning in 1965. In the early years, record keeping was more than a bit sketchy, but after lots of phone calls and e-mails to alums and opponents, a more comprehensive history emerged. With the help of Helen and Michelle, the computer-savvy secretary in the German office, this material could be easily stored and quickly updated. A stroke of good fortune was the appointment in 1999 of Dave Reed as Associate Sports Information Director. He became invaluable to our history efforts and assisted in organizing and storing all this information for instant recall on our men's soccer page. Dave also became a tireless promoter of D-III sports at CC. As a consequence, more and more of our players became recognized with deserved regional and national awards.

2001

The 2001 season commenced with a festive social event in our backyard. Helen and I had invited both the men's and the women's soccer team for a BBQ. My former assistant, Greg Ryan, had done a terrific job with our women's program and he and his family were our good friends. (I still regret that his son, Ben, elected not to attend CC. What a talent!) Players on both teams supported each others' efforts with genuine enthusiasm.

Greg and I had received top accolades from the NSCAA at the coaches convention and I had been to Jordan on an invitation from the founder of CC soccer, Saad Sahawneh. We were eager to begin the new season. A new full-time assistant, Scott Lamphear, an All-American from D-I champion Wisconsin, had joined the Tiger effort and Jason Christian,

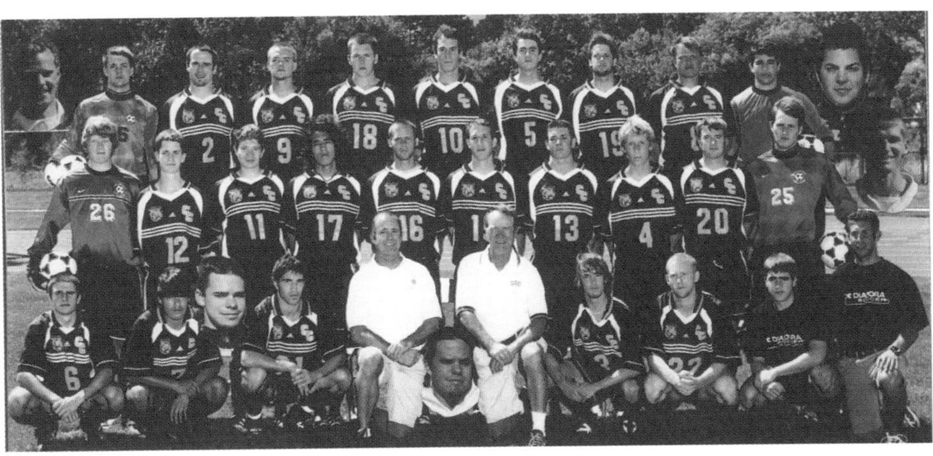

2001 | 9-6-3
Front row, left to right: Jack Simons, Alex Aguirre, Greg Miller, Nick Zinn, Trainer Richard Quincy, Clayton Miller, Coach Horst Richardson, Tim Campbell, Martin Quinn, Chris Aubin, Assistant Coach Adrian Marrero. **Middle row:** Patrick Gannon, Nathan Hamilton, Guenther Dendl, Paquito Lopez, Mike Gossen, Tim Ambruso, H.C. Martensen, John Cropper, Rob Backlund, Jon Holdorf, Assistant Coach Scott Lamphear. **Back row:** Goalie Coach Jason Christian, Ben McVeigh, Kevin Vicente (captain), Collin Eder (captain), Ethan Anderson, Sean McGinnis, Jake Lambert, Gem McLaughlin, Keith Connaghan-Jones, Zac Rubin, Greg Lestikow.

as well as Adrian Marrero, volunteered. On top of that, "Chip" Sagal, former player and now sports psychologist, spent a couple of days with us in pre-season preparation to "get into the players' heads." Our two co-captains, both back from a semester abroad, were Collin Eder and Kevin Vicente. And Richard Quincy took over the trainer position for Bruce Kola that year.

Among the freshmen players was a set of identical twins, Greg and Clayton Miller. I could not tell them apart, and I was not the only one in that predicament. Greg Miller '05 reflects on my frequent consternation when trying to identify them:

> *Having to do with my Twin-ness, many people had a hard time telling Clayton and me apart. That was especially the case for Coach Horst. I think he decided early on that it wasn't worth trying to keep up with our changing facial hair, haircuts, style of play, or personality. He figured it would just be easier to call us by "Miller 6" or "Miller 8" (our respective numbers on our uniforms), and know which number corresponded with which position. I have had so many people over the years tell me: "You two just need to wear name tags to make this easy on everyone." And lucky for Horst, our name tags were our numbers on our uniforms. I don't think he ever confused us, unless of course we were off the field without our "name tags."*

Nick Zinn '05, a promising talent from Michigan, came into pre-season with solid recommendations that year. He remembers the tense early days of his arrival and the subsequent weeks of the fall season:

> *I was an only child of two extremely involved parents. The day my father dropped me off at CC, he drove all 22 hours back to Michigan, sobbing. Horst did not know it, but it was a transformative event in my parents' life and marriage, as much as it was in my life.*
>
> *While I was scared and lacking in confidence, I put up my best face and tried as hard as I could to make the team. A few days went by and my dad had not heard from me (pre-cell/wi-fi days?!) when he received a call, without prompt, from Coach, letting him know that I scored that day at try-outs and that I was looking good. My mother and father sat down on our living room sofa and cried, because they knew I was in the hands of a great man and a great tradition.*
>
> *A few months later, when they came out for Homecoming, they saw not only great soccer, but great friendship as well. We played hard, we laughed all the time, and we*

genuinely loved each other. When I was a freshman, my parents went to the soccer house for the Homecoming after-party, and they immediately sensed something so unique and so fun that they never inquired again about how I was doing. They knew, in one weekend and from one phone call, that I had a new, completely interconnected family to take me into the next chapter of my life.

The season started with an ominous event. A freak rainstorm dumped an inordinate amount of water in a short period of time on Colorado Springs. The newly constructed dormitories on the Western Ridge had been completed, but landscaping was missing. A great amount of sand and gravel washed down onto Stewart Field, making the southeast side of the field unplayable. Therefore, our first game of the 2001 campaign had to be moved south of town to the Fountain Valley School.

Our opponent was the University of Redlands, a Southern California powerhouse. We lost the match 2-1 on a free kick while I was trying to make a substitution, bringing in Gunther Dendl, a foreign student from Germany. Even though the referee had signaled for the substitute to come onto the field, he didn't stop the game for us to realign ourselves. The opposition took advantage of what should have been a stoppage of play.

Back on Stewart Field for our second game, against the eventual D-III champion Richard Stockton College from New Jersey, we remained very competitive in a close 1-0 loss. Noteworthy for that opening weekend, however, is the fact that CC had hosted a mini tournament with teams from both the East and West Coasts, a first for the college. A win and a loss, both one-goal games followed, and we were confident that our first road trip, west to Walla Walla, Washington, would produce two victories.

AND THEN 9/11 HAPPENED and our world suddenly changed!

September 11th, 2001 was a Tuesday. By Thursday afternoon we would have been in the air on our way to Portland, Oregon, and then on to Whitman College in eastern Washington with vans. All flights in the country were grounded. I tried to rearrange the weekend games for Salt Lake City, but the logistics were overwhelming. The coaches tentatively agreed to reschedule the games for the end of the season, but that didn't work out either.

By the end of Block 1, flights had resumed and the team flew to Minneapolis for two games against Minnesota Intercollegiate Athletic Conference opponents. Needless to say, there were some anxious faces as we boarded the plane. Half an hour before landing, no one on the plane was allowed to get up or move around. The Twin City airport was like a ghost town; hardly anyone could be seen in the arrival halls.

We recorded a 1-1-1 record in Minnesota, had good CC fan support at our matches, and enjoyed a wonderful reception and meal at the home of Jamie and Jean Peters, Jamie being a soccer alum from the '70s and a physician at the University of Minnesota health center.

At Homecoming the resurgent Tigers scored 12 goals in two games and earned a winning record for the first time that season. New on Stewart Field was the Victory Bell, which was dedicated at Homecoming Weekend. If victorious at a home game, the team would henceforth ring the bell, one ring cumulatively for every victory during the season. The tradition which started then is still with us today.

By mid-October, the team was on a hot streak. For the first time since its inception, we won the Boddington Memorial Tournament. The win against MacMurray College proved to be my 400th career victory, (the team doused me with a cooler of Gatorade) and I kissed Martin Quinn's bald head for being assist king!

After an away do-or-die win to Chapman University in California, the squad knew it had an outside chance for an NCAA tournament berth. And indeed, the NCAA selection committee chose the Tigers! But the boys had to pack their bags for Spokane, Washington, to battle against the Northwest champion Whitworth College, a team we had intended to play before the 9/11 attack caused cancellation. In spite of exuberant play in the second half, and a swerving free kick by Martin Quinn, which the opponent's goalkeeper miraculously saved, we had to settle for a 1-0 loss.

Once at the airport, about to board the flight home, a curious incident occurred. Members of the local police force apprehended our trainer Richard Quincy and Assistant Coach Adrian Marrero. Apparently an incident at our motel produced a case of mistaken identity, and the police officers wanted to make certain that members of our team weren't the culprits in question!! And indeed we weren't and all of us proceeded to board.

Assistant Coach Scott Lamphear reminds me that I had made a deal with the team about offering my head for a shave if we made the tournament. Here is what he recollects:

> *2001 was my first experience coaching at the collegiate level ... and what a season it was. Rejoining the team in September, sporting a 1-3 record, I got to see a bunch of young men deal with adversity and come out on top. With major victories over Macalaster, Chapman, UW-Platteville and others, including Horst's 400th victory, the team was selected to the NCAA Tournament.*

What many of you may not know is Horst made an offer to the team in those early stages of the season that, if they rebound from the rocky start and advance in the NCAA Tournament, they could shave his head.

When all was said and done, Horst stood by his word. He was ready to sit in the locker room ready for a shave — Martin Quinn and Steve Heitkamp style, both of whom were bald. The shave, however, never happened. The team wasn't finished with what they started. A win over a very disciplined Whitworth wasn't in the cards, but every one of those Tigers left knowing they gave everything they had for each other. Horst left with his hair, and those players left with great memories and friends for life. It was an honor to have played a small part in the success and adventures of the 2001 Tiger men's soccer team. Thanks, boys and thanks, Horst.

A season during which our country had experienced a horrendous and shocking terrorist attack had come to an end. Four terrific seniors were about to graduate: Captains Collin Eder and Kevin Vicente, Keith Connaghan-Jones, and Ethan Anderson. Thanks for your commitment and dedication!!

And three weddings of CC soccer folks were celebrated that year: former assistant Jerry McNeal to Michelle, ex-captain and standout player Jon Whitfield to Hilary, and razzle-dazzle trickster Fernando Regueiro to CC coed Dakota.

2002

The 2002 season was a banner year, with a 15-6 record and a trip to the NCAAs. 2002 was a World Cup year as well, with Helen and me watching the action in the summer in Kuala Lumpur, Malaysia, where our son Erik '92 was teaching and coaching.

In pre-season at home, we were able to schedule a match against the U.S. Para-Olympic team on the small Autry intramural field. It was a fun affair. And the fun continued with a second annual men's and women's social at our home, a BBQ with lots of food prepared by Helen and Coach Ryan's wife, Janet.

Scott Lamphear and Jason Christian continued as assistant coaches, Bruce Kola returned as trainer, and Martin Quinn and Sean McGinnis were the captains. CC President Dick Celeste and his wife, Jacqueline, became super soccer fans, supporting both the men's and women's efforts at our respective home games. Pre-season ended with a trip to Denver to

2002 | 15-6-0

Front row, left to right: Tim Campbell, Jon Holdorf, Patrick Gannon, Miller Resor, James Kerrigan, Nate Hamilton. **Second row:** Coach Horst Richardson, Clayton Miller, Alex Aguirre, John Cropper, Nick Zinn, Martin Quinn (captain), Greg Miller, Abdou N'Dir, Equipment Manager Julie Sheely. **Third row:** Tim Ambruso, Brian Svigel, Stephen Heitkamp, H.C. Martensen, Pat McGinnis, Rob Backlund, Paquito Lopez. **Back row:** Assistant Coach Scott Lamphear, Gem McLaughlin, Brian Tafel, Sean McGinnis (captain), Kyle Marshall, Mitch Bacon, Jake Lambert, Mike Gossen, Goalie Coach Jason Christian. **Top right:** Andrew Henscheid, Dash Feierabend, Trainer Bruce Kola, Student Trainer Corinne Bianca.

---

watch a professional soccer match between the Colorado Rapids and San Jose. It was a real thriller, the home team winning 3-0.

In late August before our first game, a number of alums and I had gathered in Southern California to celebrate Brigham Olson's 40th birthday. We presented Brigham, our stellar captain from the mid '80s, with a CC soccer jersey and a plaque, which announced his induction into the CC Athletic Hall of Fame. Brigham was dying of a brain tumor. In attendance at this sad and difficult event were his teammates Pat Shea, Brad Wolf, Sam Schwartz, Charlie Stanzione, Tom Hyland, Scott Evans, Dickie Hertel, Jamie Hull, and Tom MacKenzie. Many a tear was shed at this emotional and joyful farewell.

A major recruiting coup for that year was the acquisition of Patrick McGinnis. Patrick was Sean McGinnis's younger brother, and even though admitted to CC after his high school graduation, he had decided to attend Dartmouth College. The two brothers were both graduates of Air Academy High School in Colorado Springs and known to us as excellent students and outstanding soccer players. Patrick, in fact, was the valedictorian at his high school. He decided to transfer back to his hometown because at D-I Dartmouth he wasn't allowed the creative freedom which was the basis of his flourish on the field.

Now we had two sets of brothers on the team, the Miller twins and the McGinnis brothers. By the way, the women's team also had a set of twins, Sarah and Kate Chadwick, and two sisters, Brittany and Stevie Kernan, relatives to us on Helen's side of the family.

As Associate Sports Information Director, Dave Reed had been assigned to men's soccer, promoting our team. Soon, more and more of our players received well-deserved recognitions. I take credit for turning Dave into a soccer junkie! Dave recollects his conversion from football to futbol:

> *When I first arrived at Colorado College, it was a month into the soccer season and I didn't have much to do with the men's soccer program. In fact, I was not much of a soccer fan since high schools in Ohio the size of mine did not have soccer teams. Everyone played football, not futbol. Krysta Nygard, who was a student, was the soccer contact for my first three years. But every now and then, especially on Monday mornings after a road trip, I would get a call that always began 'Dave, this is Horst.' It usually was to fix incorrect scoring plays, and it was my job to explain that I could not do that without the approval of the home SID.*
>
> *After Nygard graduated, I took over as the soccer contact and have become a fan of the game, but more importantly, a fan of Horst and Helen. I was welcomed into the CC soccer family, and since then have spent many days and nights at games, banquets and senior brunches, as well as dinners at the Edelweiss Restaurant. I now enthusiastically watch international soccer, especially the World Cup, European Championship and the Bundesliga, rooting for Germany and Bayern Munich!*

Our opening game was a doozie, a 2-1 win over Gustavus Adolphus. It was an expensive victory, though. The assigned referee, who traveled all the way from Cheyenne, Wyoming, to call the game, turned out to be most card-happy. Numerous yellow cards were issued, and we received two red cards! Never before had a Tiger team been docked with two red cards in one game.

For the last 35 minutes, we played with two men down. The game was tied at 1-1 at that point. Jake Lambert came off the bench with seven minutes left in the game and snuck in the winning goal on an assist from Pat McGinnis. And Jon Holdorf was a solid wall in goal!

We were eager to ring the victory bell, but as it turned out, the clapper was missing! The boys improvised and struck the bell with a metal folding chair.

Jake Lambert scored again in our second contest. He had been injured by an opponent's teeth, an injury which required two stitches. Unperturbed, he reentered the game to tally a goal. It was, however, our only goal in that match against Puget Sound, which we lost 1-2.

Alex Aguirre, our tireless and powerful midfielder, had begun a pre-game team huddle tradition with an awesome cheer. Years later, his teammate Clayton Miller '05, one of the Miller twins, wrote to me about the Aguirre huddle:

> *My favorite memory goes back to Alex Aguirre (aka Vato) and his pre-game huddle before kickoff. He did this for every single game for 4 years. I have no idea where or how he came up with it, but it still gives me chills. And to this day, I can still remember the chant word for word: "Do you dare enter the heart of the devil's den? By God have mercy on your soul, for we shall not. In this bloodied battle of rivalry and war, you dare challenge us? The immortal, the bloodthirsty Tigers? I think not my friend. So I have one question to ask you — how do you feel tonight!?!?!?!?!?! 1, 2, 3 TIGERS!!!!!!*

Zac Rubin, a goalkeeper on the team and *Catalyst* staff writer, wrote an optimistic season outlook after two victories during the second weekend of the early campaign. Encouraged by 11 goals scored in the first four games, a much better statistic than the year before, Zac lauded captain Sean McGinnis for his hat trick against Whitman College, and praised Sean's younger brother Patrick for his key assists.

The "hot start," which Zac had documented in his article, became lukewarm during the third weekend and a split on the road in Minnesota. After double victories at home a week later, a bus trip to Iowa awaited us for the first block break. Grinnell College, always a tough opponent at home, was our first challenge. The contest proved to be a physical one, but Brian Tafel, a freshman from Longmont, Colorado, who would feature prominently in future CC contests and an athlete who didn't shy away from contact, tallied the lone goal for us to seal the win. Tafel and Gem McLaughlin became a formidable defensive duo for us.

In the second contest in the Hawkeye State, even though John Cropper broke his nose, the Tigers produced another win against Buena Vista College in the heartland town of Storm Lake.

Strange as it seems, our next match against crosstown rival UCCS produced another four red cards, two for them and two for us. For our tireless and aggressive midfielder Alex Aguirre, it was his second red card for the season! Even though our two cards came late in the game and UCCS played shorthanded for a longer period of time, the Tigers couldn't produce a win in front of a huge Homecoming crowd comfortably seated on the sloping lawn in front of the brand new Western Ridge dormitories.

A foreign student from Senegal, Abdou N'Dir, scored two goals in our next match against St. Olaf to help us achieve a well-deserved win. Abdou's story is a unique one, and deserves retelling.

Abdou grew up in Gueoul, a village in rural Senegal, where he enjoyed playing soccer and dancing. A car had hit him when he was seven years old, and his right leg was badly broken and infected. That's when Judith Beggs Pierson, a lawyer from Denver and Peace Corps volunteer, found him. Judy provided antibiotics, and Abdou recovered and returned to his favorite activities, soccer and dance.

Judy recognized his talents as a dancer and brought this boy to the attention of the Cleo Parker Robinson Dance Company in Denver. And, indeed, Abdou came to the U.S. on a dance scholarship and thrived with the company. Shy, humble, and graceful, he had hidden energies and a big smile, which endeared him to audiences.

His soccer talents didn't go unnoticed either. We recruited him at CC and he was admitted with foreign student scholarship support. Once he was enrolled, the editor of *Dance Magazine* contacted me to do a story about Abdou. I am quoted in the article: "Abdou floats across the field. He is a most graceful and creative player with perplexing moves that throw the other team off. My first impression was that he was meek and withdrawn, but there was always his smile. He was just waiting for his chance." And when he received that chance, he ran with it and scored two goals in one game!

Junior Tim Campbell and sophomore Nate Hamilton experienced formidable development and helped the team achieve a respectable 13-4 record as we approached the end of the season. I sensed NCAA play-off potential, and challenged the squad to "keep the momentum going."

And then it snowed and our opponent was from snow country USA, Potsdam, upstate New York. It was a miserable day, frigid temperatures; the few spectators who showed up were huddled in the press box. We had borrowed parkas from the football team to keep the guys on the bench warm! The McGinnis brothers ruled on the field that day, hardly ever losing their footing on the slippery surface. Pat McGinnis '05 writes about that game with obvious relish and satisfaction:

> *I remember, during my sophomore year, we had a mid-week game near the end of the season. We fielded a strong team that year, including a powerful senior tier of leaders. As seemed typical, we also sported a core group of players who were totally obsessed with the sport of soccer!*
>
> *Anyway, I woke up one day, excited for our match later that afternoon. On my way to class, I enjoyed passing above the field. Somehow, on match days that season, the mowers managed to create contrasting patterns around the center-circle and penalty boxes, a la the Champions League! Sitting my way through a history lecture on this balmy morning, I peered out of the slender window, only to see something tiny and white land on the sill. Soon, a few more ...*
>
> *Oh, No! It can't be snowing! My mind raced. As most of us shortsighted sports fans and athletes will relate, a delayed training, practice, or scrimmage can threaten our whole sense of balance and life purpose! Needless to say, the prospect of a cancellation on a big game day amounts to nothing less than global devastation. So, after class I made my way dormwards through the blustery onslaught of the cold front, my insides hot with consternation.*
>
> *By this point, I felt reluctant to even glance at the field again, either from spite at the uncooperative weather or maybe just from sheer disbelief at such a heavy storm so early in the fall season. But for some reason I was pulled to take a peek anyway, perhaps just to seal my deplorable fate quickly that day with the sight of an unplayable and snow-covered pitch.*
>
> *Consider my surprise and curiosity when, overlooking the field, I could see a number of dark specks moving back and forth across the wintry expanse. Looking closer, I could discern what appeared like shovels or snow-blowers and faint patches of green temporarily re-appearing in the distance.*
>
> *Wait, I thought, that can't be the coaches, can it? ... And their wives? And the whole equipment staff?! And their wives?!!! Clearing the field by hand!!! I couldn't believe it! This was unheard of!*
>
> *In any case, we were going to be saved. From utter disappointment to complete enthrallment in a matter of seconds! Around the same time, other teammates were*

making a similar discovery. The word and excitement spread like wildfire. Game on!!! No joke, no exaggeration ...

Our team gathered a few hours later, as scheduled. I don't think any of us even remembered who we were going to play against. We seldom tried to. It didn't matter. That's how fired up we were, totally wired by the chance, by this unexpected gift of being able to even play on that day.

Well, we players felt so amped with adrenaline and the cold, and the staff so exhausted from uncovering the entire field, that Horst barely even gave a pre-game talk. No strategy, no details. Just something like: "If you guys can play even a fraction as hard as we just shoveled ..."

Clearly, we needed no extra incentive. I can only attempt to capture what happened next: Utter annihilation of the opponent! ... a slew of extra-special team-worked goals in honor of those who made it possible ... an abiding sense of gratitude ... and I can still see the equipment staff on the snow-banked end lines, throwing fists to the heavens in celebration of that score!!! Thank you! And Go Tigers!

The soccer gods were on our side as we finished the season with a crucial win over Chapman College, a regional independent affiliate like CC. Once again we achieved an NCAA bid as an independent team, i.e., not affiliated with a conference.

In Redlands, California, we lost to a superior Trinity University squad, even though Pat McGinnis had put us ahead in the first 10 minutes. A second goal, somewhat controversial, was disallowed. We never recovered from that disappointment and the momentum shifted the other way. But the boys had the satisfaction of traveling to the Sunny Southland on an NCAA nickel, and, as the guys were fond of saying, "You make the NCAAs and you get to sleep one to a bed on a road trip!"

Martin Quinn had served as a student representative from CC to the NCAA. Our then-Athletic Director, Julie Soriero, had recommended him to the NCAA for the National Student Athlete Advisory Committee, a group of 24 D-III students from around the entire country, and Martin was selected. What an honor!!

At the awards banquet we celebrated our season's achievement and enjoyed watching the highlights on video. Every year these season recaps became more elaborate, creative, and entertaining, delighting players and staff, and motivating the team to perform to maximum potential in the next campaign.

Bill Parent, CC alum and volunteer sports photographer for the soccer team, once again had provided us with innumerable exciting action shots. Helen selected a number of these for award winners. She framed the picture and labeled it pertinent to the award. These photos became meaningful mementos to award winners and graduates.

2003

In 2003, we embarked on another international trip, this time to Costa Rica. We booked a two-week soccer tour through "Costa Rica Soccer Tours" and added a week of volunteer service. We traveled the country in a comfortable bus from Caribbean to Pacific coasts, went rafting and zip-lining, saw lava flows on the volcano, enjoyed jungle settings and wildlife, frolicked on beaches, devoured excellent meals, and, of course, played a lot of soccer.

The Ticos, with their laid-back *pura vida* approach to life, are passionate about their soccer, and provided strenuous competition. At an orphanage we performed an afternoon

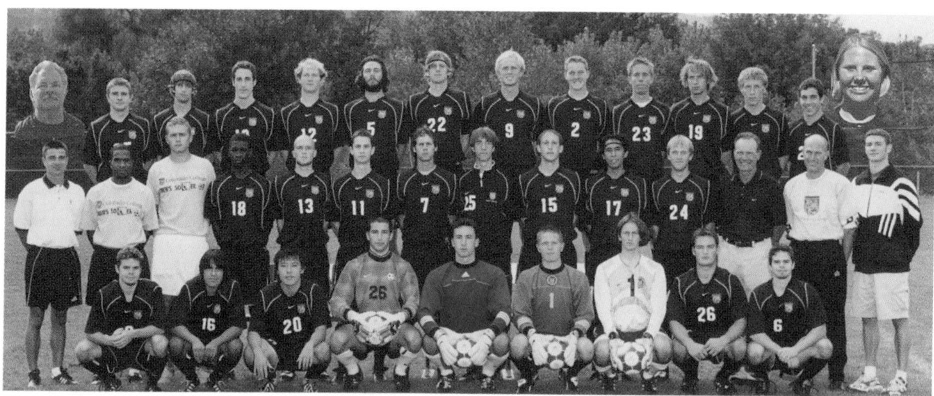

2003 | 11-6-3

Front row, left to right: Greg Miller, Alex Aguirre, Yuki Miyazaki, Zac Rubin, James Kerrigan, Pat Gannon, Jamie McCulloch, Beale Tejada, Clayton Miller. **Middle row:** Assistant Coaches Shawn Reeder and Terrance Gunnells, Nick Evans, Abdou N'Dir, Steve Heitkamp, Nate Hamilton, Mike Gossen, Logan Campbell, Tim Ambruso, Paquito Lopez, Patrick Jackson, Coach Horst Richardson, Assistant Coaches Timm Nikolajsen, H.C. Martensen. **Back row:** Trainer Bruce Kola, Jack Simons, Tim Campbell (captain), Pat McGinnis, Noah Drever, Mitch Bacon, Andrew Henscheid, Robert Brennecke, Brian Tafel, Scott Anderson, Cody McGrath, John Cropper, Nick Zinn, Student Trainer Shelby Ransdell.

of community service, engaging with elementary students; we played games with the kids, taught them some English, and learned a lot of Spanish.

The real story in Costa Rica, though, was our volunteer project in the Manuel Antonio National Park, a gorgeous seaside setting on the Pacific coast. The plan was to occupy a bunkhouse in the park, hire a cook, and build a couple of trails under the supervision of a park ranger. To get into the park, we had to wade through a swollen stream with our luggage lifted high above our heads. After this adventurous introduction to the park, we headed for the bunkhouse and after a cursory inspection were horrified! It had apparently been abandoned for many months and was marginally inhabitable with filth, spider webs, and hornet nests everywhere.

Helen, the only female amongst us, new Assistant Coach Timm Nikolajsen, a Dane with a booming voice, and I organized a clean-up in the tropical heat of the early afternoon. The guys, knowing that we had to make this place our home for the next five days, helped with muted enthusiasm and soon the bunks were ready, the outside shower worked, and the kitchen area was sanitized. All this activity did not disturb a sloth above us in a large tree who hardly moved.

The cook provided us with the same meals every day: rice, beans, and chicken. Timm and entrepreneur Zac Rubin found a back entrance to the park, which made a trip to the village possible; they returned with several cases of beer, making the evening meals much more enjoyable.

We restored several trails and poured some concrete steps, scribbling "CC Soccer" in the drying cement. (Several years later, some CC alum stumbled upon that "engraving" and sent me a picture.) Most vivid in my mind, though, as I think of that jungle stay, is a memory of Paquito Lopez, dressed in boots and shorts with a bandana on his head, soaked in sweat, weed-whacking the overgrowth in front of the ranger station, working furiously, while the ranger was sitting in an easy chair on his porch, smoking a cigarette and drinking a beer.

*B*ack at home, Brigham Olson had been inducted into the CC Athletic Hall of Fame, a new Athletic Director, Joel Nielsen, had been appointed, and in the equipment room, Doug Payton, a terrifically supportive equipment manager, took care of the players' needs. Doug came to lots of our games, brought out popsicles when the sun beat down hard during training sessions, and when it got cold, supplied hot chocolate!!

I was further blessed with an assistant, Timm Nikolajsen, who worked in the CC business office and got time off in the afternoons to train our goalkeepers. (Scott Lamphear, my assistant for the two previous years, moved on to become the assistant of the CC women's soccer program.) H.C. Martensen, a player who had just graduated and who was a fitness guru, helped get the guys in shape, and two volunteer coaches, Shawn Reeder and Terrance Gunnels, wanted to get collegiate coaching experience and helped us along the way.

I had scheduled a 20-game season and, in an incredible scheduling coup, managed to get 14 home games. A solid group of seniors had returned. Captain Tim Campbell was an able leader, and a German exchange student, Robert Brennecke, was a late addition to the squad.

In retrospect, I probably shouldn't have scheduled a strong D-II Regis College team for an opener, since they trounced us at home badly. Due to rain, we had to play the game on the artificial turf of Washburn Field, a move which most likely was advantageous to Regis, a highly skilled passing team. Our SID had figured out that this game was my 700th contest at CC, and the local paper ran a two-page story on Helen and me!!

After a second loss at home, we had only scored one goal and allowed seven. The scoring power of Sean McGinnis, the midfield expertise of Martin Quinn, the defensive strength of Gem McLaughlin, and the quality net minding of Jon Holdorf, all of whom had graduated, were sorely missed.

Fortunately, as so often is the case in amateur sports, unexpected surprises were in store. Nick Zinn and Steve Heitkamp stepped up their offensive play; Paquito Lopez, Tim Campbell and Alex Aguirre became dominant in midfield; Brian Tafel and John Cropper were solid on defense; and Pat Gannon minded the net. Pat McGinnis was waiting in the wings as an ace-in-the-hole. Two victories followed.

Our fifth opponent was Pomona College, an academically stellar institution like CC, and there is an interesting story here: Whenever we competed against Pomona, the contest was always a spirited one, and so it was in this game. The Tigers blasted twice as many shots against the Sage Hens as they were able to launch against us, but we lost 1-0 on a goal scored by a Colorado Springs player!! Matthew Lee-Ashley won the game. I had recruited him to come to CC and thought we had the inside track because both of his parents were professors at CC, Susan Ashley and Bob Lee. Susan Ashley, who was in the stands with her husband Bob, was torn whether to cheer for CC or Pomona. Here is what she remembers:

Late in the season Pomona-Pitzer, coached by Bill Swartz, came to play the Tigers. It was Pomona's only trip by air that season, a trip senior Matt Lee-Ashley, a product of Palmer High School in Colorado Springs, had campaigned for with the coach from his first year at Pomona. As might have been expected, the game produced a tough defensive battle without many serious threats on goal at either end. But in the second half, Pomona kicked a corner from the right which came in low and slithered through players in front of the net. Matt slipped in from outside the box and tapped it home with his left foot, to the delight of his parents — Robert Lee and Susan Ashley, members of the CC faculty — and to the dismay of almost everyone else watching the game. That goal decided the match.

A block break bus trip to Iowa produced two victories, giving us a 5-3-1 record. At Wartburg College, starting goalkeeper Pat Gannon jammed his finger and trainer Bruce Kola ruled him out of the lineup. Back-up keeper Zac Rubin stepped in and did an admirable job minding the net. For the next match vs. Simpson College, then a better team than Wartburg, two more starters, John Cropper and Alex Aguirre, were out with injuries and chances for a win that day were diminishing.

As it turned out, the day was a glorious one for the Tigers. Zac Rubin was amazing in goal, making several key saves, and Robert Brennecke, who had quite a bit of playing experience from his native Germany, slotted home an unassisted goal in the second half, which proved to be the winner. On that high note, and with plenty of pizza on the bus, we headed home.

In Western Nebraska, near Ogallala, the diesel engine of the bus started to overheat badly and we limped into town. The vehicle needed major repairs! We ended up with rental vans to bring the team back for Monday morning classes. This block break was a memorable one!! It certainly was a memorable one for our player from Germany. Years later Robert Brennecke still remembered this trip to the American heartland:

One of my most vivid memories was our road trip to Iowa in the first half of the season. We traveled in an historic Tiger bus, and right from the beginning I had my doubts whether we would make it all the way out of state. However, the journey began smoothly because Noah Drever had organized to replace three rows of seats in the bus with a king size mattress. For a person from a country where actions against traffic regulations are almost regarded as a felony, this was just great.

On the second day of traveling, my first assumptions became true and the bus broke down the first time. By the time the bus driver had heroically duct-taped the bus drivable again, it was clear that we might not make it on time. So Coach Richardson did let us change on the bus and he put on the football movie Rudy. *By the time we arrived at the soccer field the whole bus was chanting, "RUDY, RUDY, RUDY," as the main character of the movie finally got his first playing time after a year of hard work and many defeats.*

Even though we had spent an eternity on that bus, we were so pumped up that we got off that bus and without much of a warm-up just ran over our opponents — outplayed and outran them and got that W on the road.

It's not really important to mention that the bus broke down again on the way back and Horst had to organize mini-vans in the middle of nowhere. We made it home to CC, though, and up to now I have never seen so many cornfields again in my life as was the case in Iowa.

Much of October was a good soccer month for us. A successful Homecoming weekend was behind us and the team played well. In a late October *Catalyst* article, Greg Lestikow sums up our progress:

After recording only one loss in their last 10 games, the Tigers suffered two defeats in only three days against the University of California, Santa Cruz, and Carleton College. The Banana Slugs from California were nationally ranked, and CC played superbly. John Cropper said: "We played one of the best games we have played all year, but we just couldn't put one in the net!"

2003 was a solid, but not stellar, season. We finished the fall campaign strong at home with a win over Nebraska Wesleyan, with Pat McGinnis scoring the last goal of the season. All season long I had toyed with the idea of moving him into a striker position, but he resisted, preferring a quarterback-type midfield role. I kept up my insistence of this positional change for him and convinced him of trying the new spot for the following year. Patrick and his teammate, Tim Campbell, were named Regional All-Americans.

Several improvements had taken place that year for men's soccer: the press box on Stewart Field became flanked by covered benches, making the west side of the field much more attractive visually and more comfortable for the players. Our locker room was upgraded with a non-slip floor and I had dressed things up with team pictures from 1950 to the present installed on the perimeter of the room above the lockers. A second photographer, Charlie Lengal, a professional, provided us with additional picture documentation.

Unfortunately, a set of port-a-potties, sitting on the northeast corner of the field for the spectators, were in the field of vision when taking action shots from west to east, hardly an appealing background! Today, restroom facilities are available to the spectators in the Western Ridge common area.

Finally, Athletic Director Joel Nielsen, who had just been appointed, left to accept a position in South Dakota. And our beloved, retired, longtime equipment manager, Emily Varley, had passed away in August. She had been the kindest, most understanding, and patient individual many a CC varsity athlete had known.

2004

Without question, 2004 was a banner year! In my 50 years of coaching, the 2004 season must rank in the top five, by any measuring stick.

Much of the success of that 16-4-1 fall campaign must be credited to one man, Patrick McGinnis. I had convinced him to move from midfield to striker position, and he responded with scoring 39 goals. That was a phenomenal achievement!

Patrick majored in physics and carried a double minor in philosophy and Spanish, a heavy academic load. Both in the classroom and on the field, he was highly self-motivated and conditioned to perform. It was clear from the outset of the season that with Patrick we had an ace in the hole.

As part of New Student Orientation, the college had initiated volunteer service projects. Volleyball Coach Rick Swan and I lead a sizable contingent of first-year students to the Taos Pueblo in New Mexico to work on various projects there. Thirty football players, 12 members of the volleyball team, and 23 men's soccer players worked hard for three days, living in tents and in the sparse gym on native land. We dug foundations for sheds, installed vents in a huge greenhouse, cleared brush, and conducted sports clinics. The governor of the Pueblo, John Mirabal, sent a thank you letter to our new Athletic Director, Julie Soriero:

> *On behalf of the Taos Pueblo, I would like to thank you for the student/athlete trip August 14-17, 2004, and the enormous generosity that the CC students*

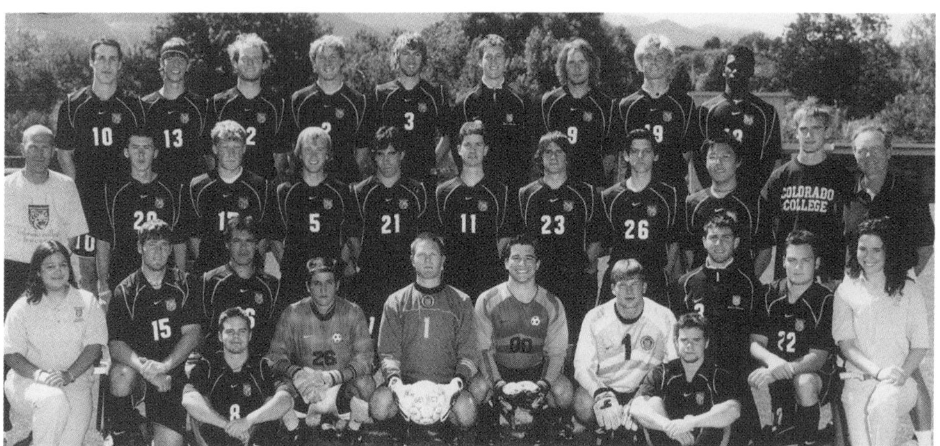

2004 | 16-4-1

Front row, left to right: Student Trainer Jessica Ledbetter, Andy Bond, Alex Aguirre (captain), Clayton Miller, Luke Abbott, Pat Gannon, Zac Rubin, David Khuen, Greg Miller, Greg Breslau, Beale Tejada, Student Trainer Megan Berry. **Middle row:** Assistant Coach Timm Nikolajsen, Pat Fagan, Brooks Robinson, Pat Jackson, Nick Zinn, Nate Hamilton, Jack Simons, Matt Samson, Yuki Miyazaki, Brian Bones, Coach Horst Richardson. **Back row:** Patrick McGinnis, Logan Campbell, Noah Drever, Brian Tafel, Grant Armour, Ben Steiner, Cody McGrath, Jason Steiert, Abdou N'Dir. **Not pictured:** Nick Evans, Aaron Hasenkrug.

---

demonstrated to the community members of the Taos Pueblo. The community work they accomplished was not only a huge benefit to several of our tribal programs, but also voiced a powerful message to our community members, particularly the younger members, about the value of community effort and the importance of teamwork. Our students also greatly enjoyed the various sports camps, both in Santa Fe and at the Pueblo, which your athletes organized and executed throughout their stay ...

Ezra Bayles, goalkeeper from the '92 team, who lived in Taos, was employed as activities director of the Pueblo and proved to be invaluable to us in our volunteer assignments. Finally, Rick Swan remembers a funny story about our days at the Pueblo:

We worked so hard during our first two days there that on the third day we had some leisure time. One of the elders, who had two horses in pasture, offered the kids some rides. Several of the kids accepted. One of the freshman boys jumped

> *on a horse, it galloped away with him, somewhat out of control, and rode into the brush. The horse came back into the open, but without a rider! The freshman returned on foot, somewhat humbled by the experience.*

Once we were back on campus, the upperclassmen joined us for pre-season with fitness, drills, chalk talks, and small-sided games on the agenda. The McGinnises and the Richardsons hosted Tiger team candidates for nourishing meals to enjoy "off-campus" dining.

Several capital improvements had occurred on Stewart Field: the covered team benches had been completed, a new scoreboard had been installed, and an attractive stone wall around the perimeter of the northern curve of the track on Washburn Field had gained us some more practice area on Stewart Field.

An experienced group of seniors led the fall effort. Pat Gannon and Zac Rubin were seasoned in the nets, captain Alex Aguirre was a pillar of strength on defense, the Miller twins, Greg and Clayton, as well as Nate Hamilton, showed deft passing in midfield, and up front Pat McGinnis and Nick Zinn baffled the opposition. Juniors Brian Tafel, Jack Simons and Abdou N'Dir provided further upperclassmen expertise. Timm Nikolajsen continued as assistant; his booming voice could be heard across the field and beyond. Bruce Kola, our trainer, received much help from two student trainers, Jessica Ledbetter and Megan Berry.

Goalkeeper Pat Gannon and a couple of the guys had come up with a team promotional gimmick that got the fans out to the home games. Under the motto "Ready and Willing," black-and-white posters of members of the team appeared all over campus advertising the forthcoming contest. The posters were "artistic" collages of players in manly poses to catch the eye of our student body. Our home attendance was substantial that year. In fact, Clay Miller remembers an awesome crowd on an Indian summer afternoon:

> *During my senior year, there was a memory I had on the soccer field that I will never forget. We were playing on a beautiful fall day in the Springs. Literally not a cloud in the sky. Between the weather and the good soccer we were playing, the crowd came by the hundreds that day and the "hill seating" under the apartments became standing-room-only. I had never seen a crowd like that in my 4 years at CC. The atmosphere was electric, and I can still remember walking into the field to "Braveheart" and seeing that crowd.*

After warm ups, the starters proceeded to the middle of the field for the routine playing of the National Anthem. Right before the close of the anthem, when you normally get chills anyway, 3 or 4 Air Force fighter jets flew overhead as if we were playing in the Super Bowl! Some of us got caught up in the moment and thought they were for us, but later learned it was just a normal fly-by that was timed perfectly …

After five games, our record stood at 4-1, the best start in years. California surfer boy Noah Drever, now a sophomore, had improved to become a starter and provided key goals and Pat Fagan, a quiet yet dynamic dribbler of small stature, could be called upon to enhance our offensive power. The victory over a strong California Lutheran squad gave us much confidence and made us believe that a bright future was in store for us that season. And once we had dispatched No. 20-ranked Rowan University from the East Coast, we knew we were on our way. Noah Drever '07 still remembers the game-winning goal he scored against Rowan as a real highlight of his CC career:

The goal that I will always remember is from a home game in 2004, CC vs. Rowan University. We knew going into the game that Rowan University would be a tough opponent. They are typically contenders in the NCAA tournament, slugging their way through a difficult East Coast conference.

The day was warm and the sun unrelenting, an advantage I was grateful for, especially as it was compounded with over a mile of altitude. We moved into the second half at 0-0. It was a battle with very few shots on goal. Finally, around the 80th minute, a breakaway occurred. The ball found its way to the left winger, Patrick Fagan, who carried it down to the edge of the field. As he prepared his left foot to cross the ball, a sensation of hyper-focus filled my body. Fagan's kick was beautiful — just a slight bend swinging it back towards the top of the box. I continued my run with a forward leap to connect, and then noticed that the ball was in the back of the net. The game ended shortly after that with a 1-0 victory for Colorado College.

I still have a picture of Horst holding my head and placing his forehead against mine. It was by far one of my proudest moments — a moment where I found myself in the right place at the right time, proud to know that Fagan's assist and my goal made the difference that day.

Central defender Brian Tafel, indicating that the best defense is a hell-of-an-offense, tickled the net with a couple of powerful shots in subsequent games, and local player Jack

Simons came into his own in midfield and supplied a huge measure of morale-boosting witticisms to boot. Like Bill Hochman, his parents (his dad is a CC English professor) have over time attended more of our games than anyone I know. Oh, and lest I forget, our fan base even included half-time entertainment from the CC dance team, a first!

Megan Berry, a first-year student from Montrose, Colorado, was a student trainer. She was a dedicated addition to the team's well-being and used to chat with Helen in the early afternoon on Mondays as Helen was updating our inspirational bulletin board in front of the locker room. Megan has become a dear family friend and recalls those hallway meetings:

> *"Deer in the headlights" is an understatement for my first few months at CC. I chose a lab course for my First Year Experience, which meant five or more hours of class per day in addition to hours and hours of homework, and I also landed a job as a student athletic trainer which, at the peak of the season, could mean upwards of 30 hours of work per week. I was homesick and exhausted, and every day was a sprint to the finish line.*
>
> *It was during said sprints, while hauling ice bags up and down the halls of El Pomar, or going to the training room after lunch to get ready for practice, that I noticed Helen diligently updating the bulletin board outside the soccer locker room. Never without her packet of newspaper clippings, stories and stats from the website, photos of players and tigers, and motivating headlines cut from magazines, Helen made sure the board was always up to date and informative, telling the story of the year's team.*
>
> *It was while she pinned and unpinned the stories on the bulletin board that Helen and I got to chatting. I was beside myself with relief and gratitude to have a friendly face in the overwhelming crowd of sweaty, beautiful (and, most days, smelly) boys. Helen took me under her wing. She was never without a smiling face and a listening ear, and the support and compassion she showed me in those early days scaffolded me when I thought I might break.*
>
> *I can't imagine how I would have survived without her, and I'm sure no one who played or coached for Horst can, either. Throughout Horst's tenure, Helen loved and served the team with a fierce devotion. Multiple times every season, she welcomed the entire team and coaching staff into her home before weekend games for a homemade breakfast, having risen early in the morning to prepare enough eggs, bacon, sausage, fruit salad and English muffins with butter for more than 30 people all by herself. She*

and Horst also hosted four dinners, one for each class of players, every season. She could regularly be seen toting Ziploc bags of homemade chocolate chip cookies to the field when players had birthdays, and the officials could always count on her to show up on game day with a cooler of water and Gatorade just for them.

Helen filmed every single home game from the announcer's box, regularly fighting through excruciating knee pain, until she could no longer do it. She crafted immaculate scrapbooks every year, creating an invaluably detailed, multi-dimensional record of the history of the team. In later years, she was known to unfurl a banner congratulating Horst on milestone victories, and she was also an unfailing source of optimism and support when the team hit a rough patch, whether for a few periods or for weeks at a time.

What's perhaps more incredible than the countless hours of logistical and culinary support Helen humbly devoted to the team for half a century is the fact that players and coaches were so much more than numbers to her. Helen learned every single player's name, and often the names of his parents and siblings. She inquired about studies, hometowns, post-graduation plans and personal interests.

Even now, years later, Helen knows where many, many players live and how their lives have progressed. She and Horst often pile into their Jetta to drive (sometimes across many state lines) to attend the wedding of a former player, and they still welcome players and their families into their home on a regular basis.

There's a magic associated with CC men's soccer. You can't quite put your finger on it, and it looks different for different people. Every time a new batch of Tigers has the honor of stepping out to practice or play in the shadow of Pikes Peak, they're building on the legacy of many, many others who came before, paving the way in pursuit of something just a little bit different, just a little bit magical. And for the way Helen gave of herself to the CC men's soccer team for fifty years, there is no other explanation: the woman is magic.

Just prior to our critical road trip to the Twin Cities, Pat McGinnis had scored an incredible four goals against Chapman College to dispatch that California squad, making him a force to be reckoned with for opponents in future contests. So it was no surprise that in our away game to Carleton College he was a marked man.

The game was a rough one, marked with lots of fouls. Brian Tafel and Pat McGinnis were ejected from the match, Pat in the last 15 seconds. The referee had warned Pat not to use the back of an opponent as a ricochet surface when throwing in the ball. Yet, at the end of the match Pat couldn't resist doing this again against an opponent who had fouled him repeatedly during the match. The referee pulled out a red card and Pat had to leave the game.

Nick Zinn, though, scored the winner even though we were down in number of players. Our loss to Macalester the next day was a temporary setback, as we finished the road trip with a win over Concordia College. Pat McGinnis had come back with a vengeance in that game after sitting out vs. Macalester. In the Concordia contest, down by one goal early in the game, Pat scored an incredible five goals to give us the win.

A huge Homecoming crowd, including many soccer alums, greeted the Tigers and cheered them on to two victories during the weekend. Teammates Beale Tejada and Jack Simons wrote with much enthusiasm for *The Catalyst* and included this memorable quote for posterity from Noah Drever, whose hairline was receding at an early age: "Heading balls into the net is perhaps the only time in life when male pattern baldness is truly an advantage!"

Our torrid scoring pace continued and we rang the victory bell with glee. Dave Reed, our very supportive SID, submits this recollection of our game against Denver-based Johnson & Wales:

> *Led by Patrick McGinnis, who would eventually be named the Division III Player of the Year, the Tigers cruised to a 9-1 victory over Johnson & Wales University. During the second half, a frustrated Wildcat decided to take out his frustrations on the referees. As Andreas Schiffner ran back and forth in front of the Colorado College bench cursing in German, Horst Richardson had heard enough. On his next run up the sideline, Richardson let the young player know, in no uncertain terms, that he understood every word that was said and did not appreciate the way he was berating the refs, even though they did not understand a word of what was said.*
>
> *Helen, whose many duties at the time included filming the game, saw the entire incident from her position on the press box deck. After the game I asked Helen what Horst said. She politely declined saying, "Oh, I could never repeat that." That's when I decided I needed to learn the German language.*

With three games remaining in regular season play, Pat McGinnis had tied Andre Zarb-Cousin's all-time CC record of 33 goals in a season. He had also become national scoring leader.

A second road trip to Minnesota was next on the agenda. Against Gustavus Adolphus in the provincial town of St. Peter, we not only faced the top ranked team in the West, but we also battled 40-mile-per-hour winds and we just couldn't score. We rectified that situation, though, in the following game against St. Thomas with a satisfying and rewarding win.

I attribute that victory to my pre-game talk, rendered dramatically at Halloween while wearing a frightening and ferocious mask. On the flight home, Brian Tafel, our giant defensive midfielder, appeared on the plane dressed as Superman, a fitting Halloween costume for him, indeed. At home, we finished the regular season with a win over Nebraska Wesleyan, giving us a terrific 16-3-1 record.

With the best season since 1992 behind us, we were invited to the NCAA tournament and had to pack our bags for Spokane, Washington, to compete against Whitworth College.

The soccer gods were not on our side that day. We had two apparent goals disallowed and still were in contention. The pivotal moment in the game occurred when we were granted a penalty shot in the second half. The game stood at a 1-1 tie, and everyone expected Pat McGinnis to step up to the penalty spot. Inexplicably, he spotted the ball for his friend and teammate Brian Tafel to take the shot. Brian's low blast hit the left post and bounced out. In spite of our consistent pressure on their goal, we had to settle for a 2-1 loss.

Nevertheless, the accolades flowed in and our banquet that year was very festive. Two new awards were established: The Dick Schulte Midfielder of the Year Award, presented to Alex Aguirre, and the Saad Sahawneh Attacker of the Year Award, unanimously to Pat McGinnis. Pat also was chosen the National Player of the Year by the National Soccer Coaches Association and traveled with me and Helen to Baltimore to receive this award at the NSCAA convention. After graduation, Pat played a season of professional soccer for the Kansas City MLS team. Today he and his family live on Maui, where they run an organic tree farm.

At the conclusion of every annual banquet, it had become customary to show a highlight video of the season. This year's video was eagerly anticipated, as rumors had spread of a special "segment." Pat Gannon had produced a video of Jack Simons, singing a spoof about trainer Bruce Kola. Associate trainer Cindy Endicott was in on the training room footage and still chuckles as she remembers this artistic endeavor:

> *My favorite memory of men's soccer is when Jack Simons wrote a song parody for Bruce Kola to the tune of "Lola." The lyrics were created and sung by Jack Simons, and the video was produced by Pat Gannon. Jack was very cunning in his efforts to sneak around the athletic training room, singing his lyrics as he performed various crazy*

exercises, sitting in the whirlpool, or getting taped as one of the student athletic trainers tried not to laugh. He stood on top of the dugouts with his guitar and threw himself onto the ground to fake an injury that would eventually be evaluated by "the K man."

My favorite part was sneaking Jack into Bruce's office, where he stood on top of Kola's desk singing his ode. The look on Bruce's face when he watched the video and saw Jack standing on his desk was fantastic. Little did Bruce know that I requested a special copy of the video, which I promptly placed in my home safe. Safe and sound for when Bruce someday would retire and I could surprise him with a reappearance of this fantastic tribute by men's soccer. This video truly was a memorable one. We roared with laughter as we viewed it!

2005

2005, a new season with new stories and players determined to succeed. The *CC Bulletin* publication for August had featured a story on me as professor and coach in the Block Plan. I lauded our student/athletes who had to learn quickly how to manage their time and commitments while studying intensively and playing competitively. I considered the Block Plan a "fabulous preparation for life."

Volleyball Coach Rick Swan and I once again collaborated to take new students to the Taos Pueblo for New Student Orientation volunteer work. But this time there was a surprise of sorts in store for us on the trip south.

We stopped at the Fort Union ranch in northern New Mexico for an historic tour and a ranch work-out. Imagine the surprise of our players when none other than Pat Gannon, our goalkeeper and now graduate, rode up as a cowboy on a horse to greet us! Pat had spent the summer as a ranch hand, gathering experience in hard labor, and he was eager to pass that on to us. So we spent several hours cleaning out cattle watering holes, wallowing in muck!

For Coach Swan and me, the Taos pre-season trip became an annual event for a number of years. The students, for the most part, were enthusiastically engaged and the coaches and camp counselors were able to observe their work habits.

A fun addition to the CC contingent that summer was talkative and energetic Glen Luther, husband to Athletic Department secretary Nancy Luther. Glen, who ran the CC ice rink on campus, had lots of tall tales to relate from his interesting past. As a conclusion to New Student Orientation and in the spirit of the liberal arts, I had in mind to take the team to see *Macbeth*, as part of the Colorado Springs Shakespeare in the Park theater program; but alas, the lead actor, Macbeth himself, was sick that day and the show had to be canceled.

Two new staff members, joining me and Timm Nikolajsen, greeted the team for try-outs: Jesse Perez as assistant coach, and Jason Fox, trainer, as temporary replacement for Bruce Kola. Jesse had played semi-pro soccer in Mexico and California and was now active in local adult soccer. He and his wife, Lily, owned a Mexican restaurant in town where the team would eat on special occasions. Jesse, dressed in a black leather jacket, had a habit of coming to practice on his Harley motorcycle, which additionally impressed the boys.

Just in time for the first practice, Pat McGinnis, now a pro with the Sporting Kansas City MLS team, sent us a letter wishing us a terrific season. Also, our program was chosen to conduct a pilot referee project to test the feasibility of "spray and stay," a foam demarcation line sprayed by the referee to indicate a 10-yard distance for the wall on a free kick.

Once the dust had settled from pre-season try-outs, 11 new players had been selected to join the squad. A number of these men were to play a substantial part for our

2005 | 12-8-0

Front row: Berk Korustan, Lee Smith, Pat Fagan, Brooks Robinson, Beale Tejada, Matt Samson, Warren Takashima, Ben Beadle-Ryby. **Middle row:** Brian Wohlner, Chris Quon, Jimmer Comerford, Hunter Oliver-Allen, Luke Abbott, David Khuen, Joey Wykowski, Jason Steiert, Wes Rikkers, Jeff Smith, Julian Holscher. **Back row:** Trainer Andrew L.T. Mahar, Assistant Coach Jesse Perez, Coach Horst Richardson, Jack Simons, Abdou N'Dir, Brian Tafel (captain), Grant Armour, Cody McGrath (captain), Noah Drever, Assistant Coach Timm Nikolajsen, Trainer Jason Fox. **Not pictured:** Hunter Allen.

program, including Jimmer Comerford, Ben Beadle-Ryby, Wes Rikkers, Joey Wykowski and Chris Quon.

We lost the Bill Boddington Tournament during the opening weekend in the final by a 2-1 score to visiting Southwestern College from Texas. They snuck one in with two minutes left in the game. A much worse blow, though, happened on the second weekend of the season, as we lost senior captain Brian Tafel to a torn ACL. This serious injury kept him out for the rest of the season.

Jack Simons '06, our midfielder who wrote for *The Catalyst*, paid tribute to Brian in an incredibly caring and compassionate article. It was a masterful homage to Tafel, written from a friend for a friend:

> *The play looked so innocent — a pass played just behind him; he tried to stop himself to get to the ball. He had to; he tried to get to every ball … And his right foot dragged for a second. Only for a second, and then, a second later, he was lying on the field. He was writhing. He tried, and failed, to get to his feet.*
>
> *On the sideline, on our bench, confidence. He's fine, we assured ourselves and each other. That's Brian Tafel out there. He's only gone knee-to-knee with a defender. Soon the pain will wear off and he will climb to his feet. He'll climb to his feet and resume his position in the middle of the field. And yet, there he remained. On the grass. Jason Fox, the trainer, assisted him off the field and took him to the training room. He came back in the second half on crutches. The captain was out for the season.*

Years after this injury to Tafel occurred, Jack Simons confided in me that on that day his life changed, because "when Tafel went down, I got up." You see, Jack had experienced several tough years: the death of two friends, heavy substance abuse, dropping in and out of CC, almost making the team and then suffering an injury, and yet showing occasional signs of brilliance and creativity both on the field and in the classroom. But his life showed little purpose. So when Tafel "went down," Jack told himself, "Enough is enough!" He rolled up his sleeves and got a grip on his life. Now a senior, he practiced hard, started to play, scored a couple of goals, and blossomed.

I have a letter from Jack in which he pours out his heart and bares his soul, incredibly candid and honest:

... so I did come back for one last season in 2005. In fact, I almost quit that team as well. After a terrible, nagging turf toe injury I really thought I was done and I announced it through tears to the team. But something or someone finally smiled on me and after our captain Brian Tafel (whom I really miss) was lost for the season with an injury, I felt compelled to give it one more try. And it worked out and I played a bunch, even scoring a few goals including one on a header vs. Augustana. I still consider that goal the single most enjoyable moment of my life. And then my old life really was over.

Today Jack is a successful and caring high school English teacher and soccer coach in Des Moines at a multi-ethnic school doing great things for troubled kids.

On a national scale, the tragedy of Hurricane Katrina unfolded as the monster storm unleashed its destructive strength in Louisiana. Our team, under Chris Quon's leadership, responded by raising $1,600 for the victims of the catastrophe through the sale of CC folding chairs to our spectators.

Three grueling back-to-back road trips rounded out September. Two narrow victories in Portland, Oregon, were followed by two one-goal losses in Southern California. In Portland, at the Rhinelander Restaurant after the second victory, I entertained the team and their parents by singing Oktoberfest songs, but in California the mood was less festive.

And then came the bus trip to Iowa. It proved to be a disaster. Jason Steiert, who with Wes Rikkers and Berk Korustan had formed a considerable defensive link, lost his cool during the first game in the heartland against Buena Vista College. After he was provoked, he slugged the opponent and was ejected from the game.

Next we faced Wartburg College, the sixth road game in succession. The rural program, amidst corn and soybean fields, had surprised quite a few opponents, us included. Their high-scorer, a foreign student from Ghana, was an incredible player and sliced us apart with four goals. The only redeeming factor in Iowa was a side trip to a wind farm, one of the early attempts at sustainable energy production. Joey Wykowski '09, first-year goalkeeper, was on that trip and reminisces:

One trip that really stands out in my mind is my freshman year, when we traveled to Iowa. Besides the endless fields of corn, my mind is immediately flooded with specific visuals from that trip. I remember Horst using a watering hose at Coe College to demonstrate the diagonal balls he wanted played to the corners. I remember coming

> *in for the second half of a hard fought game where we came back from a significant deficit. Our next stop on the trip brought us to Wartburg College, where Horst waxed poetic about the German history of the college and the significance of Martin Luther, the Protestant reformer. The trip came to a screeching halt with a tough result against a strong Wartburg side. A couple of the upperclassmen absconded with some of the pillows from our motel for a long drive home to Colorado. (I remember that the proprietor sent our athletic department a bill for those pillows!) Nevertheless, this was a trip where I felt the team really bonded and came together, leading to a strong overall season.*

At Homecoming, Steve Wong, our 1975 goalkeeper and now a Jungian psychotherapist, author, documentary filmmaker, and tai chi instructor, was honored with the Louis T. Benezet Award at the convocation ceremony and our intrepid *Catalyst* writer, Jack Simons, delighted his campus-wide readership with a cryptic article about the ostentatiously loud "X-factor fan."

Jack could have been thinking about CC president Dick Celeste, who normally sat in the front row of the fan section both for men's and women's home games. Due to a wrist injury on his right arm, he was sporting a cast painted in Tiger colors. He was known to gesticulate wildly and would encourage the fans to cheer.

The major Homecoming event was our grudge match against crosstown rival UCCS. It was a wonderful Indian summer afternoon with lots of spectators on the hill, including numerous soccer alums. Ben Beadle-Ryby '09, then a first-year player in midfield, sent me his memories of the match:

> *At the outset of my career, our Homecoming game against crosstown rival UCCS rings loudly in my mind. At this stage in my freshman season, I had grown accustomed to our pre-game rituals of the familial brunch at Horst and Helen's, our pre-game talk, and our locker room prep. What I was not fully prepared for was the size of the crowd or the magnitude of the game. With the hill packed with current students and CC alums, as well as UCCS fans, the atmosphere was simply electric.*
>
> *Of course, once the game gets going we all tend to get lost in the action ... but midway through the first half I was brought back to the magnitude of the event as I received a flick-on from Julian Holscher (foreign student from Germany) that left me with a single touch to get the ball by the keeper; as the ball hit the back of the net to*

put us up 1-0, I was immediately reminded of the size of the crowd as it erupted in cheers. That's a feeling that I'll always remember.

From there, we managed to control the game and emerged victorious with a 3-1 finish. All of this was nothing less than glorious, but it became a truly treasured memory when it came to light that the victory marked the 450th of Horst's career. 450 hard-fought wins seems unfathomable, and it was a real treat to celebrate it in front of such a large group of alums that had witnessed those types of victories for dozens of years. During my senior year, we helped Horst cross the 500-win milestone and only at that point, after having earned so many victories and suffered some tough losses across my career, did I fully appreciate this accomplishment.

Jimmer Comerford '09, in his first year in 2005, also decided to highlight the UCCS game for his "memorable moment," focusing on a locker room ritual:

A pillar of CC soccer was (and forever will be) the dynamics of the locker room shower. One of my fondest memories of CC soccer, which set the tone for my four years to follow, concluded in this sacred location.

It was Homecoming week, and our team was preparing for a match against crosstown foe UCCS. While local bragging rights and the fact they played in NCAA Division II (a division above our own) were points of emphasis, our senior leaders made a poster that conveyed some history. It detailed every loss CC had suffered at the hands of UCCS over the past decade, back to our most recent victory in 1994. Needless to say, motivation was abundant.

Skip ahead to a typically gorgeous Colorado fall Saturday, with the hillside above Stewart Field covered with loyal fans, families, and alumni partaking in the Homecoming festivities. We put on a show! In an exciting and high-energy match, we dominated play, snapped the 10-year skid, and beat UCCS 3-1.

Amidst the history with this particular opponent and the emotion of the crowd, as a team and a community, we were overjoyed and proud to celebrate Horst's 450th career victory as a coach following our win. What a tremendous accomplishment! As the banner was unveiled and we gathered for pictures with our teammates and generations past of CC soccer players and supporters, one thing became very clear to me — I was in a special place, and part of a truly special program.

I returned to the locker room with my team where that motivational poster was still hanging on the wall. All it took was the unabashed leadership of Jack Simons and the lyrical stylings of Eddie Money ("Take Me Home Tonight"), for that symbol of

> *defeat to be ripped from its place, dragged into the shower, and almost ritualistically destroyed by the team. While the weather, the crowd, the competition, the outcome, and the history made on this day showed me what CC soccer was all about, it was the time in the shower that made me realize the brotherhood I was now a part of, and what a remarkable four-year ride I was about to take.*
>
> *Recently, the entire El Pomar Sports Complex was renovated with amazing upgrades to technologies, facilities, and amenities. But the communal shower in our old locker room was untouched, left exactly as it always has been. I can't say I'm surprised.*

At the end of the game, after the team had rung the victory bell, I was surrounded by players, alums and fans, and Helen, who had pre-planned this surprise, presented me with a portrait of myself in coaching attire, sketched by CC artist Rick Specht, which now hangs in our living room.

The joyful mood of this celebration quickly turned somber that afternoon because of another scheduled Homecoming event. That afternoon also saw us dedicate the north end practice field area as Olson Field, in memory of former captain Brigham Olson, class of 1985. Brigham had passed away two years ago, and now his family, his teammates, and his friends had gathered in the northeast corner of the grass pitch to honor him by unveiling a plaque, which was affixed to the stone retaining wall.

A teammate spoke, his father spoke lovingly of his son, our athletic director represented the college, and I offered concluding remarks. At the end of my comments, I was so overwhelmed with emotion that I wept. In a beautifully written *Catalyst* article entitled "A Perfect Day," Jack Simons captured the depth of feelings on that October 8 day:

> *... where only minutes earlier our coach had worn an ear-to-ear grin, here he was in tears. And, though the tears seemed to change him, those who really looked saw the same Horst there at the dedication ceremony as in the portrait ... The man was smiling inside. He was smiling inside not because the ceremony didn't affect him — Horst described Brigham with such reverence — but because he couldn't help but be pleased to have known so well a man whose memory alone could carry such a day. "You don't get many perfect days," Horst told the team the next day, "and you guys gave me one yesterday."*

After Homecoming, we won six games and lost three to finish off the season. Pat Fagan had moved into the season's high-scorer position, and his teammates, particularly Jason Steiert and Abdou N'Dir, spread the rumor of his "serial killer stare!"

"His stare is like ice," said sweeper Jason Steiert '08, "really intense ice. You never really know what he is thinking when he has that look in his eyes. The thing is, you really don't want to know." Abdou '06 added: "You gotta trust that serial killer stare, even if it scares you. It means he is cool, he is composed." Fagan himself attributed his intense stare to his hometown of St. Louis, where the streets are dangerous and you "gotta stare the man down."

At the banquet at Jesse's Mexican restaurant, Brian Tafel presented another entertaining highlight tape and announced that, having missed his entire senior season due to injury, he was going to come back for a super senior semester to play out his eligibility. (I was noticeably relieved by this announcement.) And I, in turn, announced that the team was going to take another international trip at the end of the academic year, this one to the 2006 World Cup in Germany!!

2006

For three weeks in June 2006, the CC Tigers toured throughout Germany, playing friendly matches and watching the World Cup competition in the host country. Our traveling party consisted of 21 players, surgeon Dr. John Middleton, co-captain in 1973, his wife Melinda, former CC German major, their three children, Anne, Davy and Julie, and Helen and me.

Through a friend who had a car dealership, I was able to rent three Mercedes-Benz nine-passenger vans to haul us around the country in relative luxury. Julian Holscher, a German university student who had been on the CC team the year before, agreed to be one of the drivers during our Germany stay. He expressed his satisfaction for driving us around because he saw parts of his home country previously unknown to him:

> *After getting a deep insight into the U.S. and soccer culture through training, games, and trips but also by lots of leisure activities with the boys, it was a pleasure to show them my home country during the World Cup 2006 in Germany. I drove one of the vans and not only got to know new places myself but also numerous CC alumni in Germany. We played almost every other day, watched World Cup games and enjoyed typical German food and not very typical German weather — it was one of the nicest and hottest summers in a long time. Many thanks to you, Horst and Helen, for this exceptional time.*

Horst's friends and soccer buddies in his home country outdid themselves hosting our group. Here's what the sweeper on the team, Jason Steiert, had to say about the trip:

> *Coach Richardson had planned an excellent adventure for the team in Germany. Our days were filled with cultural activities, historical sites, bratwurst, beer, and, of course, soccer. We visited ten cities; most memorable were Freiburg in the Black Forest, where we watched Germany's opening match against Costa Rica in a local park jammed with people; Munich, where, in the Olympia Park on huge TV screens, we watched the United States compete in their first game against the Czech Republic; going underground in Nuremberg to see the medieval dungeons; in Berlin, home of the fan mile in front of the Brandenburg Gate, where 900,000 fans cheered on their team.*
>
> *Check Point Charlie, the Holocaust Memorial, a stop along the former Iron Curtain, and attending a World Cup match in the Hamburg stadium were on the itinerary. But the most beautiful part of the trip was Horst's return to his hometown village of Rosstal, where we were treated like celebrities and got a peek*

2006 | 14-4-2

Front row, left to right: Ben Beadle-Ryby, Jordan Reese, Luke Abbott, Joey Wykowski, David Khuen, Chris Ellis, Berk Korustan. **Middle row:** Warren Takashima, Pat Fagan, Brian Wohlner, Logan Boccard, Brooks Robinson, Ben Hancock, Matt Samson, Beale Tejada, Brendan Douglas, Lee Smith. **Back row:** Assistant Coach Jesse Perez, student trainer, Chris Quon, Trevor Cobb, Jimmer Comerford, Hunter Oliver-Allen, Brian Tafel (captain), Wes Rikkers, Jason Steiert (captain), George Hicks, David Van Sicklen, Coach Horst Richardson. **Not pictured:** Jeff Smith, Ben Steiner.

into his childhood. Even got into the newspaper! ... We left Germany with a solid winning record of 5-4-1.

Germany did indeed put its best foot forward that summer and the *Weltmeisterschaft* did much to elevate Germany's status amongst the nations of the world. And, as a footnote, the national coach of the Germany team, Juergen Klinsmann, was hired as national team coach for the United States after the tournament.

Finally, a huge thanks to several former CC German House head residents (Sonni Boeckenfoerde, Cornelia Foerster-Gress, Claudia Stemmler, Barbara Steiger, Joseph Irl), former German exchange students who played for the Tigers (Robert Brennecke, Gunther Karsten, Andreas Wolff, and Gunther Dendl), Andrea Koops, part-time CC student at one time, and in particular Ralph Rieker, CC graduate in economics in 1985, who, as president of the Ricosta Shoe Company, gave the team a royal reception in Donaueschingen and, on my birthday, invited me on a breathtaking helicopter ride to the Swiss border!!

As with previous international soccer journeys, my hope was that the experience in soccer gathered abroad would pay dividends in the forthcoming season. Veteran Brian Tafel provided leadership as captain. Co-captain Jason Steiert joined him in leadership responsibilities. Former CC star player and ex-UCCS coach Eddy Dietz worked with Jesse Perez as assistants, complemented by Adam Ewig as goalie coach. Isaac Jones '96, outstanding defender from 10 years ago, volunteered his time as an assistant. A relatively young but highly motivated and enthusiastic squad looked forward to a successful season in late August.

The press box had been remodeled during the summer, now featuring a new set of stairs behind the home dugout to the observation deck, which also had a new awning to shield the sun, making it easier to videotape the games. On the east side of the field, an attractive set of concrete bleacher seats made the spectator area more attractive.

But the big news for D-III sports at CC that season, a real game-changer, was the fact that this was our last season as independents, for starting with 2007 we were full-fledged members of the Southern Collegiate Athletic Conference (SCAC). That had huge implications for our D-III programs.

For men's soccer that meant that I didn't have to spend a third of my time every year putting together a competitive schedule with mostly D-III opponents from all around the country based on their availability. This was an exhausting and time-consuming task every year. Furthermore, affiliation with a conference provided an automatic qualifier to NCAA tournament play and it also assured more player recognition during and after the season.

A unique "liberal arts" experiment in "laughter power" combined merriment with research in our locker room as the season commenced. CC Psychology Professor Tomi-Ann Roberts trained the players in laughing exercises to reduce stress and enhance performance. *ESPN The Magazine* wrote about us:

> *Mark Twain said that the human race has really only one effective weapon, and that is laughter. This season, the Colorado College Tigers are putting his theory to the test. After CC psych prof Tomi-Ann Roberts returned from India and a visit with Laughter Yoga International founder Madan Kataria, she told the school's coaches that she believed the endorphins released during laughter could ease pre-game anxiety and build focus. So the men's soccer team is giving chuckling a try.*
>
> *To date, its winning percentage is similar to last year's, but there may be more subtle benefits. "Players have better touch and concentrate more," says footie coach Horst Richardson. Meanwhile, Roberts is compiling data to prove her theory. Because, in the end, winning is no joke.*

In an incredible scheduling coup, I was able to lock in eight games at home to start us off. We won six of those home games. Freshmen Logan Boccard, Trevor Cobb, and Jordan Reese, all three honored at the end of the season with the Rookie of the Year Award, developed into lethal scorers. At the other end of the pitch, two super goalkeepers tended the nets, David Khuen and Joey Wykowski. Matt Samson and Jimmer Comerford became critical attacking defenders who, even though dashing up and down the sidelines, hardly ever showed signs of fatigue.

The game I remember most in those first eight matches was the 6-0 loss to Pacific Lutheran. Due to rain, not an unfamiliar phenomenon in Pacific Lutheran's northwest part of the country, we had to compete on the synthetic surface of Washburn Field, a decision which favored the opponent, whose home field was artificial turf. Nevertheless, we let the game slip away and offered little to test the opposition. I was more upset than disappointed about our effort and let the team know it. A victory under the lights on Washburn Field the following week ameliorated the Pacific Lutheran trouncing and convinced us that we needed to train and play more on artificial turf as it was clearly the surface for the future.

Anticipating competition in the SCAC conference, which we were about to join, we had scheduled several opponents from that league to play against. During the first block break the Tigers earned a 1-1-1 record on the road in Texas against three future SCAC opponents. The overwhelming lesson learned on that trip to the Lone Star state: It gets sizzling hot in Texas!

A brilliant Homecoming weekend followed. To the delight of fans and alums, the team won both matches in entertaining fashion. The night game against Minnesota powerhouse St. John's almost slipped away, as a routine back pass to the keeper bounced over David Khuen's head and trickled into our goal to temporarily tie the contest. Pat Fagan's penalty kick at the end of the match saved the evening for the home team. Beale Tejada '07, who received a prestigious El Pomar Fellowship after graduation, remembers the St. John's contest as a highlight of his career:

> *Beating St. John's my senior year was a night to remember. They came in as a formidable opponent in our region, and they were supposed to beat us because we were young and inexperienced, but instead we dominated them in all areas of the game. Also, it was a Friday night under the lights, so it gave us all more energy. Hopefully playing under the lights will become a tradition!*

Pat Hawes, the St. John's coach and a friend of mine, couldn't believe how charged up we were! And yes, we have played multiple games under the lights on Washburn since then.

Wes Rikkers and Warren Takashima harassed Millsaps College in the other weekend game with precision scoring. Tak ripped in a free kick with a vicious swerve, which earned him the "Meisterschuss Award" at the end of the season. During the Homecoming ceremonies, former captain Jay Engeln '74 and now nationally acclaimed educator, was inducted into the CC Athletic Hall of Fame, and Helen and I were honored with the Gresham Riley Award for service to the college.

Two shut-out victories and two double OT games brought us to the end of October. Unfortunately, super senior Brian Tafel had to sit out the rest of the season with a broken bone in his left foot, and we had to fly to California without our captain. At Pomona College, Beale Tejada, on an assist from Hunter Oliver-Allen, scored his first goal of the season just before the stroke of half-time to win the game for us.

A visit to the J. Paul Getty Museum followed the next day. Inspired by a visit to the world-famous art museum, Ben Beadle-Ryby and Logan Boccard combined on an artistic combination play to carry the day at Whittier College in the final minutes of the contest on a teeny-tiny field. With two victories won away, we thought our chances for another NCAA tournament invitation had been greatly enhanced.

A road trip to Lincoln, Nebraska, to play a single game against Nebraska Wesleyan concluded the season. We owed them a return game, and thus the arduous bus trip had to be made. The game ended up 2-2 in double overtime.

On the bus ride back, with a 13-4-3 record in hand, I monitored the NCAA selection committee's deliberations for post-season play. We were not selected. The committee favored UC Santa Cruz, the other independent team in contention in our region. After all, they had beaten us during the regular campaign.

Much later, the AD at Nebraska Wesleyan reported to our AD that during the match they had fielded an ineligible player and thus were required to forfeit the game, making our record 14-4-2. Too bad we didn't know that sooner. Perhaps the NCAAs would have fallen our way.

An excellent year it was! Ten shut-outs, five double OT games, lots of goals scored by numerous players, many awards earned, and NO red cards!!

Upon the request of recent graduate John Cropper, who was serving in the Peace Corps in Albania working with youngsters in a poor rural community, the team collected soccer equipment as a donation to kids in that foreign country. Cropper '04 wrote us a thoughtful note after receiving the donation: "… If you could only witness the joy you have provided this depressed town, you would understand what you have all done." And Helen received a wonderful thank you note from all the referees who whistled at our home games for all the water and juices she provided for them at every game.

Finally, the *CC Bulletin* ran a centerfold article on Brian Tafel, who, as a sports junkie, had decided to write his thesis on a basketball topic. A handsome picture of him, on the soccer field with a basketball in one hand, text books in the other, and a soccer ball curled on his right foot, highlighted the article. I said of him: "He is an unbelievable competitor with an unbending will to win. How improbable that over two successive seasons he would have two season-ending injuries."

A TIME OF TRANSITION

2007-2015

2007

During Block VIII in the late spring of 2007, David Beckham, already an international soccer icon and star, had announced his intentions to play professional soccer in this country for the LA Galaxy. On the CC campus in the same time frame, our own Pat Fagan had catapulted to stardom by becoming an underground poster boy for the Lamapalooza spring festival. Posters around campus announced him as FAGAN-PALOOZA. It was all just a lot of college fun, of course. A more serious arrival on campus was a new athletic director, Ken Ralph, young and energetic, who over 11 years would become an enormous supporter and spokesperson for CC sports.

After 42 years of teaching German Language and Literature, I had retired from academia and now occupied, for the first time in my coaching career, an office in the sports center. A hallway in the back of the El Pomar Great Hall had been converted to accommodate three mini-offices for women's lacrosse, tennis, and men's soccer. The move from my professorial office in Armstrong Hall to an office space as staff member in El Pomar was a major transition in my life. I really missed being in the classroom, but I also enjoyed extra time for family and travel.

At that time I was lucky and pleased to secure the services of a special young man to become my assistant coach. James Wagenschutz and I worked together for six years; we complemented each other well. Although he was a Denver University graduate where he had coordinated their club soccer program, his allegiance was now clearly with CC. He was an Outward Bound Wilderness man, ran the Pikes Peak Marathon, and had worked for the United States Anti-Doping Agency. His special areas became fitness training, goalkeeper coaching, electronic communication and recruiting, and road trip preparations.

The last category now was more important than ever, because we now were full-fledged members of the Southern Collegiate Athletic Conference (SCAC). Fifteen years of NCAA affiliation as an independent college had come to an end.

The SCAC in area and distances was enormous. Here's the list of the member schools in 2007.

Austin College .... *Sherman, Texas*
Birmingham-Southern College .... *Birmingham, Alabama*
Centre College .... *Danville, Kentucky*
Colorado College... *Colorado Springs, Colorado*
DePauw University...................................... *Greencastle, Indiana*
Hendrix College.. *Conway, Arkansas*
Millsaps College.. *Jackson, Mississippi*
Oglethorpe University................................ *Atlanta, Georgia*
Rhodes College.. *Memphis, Tennessee*
Sewanee-The University of the South.......... *Sewanee, Tennessee*
Southwestern University............................. *Georgetown, Texas*
Trinity University.. *San Antonio, Texas*

2007 | 13-7-0

Front row, left to right: Matt Franco, Logan Langholz, Jordan Reese, Andy McGhie, Joe Wykowski, David Khuen, Brian Engle, Berk Korustan, Chris Ellis, Ben Beadle-Ryby (captain). **Middle row:** Brendan Douglas, Warren Takashima, Ben Shapleigh, Chris Quon, Matt Samson (captain), Kevin Ecke, Logan Boccard, Ben Hancock, Matt Hall, Pat Fagan, Lee Smith, Nicky Anastas. **Back row:** Assistant Coaches James Wagenschutz and Jesse Perez, David Van Sicklen, Trevor Cobb, Jimmer Comerford, Hunter Oliver-Allen, Michael Richardson, Wes Rikkers, Jason Steiert (captain), George Hicks, Wil Nelp, Student Trainer Katie Beckmann, Coach Horst Richardson.

As one can readily see, Colorado Springs to Atlanta for a conference game is no mere trek across town. Another anomaly was the fact that four of these schools had a tiger as their mascot.

In a pre-season press release, our SID, Dave Reed, had written about the expectations of the squad:

> *After playing the last 15 years as an independent, the Tigers are eager to experience the benefits of conference membership. Building rivalries, earning individual awards, and playing for a championship are all worthwhile objectives, but the real prize is the opportunity to play for a berth in the NCAA play-offs. And, due to the strength of the conference, it is possible that more than one team could qualify. Coach Richardson says that he would be pleased if the team finished in the top three.*

With 11 games scheduled by the conference in a single round-robin set-up, a maximum of nine other games needed to be scheduled by me. Since conference competition did not begin until late September, the first four weeks of the season were devoted to non-conference matches against comparable D-III opponents from in and out of region. The SCAC had no conference championship tournament in place; the winner of the regular season was crowned champion and represented the conference in the NCAA post-season tournament.

We started the first semester with another service project at the Taos Pueblo and arrived back on campus eager and ready to hit the soccer pitch. But instead, our program was hit with a major hazing allegation, which clouded the entire season.

Initiation of new team members to sports teams was deeply ingrained in collegiate culture, and team captains and upperclassmen always devised some party event to "initiate" the newbies. However, with hazing incidents increasing nationwide, the college was no longer inclined to deal casually with these incidents. So when neighbors to an off-campus soccer house party complained to the college administration about loud and unruly behavior, the dean of students, Mike Edmonds, came down on us with a hammer, even threatening forfeiture of the entire season.

After the dust had settled and all was said and done, the team was slapped with 64 suspensions!!! Here is what our punishment consisted of:

- For the four seniors attending: three-game suspensions, miss first road trip
- For all others attending: two-game suspensions
- 16 hours of community service for the team
- Mandatory attendance at "Dangers of Hazing" lecture.

If it hadn't been for the support of the new Athletic Director, Ken Ralph, in these deliberations, our punishment could have been worse. The new assistant, James Wagenschutz, and I were faced with the challenge of monitoring all the suspensions. James sent me his reflections on his first days on the job:

> *There I was, standing behind the El Pomar athletic center with my new boss, new coach, new surroundings. It was mid-August 2007, my first pre-season had started with so much positive energy about the year and a new opportunity in coaching college soccer. I was beyond ecstatic. Then, it happened. Reality check. Horst pulls me aside and gives me the news. "James, we have some bad news. There were some neighbor complaints about our boys. Possible hazing. Going to be some issues."*
>
> *In my head I said ... Wait, what? When? Who? Where? Say that again.*
>
> *Then, after what seemed like a really long pause, he provides the details of what he knows thus far. Then with almost a sense of humor and a coy smile, Horst says, "Are you sure you want to do this? Put your life in the hands of 18- to 22-year-olds?" He then pats my back and smiles: "Welcome to college coaching."*
>
> *So, one of my first tasks as an assistant coach at this small, D-III liberal arts college was to track 64 rolling suspensions over the course of the season and report to the Head Coach and AD. I guess the coaching on the field would come later.*

The outcome of these rolling suspensions was that we never had the same team on the field in any contest during the entire season! But we still managed a 13-7 season and a third-place finish in the inaugural SCAC year. That was a magnificent indication of the fiber and the grit of this squad and a terrific lesson in overcoming adversity.

James and I, plus part-time assistants Jesse Perez and Eddy Dietz, as well as Pat McGinnis, who was back in town after his brief professional career in Kansas City, worked hard to prepare a handicapped squad for each week's series of games. It was a real credit to the team, especially to our captain Ben Beadle-Ryby, that they accepted their imposed punishment and were eager to put their best foot forward and make amends.

My approach to the rolling suspensions was to make the seniors eligible as soon as possible by sitting them out in the early season games. Sweeper Jason Steiert, defender Matt Samson, keeper David Khuen and forward Pat Fagan were soon back full-time. One stroke of good luck for us that fall was that our speedy forward, and high-scorer from the year before, Logan Boccard, had not attended the initiation party and was thus available to play for all the matches, providing needed firepower.

Of the early games that season, one stands out as an anomaly. We lost to Willamette University from Oregon in overtime, undeservedly, 3-2. We outshot the Bearcats by a wide margin and were leading the game. They then scored on three long-range set plays in a row, an unbelievable percentage of success. A lucky day for them, to be sure. Under the tutelage of Assistant Coach Jesse Perez, Trevor Cobb improved his scoring prowess, and our talented player Chris Quon, returning from injury, showed promise.

After the first eight games, fortunately all at home, we had recorded four shut-outs and six victories, including one against our first-ever SCAC opponent, Austin College. I was pleasantly surprised by our performance so far under duress.

Our first SCAC road trip, to the deep south of Mississippi and Alabama, didn't start off on a positive note, as David Van Sicklen missed the airport bus! In the heat and humidity of Jackson and Birmingham, we managed a split in two games.

A "balls-out" poster, the description of which I will leave to your imagination, advertised our Homecoming games. Again we split a SCAC weekend series, learning to recognize and respect a superior and top-ranked Trinity University squad. A supportive number of parents and alums attended our games and helped with a Homecoming BBQ reception. The parents also conducted a fundraiser to benefit the team.

After squeaking past Oglethorpe and Southwestern by identical 1-0 scores, on goals from Fagan and Reese, we had set our sights on second place in the conference, and when we defeated Sewanee as well, that second place finish definitely seemed in reach. Junior Chris Quon scored his first game-winning goal in that match. Another factor in the victory, no doubt, was an early-season snowstorm, which left the visitors from Tennessee perplexed.

The season was coming to a close. In a rough game away to Centre College in the woods of Kentucky, the host was shown two red cards, and Jordan Reese, our rising attacker, needed stitches in his left eyebrow after a high elbow knocked him to the ground. David Khuen was stellar in the nets and Boccard scored twice to lock up the win for us. Jason Steiert, our sweeper, considered that game our *tour de force* for the fall campaign:

> *Centre was highly regarded in the SCAC and had a similar record to ours. It was one of the best games we had played as a team. Our passing, shooting, and tenacity were all spot on. We played for each other and sacrificed our bodies to help each other out. There was an element of invincibility; I just know and felt that we were going*

to dominate that day. ... They had one vocal fan who shouted degrading comments against our players. After our second goal, though, he shut up. ...

Against DePauw in Greencastle, Indiana, we were unable to penetrate the opposing defense effectively and had to settle for a 1-0 loss. On the plane home from Chicago, though, much levity ensued because of a cookie incident. Our players, Warren Takashima No. 18 and George Hicks No. 15, were in possession of some delicious chocolate chip cookies, which they shared with a couple of girls from the DU women's soccer team, also on their way home, seated several rows ahead of us. Our boys attached a note to the cookie plate: "Dear Ladies — Help yourself to a delicious cookie. From one Colorado team to another. From CC Men's Soccer — the boys in rows 21 and 22, #18 and #15. (In a P.S., a *double entendre* was attached.) Let's scrimmage sometime!!"

The DU ladies actually sent a note back: "Dearest CC boys — we thankfully accept these delicious cookies. They sure beat Fritos and Sun Chips. #15 and #18 are undoubtedly the smarter ones of the group. Two men to 18 women are relatively good odds!" (Warren had saved this note and passed it on to me.)

After a stupendous win vs. Hendrix in Arkansas the following weekend, a game in which senior sweeper Matt Samson struck twice for goals, second place and a possible NCAA berth once again seemed within reach. And then came the last game of the season against Rhodes College in Memphis.

Regulation time had ended in a 2-2 tie. We were winning the statistics, but had made careless mistakes throughout the contest. With four minutes left in double overtime, the Tigers lost ball possession needlessly in the middle of the park, which gave Rhodes a breakaway on goal. They scored.

Our senior net minder David Khuen '08, in his last collegiate game, was furious! He felt the team had let him down, and I tended to agree with him. He and I sat out on the field alone for a long time, contemplating what could have happened if things had gone our way. Here are David's comments about his final college game:

The final game of the season was away at Rhodes College in Tennessee. All we needed to do was win and we were in the NCAA tournament. We were playing a mid-level team (at best) in Rhodes. We were second in the SCAC behind Trinity. However, we played like absolute garbage! We could not complete a pass, defended on our heels, and maybe had two shots on goal. We were the better team, but when you play that poorly, anything can happen.

After tying the game 1-1, they were awarded a penalty shot in the closing stages of the game. The guy put a decent strike on the ball, but I, correctly, thought he was going to my right. I made the save, and did my best to parlay that energy into breaking us out of the lull we were in all game. Unfortunately, that was not the case. In the second period of overtime, they netted the game winner. This ended our season, and my career at Colorado College.

While my last memory was not the most positive from my CC soccer career, it did nothing to diminish my time between the pipes at CC. I played with great soccer players, was part of some great wins, and even broke some records. However, and most importantly, I made lifelong friends through the CC Soccer program.

From a pimply freshman, excited to play in college, to a three-year starter helping to lead the team to multiple successful seasons, the best times I had on the pitch were on Stewart Field. I even played semi-professionally in Australia, but I have more fond memories with my teammates at CC. Horst and Helen were an integral part to both our soccer and our personal growth. Thank you both for all the memories!!

The benefit of conference affiliation became evident at the banquet when we were able to announce plenty of league awards to our players, even though we had traveled thousands of miles to earn them. Other regional accolades followed. Given the self-inflicted handicap at the beginning of the season, the team rallied to produce a winning season. I was proud of them.

A final note about the season: The campus paper, *The Catalyst*, did not carry any sports coverage that season. What a bummer!

As a footnote to the season, I must confess that several times during that fall it occurred to me that I might quit as coach of the team because of the hardships imposed on us after the hazing incident. It was a major strain, to say the least. In retrospect, I am glad I stuck it out with the team. We all learned from the experience.

2008

On occasions I would send out a pre-season announcement letter to all the alums, thanking them for their support in fundraising efforts and encouraging them to attend a game or two in the fall. I did so in 2008. The Boddington/Richardson Soccer Endowment had grown steadily over the years and was now earning substantial yields to benefit the

2008 | 13-6-1

Front row, left to right: Travis Boccard, Nicky Anastas, Andy McGhie, Brian Engle, Joey Wykowski, Colin Prather, Ben Beadle-Ryby (captain), Berk Korustan. **Middle row:** Trainer Holly Fry, David Van Sicklen, Wil Nelp, Ben Hancock, Logan Boccard, Chris Lutz, Brendan Douglas, Matt Franco, Jordan Reese, Chris Ellis, Coach Horst Richardson. **Back row:** Student Trainer Danielle Wisuri, Assistant Coach James Wagenschutz, Kevin Ecke, Jimmer Comerford (captain), Sandy Feuer, Hunter Oliver-Allen, Michael Richardson, Wes Rikkers, Chris Walker, Trevor Cobb, Warren King, Assistant Coach Pat McGinnis.

---

team. For instance, in my mailing to the alums this year, I announced that we had hired a special motivational speaker to address the team, none other than Ronn Svetich, the sports psychologist and mental coach for the Colorado Rockies. We learned from him about aspects of team dynamics and competition.

The Boddington/Richardson Fund also made possible attending a fun-filled Shakespeare-in-the-Park performance of *As You Like It*, which was welcomed recuperation from the physical training on the pitch. Finally, my alumni letter introduced the staff and the team leadership to our supporters:

> *An able staff, boosted this year by 2004 graduate Patrick McGinnis, All-American and NCAA D-III national player-of-the-year, will attempt to guide the squad to its lofty goal of challenging for the conference title. James Wagenschutz and Dan Highstead, both USSF licensed coaches, are resourceful, knowledgeable, and valuable assistants. Captain for this year's group is the talented and energetic midfielder Ben Beadle-Ryby, from Loveland, Colorado. Another Coloradan, Jimmer Comerford from Grand*

> *Junction, steady and dependable on defense, will serve in the capacity of co-captain, and the junior captain is the dynamic Trevor Cobb from Corrales, New Mexico. These three will provide considerable maturity and leadership on and off the field.*

James Wagenschutz, called Wagz, accompanied my son, my daughter and me into the Himalayas of Nepal that summer to deliver CC soccer gear to the highest elementary school in the world, the Edmund Hillary Elementary School in Pangboche, at an altitude well over 12,000 feet, continuing a service commitment towards underprivileged children. (James remembers talking soccer strategy in the Khumbu Valley. There we were, the two of us, at a tea house in the shadow of Mount Everest, moving salt and pepper shakers around, preparing for the fall season!) Wagz also ran the Pikes Peak Ascent in August, coming in No. 200.

Dan Highstead began a long career of CC assistant coaching that fall. Very British and full of jokes and esoteric drills, he became a favorite presence on the field.

I had always been reluctant at the beginning of a season to make predictions about the outcome of the campaign. My philosophy was more geared toward "one-game-at-a-time." In 2008, we were quite successful with that mentality: after nine games our record stood at 8-1. What a fantastic September it was!

Competition began with a road trip to Minnesota where, at the home of the formidable "Olies" of St. Olaf in Northfield, we crushed the host by a score of 4-1. That was unheard of! Our opening weekend at home featured a coast-to-coast tournament between us, MIT, and Cal-Tech. The brain trust of MIT provided us with the only defeat in September. If Logan Boccard's blistering shot high off the right post had scored, who knows what might have happened!

A SCAC away trip to Texas loomed on the horizon. In the SCAC, each team had a travel partner. Whenever we were scheduled to play against Trinity, it seemed that we had to first compete against their travel partner, Southwestern. Southwestern's coach and I were good friends, primarily because he rode a German BMW road bike. But when the kickoff got the game under way, our attention was focused on victory.

It was an afternoon game and the temperature at midafternoon hovered around 93 degrees. Fleet-footed Berk Korustan, of Turkish descent and dominant flank player, gave us the win with his first game-winning goal of his career.

Southwestern University is located in Georgetown, Texas, about an hour north of Austin. Since we could only afford missing one class day on an away trip, we would fly out of Denver late Thursday, rent vans, and arrive at our motel near Georgetown around 11 p.m. On Saturday morning, our off-day, we would relocate to a motel in San Antonio, have study time in the afternoon and visit the River Walk in the evening. In order to catch our flight back to Denver from Austin on Sunday, the Trinity game inevitably would start at high noon, leaving time for a quick meal and airport travel after the conclusion of the match.

The CC Tigers had not beaten Trinity since 1996. This match turned into a real shoot-out at high noon at the OK Corral. Undefeated Trinity were ranked No. 1 in the country when we faced them. A win would secure first place in the SCAC for us. Adrenaline was flowing, and everyone was eager for the contest to commence. At the end of the half the game stood scoreless. Ben Beadle-Ryby, our captain, describes the contest's conclusion:

> *On the back-end of four memorable years sits this vivid recollection of a game against a rival. This time it was on the road in the sweltering San Antonio heat against the nation's number one team, Trinity. It was our time to measure ourselves against the country's best and we didn't shy away from the challenge.*
>
> *The entire game was back and forth — truly one of the most competitive games I can remember. After coming out of the first half dead-even, I felt the momentum shifted our way in the second half. We had a couple close shots and we found ourselves in their side of the field most of the way through the second half. In the end, 90 minutes of back and forth is boiled down in a box-score to two PKs — one which we missed, and one which they made in the 89th minute. It was an insanely demoralizing defeat.*
>
> *At the time, that defeat weighed heavily on us, and we collectively failed to recognize that the game demonstrated that we were on par with the best ... As I look back, that loss was one of the highlights of my career — painful, no doubt, but a reminder that we could hang with anybody out there.*

The emotional build-up to a game like Trinity leaves repercussions. On the flight home I looked closely at the players; they were drained and most of them sound asleep in the plane. I knew that it would take time to get over the Trinity loss.

A second 1-0 loss followed vs. Nebraska Wesleyan, before we were back on track. By the time we played against Westminster College from Salt Lake City, Brian Engle had established himself as our starting goalkeeper, and super-sub Kevin Ecke gave us the winning goal.

Against the defensive specialists of DePauw University, we had to settle for a tie, even though shots were 34-7 in our favor. Nevertheless, we were on track for second place in the conference.

A severe setback occurred in Dallas where we could not overcome a stubborn University of Dallas opponent on their postage stamp-size field. Boccard and Cobb combined to give us a victory over Hendrix, but the final weekend in Tennessee and Atlanta brought a promising season to a disappointing end.

The 13-6-1 season was highlighted by scoring 54 goals while allowing only 15; 10 shut-outs for our goalkeepers; six of our players earning spots on the All-Conference team; Academic All-American honors bestowed on Logan Boccard and Jimmer Comerford; and with a team GPA average of 3.42, a No. 5 ranking in academic standing in the entire country! And it was the first season of video streaming our home games.

2009

As we delve into the 2009 season, the biggest athletic news on campus, no doubt, was the discontinuation of our football program. It became a victim of the recession, the inability to recruit the necessary number of players for the squad, and the lack of equitable competition. In 1882, on Christmas Day, the CC Tiger football team played its first game! And now, with changing times and priorities, it had faded away.

In May, our all-time leading scorer and ex-pro Arron Lujan was inducted into the CC Athletic Hall of Fame, a well-deserved honor for a soccer legend. His induction was the fifth CC soccer personality to be so honored, after Bill Boddington, Saad Sahawneh, Jay Engeln, and Brigham Olson.

In August before pre-season, the team embarked on another international tour, our sixth such venture, this time to Brazil.

Former goalkeeper Zac Rubin had returned to his native Manhattan to become an entrepreneur, opening up a successful soccer store on the Upper West Side. He also had connections in soccer-team travel to Brazil, a soccer-mad country, where he had trained during high school.

2009 | 10-9-1

Front row, left to right: Ben Shapleigh, Austin Dressen, Travis Boccard, Brian Graf, Brian Engle, Andy McGhie, Jordan Reese, Anthony Hyatt. **Middle row:** Wil Nelp (captain), Chris Lutz, Henok Yemam, Ryan Jaeger, Chris Ellis, Joel Dungan, Brendan Douglas, Daniel Wright, Ben Hanock. **Back row:** Assistant Coaches Dan Highstead and Pat McGinnis, Warren King, Trevor Cobb (captain), Keith Drury, Nick Lammers, Chris Walker, Matt Fechter, David Van Sicklen, Coach Horst Richardson, Assistant Coach James Wagenschutz. **Not pictured:** Nicky Anastas, Kevin Ecke, Forrest Marowitz.

Zac and his Brazilian friends devised a terrific adventure for us, focusing on native culture, fun on the beach, people-to-people meetings and soccer, of course. We flew into São Paolo, and after enduring the chaos at the airport there, continued on to the charming colonial city of Salvador in the northeastern state of Bahia.

Our comfortable hotel adjoined the white sands of the ocean and it didn't take long for the guys to participate in pick-up soccer and volleyball games. The local first division professional club became our training ground for a week. I was amazed that Nicky Anastas, who had missed our flight south from New York, managed to find us a couple of days late in this distant corner of Brazil. And Wil Nelp, staying out late every night under the stars on the beach, had fallen desperately in love with one of the local university coeds.

Good thing that the month of August in the southern hemisphere is a "winter" month down under, otherwise our second stop, in Belo Horizonte in the state of Minas Gerais, would have been too hot to handle for us. In "Belo," we stayed at the youth training facility of the fabled Cruzeiro Club. Assistant Coach James Wagenschutz and I observed their training methods, learned from the coaching staff, supervised our players, and on occasions took the boys out of the compound for an açai berry milkshake. Yummy!

Zac Rubin had introduced us to a New York City high school player who was training at Cruzeiro. Lorenzo Pozzolini stood out as a soccer talent and expressed interest in CC. A year later he had enrolled at our campus!!

Attending a professional game in the 100,000-seat Estadio Mineirao was, no doubt, a highlight of our tour. Watching the "beautiful game" in this electric atmosphere was exhilarating! Pele's feet, cast in bronze, greeted the spectators at the entrance to the stadium.

I made sure that the team visited another stadium in Belo Horizonte of major significance to U.S. soccer. During the 1950 World Cup, which Brazil had hosted, one of the greatest moments in U.S. soccer history had occurred there: The USA fledgling squad had defeated super power England 1-0 in a major upset. Years prior to our visit, during a coaching course, I had been to this stadium with legendary St. Louis University Coach Harry Keough, who had actually been a member of that U.S. squad. Before we left Belo, we continued our tradition of community service by engaging with a youth center in a *favela* neighborhood. This volunteer activity left a lasting impression on Chris Ellis '10:

> *In the summer before my senior year, our team took a trip to Brazil to volunteer, attend professional games, and play soccer with and against local teams. This was a truly transformative experience as we were able to experience a new culture through a game that we all love.*
>
> *While in Brazil, we spent a significant amount of time in* favelas, *impoverished neighborhoods, interacting with local kids. Although these kids lacked things that we took for granted every day, they were so happy and excited to show us around their neighborhood. They became even happier when we got to the soccer field and started to kick the ball around.*
>
> *I will never forget how these kids were able to find an escape through soccer that allowed them to take control and create. Not to mention that they were extremely talented players. I have often reflected on this trip and moments with the Brazilian youth and I am reminded to appreciate and enjoy life.*

Trevor Cobb '10, ever the philosopher and literati, chimes in about the *favela* experience with these reflections:

Wearing expensive cleats on a rock-hard dirt field is like wearing running shoes on an ice rink. And when we laced up on the favela *pitch in the Minas Gerais region of Brazil, we might as well have been playing on ice. The local squad danced circles around us in plumes of dust. The boys we were up against — and they were just that, many not more than 16 years old — had rolled out of bed that morning "ready to ball."*

With the exception of our Latin sensation, Ben Hancock (who stepped on the field with a trimmed mullet and a mustache that would have made any mariachi proud), it was clear that we were far from home. And yet, the match made us forget our differences. We spoke in butchered Portuguese, but communicated through our movements. On the field we had the same lexicon and spoke the same language. We had the same understanding of grace and fluidity, and we all craved the rush that comes from watching the ball hit the back of the opponents' net.

For two years we had planned our trip to Brazil, which required traveling some 9,500 km over the course of several weeks. When we strolled out of our air-conditioned bus onto the streets of the favela *that morning, the contrast between our lives back home and life here in this poor neighborhood felt indeed profound. By the end of the match, though, we were all mere sweat-drenched footballers.*

I had long believed that soccer, or futebol, as the Brazilians say, is the universal language. But never before had I experienced its power to bring people together, and to shadow our differences.

So I pose the question to our family of Tiger players, past, present, and future: What is our role as footballers? What is our global responsibility as native speakers of the universal language? I'd wager to say that the answer may be more important than we care to think!

Members of the team sent a daily blog of our activities to the CC athletic website, documenting our trip. We came home with an appreciation of a vibrant and diverse culture and the satisfaction that we, as soccer players, were part of a global community through sports.

When interviewed about the forthcoming 2009 season, I concluded that two challenges lay ahead: We needed to take advantage of our home dates and build momentum for the end of the season. We faced a major dilemma, though, namely an inability to balance our desire to play attractive and entertaining attack-oriented soccer with the absolute need to be efficient, simple, and defensively determined.

We addressed this dilemma all season; eventually, I think, the joy of playing attacking soccer took priority over recovery runs and consistent attention to defensive needs. As a consequence, our final season record, even though we scored 41 goals and allowed only 27, was a mediocre 10-9-1. However, of the games we lost, six were lost by only one goal, and all of those matches could have gone either way.

Our coaching staff was the same as the year before. Seven seniors returned to action from the previous campaign, including attackers Trevor Cobb and Jordan Reese, midfielders Ben Hancock, Brendan Douglas and Chris Ellis, and goalie Brian Engle. We were light on juniors — only four were on the squad, led by defensive stud Wil Nelp. Of the six sophomores, Chris Lutz had asserted himself and became a starter on the flank. The freshman class showed much promise, with giant and lanky defender Nick Lammers, razzle-dazzle dribbler Matt Fechter and two solid keepers in Brian Graf and Forrest Marowitz.

Chris Lutz '12 wrote to me about me getting mad at one of the opponents, an incident which he has never forgotten:

> *We were playing a close game, I don't remember which one, and their right mid kicked the ball out of bounds and you (Horst) yelled at him, "Not in the creek!" as it sailed over the fence. That phrase became a battle cry for the remainder of the game and season. To this day that remains a common soundbite among our group of soccer friends and we were all appreciative of the energy and trash talk coming from the head coach!*

Yes, I could get quite incensed when some defender on the other team would purposely drill the ball into the creek! Our associate director of athletics, Greg Capell, who came to many of our home games, more than once risked life and limb descending the embankment into the creek bed to retrieve errant balls. Greg, thanks for your service to the team, which was above and beyond the call of duty!!

After six games into the season, our record was a paltry 2-3-1. In game No. 4 we faced Whitworth, a squad well-known to us as a regional NCAA tournament opponent from previous years. In this game, I was ready to give a transfer student playing time. Ryan Jaeger '12, a mountain boy from Telluride, Colorado, with flaming red hair, had trained diligently and shown signs of sparkle. Ryan recollects his first playing minutes for CC:

I had just transferred to CC from Bucknell in hopes of accomplishing one thing: to play soccer on the collegiate level. After a rough start to the season, the stars aligned. I had perhaps the best week of soccer of my own career. We had a night practice before our game against Whitman, and I buried a shot from outside the 18 against the starting lineup. Horst came to talk to me after practice and I recall him saying, "I wish we could start you, but you'll get some minutes come game day."

As promised, the day came, and nearing the end of the first half, I was on the sideline warming up for my first collegiate appearance. The dream was in fact becoming a reality. My name was called over the loudspeaker as I subbed in. Minutes later a ball came from a goal kick, was flicked on by Matt Fechter, and I was on a breakaway. My first collegiate game, my first appearance, I put away a goal for the Tigers!

That moment, those seconds will mean more in my life than I can ever explain. It wasn't until then that I felt I had truly earned my spot in the Tiger family. A family that will be with me to the grave.

In overtime, Jordan Reese blasted a shot off the crossbar that could've won the game, but Whitworth walked away with a victory on a lame shot to goal, which deflected off one of our defenders and trickled into our goal.

However, the sixth game produced a splendid win over Southwestern on a Friday at home, and I sensed that we were over the hump and ready to tackle Trinity on the Sunday game, even though once again the schedule had placed Trinity as the second game in the series. I had scheduled a brief practice session for Saturday to shake out the legs and get ready for the big encounter. And right in the middle of practice, something totally unforeseen and tragic occurred.

A member of the athletic staff had come out to the field and beckoned me over to him. I was told that last year's graduate Chris Quon, a varsity member of both the soccer and lacrosse teams, had suddenly and unexpectedly died in Chicago because of heart complications. Had a bolt of lightning struck down from the clear blue sky, I couldn't have been more stunned. I circled the team around me and told them the sad news. We sobbed, trying to understand this cruel twist of fate. Our friend Chris Quon, a specimen of health and athleticism, had left us.

In a CC press release, I remembered Chris: "Chris was an inspiration to his teammates through his upbeat nature, outgoing personality and his athletic abilities." His mother, when asked to submit a memory of her son for our soccer narrative, submitted the following words:

I remember bringing Chris to visit CC for the first time as a senior in high school. It was a clear beautiful day — and Chris took one look at the soccer field with the mountains in the background and decided then and there that if CC were to accept him, it would be his home for the next four years!

Chris loved the game, but most important to him were his teammates and coaches. Our family has so many special memories of CC soccer: driving to Iowa to watch Chris play in his freshman year with his proud grandpa in the cheering section; watching Chris and his team passionately ring the CC bell after a win; seeing Chris slide on his knees in celebration after scoring a goal (which unfortunately led to an injury — oh man, Chris!); Chris sharing with me the video that he produced to pitch the school on having a house just for soccer players to live in (denied!); a life-changing soccer trip to Germany with the team during the World Cup; watching the short videos that he created to promote upcoming soccer games; meeting and spending time with his wonderful teammates — even now years later after losing our beloved Chris.

The memory that is precious to me is seeing Chris' CC teammates enter the church at his service in Chicago — it meant the world to our family to see his "brothers" there, and I know Chris knew they were there.

We are grateful for the love from the CC community, his teammates, extended CC Soccer team (assistant coaches, equipment managers, trainers), and from Coach Horst and Helen — for Chris and our family — years later.

Now the beautiful tree that was planted in Chris' memory stands at the place where Chris stood overlooking the CC fields with the mountains behind. I know Chris is with us always and cheering on his beloved CC teams.

As I write today, on April 20, 2018, I visited his tree on top of the Tiger Trail leading down to the athletic fields. The young, deciduous tree is sporting lush green leaves, growing next to a memorial bench from which one can contemplate the western view. I have a hunch that Chris sits on the bench every now and then, dreaming of the good times he had on the soccer and lacrosse fields.

We dedicated the rest of the season to the memory of our teammate. The energy and passion we displayed in competing against perennial superpower Trinity the next day was an indication of our love for Chris. However, the soccer gods showed no compassion, and we lost a hard-fought contest 1-0.

Our next match, another SCAC encounter, was a victory, which happened to be my 500th win. Yet, I was not at the game. More important that day was my presence at Chris' funeral in Lake Forest, north of Chicago. It was comforting for the Quon family to see so many representatives from CC at his service. Dave Reed, our SID, wrote to me about that weekend, which was both solemn and celebratory:

> *Under normal circumstances, a 4-0 victory over the University of Dallas would not be especially memorable. But on that particular day, the opponent did not really matter. Horst Richardson joined an exclusive group on Saturday when he picked up career victory No. 500. Unfortunately, he wasn't around to enjoy it. While the Tigers defeated the Crusaders at Stewart Field, Richardson was approximately 1,100 miles away outside of Chicago attending the funeral of Chris Quon, who passed away less than a week earlier.*
>
> *"I'm very happy about achieving the milestone," Richardson said, "but I wish I could have enjoyed it under different circumstances."*
>
> *Richardson joined Wheaton College's Joe Bean (586), Ohio Wesleyan's Jay Martin (557), Keene State's Ron Butcher (545) and Rowan's Dan Gilmore (514) as the only Division III coaches to reach the milestone. Five coaches at the Division I and II levels also have 500 career victories.*
>
> *"I'm sort of at a loss for words," Richardson said. "I knew that it was coming, but now that it's here, I'm not sure how I'm supposed to feel."*

At Homecoming the weather turned quite cold and windy. Helen and I hosted 55 alums and players for breakfast, reminiscing about the "good old days." After the Homecoming game, President Celeste presented me with a 500-win commemorative soccer ball.

The rest of the season was a see-saw affair. We tried hard to break into winning territory, but brought a 9-9-1 record into our last game away to Millsaps on astroturf in Jackson, Mississippi. Missing on our last two-game road trip was starting goalkeeper Brian Engle. He had volunteered for the women's soccer team, tending goal in a penalty training session and had fractured his wrist.

The Millsaps contest remained a nailbiter to the end, but Jordan Reese's early goal in the second half stood for the winner. His goal relieved our anxiety and assured a winning season. The flight home, though, was a losing situation for Chris Ellis and me, as we were bumped from our flight!! Oh well ...

Since the 2009 season, the college has staged the annual Quony Cup, a small-sided, co-ed soccer competition every May, to honor the memory of Chris. This event is also a fundraiser for a worthy cause and is in keeping with Chris' concern for the less fortunate. The Quony Cup has grown into a popular spring festival, both for our students and our alums. Quon's teammates, who attend in full force, have won this fun fest most of the time.

What remains to be said about this season is the birth of a son to Assistant Coach James Wagenschutz and his wife, Kat. Chase, a strapping baby, is now an intelligent 9-year-old boy who displays talent for the beautiful game.

2010

In 2010, the World Cup was staged in South Africa. Helen and I, as well as our son Erik '92, attended. In Johannesburg in Soweto Town, our host was Teddy Mattera, who had played for us in the mid '80s. We reminisced about the good old CC days, and also saw a pair of World Cup matches, including a wild one between England and USA. On the strength of Landon Donovan's goalscoring and Tim Howard's goalkeeping, the U.S. national team advanced to the second round, a terrific achievement for our squad.

At the alumni game in May, just before graduation, a star-studded alumni group had given our forthcoming varsity core group all that they could handle. Both McGinnis brothers, Brian Tafel, Kevin Vicente, Jimmer Comerford, Tim Campbell and others sparkled on Stewart Field. Also, the week before, on Sunday, April 25, the college staged the first annual Quony Cup, which was a great success. Funds were raised for the American Cancer Society and for the Chris Quon Memorial Fund.

At the end of the summer, during NSO week, the candidates for the team traveled to Crestone to camp and engage in volunteer work near the Baca Campus. Fire abatement and trail restoration were the order of the day. The boys displayed a solid work ethic handling shovels, picks and axes, and I was encouraged by their enthusiasm. We concluded our physical labor with a trip to the Great Sand Dunes National Park, where the obligatory race to the highest sand dune occurred.

Back on campus, and after player selection had taken place with inter-squad scrimmages at Sky Sox Soccer Stadium and Fountain Valley School, we participated in a goal-setting seminar, led by entrepreneur and former standout CC midfielder Dick Schulte '74, and his associate Mark Tribus, who brought with him expertise in focus work for special military forces.

2010 | 7-9-2

Front row, left to right: Elliott Levett, Henok Yemam, Lachlan Watkins, Travis Boccard, Faizan Ali-Khan, Andrew Salazar, Daniel Wright. **Second Row:** Assistant Coach Dan Highstead, Team Manager Sawyer Connelly, Joel Dungan, Anthony Hyatt, Forrest Marowitz, Andy McGhie, Brian Graf, Daniel Herz, Ben Shapleigh, Wil Nelp (captain). **Third row:** Ben Glass, Sean Parham, Chris Lutz (captain), Ryan Jaeger, Lorenzo Pozzolini, Warren King, Coach Horst Richardson, Assistant Coach James Wagenschutz. **Back row:** Assistant Coach Patrick McGinnis, Patrick Robinson, Kyle Buchwalder, Josh Feldman, Matt Fechter, Brandon Ogilvie, Nick Lammers, Chris Walker, Aaron Chin, Keith Drury.

Based on two seemingly simple questions, “Who am I?” and “Who are we?”, the players developed a comprehensive strategy for performance and success in a team setting. I was encouraged by the progress we were making, preparing the team for the forthcoming season.

Our SID, in a press release titled “Where there is a Wil, there is a Way,” echoed my sentiment and focused on senior and captain Wil Nelp. I praised Wil in a quote: “If we had 11 players like Wil on the field, I wouldn't have to worry about anything. He is a wonderful athlete and an extreme competitor. Wil has an unbending drive to compete and succeed, and he expects that from his teammates.”

Our veteran threesome of assistants, Wagenschutz, Highstead and McGinnis, were in place to help me organize, train and prepare the squad. And thanks to student Sawyer Connelly for being our team manager.

We looked forward to the fall campaign with guarded optimism. For Homecoming, a special event was planned to celebrate the 60th anniversary of CC soccer, 1950-2010. With a fairly young, talented and able group of players at hand, we had great expectations for this special season.

And yet, the end result was a rather dismal 7-9-2 losing year, only my fifth losing season in my career. We allowed 29 goals and were only able to score 18. Clearly, finishing was an issue. This season, in retrospect, was eerily similar to the 2000 season, also a losing record, when we celebrated the 50th anniversary of CC soccer. Strange indeed!

After the first five games, we had accumulated a 2-2-1 record. We hadn't scheduled any slouches to compete against, and with only three seniors on the team, I figured that a tough schedule would eventually pay off for the younger members of the team. Contest No. 6 against Carnegie Mellon from Pittsburgh, always a play-off team, turned out to be a special event because the coach of the opponent was none other than CC graduate Arron Lujan, CC's all-time high-scorer and Hall-of-Famer. They won the first half, and we the second, but we lost the game.

After a tie against perennial powerhouse Wheaton from Chicago, we were ready for SCAC conference competition. And the team surged forward with four successive wins! But Trinity and Southwestern were not kind to us on the road, and we had to come home with only one goal scored and allowing 10!! Probably the worst road trip ever.

The nail in our coffin that year was another road trip to Texas. The night before our contest against Austin College in Sherman, Texas, the fire alarm in the Dallas hotel scared us out of bed in the middle of the night because balloons from a late-night birthday party had struck the in-house sprinkler system!! And at Austin, a terrific tornado with lightning and heavy rain forced cancellation of the game. All efforts to reschedule that contest failed.

Although, in my opinion, the team showed much promise, no one had a break-out season. There were many bright moments, but no consistency. Nevertheless, morale remained high and we even engaged in a service project in the Garden of the Gods, restoring eroded trails. The Rocky Mountain Field Institute had arranged the volunteer work for us. The guys worked hard on a glorious fall day in the serene setting of the park. At the end of the season, I had the firm conviction that this losing season was an anomaly; it was a learning period for our group and I predicted that the following season would be different.

My athletic department evaluation at the end of the season was not complimentary.

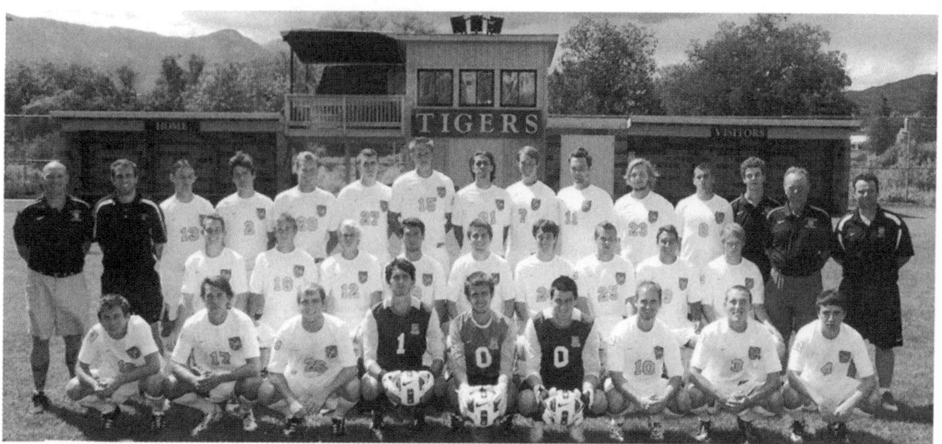

2011 | 11-5-3

Front row, left to right: Alec Martinez, Chris Edmonds, Stuart Beezley, Forrest Marowitz, Alex Spectorsky, Brian Graf, Travis Boccard, Morgan Wack, Andrew Salazar. **Middle row:** Sean Parham, Hunter Martinez, Chris Lutz (captain), Alec Lee, Ben Glass, Alec Sowers, Elliott Levett, Daniel Wright, Ryan Jaeger. **Back row:** Assistant Coaches James Wagenschutz and Dan Walsh, Patrick Robinson, Kyle Buchwalder, Brandon Ogilvie, Andrew Worthington, Nick Lammers, Keith Drury, Josh Feldman, Matt Fechter (captain), Ben Sandalow, Lorenzo Pozzolini, Team Manager Will Bowers, Coach Horst Richardson, Assistant Coach Dan Highstead.

2011

In May 2011, Hall-of-Famer Jay Engeln '74, who had been appointed CC's director of alumni affairs, and his wife, Priscilla, invited the group of alums to their home for post-alumni game refreshments. Of much interest to the alums was the athletic department plan to substantially expand and remodel the El Pomar Sports Center.

On August 14, in the local *Gazette* newspaper, these plans were unveiled and made public. Included in the design was a brand new synthetic playing surface for Washburn Field. The entire project was to be completed in a year and a half. Conceptual drawings of the project provided much excitement in anticipation of these fantastic new facilities.

Our 2011 season was a complete turnaround from the disappointing campaign the year before. We scored twice as many goals as in the previous season, scrimmaged against two D-II RMAC squads in pre-season, played seven overtime games (winning two, losing two, and tying three), competed in the semi-final of the first-ever SCAC play-off tournament, and compiled a respectable 11-5-3 record.

A number of factors contributed to this successful effort. Matt Fechter had a breakout year in our attack and earned SCAC Offensive Player of the Year honors and All-America status. Nick Lammers, at 6'7", became a giant force on defense. Kyle Buchwalder, Academic All-American, intelligent and inexhaustible as defensive midfielder, seemed to roam all over the field. Chris Lutz could sprint from the depth of our defense into the attack and delivered wicked crosses into the penalty box. We were blessed with two terrific goaltenders in Forrest Marowitz and Brian Graf and Sean Parham and Danny Wright exhibited speed and danger up top.

The biggest surprise of the season, though, was a freshman from Chicago whom Tom Lee '78 had helped recruit. Andrew Worthington, from the outset, became the perfect complement to Nick Lammers. The two were unbeatable in the air and intimidating on defense.

Lastly, a former AFA player, Dan Walsh, joined the coaching staff as a volunteer. Not only was he competent on the field, but his witty one-liners also injected much levity at practice. And, most importantly, the players were having fun!

Our conference, the SCAC, was undergoing changes. One of our member schools, DePauw University in southern Indiana, had withdrawn from our conference to join the North Coast Athletic Conference, geographically closer to them. In the SCAC, the members had agreed to subdivide the league into Eastern and Western divisions, and scheduling had become "unbalanced," in as much as not every institution played against every other one in the same season. In 2011, for example, we did not compete against Centre and Sewanee.

The two divisions lined up as follows:

EASTERN	**WESTERN**
Birmingham Southern	Austin
Centre	Colorado College
Millsaps	U-Dallas
Oglethorpe	Hendrix
Rhodes	Southwestern
Sewanee	Trinity

Together, our squad had set a team goal: to improve as a team every time we stepped onto the pitch. A worthy ambition, indeed.

In our opening game against crosstown rival UCCS, seven goals were scored in a heated overtime contest. 2:23 minutes into OT, Sean Parham sealed the victory for us off an assist from Matt Fechter. We have lots of photographs of CC soccer action, but one of the all-time great pictures has to be the one of a jubilant Sean, surrounded by Ben Glass and Matt Fechter, celebrating this winning goal. It is also one of the best memories for SID Dave Reed:

> *Sophomore forward Sean Parham scored 2:23 into overtime as Colorado College stunned CU-Colorado Springs, 4-3, in the season opener for both teams on Thursday afternoon at CC's Stewart Field. The Tigers had to regain their composure after the Division II Mountain Lions scored a pair of late goals to erase a 3-1 deficit. But unlike a year ago when Colorado College dropped a 3-2 decision in overtime, the Tigers scored the deciding goal and snapped a two-game skid against their crosstown rivals.*
>
> *"It shows a lot of character by our guys," head coach Horst Richardson said. "I'm so exceedingly proud of them to not fold because we have been snake-bitten in overtime the last two years. I can't even recall the last overtime game that we won."*
>
> *Parham struck for the first game-winning goal of his career from six yards out, putting the shot over the outstretched arms of UCCS junior goalkeeper Jarod Thomas and just under the crossbar. Matt Fechter picked up his third assist of the game, the first game-winning assist of his career, after misfiring on a bicycle kick from 15 yards out on the left side. As the Mountain Lions' defenders turned toward the goal, Parham was left unattended in the middle of the box.*
>
> *It was the most exciting conclusion to a CC game I can remember.* *(See p. 144.)*

Two overtime games followed, before a hot and humid away trip to Minnesota. Not on the Minnesota trip was Brandon Ogilvie. This promising and powerful sophomore was out for the season with a knee injury, incurred in the fourth game of the season. I kept reminding the players about our agreed-upon goal, and indeed, it seemed to me, win or lose, we were improving with each match.

Clearly we were superb back at home at the Boddington Tournament, with two shut-out victories against Wittenberg and UC Santa Cruz, the latter rated No. 17 in the country at the time. There was no better way to beat Santa Cruz than to have senior Travis Boccard '12 do the honors on the only goal in the game. It was the first game-winning goal of his career. Travis, known for his grit, desire, and hustle, speaks about this glorious moment:

It was the goal I have been waiting for all season and I am glad to have scored it to help the team to a great win. Our whole half-time conversation was about putting pressure on them from the back all the way through. We did a great job of that. We knew going into the game that they were a quality team. Our defense was awesome!

Travis rang the victory bell after the game! Chris Lutz also singles out the UC Santa Cruz game as his most memorable moment:

The best victory I had during my four years on the team was the win against Santa Cruz, then nationally ranked. It was a hard-fought 1-0 win that I credit not only to my teammates, but also to the huge number of fans who came out to support us. I remember this win so vividly because it set the tone for the rest of the season and proved to us that we could beat anyone we faced!

A curiosity about this game was the fact that referee Lance James, clutching his cell phone during the entire match, received a call from his wife informing him that she was going into labor. He stopped the game for a couple of minutes to be able to speak with the soon-to-be mother. After finishing the match, he rushed to her side. Chris Edmonds '14, better known as "Ox," distinctly remembers this incident and writes about it:

Lance, the bald ref, never got much love from the bench at Stewart Field. He would run around too aggressively like he was playing in the game. He talked more than he needed to, an all-too-obvious crutch to keep control over the games that often spiraled out of his hands. And sometimes he just made really bad calls.

Be that as it may, we will always remember the day Lance was reffing a game at Stewart when there was some commotion at the sideline. It turned out he was reffing while his wife was in the final throes of her pregnancy with their child, and she had just gone into labor. I never heard if she had gone into labor prematurely, but the fact that he chose to ref our game rather than to be with her was striking. And part of me had a renewed understanding and respect for Lance. The man loved the game, he was out there in service to soccer, and in dedication to the players who call it their sport.

During the Boddington Tournament, it became my sad duty to announce the passing of CC soccer legend Peter Morse, who had been an Olympic team candidate for CC in

1968. In honor of his legacy, we held a moment of silence before the Saturday game and I read the following statement:

> *Before introducing today's lineups, we ask you to stand for a moment of silence to honor Peter Morse, Tiger soccer captain in 1968, who passed away last month in Nigeria, where he was employed in the petroleum industry. Peter will be remembered by his family, friends, and Tiger teammates as a true sportsman, a fierce competitor, and a most caring person. It is entirely fitting that we remember Peter Morse on the occasion of the Boddington Tournament, since Peter was a longtime friend of the Boddington family.*

After two overtime games in Nebraska and a long bus trip, we were ready for league play. Our record stood at 5-1-3; keeper Brian Graf had recorded his fifth shut-out at Nebraska Wesleyan, and Dan "Frenchy" Wright, short, stocky and deadly, had scored twice in Lincoln to ease the pain of driving back to Colorado through the hundreds of miles of the high plains. Thus, we approached October and league play with confidence.

At Rhodes in Memphis, Tennessee, in another overtime game, we were "shafted" by the referee as the opponent scored the winning goal while he was aligning our defensive wall. No amount of protest would change the referee's mind: he allowed the goal, and that was that.

We were frustrated and disappointed, but an exquisite winning goal at Millsaps 48 hours later set the soccer world aright again. A delightfully executed string of give-and-go passes, between Manhattan magician Lorenzo Pozzolini and Steamboat Springs downhill racer Frenchy Wright, sliced the opponents defense apart and allowed Morgan Wack, beachcomber from San Luis Obispo, to slot home the ball.

As always, while traveling to the Deep South, I would include a visit to monuments dedicated to the struggle for human rights. The Martin Luther King Jr. Memorial in Memphis was an important historic place for us to spend serious visitor time and contemplate the life of a great American.

In the Lone Star State two weeks later, we gave Trinity our best shot, but it wasn't good enough. Their internationally star-studded squad, including a former professional player from Brazil, was too strong and seasoned to overcome. But in the second game at Southwestern, we blew out the host 5-1, a remarkable achievement. Matt Fechter was unstoppable with four goals!!

It just so happened that we, as No. 3 seed, were paired against Southwestern in the SCAC play-offs, hosted by Birmingham Southern in Birmingham, Alabama. Facing a team we had demolished two weeks earlier at their home field by a score of 5-1 presented me with major motivational issues. We certainly couldn't afford to enter that match overconfident, or worse, complacent. The guys assured me that they were primed for the match, and a tightly contested battle ensued under the lights.

Southwestern's strategy was clear: mark Matt Fechter out of the game! Yet, it was he who tied the game for us on a direct free kick early in the second half. The game was headed into overtime when a controversial call helped decide the match with a minute and a half remaining in regulation time. A late and uncontested Southwestern shot sailed wide of the goal, but it was ruled to have deflected off one of our defenders. The corner kick was served well into the box, the high ball found a Southwestern player, and he headed it past the outstretched fingertips of goaltender Brian Graf.

Game over. They won. We lost. Soccer can be such a cruel game!!

At our awards banquet, many players received well-deserved accolades from the conference, the region and the Coaches Association. The highlight of the evening, however, was a terrific video show produced by Ryan Jaeger and Andrew Worthington. The video footage was courtesy of our manager and video person, Will Bowers. Entertaining, funny, and memorable. And think of this: Matt Fechter, jersey No. 11, in 2011 scored 11 goals and had 11 assists. How about that!! A rare double-double for the SCAC's Offensive Player of the Year!

2012

Enough happened in 2012 to fill a separate soccer book!

For starters, the entire eastern half of the SCAC conference, urged on by Centre, Rhodes and Sewanee, decided to abandon ship and start their own conference, thus avoiding expensive travel out west. Fortunately for the western remnants of the SCAC, we picked up a new member school, Centenary College in Shreveport, Louisiana, and were able to retain the original name of the conference.

So the now-six-member SCAC played a double round-robin schedule and filled 10 other playing dates with available D-III opponents. In the spring, we continued with off-season practice, a five-week, one-game practice period with coaching, granted us the year before.

2012 | 14-5-3

Front row, left to right: Daniel Wright (captain), Andrew Worthington, Kyle Buchwalder, McCall Sides, Ian Horne, Matt Fechter (captain), Ryan Huettel, Max Grossenbacher, Sean Parham (captain), Willy Harris, Seth Newby. **Middle row:** Assistant Coach Dan Highstead, Alec Lee, Alec Martinez, Patrick Robinson, Ben Sandalow, Ben Glass, Stuart Beezley, Forrest Marowitz, Andrew Salazar, Morgan Wack. **Back row:** Lorenzo Pozzolini, Brian Graf, Tom Crosby, Nick Lammers, Brandon Ogilvie, Keith Drury, Josh Feldman, Alec Sowers, Hunter Martinez, Elliott Levett, Chris Edmonds, Assistant Coach James Wagenschutz, Coach Horst Richardson.

In April before the alumni game and the Quony Cup, the men's soccer team engaged in a volunteer project on the near west side of Colorado Springs, cleaning up trash, litter and debris on the mesas, mainly discarded by homeless folks over several years. It was Lorenzo Pozzolini, who while digging through old and rotten sleeping bags, discovered a decomposed corpse!! Within minutes, our work site had become a crime scene, as police cruisers, detectives and firetrucks arrived. We were interviewed, written up in the paper, and quoted on local TV.

Assistant Coach James Wagenschutz quipped: "Any other college team ever find a corpse while doing community service?"

Twenty-nine former CC "greats" showed up for the alumni game, a record number. Although they couldn't quite match the varsity in endurance, they exhibited much sparkle and enjoyed themselves immensely. It was also fabled trainer Bruce Kola's last appearance on Stewart Field, as he had decided to retire from CC. What an invaluable asset he had been over time to our athletic department in general, and to our men's soccer effort in particular. Many thanks from the coach to a dear friend!!!

At his retirement party, a list of Kola-isms was printed in the program, some unforgettable, like: "Lack of planning on your part does not constitute an emergency on mine," and "So there were three against 1,000, and so I told my men: Spread out!" and "The fake meter is spinning off the wall!" Robyn Kadel replaced Bruce as our trainer.

In early June, a CC soccer party of 29, including Brandon Ogilvie on crutches, embarked on another international tour, this time to eastern Europe. We had plans to travel to Poland and Ukraine, in particular, because these two countries were hosting the European Nations Championships, the EURO 2012, and we had secured tickets to a game in Lviv, western Ukraine, to see Germany against Denmark.

Once again I had contacted good friends in Germany and points east to assist us in making this journey possible. Without the dedicated support of my old soccer buddy Volker Brueckner, who helped with travel and housing arrangements, this logistically-difficult tour would not have happened. I also need to thank CC professor John Gould and his Slovakian wife, Simona, whose brother is a professional soccer player, for introducing us to valuable contacts in Slovakia.

We traveled by bus, train and air to reach urban and rural communities where we played matches against university and village teams. Frankfurt, Cologne, Lüneburg, Hamburg, and Berlin in Germany, and Budapest in Hungary were our early stops. I almost had a rebellion on my hands when the overnight "accommodations" in Lüneburg turned out to be the storage shelter for their local club, where the boys ended up sleeping on straw!

In Berlin, however, where the U.S. ambassador to Germany, Philip Murphy, welcomed us at our playing site, things were upbeat again, even though the van with our game gear got lost in city traffic and we ended up starting the game, to the delight of the spectators, in our T-shirts and undergarments!! It was Ben Sandalow who first dropped his trousers and proclaimed that he would take the field in his Spandex underwear! Inspired, the rest of the team soon followed. The awaiting fans were in for a real treat! As they say: The game must go on! Here is Brandon Ogilvie '15 recounting the events of that day:

> *We were staying in Berlin. A few of our teammates were fortunate and able to stay in the beautiful home of a local attorney. He had connections to Colorado College as a former host of German exchange students. Others, including myself, were less fortunate and slept in a room at an old school. To our surprise, there was a fully stocked bar at what we were told was an elementary school.*

> *It was a cold, dark night sleeping on the floor at the school, but we were happy to be given a tremendous breakfast as we met up with our other teammates back at the attorney's house. We had a game scheduled later that day, and that morning it was decided that our jerseys could be washed beforehand. Unfortunately, a lapse in communication delayed the delivery of the clean uniforms to the field, and our team took the field in nothing but our underwear for the entire first half of the game.*
>
> *The Bundestag members watching the game enjoyed this American adaptability to unforeseen circumstance! The uniforms showed up for the second half. All in all, it turned out to be a tremendous day of soccer, with some wardrobe malfunctions that we can look back at and laugh.*

To the disappointment of the crowd, our uniforms arrived at half-time and we played the second half in regular dress.

Ambassador Murphy, by the way, had good CC connections, both in President Dick Celeste and Professor Tom Cronin.

In Berlin's city quarter of Kreuzberg a day later, the team engaged in a volunteer project with immigrant children, mostly from Turkey and the Mideast, participating in conversational English and physical education.

After a flight to Budapest and a short city tour, we had an early east-bound train to catch the next morning. Even though the team was ready to leave at 6:30 a.m., our transportation to the train station was nowhere to be found. A hectic ride in seven taxis, worthy of a Keystone Cops movie, got us there a couple of minutes before departure.

In the eastern Slovakian university town of Presov, we had a reception with the university sports administration prior to our game. Assistant Coach James Wagenschutz began having severe abdominal pains during lunch. Our university-appointed translator brought James to the hospital, where he was diagnosed with acute appendicitis and needed emergency surgery. While we were losing the game against the university squad 2-1, James lost his appendix and needed to remain in the hospital there.

An adventurous overnight train ride across the Carpathian Mountains brought us into the hinterland province of the once multi-ethnic, Austro-Hungarian Empire. The midnight border crossing into Ukraine was somewhat reminiscent of former border crossings I had experienced in the Soviet days: guards with sniffing German shepherd dogs, stringent passport control, surveillance cameras and agonizing delays. On top of everything else, we had to switch to a different sleeper coach in quite a hurry and almost left goalkeeper Forrest Marowitz behind on the platform as the train was pulling out of the station. Brandon Ogilvie has distinct memories of that night on the Ukrainian border:

> *Some unfortunate members of the team were seated in the non-sleeper car section of the train and forced to vacate the train at the border. There were Ukrainian militia with assault rifles and vicious guard dogs that kept a close eye on everyone and were constantly shouting things in Ukrainian. Those that remained in the sleeper car were lifted many feet into the air so that the undercarriage could be changed on the train. Apparently Ukrainian rails were a different gauge than those used in Hungary and so our wheels needed to be swapped out so that our journey could continue.*
>
> *It was a stressful event, no doubt, but eventually everyone made it back to the train and made it to Lviv (though myself and my two roommates, Elliott and Josh, almost overslept and missed our stop. The next stop would have been Moscow!!) In Lviv, we got to watch Germany take on Denmark as part of the Euro Cup tournament.*

In Lviv, Volker's acquaintance, Oleg, met us at the train station with a rickety purple bus, which our guys quickly dubbed the "Purple Dragon."

After an informative city tour, Oleg took us to his village outside of town. The entire team stayed at his three-story brick house, which was still under construction and lacked a roof!! We had a festive reception at the village club. Their clubhouse had just been constructed, and to celebrate this accomplishment the village priest had come to the game to bless the locker rooms and both teams!! The meals at the village pub were superb!! And all of our evening meals had to be so scheduled as to coincide with a Euro match.

The day after we watched Germany defeat Denmark in the Lviv stadium, the Purple Dragon, spewing diesel fumes, delivered us to the Polish border. With our extensive luggage, we had to walk for about a mile to clear border control, and I was hoping and praying that on the other side our luxury highway bus would be there to greet us. In very hot and humid weather, our journey continued west in air-conditioning.

There was much history to appreciate in the old imperial city of Krakow, our next destination. Assistant Coach Wagenschutz, still recovering from his surgery, was waiting there for us to rejoin the group. An emotional and stressful visit to the Auschwitz concentration camp and a game in Katowice completed our brief stay in Poland. Our defender Patrick Robinson '14, a religion major, and Forrest Marowitz '13, of the Jewish faith, composed a thoughtful blog after the Auschwitz encounter:

... It's a strange atmosphere at the Auschwitz museum, busloads of tourists pass through with an ease that was never presented to the prisoners of the past. Walking through the compound, it was almost impossible to imagine what life would have been like there. Thankfully, our imaginations were not powerful enough to truly re-envision the camp during functioning times and the horrendous acts that were committed there against human beings by human beings.

Via Vienna we traveled back to Germany and concluded our trip in my hometown of Rosstal, about which sweeper Andrew Worthington '15 reflects as follows:

Upon arriving in Rosstal, Horst walked us around as if only yesterday he had been there. He told us hilarious stories about himself and his friends in the village, and also how he, while riding a bicycle, ran over a chicken, which scared the heck out of the bird and caused Horst to crash and burn on the dirt road ...

But the most moving part of the tour was when Horst described the moment when he, as a boy, left his hometown and with great pain and close to tears told us how he had left everything behind. ...

Europe was more than soccer for us. We got to see the old continent, which meant we were privileged to see cathedrals and ancient cities, the best humanity had to offer then. But we also visited less prosperous places, and Auschwitz, the worst that human beings had to offer. It was a unique and enlightening 18 days that none of us will ever forget.

We returned home with a winning record and I felt the team was ready for the rigors of the upcoming fall season.

The fall season was exceptional, exceeding my expectations by far! Undefeated at home; 12 shut-outs; Matt Fechter, two-time All-American; three Academic All-Americans in Kyle Buchwalder, Nick Lammers, and Daniel Wright; NCAA second round and a 14-5-3 record. Danny Wright '13, now into documentary film productions, remembers the cast of characters around him and writes these caring and affectionate sketches of some of his teammates:

"One of us." Three words that my teammates and I had written above lockers, tucked inside shin guards and chanted in team huddles before games. When reminiscing about my four years as a member of CC men's soccer, the memories of

our team as a whole, not my personal successes or failures, are the ones that float to the top. Of course, there are a lot of great individual moments too, but I told myself I would not take the easy road and write about myself, but rather focus on the "us" of CC men's soccer.

It's not about how I came to CC as a chubby freshman, who thought I was cut during try-outs, who only played in a single game freshman year and not many more as a sophomore. It would be irrelevant to include how I fell in love with a lady Tiger and decided to get my ass into shape to impress her, and in doing so claimed a spot as a starter. And it would be braggadocios to recount how that chubby freshman eventually became captain his senior year, scored the winning goal at NCAAs and scooped the lady Tiger away, off into the sunset. Nope, I won't write about myself, this is about "us." There are endless stories of my teammates and coaches over the four years, but I'll focus on those revolving around my seven classmates.

As we lined up for the national anthem, towering over everyone at 6 feet 7 inches, was Nick Lammers — he was more impressive than Pikes Peak looming in the background. Rumors circulated in the SCAC conference that CC had a giant from Texas as our center back, and I'm sure when our opponents saw him for themselves, many simply gave up on scoring before the game even started. It was hopeless to beat him in the air, and impossible to pass him on the dribble. The fans at our games got such a kick out of his impermeable defense, they came up with a song just for him, "You will never beat Nick Lammers!"

On road trips, it was an unspoken rule that Lammers automatically got his own bed and always rode shotgun in the team van so he could stretch out his legs. On occasion, just to see his reaction, someone would take the front seat. Lammers, unamused, would stand outside the door shaking his head until the seat was relinquished. Also, the man could eat! Every so often we were blessed with the opportunity to have a pre-game meal at the fine establishment known as The Olive Garden. The only option on the menu for Lammers was the "bottomless pasta bowl" of which he would order 4 or 5 bowls. No one else on the team even came close to finishing his third. But Lammers wasn't all brawn, he had brains to go with it. A philosophy major sporting one of the best GPAs on the team, Nick brought a refreshing perspective to the group. Before our senior season started, Lammers sent an email to the team, sending chills through everyone who read it. He was an anchor on the field and a wizard through his words.

Forrest Marowitz, a keeper from Seattle, was the musician of the team so automatically the coolest as well. His confidence and composure, both on and off the field, were contagious. As the unofficial team DJ, he was in charge of the locker room music and always had the perfect songs for whatever the moment demanded. Forrest was also very good at keeping team morale high. He had a rule that you could only sulk about a loss or a bad performance until you showered. Once you had showered, it was time to move out of the past and focus on the future. It was a lesson I took to heart in season and still adhere to today. Forrest was one of the best penalty kick savers I have ever played with. He saved several PKs throughout his career at CC, but the biggest save by far was at the NCAA tournament in Boston, freezing Babson's momentum toward a second half comeback and safeguarding our advancement to the next round of the tournament.

Practice makes perfect, right? Not for Kyle. Kyle Buchwalder spent more time in the training room than anyone else on the team, yet he was miraculously injury free each weekend in time for games. I don't know if that's a testament to the training staff, or if Kyle just had a crush on Robyn. Kyle didn't need practice because he was already perfect. Perfect GPA, perfect hair, perfect teeth, perfect dimples! He even had a perfect twin brother! He was also one of the most technically skilled midfielders in the conference. But Kyle had one flaw: he couldn't shoot to save his life. If Kyle could score goals like he could dribble, the conference would have been in big trouble. In fact, according to the stat books, Kyle played in every game since he joined the team his sophomore year, and only scored two goals. Yikes! Not so perfect now, eh Karl?

Ben Sandalow, here we go. Sandalow joined the team his junior year, but quickly made his presence known. During pre-season senior year, Sandalow's clothing and belongings for the upcoming academic year were locked in a storage locker and the only person who had the key was his roommate who would not arrive on campus until several weeks later. In typical Sandalow fashion, he quickly solved the issue and took the first shirt he saw, a yellow training penny from the locker room. Sandalow wore that penny every day at practice for the next couple of weeks, never feeling the need to wash it. Robyn, our amazing trainer – the one who Kyle had a crush on — eventually had to ask me to have a conversation with Sandalow about his personal hygiene.

Sandalow was a bare-necessities type of guy. When we traveled to Europe as a team one summer, it was recommended that everyone pack light and bring one duffel bag and a backpack. That wasn't an issue for Sandalow. He showed up to the airport with a small, half-full gym bag containing a few shirts, his cleats and a tooth brush. Another Sandalow custom that cannot go without mentioning was his post-shower routine. Once Sandalow was finished showering and still sopping wet, he would skip the towel altogether and immediately put on his jeans and shirt and jet out to wherever he was going next. On the field, Sandalow was an animal. It was not uncommon for him to roar — I'm not kidding — pound his chest or grit his teeth. In all of my years playing, Sandalow was the only person I have ever seen press his forehead against that of the referee's, and not only get away card-free, but also have the call go in his favor!

Brian Graf was the quietest of our class, but a beast when it came to the penalty box. Graf was fearless in goal and would run or punch through players to get a hand on the ball. He was known for his big saves. Graf and Forrest were always competing for a starting spot, but for one reason or another, Graf would always be in goal when we were away at Trinity — the toughest game of the year. On every occasion, Graf would come up with the game of a lifetime against our conference rivals, making fingertip saves that no one will forget for a very long time. Graf had an unfortunate back injury midway through his senior season, which was a huge loss for our team. Even though he couldn't play in games, he was our most loyal and supportive fan — an inspiring example of a true teammate.

Keith Drury was Helen's favorite, and we were all jealous about it. He was also best buds with everyone on the team, making him the most liked of our class, no doubt. If I'm not mistaken, Keith was the only one on the team who played in regular cotton underwear, not spandex like the rest of us. This was on full display during our 2012 European tour in Germany. We had a scrimmage scheduled with a local club and somehow our team laundry was misplaced. Our uniforms, shorts, and socks were nowhere to be found and all we had to play in were the clothes in which we had dressed ourselves that morning. Some of our players made the unfortunate decision to wear jeans and thus were pant-less for our match. But the show goes on and we suited up for the game as best we could. Some of us had shorts, some of us had spandex, and Keith had his cotton undies. For some reason, it was the best-attended game of our European tour. Even the passers-by stopped to watch the Americans show their stuff!

Rumor has it that Fechter's mom wrote his college essay, but we're sure glad she did! The two-time All-American hit the ground running when he arrived at CC. Well, more like hit the ground walking and maybe jogged occasionally. Matt Fechter was the laziest on the team, yet also the most impactful. He didn't need to cover much ground in order to make magic happen — every touch he took was special. Whether it was a simple pass, a flashy dribble or a screaming long-distance shot, Fechter was a great asset, making everyone around him better. He also seemed to be having the most fun. He was known to plan out his celebrations before games, sometimes getting the whole team in on them. From the shoe shiner, to a crowd dive, a shirtless victory lap or a team keg stand, Fechter knew how to get the crowd rowdy and the opposing team pissed.

But with Fechter's celebrity came high-maintenance. Maybe it was because Matt grew up not too far from the Jersey shore? Fechter needed extra time before games to pick out which pair of cleats he would wear, time to clean them, do his hair, and listen to his music playlist in full. He also was particular about his sleep before games. The first few nights of our 2012 Europe trip, Horst may or may not have forgotten to book us hotels and we ended up sleeping in the concrete locker rooms of the club that was hosting us. Played it off like it had been planned this way all along, Horst thought it would be more comfortable if we laid down straw, yes, like for horses, on the locker room floors for more padding. Needless to say not much sleep was had, and Fechter complained more than anyone. He threw a bigger fit than Sawyer who ended up with hay fever and a terrible allergic reaction. But if Fechter does get his beauty sleep — watch out!

Of course, none of these memories, friendships, successes and lessons would have been made possible without Horst. Horst, for many, is the single reason we all were fortunate enough to become part of this extensive, yet exclusive, family. He was the gatekeeper, and once the door was open, the world behind it was full of unexpected surprises. Horst's passion for the game was incessant. Soccer, in his view, was one big theatrical stage with constant twists, conflicts, new characters, beginnings and endings. Before every game, he was able to make the match ahead feel like the biggest and most important challenge of the season, and once it was over, win or lose, he did it again the next week. There was never a dull moment with Horst. From his random warm-ups, to his spontaneous headstand yoga poses, his emotional half-time speeches, or his hilarious alumni stories, Horst kept his team engaged, motivated, and inspired day in and day out.

And Helen! No one wanted to disappoint Horst, but to disappoint Helen was the end-all. The team breakfasts that Helen hosted are some of my fondest memories from my time at CC. To share a meal with teammates before our home games — the calm before the storm — was the best way to get focused yet stay relaxed. Horst was coach, but Helen was the boss. Horst and Helen were able to provide so much more than just a great soccer team, they gave us an eternal family. The fondest memories of my life were made while wearing the CC men's soccer uniform. I am honored to be one of us.

In fact, it was Dan "Frenchy" Wright who scored the golden goal in overtime on a Sean Parham assist to seal the come-from-behind victory against UT-Dallas in our opening encounter that season. It was a euphoric win, the first in 10 years against this opponent, and was key to building momentum for the rest of the campaign. Noteworthy for the second game was the fact that this match vs. Nebraska Wesleyan goes into the record books as the longest ever played at CC. Because of three lightning delays, the game, which started at 4 p.m., wasn't concluded until 7:30.

Frenchy, Fechter and Parham led the team as captains, and although we encountered two close losses on the road, including a 1-0 defeat in San Antonio against powerhouse Trinity, we were on track for success.

On another trip to Texas, this time to Dallas, we competed in a mini-tournament at the University of Dallas. Strange as it seems because of the distance separating us, U-Dallas was our travel partner in the SCAC. So when we played them, either at home or away, we always needed a second game to round out the weekend. The other team at Dallas was UC Santa Cruz, who because of their independent status, had no choice but to travel extensively to compete against D-III opponents. Chris Edmonds, who was along on this trip, didn't remember the scores of the games, but did write about a field trip we took while in Dallas:

> *I was in the American Presidency course with Professor Tom Cronin in the second block of 2012, the month leading up to Obama's election to a second term and a crescendo of the American electoral experience. I was writing a paper comparing the public perception of John F. Kennedy and Richard M. Nixon, and the disjunction I saw when comparing their contributions to public policy. It was also the weekend of the Dallas trip, and I was proud to have made the traveling list, eager to support the squad in any way I could, and I also had much work to accomplish in our motel's business center. But coach announced that on our off-day we were going on an historic excursion to the JFK Museum in downtown Dallas. Horst pulled me aside at breakfast and told me he hoped I could give a brief lecture at the grassy knoll where JFK was assassinated to discuss the lessons we were exploring in the American Presidency.*
>
> *While I don't quite remember the score of the Dallas game that weekend, I do remember piling out of the van on an overcast day in Dallas, Horst getting the attention of the boys on the grassy knoll, and turning the floor over to me. CC Soccer*

> *had a special way of not just making room in the backseat for academic priorities. Horst, Helen and their franchise at CC made every attempt to cross-pollinate the athletic and academic lives of young men simultaneously. And for that I will always be thankful.*

At the half-way point of the season we had vaulted into the national rankings and were ranked No. 3 in the West region. By the time we hosted Trinity, now ranked the No. 1 team in the country, for the return match on Stewart Field, we were physically, mentally, and emotionally ready for this do-or-die battle. Robyn Kadel, out trainer, had the boys healthy; Doug Payton, our equipment manager and former professional football player, gave us encouragement before the big game; and Andy Obringer, our events coordinator, had the playing site ready to perfection. SID Dave Reed comments about this epic encounter:

> *The Colorado College men's soccer team earned a hard-fought point against long-time nemesis and rival, Trinity University. CC, ranked No. 22 in Division III, used a first-half goal by sophomore forward Hunter Martinez and a stellar performance by senior goalkeeper Forrest Marowitz in the second half, to forge a 1-1 tie with No. 1 Trinity.*
>
> *"We made history today at Stewart Field," head coach Horst Richardson said. "That was a wonderful, hard-fought game that was very competitive. Trinity is a Division I team in Division III disguise. They have so much talent and they are very organized.*
>
> *"I'm not disappointed with a tie. It's a real indication of how the game went. This demonstrates we can play with anybody."*
>
> *Making only his fourth appearance of the season, Martinez won possession of sophomore defender Andrew Worthington's long header just inside the Trinity penalty box, worked his way free 15 yards in front of the left post, and scored his first career goal on a high shot to the far side.*
>
> *"What a wonderful thing to have Hunter Martinez score," Richardson said. "He hasn't played much this year because he is overloaded with residential advisor responsibilities. He's a typical CC Division III student-athlete."*

Paul McGinley, the Trinity coach, complimented us after the game and told me that with this tie we were definitely in contention for the NCAAs. In spite of a slip-up versus Centenary away, we recovered to beat Austin in the last regular season game to assure a second-place finish in the SCAC. And once again we faced Southwestern in the semis, and once again we had just beaten them handily in conference play.

The SCAC play-offs were hosted by Trinity and our Southwestern match ended a 0-0 tie in double overtime. To break the tie, we had to go to penalties, and we lost. BUT, for the purposes of record and NCAA selection, the Southwestern game stood as a tie, and since Trinity crushed them in the SCAC championship game, we must have looked better to the NCAA selection committee, because we, as a bubble team, received a bid. Our opponent? Babson College in Boston.

Even though so much had already happened in 2012, there was another adventure in store for us. Since missed class time is a criterion for NCAA tournament flight arrangements, we couldn't depart for Boston until Thursday after classes. The NCAA tried for several days to send us to the East Coast on commercial flights, but to no avail. CC was the only team in the entire first round which couldn't get to a distant game. Finally the NCAA had no other choice but to fly us to Bean Town on a PRIVATE JET. What a thrill for our team! Flying east, we felt we were almost Real Madrid! Catered meals, no standing in line at airports, no security hassles; our CC bus drove up to the jet waiting on the tarmac, and in Boston a bus was waiting for us on the tarmac to speed us to our hotel on the Babson campus.

As host, the athletic staff at Babson had done a terrific job preparing the site of competition and their team was favored to advance. Our senior forward, Danny Wright, however, had other ideas. On that day he played the best game of his career and scored two fabulous goals to lead us to victory. Keeper Forrest Marowitz denied Babson a goal on a penalty kick to smother a late Babson rally. Final score: CC 3, Babson 1. Our private jet had to stick around for another day!

Scranton University had had an easy game to advance to the next round and faced us the following day. In a see-saw battle, the match remained scoreless until the 82nd minute when wonder boy Wright scored his third goal of the weekend. With less than two minutes remaining on the clock, Scranton was awarded a penalty kick as one of our defenders had fouled their front runner in the box. They tied up the game, and early in overtime scored again to win and eliminate us from further advance. We had come a long way that season and held our heads high flying west in the comfort of our private jet.

At the conclusion of the 2012 review, I want to include excerpts from two inspirational letters which frame the season. During pre-season we discussed our ambitions for the fall.

Our gentle giant from Texas, Nick Lammers '13, contemplated the question what we, as a group, wanted to be remembered for. He writes about the calm before the storm:

> *... Ours is the calm of the storm. Our adversaries will look on the writhing towers of clouds, and quail before the thunder ... They will cry out at the intensity of the gale, at the turbulence, at the ferocity of the tumult ... Our storm will ravage opponents, decimate and destroy them utterly — but we will not do it out of malicious intent. No. We will do it because we want to become ourselves and reach all the lofty heights which that entails ... Word will spread, fear will grow, and soon enough, when opponents feel the icy stirrings of our coming, they will not even think to marshal their forces. Hide, wait, and hope will be their mantra. You cannot defeat this storm; your only hope is to weather it.*

Having achieved our objective of making it to the NCAA play-offs, admittedly with a little bit of luck, up-and-coming defender Patrick Robinson, echoing Nick's early season sentiment, put fire into the squad with this letter, written right after we received word of our selection:

> *Brothers: Usually we speak of the soccer gods when our luck has failed; when we feel we have been slighted, ignored, or overlooked. Not often do the soccer gods sit on our bench. But today, boys, they have smiled upon us. Today they have embraced us. And this is a gift we must not, we cannot squander. Such gifts are few and far between. Let us take it and run. The glory is ours to grasp! ... This is CC soccer. We will play our game, and they will too. We will build a legacy, and we will take that legacy to them. ...This weekend, the clouds will amass over Babson, and the NCAA will know: A storm is coming from out of the west.*

Ah, the power of words. Teddy Roosevelt, in his address "To the Man in the Arena," couldn't have said it any better than these two passionate young teammates of ours.

Of the group of 2012 seniors, no one had suffered more disappointment and shown more tenacity than Brian Graf '13, a talented goalkeeper whose nagging back injury kept him sidelined for much of his junior and senior years. Even though he couldn't practice with us or play for us, he remained an ardent supporter of the team. His recollection speaks volumes for the "Band of Brothers" who were about to graduate:

To say that being a part of the Colorado College men's soccer team was a formative experience would be an understatement. When I stepped onto the CC campus, as a freshman, I was just a kid, with all the issues and anxieties that come along with being in a new environment. I was anxious about fitting in, I missed my home, and I was still figuring out who I was. Upon making the team, I discovered the best group of guys I'll probably ever have the privilege of meeting and I was immediately accepted.

Very quickly, I became proud to call myself a Tiger. I began to embody the beliefs and attributes that my teammates displayed, and I admired so much. As I grew, I became a better keeper and a better person, as I learned and grew from this incredible group. Each day that we went to practice, we developed, and our bond became stronger. I thought that I was finally realizing what the CC men's soccer team was all about.

However, it wasn't until I got injured that I realized how unique the group that Horst created was. Starting late in my junior year, I became plagued with a line of back injuries, which not only kept me from playing most of my senior season, but also restricted me to the point where I could barely walk. It was a dark time while I helplessly watched from the sideline as my team carried on through the rest of my senior season. But throughout my injury, my teammates were there for me, whether it was visiting me after surgery, buying me groceries when I couldn't, or just coming by to keep me company as I recovered. These seemingly small gestures gave me an early glimpse into the bond that Horst facilitated between the members of the men's soccer team. I was able to see how incredibly unique that bond is and, more importantly, how it transcends soccer and college altogether.

I graduated from CC much more than a young man who played soccer. I graduated with a group of lifelong friends at my side whom I still visit and think of often. When I got into CC, I was excited to be able to play soccer in college. But looking back, I see that soccer was much less important than Horst's grand vision. Under the disguise of soccer, Horst gave us confidence, character, and a brotherhood to last a lifetime.

2013

By 2013, the new El Pomar Sports Center had been completed. We now had a facility for our students and athletes that was second to none in the country. Our coaches had moved out of their office cubicles and now sat in sunlit and comfortable spaces, ready for 21st century recruits. Furthermore, not only had the old gym been renovated, expanded, and refurbished, including the installation of elevators, but we also acquired a super facility for recreational use in the Adam Press Center. Many thanks to Athletic Director Ken Ralph for his leadership during this major reconstruction project.

Unusual was the fact that 10 varsity players had been around on campus for the summer, working with the grounds crew or doing research. They were so motivated and dedicated to prepare themselves for the upcoming season that they met several times a week very early in the morning with strength and conditioning coach Kevin Cronin in the varsity weight room. In particular, Kevin focused on Lorenzo Pozzolini to rehab his shoulder. Here's Kevin's recollection of Manhattan kid Lorenzo:

> *In the summer of 2013, I was fortunate enough to have 10 men's soccer players work and train on campus. These athletes trained with me in the newly renovated varsity weight room at 5:30 a.m. The crew was not always awake, but they sure kept me on my toes. One athlete in particular always made sure I was on top of my game – Lorenzo Pozzolini.*

2013 | 14-6-2

Front row, left to right: Chris Edmonds, Ben Glass, Alex Weber, Hunter Martinez, Ian Horne, Kai Thompson, Tom Crosby, Sean Parham (captain), Tommy Riley, Max Grossenbacher, Caden MacKenzie. **Middle row:** Coach Horst Richardson, Alec Lee, Oliver Skelly, Toby Sides, Jack McCormick, Andrew Worthington (captain), Brandon Ogilvie, Nathan Andersen, Patrick Robinson, Lorenzo Pozzolini, Christian Wulff, Assistant Coach Scott Palguta. **Back row:** Trainer Robyn Kadel, Ryan Huettel, Elliott Hiller, Trevor Houghton, Stuart Beezley, Alec Sowers, Morgan Wack, Seth Newby, Andrew Salazar, Student Trainer Mackie Greason, Assistant Coach Dan Highstead. **Not pictured:** Alec Martinez.

Lorenzo had had shoulder surgery to repair a torn labrum earlier in the year and he was progressing nicely with his rehab. We got to a point where he was able to attempt pull ups — we were told to be careful with him and make sure he didn't "hit" his shoulder on anything. Lorenzo hopped up to the pull-up bar to attempt a few pull-ups (pain free)…he completed about five pull-ups and then proceeded to fall from about five feet to the floor below … luckily he had learned how to barrel roll in rehab (to protect his surgically repaired shoulder if he ever fell ...) or he probably would have gone back for another surgery if he had not rolled out of it … the entire room stopped to see if he was "okay" … he picked himself up off the floor and looked at all of us like we were crazy and said "What the f…?!?!" (in a thick New York accent) — we all went about our business and finished the training session ... incident free.

Later that summer Lorenzo cut off a small piece of his finger while working in the wood shop on campus — for those who know Lorenzo — there was never a dull moment around him.

When Lorenzo graduated he gave me a small wooden bowl, which he had made in the same wood shop where he cut his finger. That bowl still decorates my desk!

My longtime and competent assistant James Wagenschutz, with whom I had worked together well for six years, decided to move on. I am very grateful for his dedicated service and for the unbending support he committed to our program.

His replacement as full-time assistant was Scott Palguta. What a coup to hire Scott, a Cornell University graduate and soccer star who had several years of pro soccer behind him, including three years as a defender with the Colorado Rapids Club! He was a perfect fit for CC. In a relatively short period he became an articulate spokesperson for our recruiting efforts, excelled at field sessions, helped prepare road trips, and turned into a caring friend.

At the Convocation before the 2013 graduation, several of our seniors were honored. In fact, men's soccer had a presence there as never before. Matt Fechter received the Van Diest Award as Outstanding Athlete; Nick Lammers was lauded by the physics department as Outstanding Student (he was also recognized with the SCAC's inaugural "Man of the Year" Award); Kyle Buchwalder received the Outstanding Student Award in biochemistry; and Keith Drury was honored with the Bill Hochman Prize in history. As faculty member and coach, I was extremely proud of the accomplishments of our players. And Ted Nusbaum '94 was inducted into the CC Athletic Hall of Fame for his dominant participation in both lacrosse and soccer. A festive alumni game, well-attended and well-played, concluded the spring season.

In the fall, our conference, the SCAC, welcomed two new members: Schreiner University from Kerrville, Texas, and Texas Lutheran University from Sequin, Texas. The University of Dallas remained our travel partner. The double round-robin conference schedule allowed us six non-conference games. As we gathered for pre-season after our volunteer work in the San Luis Valley, Andrew Worthington and Sean Parham stood ready to lead the squad into the fall campaign as captains.

In a press release, I was quoted about the season outlook: "Compared to last year's veteran and NCAA tournament team, the current squad is young, enthusiastic, and in need of experience. Fortunately, we will encounter solid competition before we begin conference play, and thus have several opportunities to solidify the group. This year's squad features senior captain Sean Parham from Arkansas and junior captain Andrew Worthington from Chicago. Both bring admirable leadership qualities to motivate their teammates. Senior Patrick Robinson from California helps consolidate our defensive efforts, and Ben Glass, a senior from Colorado Springs, has shown midfield dominance. We expect offensive punch from senior Brandon Ogilvie, who has had several injuries during his career at CC thus far and is now fully recovered. Alec Martinez, also a midfielder and from St. Louis, is impressive in the middle of the park, and sophomore Max Grossenbacher from Austin, Texas, controls opponents' thrusts forward. (Max is also an accomplished pianist.) Two dynamic freshmen are Christian Wulff, who decided against West Point to attend CC, and Caden MacKenzie from Denver, whose father Tom played soccer at CC many moons ago."

I could've added that inexperience and inconsistency in goalkeeping might be our biggest weakness. Veterans Brian Graf and Forrest Marowitz had graduated; it would be tough to replace them.

Caden MacKenzie '17, whose alum father took more pictures of Caden in action than any parent ever before him, remembers his time as a Tiger:

> *Some of my most memorable moments come from the first couple months as a CC Tiger. As a young, excited, and new member of the team, my longtime fascination with those who came before me became a reality. It's safe to say I was pretty excited to become a Tiger after growing up in a house where names like Horst Richardson, Charlie Stanzione, Patrick Shea and many others from my old man's era were up*

> *there with the likes of worldwide soccer legends. Being welcomed to that group was one-of-a-kind and it came in all forms. From on-the-field strong words of constructive criticism from then-captain Andrew Worthington to off-the-field with friendly open arms, hotel beds, and bananas by Pat and Ox (Pat Robinson and Chris Edmonds). I know I speak for all of those who were experiencing those times with me, it was damn good to finally be a part of the fun.*

The season did not start off well. An opening scoreless tie against Whitman (my 900th game at CC) and a rained-out game vs. UT-Dallas produced less than we had hoped for; in a goodwill gesture we invited the Texas team to dinner before their long bus trip back to the Lone Star State.

We owed Ohio Wesleyan a return game from several years ago and as we approached the away trip, I was full of apprehension, knowing full well what a traditional powerhouse we were about to face. Bad luck and a key defensive blunder served us a needless defeat in the opening match there, even though we dominated the match statistically. I was very much encouraged with our play in the first half against Ohio Wesleyan, which stood at 2-2. But in the second half they were not kind to us; an unbelievable full volley goal struck from 25 yards out broke our spirit. And after another tie on the following weekend at home we had no wins to show for the first five encounters.

But as is so often the case in sports, one never knows what can happen. By the end of September we had been on a six-game winning streak and were back in business. Yet, even though we had built valuable momentum, we couldn't get by the No. 1 and No. 2 teams in the conference, Trinity and Southwestern, respectively, losing to each team twice.

A strange incident occurred on the Trinity field on the way to our loss. Brandon Ogilvie, on a breakaway to the opponent's goal, was stopped in the middle of his sprint by a whistle, but it wasn't the whistle of the referee. We all heard it, we were all confused, and the sound had come from the field of play. To this day I suspect that one of Trinity's foreign and savvy stallions had caused this breakdown in our attack. This incident has gone down in the annals of CC soccer as the "Whistle Incident," and shall live in infamy evermore.

Nevertheless, a seven-game winning streak followed, which assured us a third place position in the conference play-offs, which now had been expanded to include the top six teams. In the last two regular season games, our team had scored eight goals. One player was involved in all of them, scoring five by himself and assisting on the remaining three.

Andrew Salazar achieved this marvelous outpouring of offensive skill, which earned him Offensive Player of the Week in the SCAC. To appreciate this feat, one has to recognize the fact that "Sally" is a mere 5'6" tall and doesn't weigh an ounce more than 130 pounds. But, like little Messi, during those two games "Sally" waltzed through the opposition's defense as if they weren't even there!!

Given our relative geographic isolation at CC from comparable D-III competition, road trips by vans, bus and air are an integral part of our various sports programs. Many a "memorable moment" occurred during these sometimes adventurous travels, and players speak fondly about bonding experiences on the road. Our then-captain, Andrew Worthington, a pillar of strength on defense and an exceptional leader of men, captures the essence of "The Road Trip" with this contribution to our narrative:

ON THE ROAD IN THE SCAC

After ending my phone call with my parents in the parking lot of the hotel, having provided them with a review of Friday's game, I see a text from Assistant Coach Scott Palguta, "Dinner at 5:30, please have everyone in the lobby by 5:15." With my instructions in hand, I quickly walk inside, eager to escape the heat. It's always too hot in Texas.

In the lobby of the motel of this hypothetical SCAC trip, you will most likely find the brightest minds on the team. Studying and writing away, the freshmen, sophomores and juniors, most responsible for our team's high GPA, are seriously busy. My reminder to be ready in the lobby at 5:15 is met with a series of conforming nods. Without a doubt the easiest stop of the day.

On away trips, we were always able to select our roommates. Classes tended to stick with one another for the most part. The three seniors who consistently traveled that year, myself, Brandon Ogilvie, and Stuart Beezley, always roomed together and never did any homework. My knock on the door of the sophomores' room is met with a loud cry, "Who is it?"

"Open the door," I calmly reply. Some scrambling footsteps grow louder as the door swings open. Standing before me is Caden MacKenzie: "Uncle Andy! How the heck are ya!?" As a part of our running joke, Caden and I greet each other like a couple of auto parts salesmen who haven't seen each other in months. Caden, shirtless and with a mustache you would expect a 14-year-old kid to grow, invites me into the room.

The other three sophomores, Christian Wulff, Jack McCormick, and Tommy Riley, are sprawled on the bed — also shirtless. Caden jumps back in with the group, and resumes watching some video on Jack's phone. I abruptly grab their attention and remind them to be ready at 5:15. "Whatever you say, Uncle! Hey, do you want to watch with us, this guy's technique is remarkable." Don't be mistaken, they are not watching soccer.

A couple of doors down, the door to the juniors' room is cracked open. Inside there is one lone, old soul. Seth Newby is sitting on the bed reading a thick, old book. With the gusto of a 90-year-old man, Seth, who is still in his 20s, drops his head to have a view unobstructed by his glasses. "They are all next door, I think they are watching baseball." Seth's middle name is Shenkel, if you needed more detail.

"Thanks. We leave for dinner at 5:15. I know that is a late dinner time for you, but you should be able to get to bed by 7:30, Shenkel."

"Hilarious."

Seth's deadpan tone all but shows me the way out.

The next door is also propped. As I enter, a symphony of laughter fills my ears. The guys are not watching baseball. Instead, the blinds are drawn and Will Ferrell is on the screen, but his comedic prowess does not have my attention. What is impressing me at the moment is the fact that this hotel room, equipped with two queen beds, a swivel chair, and a small amount of floor space, is currently accommodating 12 of my teammates. Every class is represented. The seniors, of course, found themselves a spot on the bed. I pass on the news about dinner, and grab a spot on the floor next to a couple of freshmen and prop myself up against the bed. The air-conditioning unit is waging a losing battle against all of us, as the musty mugginess of 13 guys finally hits me.

Most guys are barely watching as they fling insults at one another. One of the freshmen gets himself into trouble and is put in a headlock as we all hoot and holler. To some, this scene may be a bit too much, but to me, it's perfect.

Away trips were my favorite part of Colorado College men's soccer. While I loved playing in the away games, it was the time in between those matches that I miss so much. On the field we fight with and for each other as we strive towards our common goal. On the buses, planes, in the restaurants and hotel rooms, we all get to relax, study, and hang out. Growing up, my family consisted of myself, mom, dad, and two sisters. After CC, I had about 50 brothers!

The parents of our graduating seniors had started a tradition to honor their sons after the last home game by inviting the entire team to a dinner at which not only food was served, but part of the evening was also dedicated to a "roasting" of the seniors by the juniors. The juniors always think of funny stories with inside humor to entertain their teammates and the guests. Players look forward to this event every year with great anticipation.

We defeated Austin College to advance to the semi-final against host Southwestern. It was a heated affair, and we could have won the game as we were awarded a late penalty in regulation time. But we misplaced the shot, and lost the game in overtime. Once again Trinity was crowned league champion after their victory in the final and went on to represent the SCAC in the NCAA play-offs.

We have a wonderful action shot of Max Grossenbacher and Andrew Worthington, celebrating Max's first collegiate goal scored with one minute remaining on the clock at Washburn Field in a night game against Austin College. His goal was the only one scored in that tight contest.

It is said that a picture is worth a thousand words and this one expresses the joy of camaraderie, the euphoria of winning, and the satisfaction of achievement under pressure. What a moment it was to cherish in a rewarding 14-6-2 season!

Brandon Ogilvie received Academic All-America status and, to the delight of the coaching staff, decided to return for a super senior semester to play out his remaining eligibility.

2014

As it turned out, 2014 was my last year of coaching. However, at the beginning of the season I did not know that.

In the spring of that year, I had had the good fortune of being inducted into the Colorado Springs Sports Hall of Fame, along with CC hockey scoring legend Pete Geronazzo. "My job has been a very joyous and rewarding experience," I was quoted as saying in my acceptance speech. "My association with so many terrific people in a sport that I love has been wonderful. To have on top of that a very understanding and supportive wife, I mean that's doubly rewarding ..."

The World Cup was staged in Brazil that summer, and, in an unbelievable semi-final between host Brazil and Germany, *Die Mannschaft* routed the host country 7-1. I will never forget that game. Helen and I were in Casper, Wyoming, visiting Jon Nicolaysen,

2014 | 15-4-2

Front row, left to right: Tim Huettel, Ryan Huettel, Seth Newby, Brian Rubin, Nick Zuschneid, Stuart Beezley, Sam Block, Sam Markin, Trevor Houghton, Shin Olsan, Jake Battock, Coach Horst Richardson. **Middle row:** Connor Rademacher, Soren Frykholm, Alec Sowers, Ian Horne, Theo Hooker, Tom Crosby, Sam Clement, Caden MacKenzie, Max Grossenbacher (captain), Tommy Riley. **Back row:** Assistant Coaches Dan Highstead and Tomas Martinez, Hunter Martinez, Christian Wulff, Victor Benthack, Jack McCormick, Kilian Morales-Coskran, Nathan Andersen, Andrew Worthington (captain), Brandon Ogilvie, Austin Hammer, Alec Lee, Assistant Coaches Scott Palguta and Dustin Trujillo. **Not pictured:** Elliott Hiller.

---

who played on the very first CC squad I coached in 1965. Jon has a ranch up there, showed us his spread, and then invited us to a cowboy sports bar to see the game, where a life-size screen depicted all the action. What an exhilarating day that was!

Another joyous day that summer was the wedding of Assistant Coach Scott Palguta to Melissa Meyer, a festive affair.

An impressive recruiting class joined a strong nucleus of veterans. Assistant Coach Scott Palguta and I decided to build the squad around a strong spine, with Andrew Worthington as center back, Max Grossenbacher in central midfield, and fifth-year returner Brandon Ogilvie up top. The two biggest surprises that year were newcomer Theo Hooker, a lanky and tall goalkeeper from Albuquerque and transfer student Soren Frykholm, a roaming midfielder. On the way to our new student orientation service project, Theo Hooker '18 was surprised that I stopped the vans and gave a mini lecture:

> *I had just arrived at CC for the New Student Orientation in August 2014. There were 20 freshmen that showed up for try-outs, including four goalkeepers. I was a bit surprised and somewhat apprehensive, to say the least. We hop in the CC vans and*

head to the San Luis Valley to do some trail maintenance. An hour into the drive, Horst stops our caravan. We pull over to the side of the road, and Horst proceeds to give us a brief history of Zebulon Pike (the namesake of Pikes Peak) and his journey through the Rocky Mountains. Coach turns out to be a teacher as well.

(At the 2011 awards banquet, then-captain Chris Lutz and the graduating seniors had presented me with a two-volume set of Zebulon Pike's Journals, knowing how fond I was of this early western explorer. I appreciated that thoughtful gift very much and learned quite a bit from reading the journals.)

After several games it was clear that Hooker would be the starting keeper, a position he kept for four years! Soren, whom I had recruited from Boulder, Colorado, had decided to attend D-III St. Olaf in Minnesota, even though he had been admitted to CC and even though several members of his family were CC alums.

Two years earlier we had played St. Olaf away, and I observed his obvious skills there. He decided to take a year off from college, reapplied to CC as a transfer, and enrolled. Once he was a Tiger, he became an immediate impact player for us. After graduating with a distinguished NCAA post-graduate scholarship in hand, Soren sent me this memory of his time at CC:

As is the case for the Richardsons, my family loves stories. At all family gatherings, particularly on my dad's side, storytelling takes center stage. One popular theme is "the Colorado Springs era," which comprised the two decades (the 1970s and 1980s) that my dad grew up with his three siblings in Colorado Springs.

Also like the Richardsons, my family is through and through a soccer family. Naturally our families knew each other, both being involved in the growing Colorado Springs soccer scene. Indeed, my dad's younger brother, Peter, was able to play with Horst's son Erik at various points during their middle school and prep years.

When my dad, uncles, and grandpa would talk about their time living in Colorado Springs, I noticed that they brought up one name quite a lot: it sounded like "horse." I can remember the earliest mentions of the name because it sounded so funny. Right away, I began associating the name with the word, "legend," because that was the word they kept using to describe this guy. And when my grandpa would talk about this man from Germany who brought soccer to Colorado Springs, he'd also always mention that he coached the CC Tigers.

> *"Maybe one day," I remember him telling me, "you could go to Colorado College and play for Horst, too."*
>
> *"Of course," my dad and uncles would add, "he's been around forever, and he has to retire at some point. So you'll have to hurry."*
>
> *Well, I almost missed my chance of playing for Horst after beginning my undergraduate career elsewhere, but I ended up transferring to CC shortly thereafter. And how fortunate I was to get a year playing under the legendary Horst Richardson!*
>
> *Just in time for his last season, I came to Colorado College in the fall of 2014. Though it was only one season, I strongly associate many of my best memories at Colorado College with Horst — team breakfasts at the Richardson house (which continued even after Horst's retirement), our unforgettable team trip through England, Denmark, Sweden, and Germany in 2015, and renowned pre-game talks, to name just a few.*
>
> *Truly, my appreciation for the program, the College, and the sport of soccer would not be the same without the intimate relationship I developed with Horst, Helen, and their extended family. Thanks from the bottom of my heart.*

We staged a most competitive pre-season, and the selection process was difficult, since a talented group had reported for the try-outs. To additionally motivate the candidates, I announced that we were planning another international soccer tour after graduation, this time to Northern Europe, specifically to England, Sweden, Denmark, and Northern Germany. (More about that trip at the end of the 2014 report.) To celebrate the conclusion of pre-season, the selected players spent an overnight in the CC cabin near Florissant. Theo Hooker, an observant freshman, reports on the activities up there:

> *After two weeks of pre-season, the team had been finalized. We took a celebratory trip to the CC cabin, just past Divide, Colorado. We went up on a Friday afternoon. We spent the first hours doing some team bonding on the ropes course. As the sun went down, we went inside and the freshmen prepared a fantastic meal of spaghetti and meatballs.*
>
> *After dinner the games began, most notably a gambling game called "Guts." It is accurately named because there is really no skill involved, only guts. Each player is dealt two cards to look at. The players hold their cards face down above the table. On the count of three, you can either hold or drop your cards. If you are the only player to hold cards, you win the pot. If there are multiple people, the player with the highest hand wins.*

> *We had been playing for quite some time, and the pots had gotten large. It was so popular we had three different games playing. All of a sudden there is a huge cheer from one of the tables and Brandon Ogilvie jumps up, takes his shirt off and starts waving it around and screaming. He had just won $84. Wow ... welcome to college!*

With great expectations, the Tiger squad took the field against Occidental College in the opener, a game I was confident that we could win. The effort was there, the statistics were overwhelmingly in our favor, but the result went to the visitors.

Good thing we didn't panic, but instead dug down deep and came up with 10 subsequent wins in a row. Seven of the games were shut-outs for freshman keeper Theo Hooker.

By the time we faced our perennial nemesis Trinity, our record stood at 10-1. Within a week we competed with them twice, to identical 1-0 losses. The defeat at home really hurt, because fleet-footed senior Ryan Huettel received a nasty elbow to the face from Trinity's Brazilian and suffered a concussion, and super-senior Brandon Ogilvie had to leave the game after a blow to the face, which required 11 stitches inside his mouth.

Yet, the two narrow losses to powerhouse Trinity counted as a moral victory for us. The team had developed a super defense, anchored by Andrew Worthington. He was complemented in the center by fearless Jack McCormick. On the flanks, Trevor Houghton, Alec Sowers, Alec Lee and Nathan Andersen rotated positions and were tireless in chasing attackers down and in initiating the wing attacks. Senior Stewart Beezley ran his heart out as an attacker and scored goals based on sheer determination, and Seth Newby, a junior, showed sophisticated passing in midfield with Grossenbacher and Frykholm. And then there was Mr. Unpredictable, Caden MacKenzie, who had a bag of tricks up his sleeve up front and loved to dribble, producing several glorious goals. Ogilvie was high-scorer, but now was out with an injury.

Good thing we won the Homecoming game against Southwestern, because a huge party was planned to celebrate my 50th season. A clever sports promoter had come up with a catchy title for this athletic department-sponsored event: HORSTOBERFEST. The word says it all! German food and beer, a two-person German band, speeches, displays, pictures, lots of alums and friends, great stories, and an unexpected highlight from Singapore as my son Erik, who attended, brought along 150 black and gold jerseys, which were copies of the uniforms our CC teams wore in the early '70s. The new intramural gym in the Adam Press Center was awash in a sea of gold jerseys with black letters on the back pronouncing, "HORST - 50."

It was an emotional evening for me, and I was overcome with gratitude and close to tears several times. And everybody who came received a beer mug with a picture of me on it. Athletic Director Ken Ralph spoke to the crowd, saying: "Horst is a true educator who showed everyone that athletic excellence and academic achievement are not mutually exclusive." Thanks, Ken.

Our daughter, Stacia Arcila, a '95 CC graduate and a lifelong supporter of our men's soccer teams, spoke at the Horstoberfest. She later expanded her remarks and submits them here as an indication of her fondness for our program:

> *I have been going to the CC soccer field my entire life. It was like a second home to me. Going to the field to see my dad was always fun. I enjoyed the smell of the grass, walking barefooted, seeing the vistas of Pikes Peak, and hearing the banter and laughs between the players. I could sit on the same side of the field as the team to watch the games, too.*
>
> *It's hard for me to think of just one CC men's soccer story that represents my journey as the coach's daughter. Therefore, here is my own personal highlight tape of memories:*
>
> - *As a kid, I remember helping my dad with pre-season. I always had a special job, i.e., shagging balls, setting up cones, collecting bibs, or even taking stats. Clipboards were so cool!*
> - *Helping my mom preparing team breakfasts!!*
> - *The many cool players over the years whom I've looked up to as big brothers, specifically Brigham Olson and Kristian Sundborn. By the way, in Erik I already have the best big brother ever!*
> - *The 1988 team trip to China, bus crash and all!*
> - *Those extra special years when my brother and I were both students at CC and Erik played soccer for my dad. We sure did have some great times.*
> - *Laughing my ass off, hanging out with my brother and Jon Whitfield.*
> - *Witnessing the best season ever in 1992. What a fantastic group of guys!*
> - *Watching soccer practice from my ballet class in Cossitt Hall.*
> - *Choreographing a dance piece based on the movement of soccer players as my senior thesis project. Thanks to all the athletes who performed. It was a very special moment for me.*
> - *Bringing my daughter Indigo to the field on one of those perfect Colorado fall days to watch a game and to see her Opa in action.*
> - *HORSTOBERFEST!*

- *Belonging to a huge network of CC men's soccer players. It's like having an international second family.*
- *And most of all, I just want to thank my Mom and Dad for their hard work, generosity, dedication, and adventurous spirits. Thanks for making me feel like I was part of the team!! Go Tigers!*

Stacia's daughter Indigo, our 13-year-old granddaughter, also has fond memories of the soccer program. Here is what she has to say:

> *I've been helping out on the soccer field since I was little, maybe four years old; I can't remember exactly. Always close to my Opa's (Horst's) side, listening to him yell and blow his whistle at the players. I distinctly remember looking at him when I was a little kid and laughing because his face was pink from the sun.*
>
> *I had my friends I would play with on the field; most were the children of the assistant coaches. Sitting on the grass with the team during a game, I felt pretty grown up, a six- or seven-year-old hanging out with all those college boys who all knew my name. I always had little jobs to do, like getting the guys water, running after the balls, handing out awards at the soccer banquets.*
>
> *That's how I spent a good portion of my time in the fall for 10 years straight. It was always fun, though. My favorite part was when the team all got chocolate milk after every game, and every time there was an extra one for me!*

Two ties and three victories closed out the 2014 season, giving us sole claim to second place in the SCAC. In our last regular season game away to Centenary in Shreveport, both teams were ready for kick-off, lacking one key ingredient: there were NO referees!! An apparent mix-up in dates was about to cancel the game.

That's when I pulled out my whistle and said that we didn't come all this way not to play, and I would referee the game. The opposing coach agreed: I would do the first half, and he the second.

Our Associate Athletic Director, Greg Capell, who had traveled with us for this contest, couldn't believe that two coaches and teams would agree to such a unconventional arrangement, but the game was played, and we won! And there were no arguments or controversies. Scott Palguta, then-assistant coach and on this road trip, remembers this event well:

I'll always remember my first game "in charge" of the CC men's soccer team. Still Horst's assistant coach at the time, the team readied for a quick trip to Shreveport, Louisiana, to close out the 2014 regular season with a SCAC matchup against Centenary College. Once a year an athletics administrator accompanies the team on a road trip. On this trip, Associate Director of Athletics, Greg Capell, came along. Of course, all road trips tend to go smoothly EXCEPT for the one the boss comes on. Murphy's Law, I guess.

After a lengthy flight delay put our arrival time for kickoff in jeopardy, we found a flat tire on Horst's 12-passenger van before we could get out of the airport parking lot. There were early signs that this trip was not meant to be. The worst circumstances, though, were waiting for us at Centenary (yes, we finally made it): Again, no referees! Apparently, there was a miscommunication and our referees from Dallas — a mere three hours away — would not be coming. What to do?

After a lengthy deliberation with Greg and Centenary coach Emmett Rutkowski — cancel the game, play tomorrow? — Horst decided to take matters into his own hands. He pulled me and the Centenary coach aside, pulled a whistle out of his cargo pants, and said: "Here's what we're gonna do. Emmett, you're going to coach your team. Scott, you're going to coach our team. And I will referee." He blew his whistle, called for captains, and we were underway in just a few minutes.

Both teams handled the situation really well. We went on to win the game 2-1 and thankfully, Horst did not need to make any decisive, game-altering decisions. Of course, this game was not exactly played "by the book." Fortunately, after a post-game call with our conference commissioner, Dwayne Hanberry, it was agreed that the game was played fairly and the result would count in the standings. All's well that ends well.

(By the way, it was the second time in my coaching career that I had refereed my own game.)

Texas Lutheran in Sequin hosted the play-offs. By virtue of our standing, we received a bye for the first round and faced Southwestern on Saturday, November 8. I had probably given one of my best pre-game talks ever on that day, even though it was in the back room of the restaurant where we had breakfast. And the boys responded, crushing Southwestern 5-0. An incredible victory for us! Max Grossenbacher's parents, who lived in Austin, invited the team and a cheering crowd of parents out to their lake house after the match for a BBQ. Food never tasted so good!

Helen and I had driven our car to Austin, since we had time and the inclination to do so. That freed up an airplane ticket for Assistant Coach Dan Highstead, who, with Scott Palguta, had brought the team to Texas. We all met at the same motel. (Ryan Huettel, Soren Frykholm and Brandon Ogilvie, all integral members of the team, were out with injuries.)

Buoyed by the terrific win from the day before, our group was ready to face Trinity for the third time in this season. You could tell during the warm-ups: the boys were pumped!! And we did take the game to them from the start. Our pressure paid off as Max Grossenbacher scored in the 29th minute on assists from Caden MacKenzie and Alec Sowers. This score stood at half-time.

We were still ahead at minute 50, at minute 60, at minute 70, at minute 80. Was there an upset in the making?? In the 82nd minute they were granted a penalty and scored, and two minutes before time ran out, they scored on a break away. Game over!

Their team whooped it up in front of their bench, singing "We are the Champions," while we gathered in devastation on our end of the field. Our final record that season was 15-4-2. Three of our losses had been to Trinity, all by one goal. Had our conference, as a whole, had a higher strength-of-schedule index, we probably would have earned a spot in the NCAAs.

In spite of the disappointing finale, our team earned numerous SCAC accolades at the conclusion of the season:

- Theo Hooker, 11 shut-outs, Newcomer of the Year!
- Andrew Worthington, Defender of the Year!
- Horst Richardson, Coach of the Year!
- And Brandon Ogilvie, Academic All-American!!

Once the team had sufficiently recovered from the stress of the play-off match, we had a brief team meeting. I told them how proud I was of them for having played a super season and, while they were flying back, Helen and I would be driving home through the endless expanse of Texas.

On the drive home, Helen and I had plenty of time to discuss our future with CC soccer. Somewhere near Amarillo, we decided that after half a century of coaching, it was a good time to say good-bye. After 50 years my record stood at 567-304-71, for a total of 942 games. If one adds the games we played overseas and during the off-season, the total number of games coached would reach well over 1,000. That's a lot of games!

At the next athletic staff meeting I was going to announce my decision to retire at the end of the academic year, and shortly thereafter, in a locker room meeting with the team, tell them as well — with the proviso that our Europe trip, as announced, was still going to happen. That Europe trip with the players would be my last official engagement as coach of Colorado College men's soccer.

Before we left campus for the SCAC conference play-offs, *The Catalyst*, on November 7, published a 10-question interview with me about my 50 years at CC. As we come to the end of our narrative, it seems fitting to include it here. Jack Burger, staff writer for the campus paper, conducted the interview:

CATALYST: What has it been like to coach at CC for 50 years?

HORST: Fifty years! When I started here, the Vietnam War was going on, racial issues in the South were in full swing, and that's ancient history now, a long, long time ago. I was hired as a German instructor for just one year that turned into 50. I just happened to walk by the soccer field one day in September of my first year in 1965, and saw these guys kicking the ball around. Bill Boddington, who was coaching the team, was a volunteer whose son played on the squad. He was a businessman in town and he told me: 'If you want to coach the team, it's yours.'

CATALYST: How has the program developed since you have been here?

HORST: In those days, to get a team together, we would put posters around campus and say: 'Hey, we are going to have try-outs next week; if anyone wants to show up.' We would have 14 candidates show up, and several of them would be international students. Those were the early days. Now we have hundreds of e-mails coming in, and we want to answer them all, and find that particular student/athlete who would fit our environment, someone who likes the Block Plan and can play. It's hard.

CATALYST: What has kept you at CC for so long? What do you enjoy about working for this school?

HORST: CC has given me an opportunity to engage in the three things I like most. That was teaching, and I retired several years ago from doing that. I directed a lot of plays in the German Department, enjoying stage activities. And then, of course, coaching the team over all these years. I am going out to practice in an hour. I mean, there is snow on the Peak. It is a beautiful Indian summer day. It is a gorgeous environment and I have enjoyed working with all the wonderful student/athletes we have here. They kept me engaged, motivated, and sharp.

CATALYST: How has your experience helped you coach teams with a variety of strengths and weaknesses?

HORST: I have seen a lot. I have learned from all of those experiences over time and I am still learning because there are things that happen every year that you haven't ever addressed or anticipated. I didn't have any professional experience prior to coming here; I grew up in my native Germany, playing the game as everybody did there and I brought that passion to CC. I think I have been able to pass on my enthusiasm for the sport, my interest in it, and my personal development over time, to the kids and players. I hope I have helped at least a little bit in their education on the field. Seeing them be successful, by growing, nurturing, maturing, I think that has been my biggest reward.

CATALYST: What is the most memorable moment of your coaching career?

HORST: Well, there have been many, and I could entertain that question ad infinitum. *I have all sorts of stories and memories. I think probably the 1992 team, that went to the Final Four was a great run. We had a fabulous record. We didn't get a home bid from the NCAA because we were isolated here in the Rockies, and they didn't want to fly three teams here. We had to first travel to California, to St. Louis, and then to New Jersey, and we were wiped out by the time we went to the Final Four. But it was a great run.*

There is a terrific story from that team. We had an All-American, Noah Epstein, who now is an orthopedic surgeon. He got injured early in the season and while rehabbing, he tried out for a theater production and was cast as Romeo in "Romeo and Juliet." He really got into acting! When he returned to the team, he was very successful and scored a lot of goals. We came to find out that our regional final in California conflicted with the opening night of the Shakespearean play. So, what to do? We made a deal with the Drama Department, in CC liberal arts fashion, that if we won the first game on Friday, we would fly him out Saturday morning, he would play in the game, and then we would have him back on campus for a late night performance. He came, he played, he assisted on the winning goal, we won the game, and he was back for his part of Romeo on campus that same night. That is a wonderful story!!

CATALYST: What has been your toughest moment as a coach?

HORST: To use a current example, in our SCAC conference right now, we are perennially faced with Trinity, in San Antonio, Texas. Right now they are ranked # 3 in the country, and we have played them twice already this season. We lost twice 1-0, in tough games, errors on our part. We probably will have another shot against them at the conference play-offs. I think for me, personally, this season playing them has been very tough.

CATALYST: What are your goals as the season comes to a close?

HORST: We have a good record, 14-3-2. We locked up second place in the conference. We would like to have a good two games in the conference play-offs and do well enough so that we might be in contention for an NCAA bid next week.

CATALYST: What do you enjoy doing outside of coaching?

HORST: I love to travel. I have been all over the world. Our team has traveled a lot internationally, and we are even planning another trip to Scandinavia in May and June. I enjoy music, and the fine arts, and I attend a lot of performances locally. Obviously, I enjoy spending time with my family, especially with my two granddaughters.

CATALYST: Do you have any plans after retirement?

HORST: One of these days I will have to retire, I suppose. We haven't made that decision, but 50 years is a good run. My wife, Helen, and I have talked about it, and eventually we will make a decision.

CATALYST: What legacy do you wish to leave at CC?

HORST: I think my biggest reward would be to have a group of alums, former players, out there who have enjoyed playing at CC during my tenure, who learned a few things from me on the playing field that they could carry over to their personal lives as they grow up, get jobs, and settle down. I want to stay in touch with them, keep the extended family going, and enjoy that fraternity.

After the 2015 commencement in early June, Helen and I met the team at the Chicago airport for the last international trip which I was conducting. Destinations were London, England; Goteborg, Sweden; Helsingor and Copenhagen in Denmark; and Northern Germany. Included in the traveling party was my newly selected successor, Scott Palguta, Assistant Coach Dan Highstead, an Englishman, and our trainer Robyn Kadel, who had never been out of the USA.

The students who enrolled in the fall of 2014 had read the play *Hamlet* for their new student orientation discussions; I conceived of the idea to dedicate part of our soccer tour to Hamlet, the Shakespearean prince, for he, like our young men, was a student, an athlete, young and in love, and struggling to make good decisions. So each player received a copy of the play and was assigned a part in a scene to perform in selected places along the way.

In fact, the first scene, soldiers on guard at night at Hamlet's castle, we staged at the Chicago airport, while waiting to check in. Who could ever forget Max Grossenbacher attempting to spook us all as the ghost of Hamlet's father??

I was glad to have Dan Highstead and Cam Stopforth, both Brits, along to help us navigate through the underground of London's metro system to our youth hostel along the Thames. There was no rest for the weary travelers, however, as we needed to stay up and be alert for a London historical walk and food tour, conducted by CC alumna Celia Brooks, a longtime London resident and writer of vegetarian cookbooks.

Two games north of the metropolis followed in three days, and at one we even had a couple CC fans: Dan Highstead's family and '71 alum and former standout player David Rutherford and his family.

A visit to the Old Vic Theatre followed. We were treated to a spectacular stage sword fighting exhibition and could appreciate how skilled a swordsman Hamlet must have been. Equally entertaining was our trainer's transformation from 21st-century woman to Elizabethan lady. The costume department of the Old Vic had selected Robyn to come on stage and be dressed in period clothes. I think Robyn had the time of her life! Attorney and alum Duccio Faraoni, who is an agent for Premier League players, met us for a stroll along the Thames, and soon thereafter it was time to fly to Sweden.

In Goteborg, our host was Kristian Sundborn, former CC captain and ex-assistant coach. Goteborg is situated much further north than Colorado Springs, but the "Land of the Midnight Sun" in mid-June was not kind to us weather-wise. Our first game, a night match, was played in a driving rainstorm and it was so cold that Helen, usually a super fan, didn't leave the vehicle and our bench was huddled together to stay warm.

Post-game hospitality, however, warmed us up quickly. A city tour, another game, a great BBQ at Kristian's house, and a memorable kayak race at a sailing vessel marina were the highlights in the Volvo town. Kristian, who is an Olympic-level sailor, provided a few sailing stories for our enjoyment and made sure that we met our bus to the ferry terminal in southern Sweden on time. Thanks, Kristian.

Although the European Common Market and the Euro Zone currency have made travel easier in Europe, we still had to deal with four different currencies during our tour to these four European countries. At the ferry terminal, ready for the short ride across the sound to Denmark, Helen and I spent considerable time changing Swedish Kroner to Danish Kroner, making sure that we had enough funds for the next country. The players received a per diem allowance from "Helen's Bank," which covered their basic daily food needs. Accommodations were provided in gyms, youth hostels and budget hotels.

As we approached the Danish coast, Hamlet's Kronborg castle in Helsingor loomed large on the distant coast. Continuing our exploration of Hamlet in our travels, we had an educational tour of the fortress and staged a couple scenes of the play in the compound, highlighted by Christian Wulff's King Claudius' monologue, delivered within sight of the ancient ramparts. But we needed to get to our next game, and in a hurry. And public transportation was expensive, and we had limited funds. Ryan Huettel '16 wrote a marvelous reflection about my method of payment:

> *The running joke of our 2016 Europe trip were the gifts that Horst brought for the CC alums we met on our travels, namely the Colorado College Men's Soccer bumper stickers. He must have brought at least 700 of them, replete with the phrase "What a Kick," below the school's name.*
>
> *So at every stop (Camden Market, Kullavik Harbor, Rhein Energie Stadion), Horst liberally dispensed bumper stickers to anyone in the near vicinity. Former CC captain Kristian Sundborn? Bumper Sticker. Horst's tour guide friend Timm, who took the Unabomber's approach to traffic lights? Bumper Sticker. The Hamlet impersonator at Kronborg Castle? Bumper Stickered — no one was safe.*
>
> *By the time we arrived in Denmark, Horst had to be down to his last 100 bumper stickers. We had just ferried in from Sweden and had not been told that over the past decade, Denmark had transitioned to a cashless society. By the time we reached Kronborg soil, the team was already late for our game against the city's academy team. As we tried to pile on the state-of-the-art public bus, the driver refused our silver Kroners, patiently trying to explain that he couldn't accept hard currency.*
>
> *Horst, being Horst, saw the situation unfolding and quickly stepped in to mediate, acting as translator between the English-speaking Americans and the English-speaking Dane. Horst told us all to move to the back of the bus so he could pay the driver by card … only to converse with him for about a minute, and then hand over a bumper sticker. Thumbs up. Somehow we had been deemed acceptable to stay on.*
>
> *I still wonder what Horst must have said to the driver. Did he try and speak with him in German? Maybe tell him about the Black Attack, or praise the virtues of a well-timed back heel? While the world might never know the full truth, one thing is for certain — only Horst could pay for thirty bus fares simply with a story and a bumper sticker.*

Timm Nikolajsen, a native Dane and former assistant coach, facilitated our stay in Copenhagen. He showed us a lot of the city, including the famous mermaid, on a harbor tour. A long walk in the summer heat to the distant playing field for our game was exhausting, but the opposition was second-rate. Good party after the game, though.

Seth Newby had injured himself at the game; fortunately Timm knew a friend who could lend us crutches for Seth. One of the first-year students needed more than crutches to help him get back to the youth hostel, though, as he, after some barhopping, lost his way late at night and could have ended up in the Danish Navy. But all of the CC boys were at the main railroad station the next day at 6:15 in the morning to catch the train to the German border.

At the border town of Flensburg, my loyal and reliable soccer buddy, Volker Brueckner, was waiting for us with rental vans. Four games awaited us in Germany, two tough ones in Muenster and Lüneburg, and two easier ones in the country north of Hamburg and one in Berlin.

We had been lucky in acquiring tickets to a friendly match between the German and U.S. national teams who would play in Cologne. Getting to the match in heavy traffic was an ordeal, but we were in our seats for the kick-off. And what a treat for us Americans: we beat the reigning World Cup champion on their home field 2-1!!!

On the way back to our distant lodgings, shortly after midnight, the German police stopped our vans for a routine traffic stop. Robyn Kadel was driving one of the vehicles, and I remember how nervous she was when the police approached her car. As it turned out, she had an extra occupant in the seven-passenger vehicle. So they hid Soren Frykholm underneath a bunch of blankets, hoping the police would not discover the No. 8 person in the car. (A ticket, a fine, and a major delay would have been likely consequences.) We survived the police check. Robyn, who has moved on from CC to become trainer at a D-I program in Kansas for their track and field program, was quite fond of working with the Tigers and submitted a number of memories which I am including here:

> *Of course, the Europe trip was a great time and provided many learning experiences. So many adventures during those three weeks! The bike tour of Berlin stands out. We learned about the history of the city and saw some beautiful sights. We went to an old airport that had been converted into a park. The team raced, and Max crashed. (Luckily he was not injured.)*

Other memories include:

- *Learning how to be a soccer athletic trainer from the best: Bruce Kola.*
- *Hearing the athletes speak at team banquets and roasts. Such intelligent, funny, well-spoken young men.*
- *Working out of Boettcher Health Center during pre-season of 2012 while El Pomar was being renovated.*
- *Horst officiating the game at Centenary.*
- *Having to call so many lightning delays during practices and games, and the groans from coaches and athletes.*
- *Enjoying Helen's cookies and team dinners at the Richardson house.*
- *Receiving postcards from all over the world as the Men's Soccer student athletes traveled abroad.*
- *The amazing farewell video that the team made for me when I left Colorado to move back to Kansas. So thoughtful!*

A couple of days later on the former East-West German border, we inspected the remnants of much tougher police search and seizure procedures, and the guys received some idea of what it must have been like to live in a police state. And in Berlin, Andrea and Sven Johns extended their amazing welcome and hospitality to us, as they had done several times before for CC visitors.

Sven had organized a half-day bicycle tour of Berlin, riding at a leisurely pace past all the important sights. A special treat was a visit to the fabled Tempelhof Airfield, the site of the post-World War II American airlift. Leave it to our group of players to stage a bicycle race on the runway!! The rental bikes were not in the best of shape, and the unlucky Max Grossenbacher crashed and burned before take-off speed could be attained. Fortunately Robyn was along to tend to his cuts and bruises.

And surprise, surprise! Former captain Matt Atencio, now professor of kinesiology and in Berlin for a conference, showed up to our final game and played for the opposition. Right on, Matt!

Inexplicable, and most unfortunate, were two serious injuries to two of our players in the very last game on this trip. Both Killian Morales-Coskran and Caden MacKenzie tore their ACLs, which meant that they would miss the fall season. Incredible bad luck!

On the flight home across the Atlantic, I slowly came to terms with the fact that my half century of coaching, guiding, and counseling student/athletes at CC had come to an end. It seemed so abrupt after so many years, and now it was over. I am grateful for all the memories, and Helen and I will reread this narrative annually to let the good times roll on.

In the fall of 2015, Helen and I, now retired, sat on the grassy hill on Stewart Field as spectators, as the CC Tigers once again faced nemesis Trinity, and we cheered our hearts out. Senior captain Max Grossenbacher '16 reports on his career and the outcome of the game:

When I think of the CC men's soccer program, I think of a group of guys dedicated to playing the sport that they love. No one is forcing them to play, we just do it for the love of the game; and at CC, I rediscovered my love of the game. Every tackle, every pass, every shot, every practice and every game, I stepped onto the field excited and nervous and stepped off a better player and a better man.

Entering CC as a scrawny teenager 5' 7" on my tip toes and 125 lbs., if I had eaten a big lunch that day, I was not immediately pegged as a player with vast, untapped potential; and disappointed after a weak showing in my first season, I had a lot to think about. Is soccer something I really want to do in college? Or should I dedicate my time elsewhere?

In the end, it was my teammates who brought me back. Waking up early Sunday mornings and running, passing and shooting drills with Chris "Ox" Edmonds and Morgan Wack, until Darrold Hughes, the groundskeeper, would yell at us to get off the field. Making goalkeepers Tom Crosby and Theo Hooker stay sometimes hours after practice as I would shoot and shoot and shoot.

It was Andrew Worthington who taught me how to be a leader on and off the field, and I am honored to have served as his co-captain. 6 a.m. lifting sessions with Kevin Cronin in the locker room required a team effort to make sure everyone got out of bed and down to the weight room in time; but no matter how exhausted you felt, you were all in it together.

I played Trinity nine times in my career. Every year, the team mantra was, "We have to outwork Trinity." What can we be doing that they are not? What will give us the advantage that we need?

My senior year, we finally were able to defeat Trinity for the first time since 1996!! However, the hours leading to the game were filled with more confusion than focus on the task at hand. Soren Frykholm, our center defensive midfielder and one of our best and most consistent players, had gone home to Boulder for the weekend and confused the game time. He was going to be late and miss the first half.

Despite a slow warm-up and all the distractions from the morning, CC came out strong in the first half. Christian Wulff, looking like Batman with a mask to protect his recently broken nose, scored, giving CC a 1-0 advantage at half-time. Leading Trinity was not new to CC teams, but could we hold it? In the 76th minute, Trinity evened the score 1-1. How many times had CC teams held a late lead over Trinity only to see it slip away in the final minutes? The previous year, CC was up 1-0 in the SCAC final and gave up 2 goals in the final 10 minutes to lose 2-1. I even heard a rumor that on the sideline longtime Assistant Coach Dan Highstead said, "Here we go again ..."

But this time was different. What does redemption look like? In almost storybook fashion, Soren Frykholm scored with 7:44 remaining, giving CC a 2-1 lead and 19 seconds later I chased down a long ball on the left flank and slotted away the insurance goal, sealing Trinity's fate.

This game was a complete team effort. From top to bottom, everyone had to step up and perform. We had stuck together and played for each other despite all the distractions, and that is what playing for the CC men's soccer team is all about. After scoring, I sprinted to the bench to celebrate with my teammates. We had finally done it. We had finally beaten Trinity.

The team rushed over to the stands after the victory to thank their faithful fans. The boys came up to me, gave me a hug, and I will never forget Trevor Houghton saying: "We did it for you, Coach!"

That was the best retirement gift anyone could have given me!!!

*I*t is entirely fitting that this narrative about CC soccer concludes with reflections by my wife, Helen Richardson, who has given so much of her life to the men's soccer program. In 1979, Helen wrote a story for the Soccer Organization for Colorado Springs Youth (SOCSY) newsletter:

SUPPORT YOUR FAVORITE COACH

Thirteen years ago, needing some diversion from my two jobs — the primary one as a 5th grade teacher at Steele School and secondary one as a head resident of a

Colorado College dormitory — I went to my first soccer game, CC vs. CSU at Bonny Park in late October of 1966. At the end of the game, I was introduced to the CC coach, Horst Richardson, by the mother of one of my fifth-grade students and by her friend, who was secretary in the CC foreign language department. It was the beginning of a romantic triangle, which still exists today between Horst, myself, and soccer!

A year after we met, and just a week before our wedding in late November, an article appeared in the local newspaper entitled: Wedding Plans in Doubt for Coach! CC in play-offs! I should have known that I was marrying not only Horst, but also CC soccer. (By the way, due to a CC loss against St. Louis University a few days before the wedding, we were married on schedule on November 25th, 1967, with the soccer team seated in the front pew.)

No doubt there are many of you who are either a spouse or friend of an aspiring soccer coach, so it is with you that I want to share my years of experience as a coach's wife. You must possess various saintly attributes to endure without complaint all the unexpected and time-consuming activities of your favorite coach.

One must spend countless hours on the sidelines, in all types of extreme weather, giving support in winning and losing seasons, and encouraging your favorite coach to continue this supreme act of volunteerism while ignoring those frequent despairing tendencies.

One must undergo separations for the cause of soccer; trips to National Soccer Coaches Conventions, national licensing clinics, and summer soccer camps; jaunts to Brazil in conjunction with the Partners of the Americas Sports Exchange Program; and to Mexico and Germany to view World Cup soccer competition.

Additionally, one must be willing to give freely of one's time to type until midnight when the Far-West Soccer Ratings are due, and take complicated phone messages — sometimes in German — for your favorite coach while he watches Soccer Made in Germany on TV, not wanting to miss the instant replay of Klaus Fischer's diving header.

One must have a sense of humor (or be totally crazy) to cook for 25 starving soccer players for their annual banquet, to pick up the team at the airport at 1 a.m. after a California trip where they lost miserably, to lend a sympathetic ear to the players' numerous and complicated problems, and to drive to King Soopers before it closes to buy a relief-giving box of Rolaids.

However, a few years ago, to battle against my soccer widowhood, and having had enough vicarious experiences, I became involved with the sport myself. I have earned my State E coaching license, at a clinic directed by my favorite coach! And now I teach the basics to 23 enthusiastic E-division players at Westmoor Park, with the generous help from a few tireless moms, our nine-year-old son, Erik, who demonstrates the skills and our seven-year-old daughter, Stacia, who enjoys doing headstands while I try to explain a wall pass!! For three years, I have tried to play soccer, most recently with the Rolls Royce Classics, in the adult league, which has been a great source of genuine fun and camaraderie, and many aches, pains, and hematomas (Go to the soccer clinics to learn about these!)

Now that I can appreciate the finer points of soccer, I heartily recommend that you supporters of your favorite coach read up on the sport. I understand now why my favorite coach gives of his time so unselfishly for this exciting and creative sport. Our lives have been enriched by our relationships with so many great coaches, players, and their parents. We have been overjoyed by the huge growth of soccer at CC; in 1967, CC played seven games, all against teams within the state of Colorado; now in 1979, CC will play 18 games, with two scheduled trips to California — one game to challenge UCLA. I am proud of my favorite coach for all his successes and his work to keep CC on the U.S. soccer map.

So, if you supporters need some encouragement, come to the CC soccer games — one of the last free entertainments left and say Hi to me. I am easy to spot. I am the older woman with wrinkles, pacing the sidelines, taking stats, and sometimes up on a platform filming the game.

Well, there it is. It's been an incredible ride for Helen and me. Thanks to all for the wonderful memories!!!

Photo: Mark Reis, *The Gazette*, September 11, 2003.

Horst Richardson was born in Germany in 1941, during World War II. His mother, a war widow, married an American soldier after the war who brought the family to California. Horst earned a B.A. and M.A. from the University of California, Riverside, a Ph.D. in German Language and Literature from the University of Connecticut and an A coaching license from the U.S. Soccer Federation. He taught and coached at Colorado College beginning in 1965, retiring in 2015. German culture and history, German theatre, and soccer have been his passions at CC. Horst has served the National Soccer Coaches Association, the local Colorado Springs School Board, has sung in the Colorado Springs Chorale, enjoys hiking and traveling, has a number of publications to his name, and most importantly, has been married to Helen for 51 years. The couple have two children, Erik and Stacia, who both graduated from CC, and two talented granddaughters, Indigo and Steffi.

Helen was born and raised in Minneapolis, Minnesota, graduated from The College of St. Catherine in St. Paul, and moved to Colorado Springs in 1965 to teach at Steele Elementary School. In 1966, at the first soccer game she ever attended, she met Horst, the handsome, young CC coach, fell in love, married a year later, and had two wonderful children, Erik and Stacia. After her teaching career, she worked at Colorado College in the Education Department as a supervisor of student teachers and in the Communications Department as a proofreader. She also enjoyed her involvement in Horst's annual German play production, videotaped the CC home soccer games for three decades, and cooked innumerable, motivational team breakfasts before important matches. What a fun life!